The Slave Narrative

Marion Wilson Starling

The Slave Narrative
Its Place in American History

Second Edition

Howard University Press   Washington, D.C.   1988

Printed in the United States of America

Library of Congress Cataloging-in-Publication Data

Starling, Marion Wilson , 1907–
  The slave narrative.

  Originally presented as the author's thesis (Ph.D.—
New York University, 1946)
  Bibliography: p.
  Includes index.
  1. Slaves—United States—Biography. 2. Afro-Americans—
Biography. 3. Biography (as a literary form) I. Title.
E444.S8 1988   973'.0496073   87–2744
ISBN 0–88258–165–1

To my daughter Tiffany Starling, whose life is a precious flowering of the dream of her indomitable great-grandfather, Edward Wilson, slave of one Colonel Wilson of Culpepper County, Virginia, until freed by the Emancipation Act at the age of ten.

Contents

Editors' Preface

Scholars have been myopic when examining black thought and behavior. The quintessence of this myopia appears when the scholars write about slaves. "What was it like to be a slave?," the historian John S. Kendall asked in 1939. He answered unequivocally:

> We do not know. The slaves themselves have never told. There were always . . . negroes who had secured their freedom. . . . But they had no literary gift. If they were capable of self-analysis to the degree of distinguishing their sentiments in one estate from those in the other, they have omitted to set down the result in writing. Still less have we the story of a slave—of a slave who was nothing but a slave.

When scholars more knowledgeable than Kendall discovered some slave sources, they were incredulous. The historian Kenneth Stampp, for instance, asserted in 1956: "Since there are few reliable records of what went on in the minds of slaves, one can only infer their thoughts and feelings from their behavior, that of their masters, and the logic of their situation."

While twentieth-century historians claimed the slaves left no records, a writer in 1849 declared: "America has the mournful honor of adding a new department to the literature of civilization—the autobiographies of escaped slaves." Nineteenth-century readers found that the slave narrative was one of the major sources of accurate information about bondage. An 1882 reviewer gave the general view when he wrote: "The daily life and condition of the slave cannot but give interest to a story told by the actor in the scenes which he describes; and the historical facts stated cannot but prove of high value in the formation of a just opinion of the real status of the actual system of slavery as it existed in the South."

Marion Wilson Starling heard the echoes of the nineteenth-century and followed the historian's instinct in tracking down hundreds of authentic, reliable slave autobiographies. Although there was a criminal time lag, Starling's impeccably researched 1946 dissertation inaugurated the modern era of Afro-American historical writing with its focus on giving a voice to the oppressed.

For decades, her pioneering work inspired historians and literary scholars to reject the received wisdom propounded by the Stampps and Kendalls.

Combing meticulously through antebellum newspapers and court proceedings, Starling found such a wealth of slave testimony that more than three decades later scholars had not fully explored or tested her findings. One is struck by such masterful historical research in a work centered on the study of literature.

This historical research assumed several forms. In 1946 it was, first of all, a matter of discovery—that is to say, a search for those narratives that contributed to our picture of what life was like for the slave before 1860. The emphasis here was upon individual differences in point of view, destroying as a consequence any simple notion of what constituted the slave's world. Certainly this complex and varying life could not be inferred from the behavior of masters. A second achievement by Starling was classification: outlining the distinction that existed between those narratives printed before 1836 and those that followed the emergence of radical Abolition. The earlier narratives described the adventures of individuals, while the later ones added a consideration of questions of class, race, and position in society. Another form of classificaton had to do with the nature of the elements within the narratives. If these were fanciful rather than real, they represented parts of idealized slave sketches or imaginative narratives with strong evidences of the sentimental. If these were accurate representations of life, they gave shape to a disturbing record of the slave's experience, expressed at times with minimal skill. The "real slave story" was what mattered to the historian in Marion Starling, but she was forced as a literary scholar to acknowledge the power and the influence of the fanciful tale as well.

Determining the authenticity of the slave narrative was the most challenging of the historical problems which Starling faced and solved. For years American historians had ignored the narratives because they were convinced that these tales were the creations of Abolitionist propagandists. Scholars were untouched even by the comments of the most scrupulous antislavery editors, who described with care what they had or had not done to make appealing narratives. So embedded in the American mind was the notion of the union of slave narrative and reformist editor that it is a surprise to discover that one-half of the slave narratives came from sources other than antislavery periodicals. These are judicial records, broadsides, private printings, scholarly journals, church records, unpublished collections, regular publications, and sensational journals, not to mention the materials gathered by the Federal Writers' Project Administration during the 1930s. A basis exists for two kinds of comparison, both likely to exert an influence upon a skeptical reading public. One consists of a comparative examination of documents within the period during which a given slave narrative was written. And here little in substance or fact separates the edited narrative from that, say, in a court or church record. Another form of comparison involves narratives written before 1860 and documents in the WPA Collection, recorded oral accounts lacking the strident background of the antebellum period and dependent only upon the memory of the ex-slave. Once again the evidence sustains the compelling truth of the earlier slave narrative.

Starling considers the slave narrative as being essentially a form of sub-literature. Its chief literary value rests for her in the fact that the raw account of the bitter experience of the slave provided matter and inspiration for talented writers like Harriet Beecher Stowe. Her work also suggests that adherence to conventions, whether they derive from the sentimental novel or the religious confession, is to be found within the slave narratives as well as in the more obviously literary forms which these narratives inspired. A closer look at the slave autobiographies reveals varying skills in the use of these conventions, and assurance that ex-slaves possessed imagination and dexterity of a purely literary kind comes from reading the narratives of Frederick Douglass, William Wells Brown, and Henry Bibb, among others. Something good can be said, in this regard, of the narrative of James Williams, whose ability to separate fact from fiction was much questioned by Southern critics.

Starling was a prime mover in a profound revolution in the academic world. Her work gave a voice to the black slave, who before the 1940s was a dumb ghost nagging the conscience of some American historians. Starling contributed substantially to establishing the narratives as acceptable historical evidence and promoted in this way the long-deferred revision in the way historians looked at slavery and the world that was the old South.

JOHN W. BLASSINGAME
and CHARLES T. DAVIS

New Haven, 1981

Author's Prologue

The place of the slave narrative is assured today—especially when compared with its status two hundred years ago, when the framers of the Constitution of the United States of America wrangled for days over how to count slaves so as to determine a state's apportionment in the House of Representatives. A compromise reached, the count was set at three-fifths of a person for each slave owned; the document was signed; and the Founding Fathers set off for home. There were some slave narratives which existed at the time, but probably no one among those leaders had looked into one or cared to. "Three-fifths of a person": that was what they had settled for!

Today the slave narrative is of critical interest to scholars in Afro-American studies. I take pride in John W. Blassingame's identification of this book as having "inaugurated the modern era of Afro-American historical writing." His recognition that today's almost feverish scholarship in the field would have had to wait a while, without my pioneering work, is gratifying.

The greatest help in launching my study of slave narratives was the Federal Writers' Project, a part of the Federal Works Progress Administration, which was formed to create jobs during the Great Depression of the 1930s. The Federal Writers' Project was started in 1933 and added a slave narrative section to its Folklore Divison, possibly motivated by a dissertation, *The Negro Author and His Development in America* (Columbia University Press, 1931), by Vernon Loggins, a member of the Columbia University English Department. The subject for Loggins's dissertation had been suggested by his advisor, Professor Ashley H. Thorndike. In that volume, Dr. Loggins surveys slave narratives as literature, along with Negro fiction, poetry, historical and sociological treatises, and oratorical and theological writings from 1760 to 1900. Loggins was greatly assisted in his task by Arthur A. Schomburg, a black scholar who became the first curator for the Schomburg Center for Research in Black Culture, the New York Public Library.

Loggins's book included twenty slave narratives. Chapter 4 was devoted to the slave narratives of Gronniosaw, Archy Moore, Abraham Johnstone, Moses Roper, Venture Smith, James Williams, Solomon Bailey, Charles Ball, and Eleanor Eldridge. Chapter 6 included the narratives of Henry Bibb, Josiah Henson, Lewis Clarke, Sojourner Truth, Rev. J. M. Loguen, Lunceford Lane, Henry Box Brown, William and Ellen Craft, Noah Davis, Zamba, and a "female slave" (unnamed by Loggins but identified by recent scholarship as Harriet Jacobs). As the noted scholar Dr. Henry Louis Gates, Jr., has surmised, the Folklore Division may have been so impressed by Loggins's accounts of the narratives in these two chapters that it added the genre to its roster. By 1938, when the slave narrative project ended, oral interviews had been conducted with twenty-five hundred former slaves in seventeen states, an estimated sixteen percent of whom were six years of age, or under, in 1865. Ten thousand pages of interviews were stored in barrels in the basement of the Library of Congress, under the control of the chief librarian. The papers were off limits to scholars until 1944, when they were released by Dr. Benjamin A. Botkin, the librarian, whose book on the narratives—*Lay My Burden Down*—was published in 1945 by the University of Chicago Press.

The Library of Congress collection has proved indispensable. Prior to 1944, twentieth-century scholars had no means of refuting the warning of the "historians' historian," Ulrich B. Phillips, against using slave narratives as reliable source material. "Ex-slave narratives in general were issued with so much abolitionist editing," he wrote in his *Life and Labor in the Old South* (Boston: Little, Brown, 1929, 219), "that as a class, their authenticity is doubtful."

From the time that scholars gained access to the ten thousand typewritten pages of the Federal Writers' Project Administration's interviews with ex-slaves (known as the Slave Narrative Collection) scholars' acceptance of Phillips's one-sided view of the slave narrative began to change. Studies of the contents of the narratives began in earnest, and within a generation black scholars were vying with white scholars for use of the typescripts. A young white scholar, Eugene Genovese, teased a competing white scholar, Kenneth Stampp, for "standing [Ulrich B.] Phillips on his head" as a result of the high praise Stampp was receiving for his study *The Peculiar Institution: Slavery in the Ante-Bellum South* (New York: Knopf, 1956), in which Stampp made wide use of those narratives. But Stampp did not hold the position of supreme authority on American slavery nearly as long as the four decades of Ulrich Phillips's reign. In 1968, Stanley Elkins, a white sociologist who had received praise for his provocative study *Slavery: A Problem in American Institutional and Intellectual Life* (Chicago: University of Chicago Press, 1958), received even greater attention upon the appearance of the second edition of the book, ten years later. The year 1972 achieved landmark distinction, however. In 1972, not only did Genovese match Stampp's attainment for significant performance in the field of black studies with his *Roll, Jordan, Roll: The World the Slaves Made* (New York: Random House), but 1972 also marked the emergence of two monumental publications: *The American Slave: A Composite Autobiography,* edited by George P. Rawick (Westport, Conn.: Greenwood Press), and *The Slave Community: Plantation Life in the Antebellum South,* by John W. Blassingame (New York: Oxford University Press). Both publications are distinguished results of black scholars assuming leadership in the field. The outstanding productivity that commenced in the 1970s has continued in the 1980s, notably in the work of William L. Andrews.

Rawick performed a great service for scholarship in the forty-volume production conjoining the large Slave Narrative Collection of the WPA endeavor. The typescripts were a part of the Rare Books Division of the Library of Congress, and prior to Rawick's efforts scholars had to compete for use of these original materials. Rawick directed the preparation of the original slave narrative typescripts into books. It was a matter of great joy among scholars in the field of Afro-American studies when the entire collection, previously available for reference use only, became available as books.

Blassingame, in his *The Slave Community,* has been credited with actually breaking the historiographical tradition established by Phillips almost half a century earlier. *The Slave Community* is the first major study of slavery to employ the methodology of focusing on the institution from the perspective of the slave. Blassingame believed that the slaves, through the slave narratives, should speak for themselves. He also held that a scholar had to separate the slave narrative editor from the slave. As he is quoted in an essay "Testimony of Ex-Slaves: Approaches and Problems" in *The Slave's Narrative* (Charles T. Davis & Henry L. Gates, Jr., editors [New York: Oxford University Press], 1985), Blassingame declares:

> The fundamental problem confronting anyone interested in studying black views of bondage is that the slaves had few opportunities to tell what it meant to be a chattel. Since the antebellum narratives were frequently dictated to and written by whites, any study of such sources must begin with an assessment of the editors. An editor's education, religious beliefs, literary skill, attitudes toward slavery, and occupation all affected how he recorded the account of the slave's life. Generally, the editors were mostly professional journalists, preachers, lawyers, teachers, and

physicians who had gained a great deal of prior experience in
separating truth from fiction, applying rules of evidence, and
accurately portraying men and events. (79)

Except for an estimated dozen slave narratives, all the narratives were
produced with the aid of white abolitionist editors, whose chief mission
was to participate in the destruction of the institution of slavery in the
United States. More dedicated, principled individuals could not be
found; and their success with fugitive slaves, who had never in their lives
received formal training in writing and reading, was incredible. From
1670 to the Emancipation, abolitionist editors worked diligently to bring
about the downfall of slavery, with as much cooperation from slaves and
ex-slaves as they could muster.

The abolitionists were ever alert to discover potential speakers among
newly arrived slaves fleeing from the South to hoped-for freedom in the
North. Those who showed capability for public speaking were encouraged to try out their skills in a slave narrative, usually following a definite
form. Generally, this form contained a dictated "story" preceded or followed by any or all of the following items: an engraved portrait or photo-
graph of the subject of the narrative; authenticating testimonials; poetry;
illustrations of various kinds of topics; declamatory addresses; letters to
the narrator; newspaper clippings; notices of slave auctions, and of escaped slaves; certificates of marriage or manumission, of birth and death;
extracts from legal codes; wills; antislavery speeches and other notices of
the narrator's activities.

Though the slave narrative might be somewhat cramped by this assem-
blage, there was a need for this structure if the account were skimpy. Effort was made to change as little in the narrative as possible and to use
only easily grasped words. Sometimes it was difficult for fugitive and editor to come to an understanding, especially when it was a matter of the
fugitive's not repeating himself.

Another characteristic of the slave narratives was that the characters
placed a great deal of stress on the use of corporal punishment, which
some scholars have felt was inordinate. Yet as reported by Gerald Jaynes
in his "Plantation Factories and the Slave Work Ethic," "No single sentence in all the slave narratives I have read captures better the overwhelming presence of the whip in the minds of the slaves and their testimony
[than] 'The whip is all in all' " (Davis & Gates, *The Slave's Narrative*,
111–12). However repetitious, corporal punishment was common to the
slave.

In some early narratives as well as later ones, scholars have noted the slaves' motivations for escape. The slaves give their decision to learn to read and write, just barely second to the whip, as the reason for escaping.

Beneath all of the narratives there is a tragic message conveyed by slave and ex-slave alike: *I have been considered a non-being.* In an unusually perceptive essay, "I Was Born: Slave Narratives, Their Status as Autobiography and as Literature" (Davis & Gates, *The Slave Narrative,* 148–70), James Olney has analyzed the beginnings of slave narratives with the intention of identifying their original thought. Olney studies a dozen narratives in which the sentence "I was born" is the first or almost first sentence in the narrative. The sensitive reader can get the serious tone. The narrator is declaring that he actually exists—for proof, he appends the authenticating documents. Once having proved his existence, the narrator would recount the inhumane events of his life.

A major characteristic that the abolitionist editors deemed necessary was the inclusion of an exciting character. What kept the reader of popular slave narratives enthralled was undoubtedly the element of danger. One shivered, unable to foretell what the next shock would contain. Abolitionist editors had to keep in mind this entertainment requirement. Dynamic personalities like Lewis Clarke, William Wells Brown, Harriet Tubman, Solomon Northup, and others had an ability to render an entertaining account even though the story was not interesting. Very often, however, editors had to resort to the use of planned inserts to provide colorful material that might improve the support for the cause.

Probably the slave narratives that fulfilled these requirements most ably, and proved to be the most popular, were those by Frederick Douglass, Olaudah Equiano, and Josiah Henson—listed in order of popularity. Douglass's 125-page first edition of 1845, which ranks first among all the slave narratives, is considered the most perfect representative of the slave narrative and precedes, not only in the date of composition but also in quality, the successive editions that appeared in 1855, 1881, and 1892. The first slave narrative I ever heard of, and I have no idea how it happened, Douglass's little book stands for the entire genre, in my mind. Almost flawlessly inclusive, it achieves the aims Blassingame describes in his preface to *The Slave Community:* to describe and analyze the life of the black slave, his African heritage, culture, family, acculturation, behavior, religion, and personality. Equiano's narrative (1789; 1790) has been known for two hundred years. It is one of the longest and, at the same time, most interesting accounts of a slave's experiences. Equiano is one of the few narrators to describe his early years in Africa and to give vivid accounts of his distressing life as a widely traveled slave. Josiah Henson's narrative has maintained its place on the popularity list through the peculiarities of fate. In 1849 it appeared, along with four other narratives by fugitive slaves, in the July edition of a periodical subscribed to by the family of Harriet Beecher Stowe. The narrative caught the attention of Mrs. Stowe, who decided to use a character in the narrative for a story she was about to write, "Uncle Tom's Cabin." She would be trying her hand on her first story about slavery. Luck had its way: she discarded most of the features in Josiah Henson's narrative; substituted Solomon Northup from another narrative for Josiah Henson; and went on to spectacular success. There was little more than an assumed name for that first identification with Josiah Henson. *Uncle Tom's Cabin* had a spectacular history, on Mrs. Stowe's fictional strength.

Today these three narratives are being studied, along with others, to determine the slave's world. Important studies have emerged from most diligent Afro-American scholars, working and re-working narratives ranging from Briton Hammon (1760) to George Washington Carver (c1929) and engaging in every special technique known in the field. The most frequently studied narratives, aside from Douglass's, Equiano's, and Henson's, include the ones by Solomon Bailey (1820), Henry Bibb (1849), William Wells Brown (1847), Lewis Clarke (1848), J. D. Green (1839; 1846; 1864), Harriet Jacobs (1861), and Solomon Northup (1853). In addition to studies that centered on an individual, there are numerous studies that focus on special themes.

William Andrews, probably the most accomplished researcher in the field, has produced *two* special studies recently, an essay entitled "The First Fifty Years of the Slave Narrative, 1760–1810," and a set of studies all seriously investigating the role of literary theory in elevating the language and ideas by and through which we speak about Afro-American literature. Andrews's investigations are having a tremendous influence on many black scholars, many of whom are interested in experimental studies fusing the crafts of the historian and the literary critic. These gifted readers are uncovering interesting problems, as indicated in the current work of Robert Stepto, James Olney, Henry Louis Gates, Jr., Houston Baker, Jr., Eric Sundquist, Gerald Early, Vincent Harding, Robin Winks, Stephen Butterfield, William J. Moses, and Jacqueline Jones. As a result of their example, black slaves' texts are receiving close analysis. Through Andrews and Blassingame, the field of slave narratives is being substantially reconsidered.

Andrews's notion that abolitionists began to use editors to facilitate organizing the fugitives' accounts and to put the materials into written form led him to a revolutionary discovery. Translation was taking place unconsciously, he astutely deducted, in the transfer of ideas from the black fugitive's to the white editor's mind. Several years of study of the language patterns in narratives written before 1810, compared with patterns used after editors were employed in preparation of the accounts, corroborated his discovery. It was henceforth to be realized that there is more involved in recording an oral delivery than reaches the ear. Andrews's isolation of narratives published between 1770 and 1810, years before the abolitionists were using editors, made possible the close comparative readings that brought about his revelation. Never before had it been discerned that there could be racial distinctions in one's tonal patterns that would alter the meaning of one's words.

Possibilities for learning about the experience of being black in the United States of America have increased dramatically since Rawick's marshalling of the WPA narratives into print (1972); the reprinting of early slave narratives; the publication of Blassingame's analysis of plantation life in the antebellum South (1972); and the quite recent appearance of Andrews's in-depth expositions linking slave narratives and new literary theory. Still exciting activities lie ahead in the area of slave narratives of the nineteenth century.

All this activity in the field of literary analyses of slave narratives is particularly gratifying to me. The actual title of my dissertation submitted to New York University in 1946 was: "The Slave Narrative: Its Place in American Literary History"—that had been the plan in 1943. But at that time, in my ignorance of *any* slave narrative but Frederick Douglass's, I was unaware that there *were* no narratives lined up in libraries across the land awaiting my research. So research it certainly proved to be, starting with a frantic searching everywhere. With wonderful help and some luck, I assembled "my" narratives and started to get to the real job. As a candidate in the Department of English, with a minor in history, I decided, with the help of my advisor, Professor Oscar Cargill, that it would be feasible to set the narratives up historically first; then delve into the literary analyses. And so I did.

Time ran out before I could get to what I had anticipated would be the real body of my study. But now—as I revel over the brilliant studies that have followed upon my pioneering trail—I glow over the feeling that these studies are extensions of my dream, in a way, of illuminating our black past and helping construct our future. Studies are building upon studies. Well trained in research, scholars are able to see, *and* to hear, the constrained ancestors who managed to survive. Most remarkable of all, these young scholars are proud of their Afro-American heritage, an attitude that has not been met with before. The more deeply they understand our stony past, the more they are astounded by the race they have sprung from. It is a heritage to build upon.

Richard Wright and Ralph Ellison—their *Black Boy* and *Invisible Man* tell our story. Alex Haley has called it *Roots*. Maya Angelou and Toni Morrison bring all black women into the picture. With the concerted effort of our Afro-American scholars, by their ever closer readings, by hearing patterns of speech heretofore undiscerned, by bringing into our psyche the total scope of "being": with the help of the slave narratives, we shall be "made whole."

MARION WILSON STARLING

New York, New York
June 1, 1988

Author's Prologue to the First Edition

My gathering of narratives of the lives of American slaves written by the slaves themselves was undertaken against the backdrop of World War II. The general atmosphere of the time was somber and unnerving, in tune with the narratives. Franklin D. Roosevelt's efforts to establish a successor to the League of Nations were periodically reported; increasing signs of cooperation by the Allies were hopeful omens that man's inhumanity to man could be curbed. Meanwhile morning newspapers often jolted me with horror stories, just received from combat zones, that paralleled accounts of atrocious treatment of human beings in slave narrative after slave narrative. The treatment was similar, but not the setting. For the slave narrators it had not been a state of war, but of life—daily life.

The war ended shortly before my study was completed. President Roosevelt's dream of a United Nations organization became reality six months after his death, in 1945, with 51 nations as members. The membership roll has expanded to 154 as of March 1981. Understandably, the organization has been beset by problems. The 103 members added since 1945 include nearly a third that are new to being free nations. Most of the new members joined in the late 1950s and early 1960s, seven from Africa in the year 1960 alone. The new nations, especially, were drawn to the purposes expressed in the United Nations Charter—to maintain international peace and security; to develop friendly relations between states; to achieve cooperation in solving international economic, social, cultural, and humanitarian problems; and to strive to promote a policy of equality for all people and the expansion of basic freedoms. As I have tracked the entry of members into the United Nations family, I have recognized homelands of men and women among our slave narrators who were stolen away more than a hundred and fifty years ago to be sold by exploiters to slave-traders—Ghana, Dahomey, Ivory Coast, Rwanda, Senegal, Sierra Leone, Somalia. As the sun has been setting on colonial powers, independent nations have somehow evolved despite exploitation and neglect, to the level of recognition as members of the United Nations. Compared with their exploited past, difficulties that have arisen in that body because of their admittance have been miniscule. Their losses from the theft of human power and raw materials, the uncaring exploitation over the years, explain the "underdeveloped" label.

For the slave, the uncertainty of the future was what made life hell. Americans were recently afforded a tinge of what forced confinement can mean, in the nightmare experienced by fifty-two of our diplomats held hostage by the Iranians from November 4, 1979 to January 20, 1981. Radio stations began their daily programs by identifying the number of each day they were held. The joy that broke loose nationwide upon their release and return to the United States was unfettered hysteria: "but for the grace of God" each one of us was a free ex-hostage! Trapped 444 days!!

Promises made to the slave were not considered binding. No matter how "comfortable" the circumstances of a slave's life might seem, conditions could change without notice. A kindly master might suddenly be forced to sell a slave in order to pay debts. Grown children might insist upon being given certain slaves, even when it meant separating members of a slave family. Anger at a slave for some mishap might result in deportation to the dreaded "Black Belt," if death had not already resulted from the brutal beating administered. Slaves promised their freedom for a set sum of money, to be earned by being hired out as laborers, were often denied free papers when they had raised the amount and were forced to earn the sum over again. Deathbed promises of manumission were often ignored, slave families were sold apart, free papers were torn up in the distraught slave's presence.

New Year's Day was the most dreaded of the year, for it marked the auction of slaves to the highest bidders among traders who had been skulking around for weeks, examining the slaves like cattle. There were few slave families that had not suffered the loss of relatives on New Year's Day, sold and taken away never to be seen again. The custom was officially replaced by Emancipation Day, beginning January 1, 1863. Lamentably, President Lincoln had not been able to persuade Congress to authorize monetary compensation to the slave-holders, as had Britain when it freed the slaves in the British West Indies in 1834. Feelings of inferiority, embarrassment, and shame that have often plagued descendants of American, but not West Indian, slaves might not have arisen had federal compensation accompanied the ending of this dreadful institution.

Members of my family have suffered from this complex. Enjoying a measure of distinction because of luck of various kinds, there was an emphasis upon an ostrich-like ignoring of racial identification. We were the only black family in the town in which I was born—Zion, Illinois. My father was organist of the huge tabernacle of this town, which had been founded at the turn of the century by an evangelist from Scotland by way of Australia. It had a population of about 20,000 when I was born, people from all over the world. I did not understand at the time, though I do now, why my parents were so disturbed when they learned that my father's father was coming to visit us. They apparently tried to keep him out of sight of the citizens of Zion, but he insisted on going to church to hear my father play the organ. I remember overhearing my parents angrily discussing my grandfather's behavior at the tabernacle, where he beamed at every one and constantly referred to my father as "Dr. Wilson, my son." What had apparently inflamed them was that my grandfather had told people he was "Janitor of Public School 9, in Brooklyn, New York." My father had said that he was a "civil engineer." Years later I learned that both my father and my grandfather were right: a "janitor" is a "civil engineer" in a schedule of school salaries I had reason to consult. But to my father and mother it was a death blow. "Civil engineer" sounded genteel; "janitor" was low-class. The fact that my grandfather had provided his three children with an education that landed each in the realm of professionals seems never to have earned *him* a position of respect in their minds.

The oldest of six children, I was the only one who remembered hearing my grandfather tell about his childhood one Sunday afternoon in his small dining room in Brooklyn. My aunt, secretary to a bishop, was taking stenographic notes right beside me, and I was watching those odd swirls rather than listening intently. But suddenly she stopped writing. I realized that Grandpa's voice had changed from its usual gentle tones to loud, agitated shouting. He was recalling the day when "Master" had brought all the slaves together in the "Big House," and had told them that they were "free." In the pandemonium that followed, the little ten-year-old boy was pushed aside, and he was soon standing alone, not understanding what was going on. When he suddenly realized that the slave-holder was walking toward him yelling, "You are FREE, I told you!" my grandfather jumped back in fright, and crashed into the large hall mirror behind him.

Years have magnified my admiration for my grandfather. I am not sure that he ever received thanks for anything he ever did for his children and grandchildren. He died before I had developed sense enough to appreciate this kindly, hardworking, God-fearing citizen who was a revered deacon of his church, respected by his community, and admired by everyone but the children he had slaved for, to make them "gentlefolk."

My mother never forgave me for accepting a position on the faculty of Spelman College, the women's college of Atlanta University, after my graduation from Hunter and Columbia, with B.A. and M.A. degrees. She wanted me to wait for my name to be reached on the Board of Education's list of candidates to become teachers of English in New York City high schools. In my mother's eyes, this would have been a dream position. But I had asked advice from Dr. DuBois, a family friend who was returning to Atlanta University after a prolonged absence. When he learned that I had an offer to teach at Spelman College, he immediately advised me to accept it. "You do not know your roots," he explained. How right he was; my thirteen years with black people of all kinds, especially the hundreds of students from whom I learned more than I taught them, broadened my vision of what it means to be alive.

Finding slave narratives became a passion. Through those slim, battered pamphlets I learned what evil is, the meaning of courage, how precious the power of love. The accounts of the demonic beatings drenched me in tears; the heroic determination of slaves to help each other made me realize how true it is that man should be his brother's keeper. As the work of analyzing the narratives progressed, I became calm—and proud. Through me, these narratives would be reborn. The lives of the slaves would live, in their own words.

Out of deference to my family I have kept my work from publication, though with an aching heart. Happily, scholars have found it anyway. When I was asked by Professor Henry Louis Gates, Jr., of the Yale University Afro-American Studies Program for permission to publish the work, to my great surprise I was told by my daughter, "Fine. Go ahead." It was the association with Yale that had won consent!

MARION WILSON STARLING

New York City
March 7, 1981

Foreword

The present study is an endeavor to contribute to the field of American literary history a bibliography of the extant narratives of American Negro slaves and an introductory survey of these group autobiographic records.

Notably little attention has been accorded the slave narrative by American social and literary historians until very recently. One combs the pages of the most outstanding studies in American slavery in vain for reference to or mention of the existence of any of the narratives. None of the published writings of Ulrich Bonnell Phillips contains any reference to these records; nor was any slave narrative to be discovered among the uncatalogued papers deposited in the Yale University Library from his estate. Special studies of slavery in the various states make no mention of slave narratives.[1] W. E. Burghardt DuBois, in his long career of important studies in the field beginning in 1895, first presents the slave narratives in 1945, at which time he lists seventeen.[2] Carter G. Woodson's *The Negro in Our History*, which appeared in seven different editions between 1922 and 1941, contains only one oblique reference to a slave narrative in the seventh edition.[3] A dissertation entitled "Anti-Slavery Sentiment in American Literature prior to 1865" does not name a single slave narrative.[4] Some recent studies, on the other hand, have begun to make note of the slave narratives as valid sources of information.[5] About fifty slave narrative sketches have been published in the pages of the *Journal of Negro History*, some of the sketches having been personally collected by Dr. Woodson, the founder and editor of that publication, for the purpose of discovering and preserving records of Negro life and history.[6] On the basis of the interest of the reading public upon publication in November of 1945 of Benjamin A. Botkin's *Lay My Burden Down: A Folk History of Slavery*, it seems likely that future studies in American slavery will take the material of the slave narratives into account.[7]

In the absence of reasons from the historians themselves for their neglect of an area of "such illuminating documents" recording the "workaday life of the antebellum South," a neglect which one of the few students of the narratives has called inexcusable,[8] the author of the present study offers three conjectures: the general inaccessibility of the slave narratives; hesitancy to use sources traditionally enmeshed with abolitionist propaganda; and hesitancy to use sources preserved by way of the Federal Writers' Project. The problem of finding the slave narratives is discussed in this study,[9] and a bibliographic guide to the location of 6006 narrative records is provided.[10] With regard to the problem of the authenticity of this material, the writer has used every available means of testing the narratives, relying heavily upon the method for determining the validity of testimonial evidence as outlined by John Henry Wigmore, noted authority on judicial proof,[11] and upon the attitude of several authorities toward acceptance of the slave narratives they have come to know.[12]

The slave narrative records extend from 1703 to 1944. They are to be discovered in judicial records, broadsides, private printings, abolitionist newspapers and volumes, scholarly journals, church records, unpublished collections, and a few regular publications.[13] Because the period extending from 1836 to 1860 was the most significant period in the literary history of the slave narratives, this study has centered its interest upon evaluation of the narratives of that period. Lacking direct guidance for collecting the narratives, the writer felt justified in amassing records from the same abolitionist sources that Dr. Woodson consulted in preparation of his *Education of the Negro Prior to 1861*. He does not question the validity of material; instead, he punctuates it with such observations as the following: "The instances of Negroes struggling to obtain an education read like the beautiful romances of a people in an heroic age."[14] This book contains the only direct reference in book form that Dr. Woodson makes to a slave narrative, a reference to the 1849 edition of Josiah Henson's *Life of Josiah Henson*.[15]

Acceptance of Garrison's *Liberator* as an important source of original material by the slave is illustrated in a later work by Dr. Woodson, *The Mind of the Negro as Reflected in Letters Written during the Crisis 1800–1860*. In the foreword to that volume he states: "Most of the letters to antislavery workers and agencies were extracted from books and newspapers. The chief source of the latter was the *Liberator*, published by William Lloyd Garrison in Boston. A score or more of them, however, were taken from the *National Anti-Slavery Standard*, published by various editors in New York City. Copies of some of these same letters may be found in other anti-slavery publications."[16] Included in this study are letters regarded by Woodson as "excellent historical evidence" by the slaves Jupiter Hammon, Phillis Wheatley, Austin Steward, Frederick Douglass, William Wells Brown, Jermain W. Loguen, Samuel Ringgold Ward, Henry Bibb, J. W. C. Pennington, William Still, John Thompson, and Anthony Burns, whose narratives or narrative accounts are discussed in this study.[17] Dr. Woodson's assertion concerning the value to be placed upon those letters may have pertinence here, in view of the acceptance by this eminent authority on Negro history of materials from abolitionist publications:

From the point of view of psychology of the Negro, which must be taken into consideration as an important factor in the study of history, these letters are of still larger value. The mind of a people, the development of the public mind, has become a new factor in historical interpretation. This factor is now being considered not only as important as the social, political, and economic, but also as productive of these forces. . . . These letters herein given were written when modern facilities had not developed beyond that of frequent use of copyists, and practically all of these letters were written by the Negroes themselves. Here, therefore, we have the opportunity to judge hundreds of Negroes as they really expressed themselves.[18]

Among recent studies depending upon slave narratives published by abolitionists for "facts" concerning slavery, there is the definitive study by E. Franklin Frazier, *The Negro Family in the United States*. The material for the first two chapters on the slave family comes from seventeen slave narratives discussed in this present study. Frazier's references to slave narratives are also cited, indirectly, by Melville Herskovits in his *Myth of the Negro Past.*[20] Herbert Aptheker's *American Negro Slave Revolts* cites nine different slave narratives in the course of presenting a view of the slave scene very different from that indicated by Ulrich Phillips, in such passages as one beginning: "Slave revolts and plots very seldom occurred in the United States."[21] Merle Curti, in his *Growth of American Thought*, gives the slave narrative its first presentation in the general pattern of American history.[22] The apparent inclination of the reviewers of Botkin's *Lay My Burden Down* toward accepting the slave narratives collected by the Federal Writers' Project as a "kind of collective saga of slavery" with which materials one might "contrast the plantation tradition of the whites with that of the ex-slaves,"[23] suggests the coming of a new day for the slave narratives as a whole.

Admitting that the credibility of many of the slave narratives in the Federal Writers' Project is weakened or damaged by "internal contradictions and inconsistencies; obvious errors of historical fact; vague, confused, or ambiguous statements; lapses of memory; and reliance on hearsay rather than firsthand experience," Dr. Botkin still insists upon the intrinsic worth of the slave records, which he considers very important for social scientists as well as for students of folklore.[24] One reviewer of this book of selections from ten thousand typescript pages, in stressing the values of the slave narratives as social history, even goes so far as to upbraid the University of Chicago Press for doing a "disservice both to the studious and to the casual reader by the omission of an index."[25] Another reviewer, who especially emphasizes the value of the picture of "the social history of the South" to be found in Botkin's selections, writes:

As history it is subject to the skepticism which must always meet the thing that is long remembered and seen through the tangled vistas of vanished generations. But after all allowances have been made for the romanticism of memory—the old men's desire to tell a good story—there remains the historical conviction that slavery was not, for the Negro, the state of sleek bliss which so many apologists for the "peculiar institution" have maintained.[26]

The writer of this study readily admits that both the questionnaire method of obtaining information and reliance upon memory tend to weaken credibility. As to the latter effect, however, there is the ballast of Dean Wigmore's assertion that the memory of the aged is more active in the recollection of earlier experiences than of more recent events.[27] The general reputation of the conduct of Federal Writers' Projects, furthermore, does not guarantee the trustworthiness of individual projects. It was with gratitude, therefore, that Dr. Woodson's statement of acceptance of the particular project including the collection of the slave narratives was received. Reviewing Dr. Botkin's book, he says:

While it is generally conceded that so much money made available for this purpose in such a short time gave opportunity for much loss, waste and robbery, when we see such results as this volume from the Federal Writers' Project we have to revise our estimate of the good thereby accomplished. It was fortunate that some of the funds made available were used to collect the records of the Negro and to penetrate the past of this race by such interpretation as the facts warrant. . . .

Whether or not the editor did his work properly only those acquainted with that large bulk of material with which he worked can actually tell. He produced samples to show the various aspects of the institution of slavery and how it affected both master and slave. Who knows, for example, whether the number of narratives showing the benevolence of masters is out of proportion to the number showing the cruelty of the system, without examining all the data with which he dealt? He included so many narratives of Negroes who were well treated and content with their lot that at times one receives the impression that he was inclined to document the pro-slavery contention that the bondage of the Negro was a benevolent institution. He doubtless included a disproportionate number of narratives of Negroes who were satisfied with slavery and unwillingly accepted freedom when it finally came. Other collections of slave narratives do not give such a bright picture as we find in this narrative. The author does not scientifically show the proportion of those abused in contradistinction to those who received apparently human treatment. It is evident that, unless studied scientifically, this large collection of over 10,000 narratives would enable one writer to tell one story and some other writer a different story. It depends in this case altogether on the attitude of the writer concerned, and most younger writers who have paid attention to American history have been influenced by such proslavery apologists as Lloyd, Phillips, Bowers, Fleming and Craven. . . . Much light is thrown here on the working of the mind of the untutored Negro, imprisoned in a system by which he had control of neither mind nor body. . . . This mass of information has a value beyond the use of the historian who tells us what happened; it will serve the psychologist and the anthropologist to interpret that past from other points of view.[28]

The present writer is in a position to answer Dr. Woodson's question in the above passage, having carefully studied the ten thousand pages (*not* "narratives") in the seventeen-volume, thirty-three-part Slave Narrative Collection of the Federal Writers' Project, as deposited in the Library of Congress. After tabulating various kinds of material in these narratives for the purpose of arriving at generalizations about the same kind of material in the narratives published before 1860, the results were compared with a smaller set of narratives collected as the first project of its type under the Federal Writers' Project, under the direction of L. D. Reddick. The statistical findings of this analysis formed the basis for all conclusions stated in this study concerning the mass testimony of the slave narratives. Adhering to Dean Wigmore's criteria concerning the validity of mass evidence, this study has hoped to establish the slave narrative records as source materials of importance. Though of subliterary quality for the most part, the narratives contain the nucleus of the creative thinking of an oppressed race during a period of nearly two hundred fifty years.

The chief literary importance of the slave narratives lies in their generic relationship to the popular slave novels of the 1850s. For this reason, the final chapter of this study of the narratives as a whole consists of an analysis of the fusion of the slave's own materials with the Romanticist's methods. Throughout the study the emphasis has been upon the individual slave narrator, and for this reason similar experiences are quoted from the various narratives in order to show individual differences within the same general framework.

It is pleasant to make formal acknowledgement of the many persons whose aid and encouragement have helped bring this study to its present state. Interested at the outset in preparing a variorum edition of a single slave narrative, I owe my change of emphasis to a question asked me by Professor William Charvat: "How many slave narratives are there?" Professor Homer A. Watt encouraged me in setting out upon the quest of finding an answer, and Professor Oscar Cargill consented to become the advisor for the study.

Librarians and members of library staffs have been unusually generous with their professional skills and their time in all of the libraries visited. I am especially indebted for the privileges granted and the kind aid given me by Dr. L. D. Reddick and Mrs. Ernestine Anthony Lipscomb of the Schomburg Collection of the New York Public Library; by Dr. Benjamin A. Botkin of the Library of Congress; and by Mr. Bradstreet of the Boston Public Library. Courtesies have been unfailingly extended me also at the libraries of the American Antiquarian Society, Atlanta University, the Boston Athenaeum, Cornell University, Harvard College, Howard University, the Massachusetts Historical Society, the Massachusetts State Library, the New York Historical Society, the New York Public Library at Forty-second Street, Oberlin College, Pennsylvania University, and Yale University.

Special acknowledgement for their generosity in allowing me to use manuscript materials in their possession goes to Professor John B. Cade of Southern University, Dr. L. D. Reddick of the Schomburg Collection of the New York Public Library, Professor Wilbur H. Siebert of Ohio State University, and Mr. Arthur B. Spingarn of New York City.

The labor of counseling and guiding the mounting bulk of data was cheerfully borne by Professor Cargill. Background help in interpreting the role of the slave narratives in the social history of the United States was given by Dr. Reddick.

Finally, I wish to acknowledge the generous fellowship grant from the Rockefeller Foundation, without which help it would not have been possible for me to have undertaken this research.

M. W. S.

The Slave Narrative

Chapter 1

The Background of the Slave Narrative

The autobiographical record of George Washington Carver, published in 1944, is the last of more than six thousand extant narratives of American Negro slaves, the first of which was published nearly two and a half centuries ago, the narrative of one Adam, "servant of John Saffin, Esquire," printed in Boston in 1703. Considered together here for the first time, these narratives make up an interesting supplement to the literature of the institution of slavery in America, a literature recognized as having special significance as "a summary of the literature of the world on the subject."[1] The group furnishes a continuous record of that institution, from the time that slavery first achieved a definite place in the American scheme until long after the decree to eradicate the system had been officially uttered.

Before 1865, the history of the slave narrative ebbs and flows in the same general rhythm as the history of the antislavery crusade in America. It begins in the wake of the humanitarian efforts of Judge Samuel Sewall of Boston, the publication of whose *Selling of Joseph* in 1701 launched the literature of abolitionism in this country.[2] In the course of the eighteenth century it eddies about for a time, in company with narratives of the picaresque type. Except for this digression, occasioned by recognition of a resemblance between the career of the swashbuckling slave out for adventure and the then popular "rake's progress" literature, the slave narrative is apparently dependent upon antislavery sympathies for its progress.

At the end of the eighteenth century, in England and then in America, it achieves its first literary significance as a vehicle of propaganda in the English abolitionists' campaign, one of the earliest manifestations of the wave of Romanticism sweeping Europe. Its boom years come with the rise of abolitionism in New England, from the 1830s to the 1860s when, as one critic points out, "the strange anomaly of Negro bondage in the first democratic state became the motive force of a humanitarian protest which may be called the second wave of the romantic movement in the social realm, and which gathered intensity second only to the original agitation for human rights in the eighteenth century."[3] By the late 1840s, the slave narrative has become such a popular feature of the antislavery crusade that one contemporary critic, calling attention to its "very wide influence on public opinion," claimed that it represented "a new department to the literature of civilization," which America had the "mournful honor of adding."[4] Another critic, writing in the early 1850s, complained that the "whole literary atmosphere has become tainted" with "those literary nigritudes—little tadpoles of the press . . . which run to editions of hundreds of thousands."[5]

After the romantic fanfare that hoisted the literature of the slave into the public eye had died down, however, the slave narrative that was such a fascinating part of the antislavery program of the 1850s, revealing "the index of [the slaves'] inner life, and of their habits of thought,"[6] all but vanished from common knowledge. Slave narrative volumes trickled occasionally from the press, passing unnoticed into the vast waters of post-Civil War turmoil. The coming of the scholars' crusade in the middle 1920s, with its goal of formulating a "usable past," brought attention to some twenty slave narratives rediscovered in uncatalogued library deposits, secondhand stalls, or attics. Enlisting the aid of federal subsidies, social historians in the 1930s started projects for collecting slave narratives from the lips of ex-slaves while there was yet time. Interest in the slave narrative gained a place in the 1940s.

Antislavery sentiment manifested itself as early as 1646, when, by order of the Massachusetts General Court, a group of slaves unlawfully brought from Africa was returned to that country at its expense, accompanied by a letter expressing the indignation of the court at the infringement on Massachusetts' laws to end "bond slaveryie, villinage or captivitie amongst us." By 1776 it was an integral part of the spirit of the time throughout the country. The colonists, with Jefferson of Virginia as their scribe, expressed in blistering terms their condemnation of King George III for forcing continuation of the slave trade on them to his profit. The paragraph was struck from the original draft of the Declaration of Independence in deference to the wishes of some rice and indigo growers in South Carolina and Georgia and some owners of slave ships in New England. The discarded clause is a valuable record of the current attitude toward the slavery system, stating, in part:

> Determined to keep open market where men should be bought and sold, he has prostituted his negative for suppressing every attempt to prohibit or restrain this execrable commerce; and that this assemblage of horrors might want no fact of distinguished die, he is now exciting those very people to rise in arms among us, and to purchase that liberty of which he has deprived them by murdering the people on whom he has also obtruded them: thus paying off former crimes committed against the liberties of one people, with crimes which he urges them to commit against the lives of another.[7]

Slavery was felt to be both an unnatural evil and a nuisance by the eighteenth-century American. Sincere sympathy for the oppressed condition of the slave did not prevent the kind of reaction to the slaves as human creatures that we find in the following candid statement from such an avowed champion of the rights of the enslaved Negro as the Quaker John Woolman:

> The blacks seem far from being our kinsfolks; and did we find an agreeable disposition, and sound understanding, in some of them, which appeared as a good foundation for a true friendship between us, the disgrace arising from an open friendship with a person of so vile a stock, in the common esteem, would naturally tend to hinder it. They have neither honors, riches, outward magnificence, nor power; their dress coarse, and often ragged; their employ drudgery, and much in the dirt: they have little or nothing at command, but must wait upon and work for others, to obtain the necessaries of life; so that, in their present situation, there is not so much to engage the friendship, or move the affection of selfish men.[8]

Benjamin Franklin, while agreeing with Woolman as to the injustice to the slave of the conditions of slavery, and while interested in cooperating with the plans of Benjamin Lay and Anthony Benezet for the abolition of the system, was also personally prejudiced against the Negro as a member of a society of which he was a part. He would not employ a member of that race in his home or his business; and he issued what is probably the first expression of color prejudice in American letters, in a pamphlet entitled *Observations concerning the Increase of Mankind*, which he published in 1755 and which concludes with the following query:

> The number of purely white people in the world is proportionately very small.... I could wish their numbers were increased. And while we are, as I may call it, *scouring* our planet, by clearing America of woods, and so making this side of our globe reflect a bright light to the eyes of inhabitants in Mars or Venus, why should we in the sight of superior beings, darken its people? Why increase the sons of Africa, by planting them in America, where we have so fair an opportunity, by excluding all blacks and tawneys, of increasing the lovely white and red? But perhaps I am partial to the complexion of my Country, for such partiality is natural to mankind.[9]

The slave narratives of the eighteenth century all reveal the slaves' awareness of a social prejudice against the slave as a Negro, quite apart from his economic disadvantage at being a slave. What the slaves most frequently wanted to do about it was to get away from the America where even a kindly saint like Woolman and a cosmopolite like Franklin did not welcome him. There is dignity in the petition addressed to the representative in the Massachusetts State Legislature from the town of Thompson, April 20, 1773, by the four slaves Peter Bestes, Sambo Freeman, Felix Holbrook, and Chester Joie. They ask to leave, like gentlemen:

Boston, April 20, 1773

Sir,

The efforts made by the legislature of this province in their last sessions to free themselves from slavery, gave us, who are in that deplorable state, a high degree of satisfaction. We expect great things from men who have made such a noble stand against the designs of their *fellow-men* to enslave them. We cannot but wish and hope, Sir, that you will have the same grand object, we mean civil and religious liberty, in view in your next session. The divine spirit of *freedom* seems to fire every human breast on this continent, except such as are bribed to assist in executing the execrable plan.

We are very sensible that it would be highly detrimental to our present masters, if we were allowed to demand all that of *right* belongs to us for past services; this we disclaim. Even the *Spaniards,* who have not those sublime ideas of freedom that Englishmen have, are conscious that they have no right to all the services of their fellow-men, we mean the *Africans*, whom they have purchased with their money; therefore they allow them one day in a week to work for themselves, to enable them to earn money to purchase the residue of their time. . . . We do not pretend to dictate to you, Sir, or to the honorable Assembly of which you are a member: We acknowledge our obligations to you for what you have already done, but as the people of this province seem to be actuated by the principles of equity and justice, we cannot but expect your house will again take our deplorable case into serious consideration, and give us that ampler relief which, *as men*, we have a natural right to.

But since the wise and righteous governor of the universe has permitted our fellow men to make us slaves, we bow in submission to him, and determine to behave in such a manner, as that we may have reason to expect the divine approbation of, and assistance in, our peacable and lawful attempts to gain our freedom.

We are willing to submit to such regulations and laws, as may be made relative to us, until we leave the province, which we determine to do as soon as we can from our joynt labors procure money to transport ourselves to some part of the coast of *Africa*, where we propose a settlement. We are very desirous that you should have instructions relative to us, from your town, therefore we pray you to communicate this letter to them, and ask this favour for us.

In behalf of our fellow slaves in this province,
And by order of their Committee.[10]

There is a record of at least seven more such attempts by groups of slaves in Massachusetts to appeal to the legislature for liberation through the presentation of petitions. In June of 1773, slaves petitioned Governor Gage and the Massachusetts General Court to grant them their freedom, together with land, on the ground that they had "in common with other men a natural right to be free."[11] Another "Petition of a Grate Number of Blackes" was sent the same authorities in May, 1774, calling attention to the sinful and evil nature of the slave system, and asking for freedom as a natural right.[12] Similar petitions were presented at intervals during the next year. Slaves of Bristol and Worcester united in a petition to the Worcester Committee of Correspondence, asking the aid of that group in their efforts to obtain their freedom. The result was the calling of a convention at Worcester on June 14, 1775, at which the white persons present resolved: "That we abhor the enslaving of any of the human race, and particularly of the Negroes in this country, and that whenever there shall be a door opened, or opportunity present for anything to be done towards the emancipation of the Negroes, we will use our influence and endeavor that such a thing may be brought about."[13]

Whatever the evil to the slave of the slavery system, however, there were slaves who considered slavery a blessing rather than a curse, because it had been the means of introducing them to the Christian religion. Thus Phyllis Wheatley writes, in her panegyric "On Being Brought from Africa to America":

'Twas mercy brought me from my *Pagan* land,
Taught my benighted soul to understand
That there's a God, that there's a *Savior* too:
Once I redemption neither sought nor knew.
Some view our sable race with scornful eye,
"Their color is a diabolic die".
Remember, *Christians, Negros,* black as *Cain,*
May be refin'd, and join th'angelic train.[14]

A like depth of gratitude to the institution of slavery for having brought him to Christ is to be found in the autobiographical portions of the writings of Phillis Wheatley's contemporary, the slave Jupiter Hammon, of the estate of John Lloyd of Queens Village, Long Island. The satire that John Trumbull directed against apologists for slavery on the ground of its being a Christianizing agency, published in the *New Haven Correspondent* for July 6, 1770,[15] loses much of its pungency when read beside Hammon's solemn assertions that the slave, by utilizing the humiliation of his condition rather than by attempting to escape from that humiliation, would find his salvation in that very state.[16] Hammon felt keenly the problems of slaves less fortunately situated than he; and his grandfatherly *Address to the Negroes in the State of New York*, probably because its emphasis was so earnestly devoted to warning disgruntled young slaves against bartering their hope of an eternity in heaven for the doubtful joys of earthly freedom won by insurrection, was printed in New York and in Philadelphia in 1787 and apparently enjoyed wide circulation, extant copies showing that it was twice reprinted in the year 1806.[17]

Slave insurrections, the existence of which is indicated in the clause struck from the original draft of the Declaration of Independence as quoted above, were more prevalent from the time of the American Revolution on than has been known until very recently.[18] An authority lists forty-seven slave revolts between the generally known slave plot of 1741 in New York City and the next generally known slave revolt, the Gabriel plot in Henrico County, Virginia, in 1800—including two in Massachusetts, two in New York, five in New Jersey, five in North Carolina, five in Louisiana, six in Georgia, nine in Virginia, and thirteen in South Carolina.[19] Twenty-four of the insurrections occurred between 1774 and 1799. In September, 1774, John Adams' wife, Abigail, wrote him of the slave plot discovered among the slaves of Boston and the surrounding region, expressing a sentiment held by many persons, in her closing remark: "I wish most sincerely there was not a slave in the province; it always appeared a most iniquitous scheme to me to fight ourselves for what we are daily robbing and plundering from those who have as good a right to freedom as we have."[20] During the period of the American Revolution, there were hundreds of manumissions of slaves by owners who either shared Mrs. Adams's views, or were fearful of slave revolts; also, thousands of slaves seized the opportunity afforded by the commotion attending the revolutionary activity among the colonists, to obtain their freedom by flight and by enlistment in the opposing armies.[21]

It was a period, of course, of worldwide outburst of revolutionary activity. The cry of "Liberty, Fraternity, Equality" of the French revolutionists impressed the American Negroes still enslaved after the American Revolution ended, as representing precisely those things they were deprived of, despite the humanitarian avowals of the Declaration of Independence. Thus anarchic slave projects began to acquire formidable proportions in the newly united states, especially after the revolt of the slave in San Domingo. This revolt, which began in 1791 and brought panic to Southern slaveholders as it strode on through fourteen years of heroic determination to the victorious culmination of an independent Negro republic, became an important subject of conversation in the North and the South and caused an exodus of hundreds of slaveholders from their plantations into cities like Richmond, Norfolk, and Charleston.

The slave insurrections were labor uprisings. From the time of the slave Adam on up through the slave narratives, there are echoes of slave discontent over labor without compensation. Operating as "a commercial system of exploitation" during nine-tenths of the years of its existence and throughout approximately nine-tenths of the area it covered,[22] American slavery was subject to the cycles of prosperity alternating with depression characteristic of any system of private gain dependent upon a world market.[23] Therefore, in times of depression and panic, the slaves were the chief sufferers. Their already meager rations of food and clothing dropped to subhuman standards; slave families were separated as bankrupt slaveholders sold or leased thousands of slaves to other slaveholders; inhuman methods were employed to goad the slaves to maximum production at minimum expense to the owners. The frightful slave insurrection of 1741 in New York City occurred during the severe winter of 1740-41, when suffering among the poor of the city, generally, and among the slaves especially, was acute. Likewise, the severe economic depression of the years 1791-1802, 1810-16, 1821-31, 1835-40, and 1854-56 spanned the years of the most serious slave insurrections, of which one authority itemizes a "minimum list" of two hundred ten reported revolts.[24] Inspirited by such additional factors as the revolutionary philosophy prevalent from the 1770s on through the eighteenth century, or the rapid growth and spread of the equalitarian Methodist religion from 1785, or stirring debates in Congress in 1784 and 1808 and 1820 and 1832-60 over slavery—no amount of counsel from comfortably fixed, mellowly aging Jupiter Hammons could dissuade slavery-maddened young desperadoes from making periodical assaults upon the system. The insurrectionists felt they had nothing to lose, in the first place, unless it be that heaven they had been told about but more or less doubted. Where flight from the system was possible, they fled, by the tens of thousands, to the Dutch, the Indians, the Mexicans, the British armies, the Canadians, the French, the Northern states, the British Isles. Where their masters were willing, thousands of slaves hired themselves out nights or engaged in incredibly ingenious projects for earning money, and bought their freedom from their masters, the prices asked varying from about one hundred and fifty to six thousand dollars, with six hundred dollars as the average amount set. But there were thousands of slaves who could not brook the idea of paying for a freedom that they were learning to believe was the birthright of every man; thousands who thought the dogged labor of a Venture Smith or a Lunceford Lane, working days for the master and nights to earn money to pay the master for themselves, was idiotic. Therefore, they uprose—an estimated fifty thousand at one time in 1800. In that "most important year" in the history of the American Negro slave revolts, Nat Turner and John Brown were born, Denmark Vesey bought his freedom, and the Gabriel conspiracy took place.[25]

The notion that slavery in the North was radically different from slavery in the South seems to have begun with the enthusiastic reception given Crevecoeur's *Letters from an American Farmer*, which that enterprising Frenchman, sometime resident of frontier sections of Pennsylvania and upper New York State and onetime visitor to South Carolina, published in London in 1782, the literary market at that time being very much interested in works having the "common man" and the "noble savage" formula. No earlier record can be found stereotyping slavery above and below the Mason-Dixon line, whereas from that year onward Crevecoeur's sharp differentiation between the nature of slavery "in the Northern provinces" and in the South is to be found repeatedly: the happy condition of the slaves in the former region is contrasted with the barbarous treatment of the slaves in the latter. In the excruciating climax of "Letter XI," his description of the slave suspended in a cage on a plantation near Charleston, South Carolina, to be pecked to death by birds and devoured by insects, became a classic in Europe, after its adoption by the Romanticist Herder for the first of five *Neger-Idyllen*, with the title "Die Frucht am Baume," as part of Herder's *Briefe zu Beforderung der Humanitat*. Heralded as "the gospel of humanitarianism," Herder's work spread propaganda for the doctrines of tolerance and humanitarianism through the Europe of the Age of Romanticism.[26] Crevecoeur's picture was later borrowed, via Herder, by Kolb, Kotzebue, and Zameo. The recent discovery that the birdcage story had appeared in French literature as early as the 1750s casts doubt upon Crevecoeur's having had the actual experience he reports in "Letter XI," especially in view of the fact that the already celebrated story did not appear in the French edition of the book and was withdrawn from subsequent English editions.[27] But it is not necessary to discredit Crevecoeur's having had a firsthand acquaintance with somewhat similar conditions in and around Charleston because of this discovery that the motif for his dramatic climax was borrowed from a known source. The slave narratives include dozens of equally barbarous though not equally picturesque episodes, and it is possible therefore that Crevecoeur decided to substitute the birdcage motif for some revelation of a slaveholder's brutality that he had witnessed that was quite as atrocious but not so effective as literary material. Certainly his description of conditions on a large plantation has an authentic ring when compared with hundreds of other descriptions of large plantations. But whether Crevecoeur was reporting a bonafide experience or not, the generalization that proceeded from his story stuck. Henceforth, the best-known concept on the Continent for Southern slavery was the birdcage episode, accepted as the norm of slave experiences below the Mason-Dixon line, in contradistinction to a purportedly humane state of affairs for the slave above that line.

Contemporary records both corroborate and refute Crevecoeur's label of "happy" for the condition of slaves in the North. Since the majority of the slave establishments in the North consisted of fewer than a dozen slaves, the deplorable degradation characteristic of slave life on plantations, with hundreds or even thousands of slaves, very seldom occurred in the North. The slave narrators Abraham Johnstone, Robert Voorhis, Thomas Cooper, George White, and William Grimes tell of their dread of being sold to plantations farther south than Delaware or Maryland. As early as the 1780s, the stories of the hardships and inhuman cruelties that increased with the size of the plantation had struck the slave on the smaller, Northern farms with horror as he listened to fugitive slaves fortunate enough to escape to the North, where they changed their names and quickly settled down as laborers or craftsmen, although they were always in danger of recapture by their owners. Gronniosaw and Venture Smith, however, in their narratives of slave life in New York and Connecticut in the 1770s and 1780s, provide evidence of exploitation of slave labor by greedy slaveholders that shows that the real basis for a difference between the characteristics of slavery in the North and the South was the number of slave laborers owned and the slave labor expected. Slaveholders who really wanted to make a profit out of such labor, whether in the South or the North, had to engage in or at least countenance drastic methods to force the slaves to produce. Although no slave narratives draw so barbarous a picture of slave life in New England as Timothy Dwight in Part Two of his long poem, *Greenfield Hill*, published in 1792, Dwight gives the title "State of Negro Slavery in Connecticut" to his argument preceding the section, and being an intelligent citizen of Connecticut himself, he must have thought that he knew what he was doing.

One critic of Dwight's treatment of slavery in *Greenfield Hill* stresses the onset of sentimentalism at this time in antislavery literary productions, under the influence of the sentimentalism of European writers.[28] If by "European" he means particularly the English Denham's *Cooper Hill* and the Irish Goldsmith's *Deserted Village*, he is probably right as to literary models. But it is well to remember that the immediate source of inspiration for Dwight's poem was irritation at the reports of European travelers about the United States; that his underlying theme was his "much-lov'd native land"; and that his stated purpose was to contribute both to the amusement of his countrymen and to "their improvement in manners, and in economic, political, and moral sentiments."[29] In his implied comparison of Connecticut's "Fair Verna" and Ireland's "Sweet Auburn," Dwight links the plight of the Connecticut slave and the Irish peasant, the "uncur'd gangrene of the reasoning mind" of the first poem fitting into the "to hastn'ning ills a prey" of the second. He saw danger in a social system that shut human beings off from birth, from human blessings; and though his psychological appreciation of the slave's dilemma may be credited to the school of sentimentalism, the sociological import of such passages as the following, by one of the leading intellectuals of the state and later president of its greatest glory, Yale College, under the inscription "State of Negro Slavery in Connecticut," is more real than literary:

> See fresh to life the Afric infant spring,
> And plume its powers, and spread its little wing!
> Firm is its frame, and vigorous is its mind,
> Too young to think, and yet to misery blind.
> But soon he sees himself to slavery born;
> Soon meets the voice of power, the eye of scorn;
> Sighs for the blessings of his peers, in vain;
> Conditioned as a brute, tho' formed a man.
> Around he casts his fond, instinctive eyes,
> And sees no good, to fill his wishes, rise.
> (No motive warms, with animating beam,
> Nor praise, nor property, nor kind esteem,
> Bless'd independence, on his native ground,
> Nor sweet equality with those around . . .)
> Thus, shut from honour's paths, he turns to shame,
> And filches the small good, he cannot claim.
> To sour, and stupid, sinks his active mind;
> Find joys in drink, he cannot elsewhere find;
> Rule disobeys; of half his labour cheats;
> In some safe cot, the pilfer'd turkey eats;
> Rides hard, by night, the steed his art purloins;
> Serene from conscience' bar himself essoins;
> Sees from himself his sole redress must flow,
> And makes revenge the balsam of his woe . . .
> Thus slavery's blast bids sense and virtue die,
> Thus lower'd to dust the sons of Afric lie . . .
> O thou chief curse, since curses here began;
> First guilt, first woe, first infamy of man;
> Thou spot of hell, deep smirch'd on human kind,
> The uncur'd gangrene of the reasoning mind;
> Alike in church, in state, and household all,
> Supreme memorial of the world's dread fall;
> O slavery! laurel of the Infernal Mind,
> Proud Satan's triumph over lost mankind! . . .
> In dread procession see the pomp begin,
> Sad pomp of woe, of madness, and of sin! . . .

Awe-struck, see silken Asia silent bow!
And feeble Afric writhe in blood below!
Before, peace, freedom, virtue, bliss, move on,
The spoils, the treasures, of a world undone;
Behind, earth's bedlam millions clank the chain,
Hymn their disgrace, and celebrate their pain . . .
Why glows yon oven with a sevenfold fire?
Crisped in the flames, behold a man expire! . . .
Why shrinks yon slave, with horror, from his meat?
Heavens! 'tis his flesh, the wretch is whip'd to eat.
Why streams the life-blood from that female's throat?
She sprinkled gravy on a guest's new coat![30]

Writing as a resident of Connecticut, particularly for other residents of Connecticut and presumably about conditions in Connecticut, Dwight did not ruffle the feelings of his fellow men, exaggerated though some of his "facts" concerning the state of Negro slavery in Connecticut doubtless were. His influence, and the influence of others like him in various parts of the North—J. P. Martin of Boston, for example, who declared in 1791 that, if the American Revolution was just, "then surely a rebellion of slaves would be just"[31]—helped give impetus to antislavery agitation, so that by 1804 every Northern state had passed laws of gradual emancipation, under which the last of the slaves in those states were freed in 1829.

How freely antislavery literature circulated in the state of Virginia we know from the large collection of antislavery pamphlets gathered and annotated by George Washington.[32] The antislavery section of Jefferson's *Notes on Virginia*, emphasizing the evil effect of slavery upon the character of the slaveholding class, was published first in 1784 and passed through seven editions. Judge St. George Tucker, professor of law at William and Mary College, brought out in the late 1790s a thoughtful analysis of the problem of maintaining a system of slavery in a modern world, entitled *A Dissertation on Slavery, with a Proposal for the Gradual Aboliton of It in the State of Virginia*. From the 1770s to the end of the eighteenth century, Thomas Jefferson's opposition to slavery and to the slave trade as inimical to the concepts of individual freedom and economic independence had dominated the thought of the South's leading state. But the expanding interests of the slaveholders slowly displaced Jefferson's philosophy in the Southern mind. His agitation for insertion of a clause in the Ordinance of 1784 that would have excluded slavery after 1800 from the entire region from which came Kentucky, Tennessee, Alabama, and Mississippi brought the tantalizing result of defeat by a single vote. Commenting on the defeat, the disheartened Jefferson wrote: "Thus we see the fate of millions unborn hanging on the tongue of one man, and Heaven was silent in that awful moment."[33] Abolition societies had sprung up in the 1780s and 1790s in many cities of the South as well as in the North, meeting annually by representation in the American Convention of Delegates from Abolition Societies, but the increasing danger from slave revolts and increasing dependence upon slave labor in the newly developed cotton culture brought the South gradually to repudiation of Jeffersonian equalitarian doctrines. That Jefferson himself lost interest in continuing the campaign to free the slaveholder of the evil of irresponsible power, as well as his victim, the slave, we may infer from the fact that he found it feasible, in 1814, to apologize for his "reluctance to lead a crusade for emancipation."[34]

Meanwhile, the recurrence of slave rebellions was turning the South into a "huge fortress in which prisoners were held, at hard labor, for life,"[35] as far as about one-third of its inhabitants was concerned. By law, all men who were not Negroes became part of a standing army throughout the South after 1800. Militia companies and volunteer military units abounded, patrol duty was demanded of all white men, overseers were armed on the plantations, and guards and standing armies were to be found in all Southern cities. Fear that slaves congregated in common centers would promote further insurrections discouraged the development of industrial centers. Maryland, Kentucky, and Tennessee passed laws between 1796 and 1801 making manumission of slaves easier; but the great plantation oligarchs of eastern Virginia, North Carolina, South Carolina, Georgia, and Louisiana never seriously considered the elimination of slavery. With the phenomenal upturn in financial prospects caused by the sudden spurt in profits from the production of cotton and sugar, by 1805 it was certain to the Southerners that although slavery was a dangerous and unnatural system, it was to be encouraged and fostered rather than abolished.

With slavery disappearing in the North, which lacked such economic complications as the lure of cotton and sugar culture in the South, a tendency to criticize the South began to develop. Cognizance of this tendency can be noted in Jefferson's warning to Governor Monroe of Virginia to proceed as humanely as possible in sentencing the insurrectionists in the thwarted Gabriel plot, with the explanation that the "other states and the world at large will forever condemn us if we indulge a principle of revenge, or go one step beyond absolute necessity—they cannot lose sight of the rights of the two parties, and the object of the unsuccessful one."[36] Therefore sentences of execution were reduced to the thirty-five key slaves in the plot, ten condemned slaves being reprieved and banished before the date set. The Southern newspapers gave notably little space to the details of the trials of the conspirators and of the plot, emphasizing instead the various theories in circulation concerning a possible political origin of the conspiracy, with the intent to injure Jefferson's chance at the presidency in favor of a second term for Adams.[37] According to the *Salem Gazette* (Massachusetts) for October 7, 1800, the "minutiae of the conspiracy" were withheld from the public "through a mistaken notion of prudence and policy;" and the *New York Commercial Advertiser* for October 13, 1800, reported that the Virginia Legislature did not remove the injunction of secrecy concerning their deliberations on the conspiracy, which was understood to have involved upwards of fifty thousand slaves, and to have had some connection with San Domingan agents.[38]

A very different attitude toward making public the details of a slave plot was manifested in the proceedings connected with the projected Denmark Vesey insurrection twenty-one years later in Charleston, South Carolina. Apparently believing that a knowledge of the full history of the plot and of the plotters would be good for the public, two magistrates of the Charleston Court, including the magistrate who presided over the trial of freedman Denmark Vesey and his slave accomplices, prepared an *Official Report of the Trials of Sundry Negroes, Charged with an Attempt to Raise an Insurrection in the State of South Carolina: Preceded by an Introduction and a Narrative*, which was published in Charleston in 1822 at the request of the court. Thomas Wentworth Higginson, writing for the *Atlantic Monthly* of June, 1861, tells how a friend on a visit to South Carolina in 1841 asked to see a copy of this report but was "cautiously" informed by her hostess that the only copy in the house, "after being carefully kept for years under lock and key, lest it should reach the dangerous eyes of the slaves" had at last been burnt, the same having happened in many other homes as well.[39] Certainly it must have proved to be a document loaded with ideas for budding insurrectionists.

The character studies of Vesey and his six slave leaders provided in stenographic reports of a variety of testimonies reveal the types of Negroes found almost exclusively in the slave narratives from 1703 on. It is very interesting to learn how they went about picking their followers and winning them over to "the cause"—not so simple a thing as it might seem on the surface, yet managed with such skill that only thirty-five of many thousands of enlisted conspirators were ever discovered.[40] The enlistments appear to have been confined principally to slaves hired or working out as carters, draymen, sawyers, porters, laborers, stevedores, mechanics, and lumberyard workers. In the words of the report, "In short to those who had certain allotted hours at their own disposal, and to the neighboring country Negroes."[41] The plotters were warned to steer clear of domestic employees, especially those "waiting men who receive presents of old coats, and so forth, from their masters."[42] How right they were in entertaining suspicion concerning the attitudes of some domestic slaves is revealed in the source of betrayal of the Vesey plot, as of the Gabriel plot earlier and the Nat Turner plot yet to come. In each case a house servant was the agent of disclosure of the plans.

The speech accompanying pronouncement of the death sentence upon ten of the insurrectionists contains an exposition of Southern defense of slavery, beginning, in the words of the judge:

A moment's reflection would have convinced you, that disgrace and
ruin must have been the plot's consequence, and that it would have
probably resulted in the destruction and extermination of *your race*.
But if even complete success had crowned your efforts, what were
the golden visions which you anticipated?—Such men as you are in
general, as ignorant as you are vicious, without any settled principles, and possessing but few of the virtues of civilized life; you would
soon therefore have degenerated into a horde of barbarians, incapable of any government. But admitting that a different result might
have taken place, it is natural to inquire, what are the miseries of
which you complain?—That we should all earn our bread by the
sweat of our brow, is the decree which God pronounced at the fall
of man, extended alike to the master and the slave; to the cottage
and the throne. Every one is more or less subject to control; and the
most exalted as well as the humblest individual must bow with
deference to the laws of that community in which he is placed by
Providence. Your situation, therefore, was neither extraordinary nor
unnatural. Servitude has existed under various forms, from the
deluge to the present time, and in no age or country has the condition of slaves been milder or more humane than your own. You are,
with few exceptions, treated with kindness, and enjoy every comfort
compatible with your situation. You are exempt from many of the
miseries to which *the poor* are subject throughout the world. In
many countries the life of the slave is at the disposal of the master;
here you have always been under the protection of the law.[43]

The ire of the Charleston Court fell most heavily, not on the ringleader
Denmark Vesey, but upon the "sorcerer" Gullah Jack, sometimes called
"Couter Jack." It had been admitted that the insurrectionists "employed
every principle which could operate upon the mind of man" in order to
induce the slaves to join. They had told them that God approved of their
designs; that assistance from San Domingo and from Africa was at hand; that
"the whites, perceiving that they were becoming too numerous, had resolved
to create a false alarm of fire, and as they came out in the dead of night to
kill them, in order to thin their numbers;" and even that "Congress had
emancipated them."[44] But it seems chiefly to have riled the magistrates that
Gullah Jack's pretension to occult powers had had the greatest weight in
proselytizing the slaves. There is a note of revenge in the words accompanying
Gullah Jack's sentence:

Gullah Jack—The Court after deliberately considering all the circumstances of your case, are perfectly satisfied of your guilt. In the
prosecution of your wicked designs, you were not satisfied with
resorting to natural and ordinary means, but endeavored to enlist on

your behalf, all the powers of darkness, and employed for that purpose the most disgusting mummery and superstition. You represented yourself as invulnerable; that you could neither be taken nor
destroyed, and that all who fought under your banners would be
invincible. . . . Your boasted charms have not preserved yourself,
and of course could not protect others. Your altars and your gods
have sunk together in the dust. The airy spectres, conjured by you,
have been chased away by the superior light of Truth, and you stand
exposed, the miserable and deluded victim of offended Justice. Your
days are literally numbered. You will shortly be consigned to the
cold and silent grave; and all the Powers of Darkness cannot rescue
you from your approaching Fate![45]

As in the case of the Gabriel conspirators, the condemned slaves in the
Vesey plot died like men. Their refusals to divulge the names of any accomplices, though tortured cruelly in the effort to break their silence, link their
histories with the histories of the martyrs. It is curious that the Charleston
magistrates did not realize at once what a potent argument for the abolition
of slavery was contained in their publication, which a decade later was recognized as "incendiary," albeit by home folks!

There were more than a hundred abolition societies in the South of the
1820s, earnestly laboring in the cause of the slave and ranging in scope from
one group's avowed purpose of preventing cruelty to animals[46] to projected
plans for the gradual or immediate emancipation of the slaves. Elihu Embree
established the country's first abolitionist newspaper in Jonesborough,
Tennessee, in April of 1820. Entitled *The Emancipator,* it was a straight-
forward little sheet, issued from April to October of that year, which presented stories and excerpts from speeches designed to enlist sympathizers
with the cause of emancipation.[47] In the winter of 1821-22 a second abolitionist paper appeared in the little town of Mount Pleasant, Ohio, the place in
which the founder of *The Genius of Universal Emancipation,* Benjamin
Lundy, happened to be at the time. A few months later Lundy found it
advisable to move his paper to the "more sympathetic climate" of Jonesborough,[48] where it became a quiet "feeder" for Southern abolition societies,
bringing to their attention numerous stories of the effect of slavery upon all
members of a slave society, and advocating plans of gradual emancipation.[49]
In 1825 Lundy moved his paper to Baltimore, from which city it continued
to be published until the end of 1830, when he made the decision to move
The Genius of Universal Emancipation to Washington—a decision that was
indirectly responsible for the most dramatic turn in the tide of antislavery
sentiment in America's history.

The Southerners were "extremely, perhaps excessively sensitive" on the
subject of slavery, as one enthusiast for developing the art of human relations

observed in a thoughtful discussion of the matter in 1823. Recalling the fact that slavery had been established in the country as a national rather than as a sectional practice, and that New England ship merchants had shared with British slave traders the odium of importing the African to America for that purpose, one Samuel Miller of Princeton tried to discourage the growing tendency among Northerners to indulge in "contemptuous or acrimonious language" when speaking of Southern slaveholders. In an address delivered before the Synod of New Jersey, in New-Ark, he asserted that the slaveholders "freely acknowledge the deplorable character of the evil, as it exists among themselves," 'lament it," "mourn over it," and give evidence of a desire to "apply some adequate remedy to the acknowledged calamity." Miller advocated promotion of a national effort to bring about gradual emancipation of the slaves, the interim period to be devoted to training the slaves intellectually and morally and building up a trust fund through systematic saving of a portion of the profit from the slave's labor, so that at the time of emancipation he could enter upon life as a freedman with a sum of money sufficient to give him a fair start. There might have been no wrenching apart of the Union over the slavery question if men like Lundy and Miller had been empowered to inflame the great Northern middle class with the cause of emancipation. Miller's prophecy of the muddle that unwise impatience could create possesses historic interest:

> I verily believe, judging from the language of the New Testament,
> that if the Apostle Paul were now on earth, and were to travel in the
> Southern States, and to find the laws, and the conditions of the
> country what they are, he would uniformly preach and converse on
> this subject in a manner, which, though by no means temporizing,
> would be considered as kindly, forbearing, and inoffensive by all
> classes of the people. . . . While an adequate and an early remedy
> for the multiplied and dreadful evils of slavery is earnestly to be
> desired; yet we are not to expect that any human means can be
> found, which will put an end to these evils at once. . . . It must be a
> work of time, of patient labor, and of large expenditure. We must
> pay, and pay much, as the penalty of our dreadful mistake and folly;
> and well will it be for us, if we can obtain deliverance from it almost
> at any price. Some have been so inconsiderate as to maintain, that
> because slavery is, in all cases, an evil, that therefore it ought to be
> abolished at a stroke, and every slave in our land made free in a day.
> But the idea of liberating, and turning loose on society, at once, a
> million and a half of slaves, with all the ignorance and depravity to
> which their bondage has contributed to reduce them, would surely
> be the extravagance, or rather the cruelty of benevolence. It would
> be to bring, not merely on the white population, but on the slaves

themselves, thus suddenly liberated without being prepared for it, an accumulated curse under the name and guise of a blessing.[50]

It was not by way of inspiration from reasoned addresses and indefatigable efforts for the adoption of gradual emancipation plans that slavery was destined to be scotched, however, but rather by way of one of the most recent of the industrial inventions revolutionizing the western world, the harnessing of steam to the printing press, which led immediately to the production of journals for the masses. Whereas before the middle 1820s newspapers had been organs of the professional and mercantile classes for the most part, at a subscription cost of from five to eight dollars a year, by 1828 the number of periodicals had more than doubled, the "penny newspaper" began to appear on the city street corner, and the American public launched its campaign for government support and direction of schooling throughout the North and West. The result was that, within a single generation, the ability to read and write passed from the hands of a well-educated few, into the possession of the "most numerous reading public the world has ever known," according to one historian, who adds:

> In the United States, Tom, Dick, and Harry in the thirties and forties
> hurried to express in print their whole gamut of yearnings, doubts,
> hopes, and fears, their adventures in intellectual discovery, their
> remedies for social ills, their preachments against wickedness. It
> was the most abundant outpouring the nation had ever known and a
> documentary revelation of the many-sided American mind such as
> exists for no earlier epoch.[51]

The interests of the masses expanded. The plain people began to take a more active part in intellectual matters, and hundreds of periodicals came into being to satisfy the new curiosities of the semiliterate masses. According to Lowell, "Every possible form of intellectual and physical dyspepsia brought forth its gospel."[52] There were approximately seventy-five labor weeklies, more than thirty temperance journals, and a quantity of religious, scientific, technical, propagandist, professional, agricultural, and juvenile periodicals, in addition to a small group of belletristic magazines. It was by way of this new era for journalism that the crusade that brought the slavery question into the homes and consciousness of the American people was to be waged.

Garrison was the bombshell discovery of the mild-mannered abolitionist editor, Benjamin Lundy, who met him in an editor's office in Bennington, Vermont, in the course of a walking tour which had commenced in Philadelphia for the purpose of soliciting funds for *The Genius of Universal Emancipation*. This was in 1829. Garrison was twenty-three at the time and editor of the *Bennington Journal of the Times*. He had held this position since 1827, and his editorship was marked for intrepid espousal of the cause of the oppressed, with strong leanings toward reform movements. His career as an editor had begun in his home town of Newburyport, Massachusetts, at the age of twenty, with the *Newburyport Free Press*, at the end of a struggling boyhood during which he had helped his widowed mother by working in a Newburyport printer's office and had acquired an education on the side.[55] Garrison had never been South, never had come into contact with slavery, when the itinerant Lundy met the young enthusiast for the rights of the common man, and tapped the dynamite in his being with the revelation that there were in the United States more than two million human beings who, along with their children after them, were denied their natural rights by being held as slaves for life. In a flash, Garrison's whole purpose for living changed, and when Lundy returned to Baltimore, Garrison went with him as associate editor of his abolitionist paper.

The effect of Lundy's antislavery talk on Garrison was extraordinary. Knowing nothing at all about the historic background of the slavery issue, Garrison was conscious of but one thing: man shackled by man. Abolitionists before him had all been aware of the need to reckon with the complicated basis of slavery as a system. The slaves themselves, in an overwhelming majority of the narratives, respected the business angle involved, even in the face of their own dire distress. But Garrison's conception of the institution of slavery began and ended with the vision of slavery as a sin and of slaveholders as sinners. For him, there was but one conclusion: immediate emancipation of the slave at whatever cost.

It may be imagined that Lundy, with his practical knowledge of the many problems involved in the slavery question tempering his own yearning to see an end to slavery, had few really quiet moments from the time he and the new zealot went down to his *Genius* together until their parting somewhat more than a year later. For a little while Garrison gave at least lip service to the policy of gradual emancipation upon which Lundy had founded his paper. But by September of 1829 he could no longer hold back his conviction that immediate emancipation was the only possible aim for the abolitionist. In an article under his name appearing in a September issue of the *Genius*, he therefore recanted what he had said in favor of gradual emancipation in the course of an address he had made in Baltimore on July 4 of that year. Each editor wrote under his own name from that point on. Whatever the immediate cause for dissolving the partnership the following year, the irreconcilable difference in attitude toward the position of the slaveholder in the slavery controversy was reason enough for Lundy and Garrison to have agreed to disagree at any moment at all.

Boston was a last-minute choice of a place of publication for the journal that Garrison planned to start, after his breakup with Lundy. Washington had been his earlier choice, because the upper South seemed the logical place for headquarters of any abolitionist campaign. It is a little curious that no words have been devoted to speculation about how much of the tragedy of sectional misunderstanding might have been avoided had Lundy not suddenly decided to move his paper from Baltimore to Washington, causing Garrison to alter his plans and take his paper up to Boston, thinking that the one abolitionist paper would be enough for Washington and gallantly giving up the field to his senior. *The Liberator* in Washington would undoubtedly have got Garrison into difficulties, but it would not have been an innovation there.

In an address, "To the Public," on the first page of the first issue of *The Liberator*, January 1, 1831, Garrison contrasted the interest in abolitionism in the South with the state of apathy existing in the North. The proposals he had issued the preceding August concerning the publication of *The Liberator* in Washington had been hailed in some Southern sections but were "palsied by public indifference" in Northern parts. This reception had influenced Garrison in the final decision to take his paper to a Northern city, as it was more needed by the North than by the South, he had come to believe. His own words here are important:

> During my recent tour for the purpose of exciting the minds of people by a series of discourses on the subject of slavery, every place that I visited gave fresh evidence of the fact, that a greater revolution in public sentiment was to be effected in the free states—and particularly in New England—than at the South. I found contempt more bitter, opposition more active, detraction more relentless, prejudice more stubborn, and apathy more frozen than among slave owners themselves. Of course there were individual exceptions to the contrary.

Garrison deserves a gifted biographer. So much calumny was heaped upon his name by Northern politicians, merchants, bankers, and socialites as well as by the "solid South" that there may be some like the little old lady who interrupted a lecturer on World War I by jumping up from her seat and exclaiming: "I do not *want* the facts! I *know* the Germans started the war!" The facts reveal, none the less, that Garrison's only sin was his quixotism. He singlehandedly fastened the romantic movement to the institution of slavery. Uninhibited by a knowledge of complicating factors involved in the slavery problem, he was able to cut straight through to the core, the outrage to a group of two million human beings. The result was a growing reversal in the popular attitude toward the slave above the Mason-Dixon line, which spread slowly through the five hundred subscribers to *The Liberator* by the end of 1831, who grew in number to 2300 by 1834. Through other antislavery journals founded in the 1830s, the audience increased to 1,095,000 different subscribers to the eleven antislavery periodicals established by the end of 1836.[54] Probably completely unaware that advertisements for runaway slaves owned by eighteenth-century New Englanders had repeatedly appeared in Boston papers from the time of the founding of the *Boston News Letter* in 1704 until emancipation in the 1790s, Garrison thought there had been nothing before in the history of humankind so barbarous as the advertisements for runaway slaves that he was finding in the Southern newspapers of the day. A "master of the shears,"[55] Garrison would clip an advertisement, copy it in *The Liberator*, indicate its source, and then attack it in terms of the romanticist's emphasis upon the worth of the common man.

> (Commenting upon an announcement of a slave arrested at Palmyra on the charge of stealing) What has she stolen! Why—hem—haw—*she has stolen herself*; SHE IS A RUNAWAY SLAVE. What a horrible sin! And this is the PROOF that slaveholders would ABOLISH slavery if they COULD, but would not manumit a slave on any condition; and if he steals HIMSELF, would pursue him to the ends of the earth, at any expense. This is the *abstract* abolishment of *abstract* slavery. What *abstract*, nay, what *practical* nonsense![56]

When a Bostonian recently returned from New Orleans brought a handbill announcing the coming sale at auction of thirty-four "valuable servants" to *The Liberator* office, Garrison reprinted the handbill with an eye to generous spacing and a bizarre mixture of font, adding the note:

> Read it, Americans, and blush not merely for your country, but for your species! judge ye by the panegyric passed upon them whether the slaves are not qualified for freedom.[57]

The "panegyric" included an impressive listing of the various qualifications of the slaves, the majority of whom possessed special skills and a number of whom were bilingual.

The fugitive slave Frederick Douglass tells in his narrative of the abrupt change in the attitude of the slave toward his own social condition that was effected by Garrison and his followers. Previously a fugitive slave or an ex-slave had carefully concealed the fact, because "a colored man was deemed a fool who confessed himself a runaway slave, not only because of the danger to which he had exposed himself of being retaken, but because it was a confession of a very *low* origin!"[58] But under the aegis of the Garrisonians, the stigma hitherto attached to the slave condition was supplanted by open-armed welcome as man and brother in some of the most genuinely cultured homes in the land.

It is not possible to reproduce the effect of typical Garrisonian editorials on the evils of slavery, because of the use to which he put his unusual adeptness as a printer, the heritage of his apprenticeship days. Perhaps use of the few variations that could be managed, however, will suggest the nature of Garrison's innovations in the printer's script:

There are in this country a million female slaves who have no protection for their chastity, and who may be ravished by their masters
or drivers with impunity! ! There are born every year more than
SIXTY THOUSAND infant slaves who are *illegitimate*! a large
proportion of whom have *white fathers*—some of these are the most
distinguished men at the South—who sell them as they would pigs or
sheep! ! *Is not this perdition upon earth*—A BURNING HELL IN
THE VERY BOSOM OF OUR COUNTRY—A VOLCANO OF LUST
AND IMPURITY, *threatening to blast every plant of virtue, and to
roll its lava tide over all that is beautiful to the eye, or precious in
the sight of God?* . . . And yet there are those who call themselves
men!—*patriots*! ! —*philanthropists*! ! !—*Christians*! ! ! !—MINISTERS
OF THE LORD JESUS CHRIST! ! ! ! ! who passionately insist
upon a *gradual* abolition of a system which is altogether and absolutely one of prostitution, adultery, incest, violence, robbery, blood
and slaughter! ! It shocks their *manly, patriotic, benevolent, pious*
feelings to think of ceasing immediately from plundering more than
two million of human beings of their inalienable rights and the fruits
of their toil![59]

Garrison's answer for the many protests, from Northerners as well as
Southerners, against the violence of his attacks upon the slaveholders, was:

I am aware that many object to the severity of my language; but is
there not cause for severity? I will be as harsh as truth, and as un-
compromising as justice. On this subject I do not wish to think, or
speak, or write, with moderation. No! No! Tell a man whose house is
on fire to give a moderate alarm; tell him to moderately rescue his
wife from the hands of the ravisher; tell the mother gradually to
extricate her babe from the fire into which it has fallen; but urge me
not to use moderation in a cause like the present. I am in earnest—I
will not retreat a single inch—AND I WILL BE HEARD. The apathy
of the people is enough to make every statue leap from its pedestal,
and to hasten the resurrection of the dead![60]

The foregoing samples of Garrison's own brand of abolitionism should
render easy of understanding the State of Georgia's offer of five thousand
dollars for Garrison, "dead or alive," after a single year of *The Liberator*,
as well as the offer of fifteen hundred dollars by the Vigilance Association
of Columbia, South Carolina, for the conviction of any one distributing
copies of *The Liberator*.[61] Southern postmasters seized abolitionist literature
in general to destroy it. A price was set upon the head of any Northern
abolitionist who entered the Southern States, and many who had already
entered, like Amos Dresser, were brutally harried, imprisoned, and otherwise

mistreated. The family of Angelina Grimke, one of the "first" families of Charleston, South Carolina, was advised by the City of Charleston to warn her against returning home, after the publication of her *Appeal to the Christian Women of the South* in Philadelphia in the early 1830s. "Even liberal or humane Southerners who could not accept the proslavery argument found it increasingly hard to express their ideas," observes one historian of American thought.[62] By 1835 all of the more than a hundred antislavery societies that had existed below the Mason–Dixon line had disappeared except one in Kentucky.[63] Likewise, the *Annual Report of the New Anti-Slavery Society* (Boston, 1833) admitted the increasing severity of the slave laws passed since 1831 but expressed the hope that the greater severity would ultimately result in reaction against the institution of slavery.[64]

The biographer of one of the New England abolitionists, after admitting that there were many other forces affecting the antislavery issue—cotton, North-South trade relations, transcontinental migration, competition of free and slave labor—names Garrison as the generating influence of it all:

> Underlying and permeating all these matters was that fundamental force, that continual disturber of the conscience of every decent intelligent voter, North or South; that spiritual idea launched thirty-one years before the war, seven years before Webster's Niblo's Garden speech, by William Lloyd Garrison in his *Liberator*—the idea which through that paper first became a definite factor in politics—the purely religious idea that the maintenance of slavery was a sin.[65]

Similarly, a historian of the period writes:

> It was due to Garrison and his associates that slavery became a topic of discussion at every Northern fireside. Those who had heard the new doctrine gladly tried to convince their family and friends; those who were but half convinced wished to vanquish their doubts or have put to rest the rising suspicion that they were partners in a great wrong; those who stubbornly refused to listen could not fail to feel that a new force had made its appearance with which a reckoning must be made.[66]

The group of converts to Garrison's crusade was at first small in number, but it included some of the outstanding intellectual figures of Boston. Wendell Phillips, Edmund Quincy, Thomas Shipley, Thomas Whitson, George Mellen, Maria Weston Chapman, Samuel J. May, Francis Jackson, Charles F. Hovey, Eliza Lee Follen, Sydney Howard Gay, William I. Bowditch, Charles K. Whipple, Giles B. Stebbins, Parker Tillsbury, John Greenleaf Whittier, and Lydia and David Child were among the first to be taunted by George Ticknor and other "respectable" Bostonians for espousing the cause of abolitionism. A recent historian has described these early Garrisonians as a "group of earnest, sunny people, wholly convinced of the dynamic perfectibility of man, effusive with sentimentalism, and happily indifferent to the economic and political currents affecting the masses of middle-class society."[67]

Derided by "polite society," the converts forsook their accustomed paths in order to follow this new inspiration for purposive living. Lydia Maria Child, named by the *North American Review* as the best of the women writers in the late 1820s, deliberately abandoned the career she had built as a nationally popular writer, startling the country by publishing one of the earliest antislavery books in support of "Garrison's cause," her *Appeal in Behalf of That Class of Americans Called Africans*, which appeared in 1833. This publication brought her the "ridicule and censure" which she had already said in the preface to the book that she expected. But she was far from sorry for the step she had taken, claiming that she would not have exchanged the opportunity for being the "means of advancing, even one single hour" the inevitable progress of truth and justice, for Rothchild's wealth or Sir Walter Scott's fame.[68] In a letter to a fellow abolitionist, Theodore Weld, Mrs. Child vividly describes the early 1830s:

> The memory of the early anti-slavery days is very sacred to me. The Holy Spirit did actually descend upon men and women in tongues of flame. Political and theological prejudices and personal ambitions were forgotten in sympathy for the wrongs of the help-less, and in the enthusiasm to keep the fires of freedom from being extinguished on our national altar.
>
> All suppression of selfishness makes the moment great; and mortals were never more sublimely forgetful than were the aboli-tionists in those early days, before the moral force which emanated from them had become available as a political power. Ah, my friend, that is the only true church organization; when heads and hearts unite in working for the welfare of the human race.
>
> And how wonderfully everything came as it was wanted! How quickly the "mingled flute and trumpet eloquence" of Phillips responded to the clarion call of Garrison! How the clear, rich bugle tones of Whittier wakened echoes in all living souls! How wealth poured from the ever-open hands of Arthur Tappan, Gerrit Smith, the Winslows, and thousands of others who gave even more largely in proportion to their smaller means!
>
> How the time-serving policy of Dr. Beecher Stowe drove the bold, brave boys of Lane Seminary into the battle field! Politicians said, "The abolitionists exaggerate the evil; they do not know whereof they affirm;" and in response up rose Angelina and her sister Sarah, shrinking from the task imposed upon them by conscience, but upheld by the divine power of truth to deliver this mesage to the

world: "We know whereof we affirm; for we were born and bred in South Carolina; and we know that abolitionists have not told, and could not tell, half the horrors of slavery."[69]

The chief weapons used by the abolitionists were the journal, the convention, and the Bible. Offshoots from the Garrisonian stem later chose to include political tactics as part of their equipment, notably James Birney and Gerrit Smith. In the harmonious exhilaration of the early 1830s, however, there was general agreement with Garrison's design of arousing the wrath of the people against the gangrenous evil in existence in the South. With romantic zeal and unreadiness, the Garrisonians lent their imaginations and talents to the gravest problem of the age, which they pounced upon excitedly as their own special job. William Ellery Channing joined Mrs. Child and Edmund Quincy as chief literary aides; Sumner and Gerrit Smith joined John Quincy Adams and Wendell Phillips on the antislavery platform. By 1836, the writings appeared in a dozen antislavery journals at once, and the speeches, often magnificent things, reminiscent of the days of Cicero or of Archbishop Laud, were slathered across the yard-square pages of *The Liberator* as from an endless vat of inspiration, with Garrison wielding the giant ladle. Antislavery societies sprang up all over the North, with headquarters in Boston, New York, and Philadelphia, in which centers quarterly, semiannual, and annual conventions were held beginning in 1833. Gradually the doctrines of the abolitionist leaders began to permeate the masses, helped immeasurably by the publicity given the antislavery journals by irate Southerners "replying" by way of the general press. Although the churches remained aloof from the controversy, for the most part, the common man reading his Bible aloud at night in the bosom of his family found the verses which the abolitionists were advertising in their crusade, on almost every page of his best-loved chapters. By the time that the fugitive slaves had begun to arrive more or less openly, contributing their speeches to the antislavery meetings and their narratives to the antislavery journals, the interest of the great Northern middle class had been secured.

It is lamentable that the information thus widely spread concerning the heinous blot upon the land of the institution of slavery was unaccompanied by wide understanding. Had the abolitionists only possessed the farsightedness of gods—had they known to pin their emphasis upon the nation as a whole and its laws countenancing such barbarism instead of upon the South and the slaveholder as the agent of that dreadful system; had they known the justice of compensation to the slaveholder for the emancipation of the slaves, as English abolitionists had realized it in countenancing the payment of one hundred million dollars to the owners of the slaves emancipated in the West Indies by the British government in 1834—the emotional hysteria of the Southerner in the early 1830s might have been avoided. Instead, the South was confronted suddenly with a metamorphosis in the meaning of a term that it had known for nearly half a century, designating a quiet, friendly type of humanitarian, usually a Southerner operating in the South, though there had been a few in the North in the last two decades of the eighteenth century: the abolitionist. Literally over night, on the first of January of 1831, the term had made an unbelievable leap, henceforth indicating a violently abusive Northern stranger, self-appointed enemy to the South. Two things hurt the Southerner's feelings equally: an outsider's meddling with his business and the indiscriminate branding of the slaveholder by the neophyte abolitionists as a sinner and a thief. Garrison could not have baited the wary leopard more aptly!

Some students of the period believe that the slavery controversy was not the real cause of the dissension between the South and the North. They point to the evidence that sectionalism had already begun in the 1820s over division of opinion concerning the tariff and declare that threats of secession made in that decade were forerunners of dissension bound to come in connection with the country's international trade policy.[70] It is certainly true that the growth of the "Cotton Kingdom," in the newly developed "Black Belt" stretching from South Carolina to Mississippi, had increased the South's interest in slave labor at the very time that the system was being abolished in the North. Therefore, it was natural to expect differences to arise in the national legislature between delegates from sections with increasingly different economic patterns. It is also true that the debates in Congress of the 1820s were conducted on a more democratic basis than was characteristic of the Congress of earlier decades, so that the record of differences of many kinds and between all sections reveals sectional opinions and ambitions quite frankly. A study of Southern newspapers of the 1820s, however, shows the relatively large attention paid to the problem of supplying the huge new plantations with slaves, especially the problem of transportation of the slaves by sea or by land from the Upper South to the Gulf regions. Much space is also devoted, as a rule, to advertisements of slaves for sale and of runaway slaves, with now and then a hint of the generally undiscussed slave insurrections.[71] The sensitiveness of the Southerner to outside criticism of the slavery system was not likely to decrease as it became evident that slavery had become a permanent part of the Southern pattern, rather than the temporary expedient that it had been considered previously. Calhoun and Thomas Roderick Dew and other ardent Southerners were finding it necessary to silence the doubts of fellow Virginians and South Carolinians who had likewise been brought up on Jeffersonian ideals by proving Jefferson's equalitarian system a "mistaken philosophy, blinded by romantic idealism and led astray by French humanitarianism."[72]

The ideational patterns of proslavery and antislavery enthusiasts were of such opposite natures that conflict between sections holding the opposing views was inevitable. The probability is that the unexpected violence of Garrison's attack struck the Southerner on the very spot he was doing his best to shield from the rub of his own conscience and that the yell he subsequently let out in the name of Garrison, was in a measure generated by the subconscious scourgings of his own better nature. The Garrisonians at least provided the slaveholders with an excuse for objectivism: they could turn from apology for, to defense of, the "peculiar institution," by means of which the Southerner expected to achieve imperial splendor. The New England abolitionists had just enough outlandishness about their attitude toward the slaveholder and the slavery system to make it possible to censure them. Whatever road of reasoning is preferred, it is customary to end with some such conclusion as the following:

> The rise of militant abolitionists, however sincere, domiciled in a
> section which did not have the Southern problems, frequently using
> violent language, and begetting its use by opponents, did much to
> cement the South in defense of her own way of life, and to inject
> into the slavery controversy a psychological factor henceforth never
> absent from it.[73]

Historians are in debt to the zealous energies of young Thomas Dew, professor of metaphysics, economics, and political law at William and Mary College until promoted while still a young man to the presidency of that Virginian institution, for his preservation of the data by means of which we can reconstruct the scenes in the Virginia legislature during the last antislavery debates we have record of below the Mason-Dixon line. The debates took place during the entire month of December, 1831, three months after the terror of the Nat Turner insurrection at Southampton, and in the last month of the first year of "suffering" from *The Liberator*. The subject of the debates was the abolition of slavery in Virginia. Dew tells of the great interest taken in the debates by the public, which filled the galleries every day and sent letters and petitions from every corner of the state. "No stronger utterances in condemnation of slavery were ever voiced than appear in this debate," one authority has asserted.[74] The conclusion of the speech of MacDowell, later governor of Virginia, expresses sentiments of the finest abolitionist stamp:

> You may place the slave where you please—you may put him under
> any process, which, without destroying his value as a slave, will de-
> base and crush him as a rational being—you may do all this, and the
> idea that he was born to be free will survive it all. It is allied to his
> hope of immortality—it is the ethereal part of his nature which op-
> pression cannot reach—it is a torch lit up in his soul by the hand of
> the Deity, and never meant to be extinguished by the hand of man.[75]

But Dew was quick to criticize the abolitionist members of that session of the legislature as "an unusual number of young and inexperienced members, elected in the month of April previous to the Southampton massacre."[76] While praising their oratorical powers as befitting the orators of Rome or Athens in eloquence, he considered their arguments unbecoming to Virginians:

> Their arguments, in most cases, were of a wild and intemperate character, . . . subversive of the rights of property and the order and tranquillity of society. . . . Far be it, however, from us, to accuse the abolitionists in the Virginia Legislature, of any settled malevolent design to overturn or convulse the fabric of society. We have no doubt that they were acting conscientiously for the best; but it often happens that frail imperfect man, in the too ardent and confident pursuit of imaginary good, runs upon his utter destruction.[77]

Therefore, in the impassioned articles on the progress of the debate which Dew wrote for the *Richmond Enquirer*, he called the legislators' attention to the fact that Virginia would face financial ruin if she followed the young men's advice to emancipate all the slaves of the state and transport them to a colony in Africa. In the first place, it would mean a loss of the monetary value of the approximately 500,000 slaves, or "$100,000,000, one-third of the wealth of the whole state, and almost one-half of that of Lower Virginia," plus the need to use "the remaining two-thirds to encounter the additional enormous expense of transportation and colonization on the coast of Africa." More than that, they were told:

> The loss of $100,000,000 of property is scarcely the half of what Virginia would lose. . . . It is in truth the slave labor in Virginia which gives value to her soil and her habitations—take away this and you pull down the atlas that upholds the whole system—and we risk nothing in the prediction that on the day in which it shall be accomplished . . . the Old Dominion will be a waste, howling wilderness— "the grass shall be seen growing in the streets, and the foxes peeping from their holes."[78]

Predictably, instead of emancipating the slave, the Legislature did not adjourn until it had passed a series of stringent laws against all Negroes in the state, free and slave, forbidding them to hold public meetings, proscribing their education, and imposing numerous detailed restrictions which were admitted even by the biographer of the instigating Dew to have been "of a most despotic stamp."[79] The articles which had generated this sudden about-face from liberty to despotism were reprinted in the winter issue of the *American Quarterly Review* in 1832, but Dew also had them published in February of the same year, in book form, because the magazine had of necessity shortened some of his elaborate sections on the historical justifications for slavery.[80]

One authority on the period makes an interesting inference to account for Dew's introduction of historical justifications for the system into the slavery controversy: the influence upon him of the German universities.[81] But the two years that Dew spent in Europe, in 1820 and 1821, as a precocious lad of eighteen just graduated from college, were directed largely to the end of regaining his health, which was never robust and which had suffered from excessive study. It is not known certainly just how many weeks Dew spent in study in Germany, but apparently it was not many. Therefore, though he may have owed something to the lectures at Gottingen and Leipzig, it seems more likely that Dew's excessive attachment to his native state, galled to the bursting point by Garrisonian "abuse," was sufficient cause to dedicate the outline of his course on the history of civilizations to the defense of his beloved Virginia. He assured the slaveholder that slavery was not contrary to the teachings of the Bible, despite assertions and "proofs" of the Garrisonians that it was. He argued the natural inferiority of the Negro, whom God had endowed to enjoy life as a slave but who would be depressed instead of elevated by any change of station, and rounded up his entire *Review of the Debate in the Virginia Legislature of 1831 and 1832* with the lyrical conviction that:

> The whole population of Virginia, consisting of three *castes*—of
> free white, free colored, and slave colored population, is the sound-
> est and most moral of any other, according to numbers, in the whole
> world, as far as is known to me![82]

There is no argument in Calhoun's celebrated defense of "the South's peculiar institution," from the time of his shift from apologist to defender of slavery in the spring of 1832, that does not have a counterpart in Dew's book. Since the two men had worked together in the 1820s on the banking and tariff bills and on the occasions when Dew was called in for consultation by Jackson as a member of the "Kitchen Cabinet" while Calhoun was Vice President, it is certain that Calhoun knew Dew, and quite possible that he was influenced by the latter's unblinking dream, Greek democracy and all. At any rate, in 1833 Calhoun entered the Senate as the avowed spokesman for the South, as sincere in his belief that the system of slavery was the munificent system he knew on his own beautiful plantation in the South Carolina foothills as Garrison was sincere in his belief that all slaveholders were direct exponents of the devil. From that year until his death in 1840, Calhoun challenged the North, as to a duel. John Quincy Adams leaped to pick up the gauntlet from the floor of the House of Congress and the battle royal of the South against the North was on.

In fairness to Calhoun and Dew, it should be pointed out that the reign of actual terror that existed on many of the large plantations in the "Black Belt" during the later 1830s to the 1860s was unknown to them. Neither knew the new type of Southerner of that region—the MacDuffies, Bob Toombses, L. Q. C. Lamars, and other self-made "Fire Eaters," who saw in Calhoun's dream picture things that would have given that patrician soul the horrors. While words were being shot back and forth on the Congressional stage as to the terrible crime of destroying a society against the terrible crime of enslaving human souls, and newspapers were keeping the emotions at battle-pitch on both sides of the Mason-Dixon line, the new regime of slaveholders was rapidly making Garrison's most lurid dream come true. The slave narratives before 1836, although revealing a variety of cruelties, contain no record of the notorious systems of torture of slaves who "lagged behind in their task-work" that appear very frequently in the narratives after 1836. The elaborate instruments devised for this "reign of hell" may have been imported from the West Indies after the abolition of slavery there in 1834, along with the importation of experts in that most notorious of slave systems, brought to the United States for employment as plantation overseers. Calhoun was disposed to entrust everything to the "natural benevolence" of the individual slave owner. With his mind glued to Washington and the devastating warfare there, it was not to be expected that the scouts piercing the verbal smoke-screen at the Capitol every now and then with distressed pleas for more and more territory to the West would keep him accurately informed as to conditions in Lower Dixie.

Fortunately, the slaves knew that they now had somewhere to flee, and they fled. After 1835, there was no need for a Northern editor to toy imaginatively with advertisements of runaway slaves cut from Southern newspapers. The slaves themselves began to arrive, to tell of the terrors from which they had escaped. The figure of the fugitive slave, panting in a swamp, with the slave holder brandishing a whip and surrounded by bloodhounds close upon his heels, became so popular as a symbol that dinner plates were made with the scene for a center motif; the handles of silverware were embossed with the story; the ladies of one Massachusetts town embroidered a bed quilt for Garrison of squares covered with drawings and inscriptions "illustrating the cause;"[83] and the fad even extended to the embellishment of transparent window blinds, concerning which the editor of the *New York Emancipator* wrote:

> An ingenious painter of transparent window blinds has brought to
> the office an elegant pair of blinds. The main picture represents
> the pursuit and murder of a fugitive from slavery; the hunters with
> their rifles and broad hats, the blood hound on the scent, the poor
> trembling MAN hiding behind a rock, make up one group; and in

another are seen the planters wiping their artillery, and the hounds
retiring satiated with game, while in a stream appears the wounded
and dying victim, reddening the waters with his blood; all drawn to
the life, according to the descriptions which are given in the southern papers. . . . Underneath is the American Eagle, sustaining the
Declaration of Independence, while two kneeling slaves supplicated
for the application of its sublime truths to the vindication of their
rights. The whole is surrounded with an elegant border of the sugar
cane, cotton plant, and rice grain. The article is got up with much
taste, and handsomely finished; and presents the subject of Negro
wrongs in an impressive light. We wish every parlor in New York had
such a remembrancer.[84]

Escape from slavery by means of flight soon became the purpose of many
thousands of slaves, in many cases taking the place of the slave's former
dream of emancipation, which changing laws in the Southern States rendered
a virtual impossibility by the early 1840s. Although about one-half of the
separately published slave narratives of this period tell of their author's escape
from slavery as young, unmarried men, the overwhelming majority of the
total narratives of the period tell of the flight of whole families, of fathers
going ahead on reconnoitering trips and braving incredible dangers, including
probable death if caught, in their return trips to take their families to some
"place" they had found for them. Sometimes a whole plantation would
cooperate to conceal the preparations for flight of certain individual slaves
for whom life at the hands of the master or overseer was, for different reasons, even less bearable than usual. The record of slaves who refused succor to
fugitive slaves is very meagre. A slave asked for help by a pitifully hungry,
haunted-looking fugitive would give all he had, even when discovery meant
certain flagellation, and his own food allotment barely provided him with the
strength needed to keep up with his "task work." The few slaves who be-
trayed their fellow slaves out of jealousy of their scheme or hope of ingra-
tiating themselves with their masters seem abnormally few, considering the
proportionate distribution of such natures in ordinary society. It is possible
that there were more of them than the narratives record, but if there were
their memory must have been erased by more potent factors.

The antislavery journals teemed with accounts of the slave flights, each of
which, like Tolstoi's generalization concerning the unhappy family, had a
pattern distinctively its own.[85] There was the slave who, sold from his wife
and children, to be sent from Virginia to Louisiana, was successful in escaping
from the slave gang, found his way to his family by traveling nights and
enduring remarkable privations for concealment in the daytime, hid himself
near his family in order to steal one after another of them under cover of
night until all were under his care, and then fled with them all to the North.[86]

One gigantic black slave battered his way through many trials in his escape with his wife and four children from a plantation near Savannah, Georgia, to the promised freedom of Canada.[87] One slave couple got as far as Indiana from Missouri with their thirteen-month-old baby when they were caught by the pursuers, who shot the baby dead in the mother's arms while the father grappled with them, finally killing the one who had killed the child but having to leave its dead body and flee with the mother, reaching safety, at length, in Canada.[88] One woman slave, resolved to die rather than return to slavery, could find no other means of committing suicide in the jail in which she was confined before being taken back to her master than to draw up her legs and remain hanging from the low ceiling in that position, which she did, until death took her.[89] A letter from a Pennsylvanian to the office of *The Liberator* told of the frequency with which fugitive slaves were seen:

> There is one branch of the anti-slavery movement, as I think it may
> be justly regarded, which is making remarkable progress in this
> State, and that is the self-emancipating department. I have been sur-
> prised at the number of "fugitives from justice", as Mrs. Child calls
> them, who are continually passing through the central part of the
> State, on their way to the North: and at the deep interest mani-
> fested by the inhabitants in their success and safety. . . . Many of the
> slaves were fine-looking, intelligent, and apparently deeply reli-
> gious. . . . Their flight seemed to have been the result of much pre-
> meditation and preparation. Each man had a pistol and dirk, and
> they all expressed their determination to die, rather than to be taken
> back.[90]

A new interest in clipping advertisements from the Southern newspapers began to engage abolitionist editors as the amount of rewards offered by frantic slaveholders for the recovery of their decamped property began to soar to exciting heights. A reward of fifteen hundred dollars, for example, was offered in the advertisement for the eleven fugitive slaves described in the following excerpt from a Wheeling, Virginia, journal:

> Ran away on Monday night, 23rd instant, from near Wheeling, four
> large Negro men; named Brace, Andrew, Jack, and Charles; two
> women, Ginny and Lucy; four boys, George, William, Ben, and
> Frank; and one little girl, Eliza. Brace and Andrew are both stout
> and hearty young Negroes, twenty-one or twenty-two years old.
> Brace is square built, about five feet eight inches high, with two
> front teeth broken off. Andy is rather spare and rough-boned, about
> five feet eleven inches high, with large white eyes, one little finger
> off (about half). Both of these boys have thick lips, and are remark-
> ably dull and awkward in appearance and manners; and the prop-

erty of Alexander Mitchell. Jack and Charles, aged about thirty-five years. Jack is near six feet high, stout, and rough made, with a stern and determined countenance. Ginny and Lucy, aged from thirty to thirty-three years, both of short and square make, both quite black and thick-lipped, Lucy with front teeth out. Charles is about five feet nine or ten inches high, of light, keen, and sprightly form. The boy George is fourteen years old, bow-legged and stammers when talking; William and Ben about twelve years old; Wiliam is lame with a bad sore on his hip from a fall; Frank is about eight years old; the little girl Eliza is younger. The last nine Negroes are the property of Andrew Mitchell and Susan Mitchell. These Negroes have good clothes of various kinds; the small boys generally wore linsey roundabouts and hair caps. Andy, Brace, Jack, Ginny, and Lucy are brothers and sisters, with strong family likeness; there is no doubt but this family will keep together. . . . It is thought . . . that they are headed for Canada.[91]

Theodore Weld conceived the idea of massing such advertisements as the above together, adding to the excerpts already printed in *The Liberator* hundreds of others that he found in the Southern newspapers, and publishing the material as a book, under the title *American Slavery as It is: The Testimony of a Thousand Witnesses, as Taken from Southern Papers*. This book, notwithstanding the fact that its data can be verified as having actually come from the pages of the Southern press, from the *Richmond Enquirer* to the *New Orleans Picayune*, infuriated the Southerner against the "lying" abolitionists with their "viper's brains." It had a prodigious sale, at two dollars a copy, the profits from the sale being dedicated to the relief of fugitive slaves. It was the handbook of the antislavery movement from that time until Emancipation and became such a favorite with Harriet Stowe that she is said to have kept the book in her work basket by day and to have slept with it under her pillow by night.[92]

When the fugitive slave reached the North, he was encouraged to tell of his life as a slave at hundreds of antislavery meetings arranged for the purpose. A behind-the-scenes view of the abolitionists' management of these recitals is given in one of the slave narratives:

I was generally introduced as a "chattel,"—a "thing"—a piece of Southern property—the chairman assuring the audience that *it* could speak. . . . During the first three or four months my speeches were almost exclusively made up of narrations of my own personal experience as a slave. "Let us have the facts," said the people. . . . "Give us the facts," said Collins; "we will take care of the philosophy."[93]

Often the slaveholders themselves became intrigued by the sheer drama of their slaves' attempts to escape. Numbers of them went to Northern cities after it became impossible to manumit one's slaves in the South, freeing them there. One of the most interesting of the records of this type concerns the slave Nancy, a spirited woman who fled from her master in Anson County, North Carolina, and made her way to her husband, who belonged to an owner living in a different part of the state. The husband, knowing of the dreadful punishments likely to befall recaptured slaves—brutal beatings that ended frequently in death, chains forged on necks and ankles, sale "South," shooting—was afraid to try to escape. Finally, however, they set out together and had reached the Cumberland Gap when pursuers caught up with them. Nancy escaped, but her husband was recaptured. Nancy went up North, where she remained for a while, but soon decided to return to Anson County, so broken-hearted was she over her husband's fate. She found him on his owner's plantation, and his mistress was so deeply affected by Nancy's devotion to her husband that she determined to help them by taking part in their flight. Nancy was concealed until the plans were completed, everything having to be done with the greatest secrecy, as it had become a crime to harbor a fugitive, let alone to help him escape. The old lady then took them to Cincinnati, where she freed Nancy's husband formally. Later she became a permanent resident of Ohio.[94]

The role of the Quaker in the history of the struggle of the fugitive slave for freedom is beginning to receive the recognition it deserves in modern scholarship.[95] Picture after picture comes to mind from the slave narratives of the Quaker inside the Southern States, placidly driving his lumbering cart full of hay, which four times out of five *did* have just hay. But the fifth time there might be a false bottom and two-thirds of a load full of slaves, who would be picked up at the next "station" by a Quaker looking for all the world like the first one, and so on, up to the free states. Once, in the Quaker village of Pennsville, Ohio, a company of slave hunters came looking for eight fugitives: four men and a mother with her three children. Their reception should be reported in detail:

> After a hard and tedious chase [the slave hunters] turned back, full
> of indignation, towards the Quaker village, being satisfied that they
> had been sent upon the wrong track. It was nearly night when they
> reached Pennsville. One of the inhabitants was now seen nailing up
> his smoke-house, and barricading it with great care, giving as his
> reason for so doing, that he feared someone would steal his meat.
> This was a sufficient hint to the kidnappers that the runaways were
> undoubtedly in the smoke-house. They accordingly set a watch
> around it, and went for a warrant to the Quaker justice of the peace.
> He gravely declined giving them a warrant to search for stolen goods

in the night, and they had no other alternative than to wait and watch till daylight. Two were stationed with pistols by the smoke-house, and the rest attempted to sleep. But they were hardly quiet in bed before a whistle was heard—suspicion was excited that the Quakers were carrying off the Negroes, and the whole company, with the exception of the guard at the smoke-house, started off in pursuit, through brush and brake, and swamp, and beat up the woods until daylight, when they once more returned to Pennsville, and sought the justice for a warrant. That judicious dignitary looked down the street, and pointing to the constable, who was mounted on his horse and spurring out of the village, assured them that a warrant would be of no service, unless they could catch the man who alone could serve it. Off they went in pursuit of the constable, and over-took him after a chase of about three miles. But that official had other business on his hands, which he assured them must first be attended to. They were now in greater difficulty than ever. They appealed to the Friends around them, in their extremity of distress, and were kindly informed that another constable lived in another part of the town. Accordingly, they started in pursuit of him. In the mean time, the sentinels at the smoke-house became alarmed at the conduct of its owner, who was beginning very deliberately to tear off the roof of the house, for no other reason, that they could imagine, than to enable the fugitive "chattels personal" to escape. They commanded him to desist, but the Friend supposed he had a right, if he pleased, to amuse himself by tearing his own house to pieces. They presented their pistols, and threatened him. This the Friend considered, justly, a breach of the peace, and accordingly lost no time in obtaining a warrant from the justice, which was forthwith served. . . . They raved, and swore that they would not leave the smoke-house, and thus suffer the slaves to escape; where-upon, to pacify them, the constable opened the door of the building, when lo!—there were no slaves to be found and they had the mortifi-cation of reflecting that they had been all night engaged in guarding a few flitches of bacon.[96]

No fugitive slave seems ever to have failed to find succor at a Quaker's hands. They always arrived starved, and their grateful accounts of the dinners they ate uphold the ancient slogan about the "way to a man's heart." The fugitive slave John Brown, for example, relates in amusing detail his gargan-tuan meal in one Quaker home, which the worried goodwife tried to get him to take in stages.[97] A Canadian, writing in 1899, tells of the variety of ways that the fugitives were helped by Quakers on their journey to Canada, and declares that the "history of the conscientious lawbreakers who, for a quarter of a century, directed the underground railroad is a history of heroes inspired by the noblest motives."[98] Another narrator of a fugitive's story, a Quaker from Ohio, says:

> All through Ohio today, grey-haired men and women still tell how
> their mothers warmed, fed, and often clothed the fugitives, and their
> fathers drove through storm and darkness to save from worse than
> death the people committed to their charge.[99]

One Quaker "station" on Alum Creek, in Ohio, cared for as many as two hundred runaways in five months, after passage of the Fugitive Slave Law. One of the Quakers, Aaron Benedict, had as many as sixty fugitives in his house in one month, with twenty of them for dinner on one occasion.[100] There are many stories of teamwork between Quakers and free Negroes in various cities of Pennsylvania, Ohio, and Ontario. On one occasion the Quakers blocked one passageway from the court room so that the condemned fugitive might escape from another, and a Negro once grabbed prisoners in the midst of a mob, snatched up the sheriff's horse, and flew away into the woods.[101] Together, the two groups provided searchers for fugitive slaves with constant exasperation, as well as defeat. The Quakers, especially, often seemed to turn up just in the nick of time to help the fugitive. As one group of slave hunters remarked after turning disconsolately southward, balked again in their search: "Don't know where all those Quakers came from, unless they came up out of the ground."[102]

William Wells Brown, who became one of the most popular of the romantically feted fugitive slave lecturers and autobiographers, dedicated his fast-selling narrative to the Quaker who had rescued him from the despair of flight through the frozen woods, revealing the nature of the Quaker's role through his words of gratitude:

> To Wells Brown, of Ohio. Thirteen years ago, I came to your door,
> a weary fugitive from chains and stripes. I was a stranger and you
> took me in. I was hungry, and you fed me. Even a name by which to
> be known among men, slavery had denied me. You bestowed upon
> me your own. . . .
>
> As a slight testimony of my gratitude to my earliest benefactor, I
> take the liberty to inscribe to you this little narrative of the suffer-
> ings from which I was fleeing when you had compassion upon me. In
> the multitude that you have succored, it is very possible that you
> may not remember me; but until I forget God and myself, I can
> never forget you.[103]

The "little narrative" thus dedicated, published at the Boston office of the American Anti-Slavery Society in July, 1847, was in its fourth American edition by June, 1849, eight thousand copies having been sold in the first year and a half of its appearance.[104] By July of 1849, the ten thousandth had been sold. In the same year, the narrative was published in London by Charles Gilpin, with a sale of eleven thousand copies before the end of 1849.[105] Gilpin reprinted the narrative each year until 1852. The London publisher Bennett brought it out in a slightly revised edition in 1853, and the book continued to be reprinted throughout the 1850s.[106] When one remembers Gladstone's estimation in a speech before Parliament in 1852 that not more than about five percent of the new books published in England had a sale of more than five hundred copies, the figures of sale for Brown's narrative take on significance.[107] More important still, his narrative is but one of ten slave narratives published or reprinted in England between 1835 and 1863 that "made" the five-hundred-copies-and-over group. The popularity of the book-length slave narrative was exciting publishers on both sides of the Atlantic Ocean.

Eight of the ten American Negro slave narratives listed in the *British Catalog of Books, 1835–1863* were narratives of fugitive slaves: Brown's *Narrative of William Wells Brown, a Fugitive Slave, Written by Himself*; Frederick Douglass' *Narrative of the Life of Frederick Douglass, an American Slave, Written by Himself*, originally published in Boston in 1845, and also his second version of his autobiography, *My Bondage and My Freedom*, five thousand copies of which were sold within two days of its publication in New York and Auburn in 1855; Josiah Henson's *The Life of Josiah Henson, Formerly a Slave, Now an Inhabitant of Canada, as Narrated by Himself to Samuel Eliot*, published first in Boston in 1849 and then in London by Gilpin; James W. C. Pennington's *The Fugitive Blacksmith; or, Events in the History of James W. C. Pennington, Pastor of a Presbyterian Church, New York, Formerly a Slave in the State of Maryland, United States*, published first in London by Gilpin, in 1849; Moses Roper's *A Narrative of Moses Roper's Adventures and Escape from American Slavery* published first in London in 1837; Austin Steward's *Twenty-Two Years a Slave and Forty Years a Freeman*, published first in Rochester, New York, in 1857; William Craft's *Running a Thousand Miles for Freedom; or, The Escape of William and Ellen Craft from Slavery*, published in London by Tweedie, in 1860; and Samuel Ringgold Ward's *Autobiography of a Fugitive Negro*, published in London by J. Snow, in 1855. The other two slave narratives included the manumitted South Carolinian slave Zamba's *Life and Adventures of Zamba, an African Negro King, and His Experiences of Slavery in South Carolina*, published first in London by Smith and Elder in 1847; and the kidnapped Solomon Northup's *Twelve Years a Slave, Narrative of Solomon Northup, a Citizen of New York, Kidnapped in Washington City in 1841 and Rescued in January, 1853, from a Cotton Plantation near Red River, in Louisiana*, which was published simultaneously in Buffalo, New York, and London in 1853.

Although the *Life of William Grimes, the Runaway Slave, Written by Himself* was published separately in book form in New York as early as 1825, the vogue of the fugitive slave narrative did not set in until the second half of the 1830s, when the Northern abolitionists' curiosity concerning the doings of the slaveholders had risen to the highest pitch. Some two dozen narratives in addition to the eight above listed make up the roster of narratives by popular fugitive slaves. A contemporary critic, after calling attention to the value of the slave narratives as remarkable disclosures of the machinery of slavery from the point of view of its victims, points out their worth as literature, declaring:

> There are those who fear lest the elements of poetry and romance
> should fade out of the tame and monotonous social life of modern
> times. There is no danger of it while there are any slaves left to seek
> for freedom, and to tell the story of their efforts to obtain it. There
> is that in the lives of men who have sufficient force of mind and
> heart to enable them to struggle up from hopeless bondage to the
> position of freeman, beside which the ordinary characters of
> romance are dull and tame. They encounter a whole Iliad of woes,
> not in plundering and enslaving others, but in recovering for them-
> selves those rights of which they have been deprived from birth. . . .
> A man born and bred a slave becomes so possessed by the idea of
> liberty, that neither fear, nor the habit of obedience, nor the hope-
> lessness of deliverance, can stifle the irresistible desire to be free.[108]

The immense popularity of the narratives, in the opinion of this critic, was owing both to the Northerner's curiosity concerning the South and to a "sense of justice" that predisposed men to "hear the testimony given by those who have suffered, and who have had few among their own number to describe their sufferings." He referred to the eight thousand copies of William Wells Brown's narrative already sold; said of Douglass' narrative that by 1849, "in this country alone," it had passed through seven editions and was at that time out of print; and reported of the fugitive slave narratives in general that they were "scattered through the whole of the North."[109]

In an anonymous article entitled "Black Letters," by another contemporary critic, another side of the popularity picture is given. After complaining of the way the "black books" had swamped the literary market after the appearance of *Uncle Tom's Cabin* in 1852, the writer declares:

> It is all very well for the South to talk of the Negro excitements, and
> to take things to heart. If they had to read all those Negro-books
> that overflow us, north of Mason and Dixon's line, then, indeed, we
> should despair of them. We don't want, therefore, to hear any more
> complaints from Georgia or Carolina. 'Tis we, the readers of the

> North, who are aggrieved by these blasts and counter-blasts, and
> none have a better right to be angry, and talk of nullification than
> we have. . . . They are altogether speculations in patriotism—a ques-
> tion of dollars and cents, not of slavery or liberty. . . . Many of the
> persons who are urging on this Negro crusade into the domain of
> letters, have palms with an infernal itch for gold. They would fire
> the whole republic if they could but rake the gems and precious
> stones from the ashes.[110]

Despite the difference in attitude, these two critics are agreed upon one
thing: the popularity of the slave narratives. The sales figures we have must
represent a mere fraction of the total sales, judging from other data bearing
on this phase of their history. The fugitive slave lecturer Henry Watson wrote
Garrison on the eve of the publication of his narrative, to be priced at twelve
and a half cents per copy:

> The narrative of my life and sufferings in the prisonhouse of liberty
> nearly ready for distribution, and will, I trust, yield a sufficient return
> to maintain myself and family for some time longer, and enable me
> to continue to plead the cause of "the brethren" I left behind me.[111]

With like sanguineness, the amazingly determined ex-slave Noah Davis set
about preparing his narrative for publication. Having inveigled his humane
master into letting him go North on a lecture tour to get funds wherewith to
purchase his own freedom, and having in subsequent years repeated the lecture circuit with net receipts of four thousand dollars, by means of which he
purchased his wife and five of his seven children from his wife's master, Davis
turned to the writing and publishing of his *Narrative of the Life of Reverend
Noah Davis, a Colored Man. Written by Himself*, published in Baltimore in
1859, in the confident expectation of thereby realizing the two thousand
dollars still needed to purchase two sons yet in bondage. Anything over and
above that amount, he serenely remarked in his little autobiography, would
be applied toward the raising of the mortgage on his church in Baltimore![112]
As one historian has noted, commenting in 1941 upon this trend of the
1850s: "Lest we forget, there was once a time in our history when the picture
of a Negro on the title page of a book was a boon to its sale."[113]

The fugitive slaves and their narratives undoubtedly did much to key the
country up to the Act of Emancipation of 1863. Writing of the important part
they played in the crusade to achieve that goal, a contemporary declared:

> Even now, when it is all over, the flesh creeps, and the blood curdles
> in the veins, at the account of the dreadful cruelties practised on the
> slaves in many parts of the South. I would advise no one to read such
> histories today unless his nerves are very well strung. What was it
> then when the stories were told by the fugitives themselves? What

was it when the cries of the sufferers were going up every hour?
When the slaveholders were adding new territory to defile with
blood? Under such conditions you could hardly expect from those
who knew these facts, moderate language and soft words. The anti-
slavery men were like a cannon ball which flies straight to its mark
and shatters everything in its way. They were terribly in earnest,
and, like Luther, every one of their words was half a battle.[114]

England joined the New Englanders in honoring the fugitives Roper,
Douglass, Bibb, Pennington, William Wells Brown, Henry Box Brown, John
Anderson, Henson, Ward, the Crafts, and many others. Between twenty and
thirty thousand slaves had fled from the South from the 1830s to the 1840s;
at the Fugitive Slaves Convention, over which the ex-fugitive slave Frederick
Douglass presided at Casenovia, Canada, in 1855, it was estimated that the
number of fugitives then resident in Canada alone was fifty thousand.[115]
Except in Canada, where the fugitives settled down into more or less normal
pursuits to earn their livelihood, lecturing seemed to be the chief means of
subsistence that came into the fugitive's mind, whether or not he had ever
heard a lecture in his life before. Hoping to stem a tide that could only lead
to distressing conditions, William Wells Brown sent a message by way of *The
Liberator* in 1851 to slaves planning to come to England:

> Too many of our fugitive brethren are of opinion that because they
> can tell, by the fireside, the wrongs they have suffered in the prison
> house of slavery, that they are prepared to take the field as lecturers.
> And this being the fact, there are numbers here [London], who have
> set themselves up as lecturers, and who are, in fact, little less than
> beggars. . . . I would say to our fugitive brethren, if you don't want
> to become beggars, don't come to England.[116]

The warning was timely, as the spectacular triumphs abroad of Brown,
Douglass, Pennington, Ward, and, later, Henson, had filled with luckless
aspirations the minds of thousands with lesser endowments.

The publicity and the opportunities given a few hundred of the thousands
of slaves who fled from slavery from the 1830s to the 1860s greatly furthered
the abolitionists' program, demonstrating the fact that many slaves were not
only normally capable of behaving like human beings, but were even demon-
strably superior to average men, especially in consideration of the fact that
they had grown to manhood before even the barest rudiments of an education were available to them. The role of these slaves was a curious one, however, combining the features of stunt performers, star witnesses, and charity
patients. The embarrassment to traveling Southerners caused by the overt
attention paid slave lecturers in New England, on the high seas, all over the
British Isles, and even at the Peace Conference at Paris engendered a hatred

of the slave in some quarters where it had not existed earlier. Also, to the abolitionist, the slave was likely to be viewed more as a specimen with propagandist value than as an ordinary human being.

The stage show nature of the fugitive slave's role is best illustrated by the excitement among the abolitionists on both sides of the water over whether Douglass should or should not be ransomed in 1847. There was no other slave quite like Frederick Douglass. From the time that he had ascended the antislavery platform in 1841, four years after his escape from slavery in Maryland, he had captured the public eye. His complete identification with the "noble savage" formula endeared him to the considerable numbers of romanticists in almost any audience of the day. The real strength of his oratory thrilled the enthusiastic and even woke the indifferent into attention. Garrison discovered Douglass working the bellows at a brass foundry in New Bedford and quickly engineered him into the position of chief antislavery lecturer, first at home and then abroad. For seven years they worked closely together, Douglass sometimes paying lip service to Garrison's views in a way that is reminiscent of the lip service the young Garrison had paid the views of Benjamin Lundy a dozen years earlier. Garrison and Douglass were destined to disagree over some matters of fact. Laying facts aside, however, there was always to remain the bond of deep emotional attachment to the cause of the oppressed.

The excitement over Douglass's ransom centered on that chief blind spot of the abolitionists: money. As soon as his narrative was published on the first of June, 1845, Douglass realized that it was necessary for him to leave New England for old England, because his revelation of the concrete facts of his experience in slavery had disclosed his identity, and he was at any moment thenceforth in danger of recapture.

For two years Douglass enjoyed being "Nature's nobleman" on parade in the British Isles. It started on the trip across, when the captain of the steamship *Cambria*, who had purchased a copy of Douglass's narrative as it was being circulated on the boat, invited Douglass to speak, demanding that the Southerners who rose up in violent protest go to some other part of the ship if they did not want to hear him.[117] The narrative was immediately popular in England and Ireland; newspaper notices lauded "its native eloquence" and abundant evidence that "the argument, if it can be so termed, which would uphold slavery on the ground of the slaves' natural inferiority, has no foundation as regards such men as the writer, and therefore totally fails in its general application."[118] Sixty-five hundred copies were sold in Belfast, Ireland, in three months.[119] One editor spoke of Douglass as "a fugitive slave, who, as but yesterday, escaped from a bondage that doomed him to ignorance and degradation, now stands up and rebukes oppression with a dignity and a fervor scarcely less glowing than that which Paul addressed to Agrippa."[120] The *London Enquirer* printed a letter from a Belfast correspondent telling of

Douglass's ability to attract "large and responsible assemblies which are drawn around him, perhaps, in the first instance, by the novelty of the matter, but which cannot fail to be delighted and electrified by the addresses of the lecturer."[121] In fact, Belfast went to distinct lengths to honor Douglass, as we can see in a letter to Garrison from a "gentleman of Bristol, England," dated April 10, 1846:

> . . . And now as to Frederick Douglass. I felt much interested in him
> by reading *The Liberator*, long before you mentioned him. As soon
> as I heard of his being in Ireland, I wrote to Mr. Richard D. Webb
> about him, from whom I soon received fifty copies of the *Narrative*,
> which Mr. W. had just printed. These I quickly sold to friends, and
> had fifty more. The second lot was not long on hand, and I have
> now before me a third parcel, that contained a hundred copies,
> which are rapidly diminishing. . . . I suppose you have seen, ere
> now, the account of a public breakfast given to him in Belfast,
> presided over by a member of Parliament. It is only distinguished
> persons who are thus complimented here. What would his master
> and other Southerners say, were they to hear of this proceeding?[122]

Douglass made a very favorable impression in Scotland, prolonging his stay in Glasgow, waxing strong in his discussions of slavery as a sin and in the matter of the Free Church.[123] His new friends in the British Isles raised the sum of five hundred dollars so that Douglass's family might be brought there, Douglass having won their sympathy by his declaration that his honesty in the *Narrative* had barred the way to his joining his wife and children anywhere in the United States, especially since the relatively mild Thomas Auld had transferred legal ownership of Douglass to his brother Hugh. Hugh Auld had announced his determination to reduce Douglass to slavery again, once he set foot upon American soil. He engaged the services of agents in the British Isles to watch all ships leaving for America in order to know when and where Douglass would land if he slipped away.[124]

Despite the generosity of the British abolitionists, many of whom wanted Douglass to give up all thought of America as his home and spend the rest of his days in England, Douglass had become restless by the end of the summer of 1846 and wanted to get back. As he wrote in a letter sent to the *Protestant Journal*, July 23, 1846, in answer to a young abolitionist who seemed happy over the prospects of having Douglass as a permanent resident in England:

> Not quite so fast, young man. No inducement could be offered
> strong enough to make me quit my hold upon America as my home.
> Whether a slave or a freeman, America is my home, and there I
> mean to spend and be spent in the cause of my outraged fellow-
> countrymen.[125]

Therefore, when friends raised the seven hundred and fifty dollars Hugh Auld had set as his price for Douglass, Douglass was swift to accept the money with fervent thanks; and before the end of the year he had his "free papers" in his pocket, able to return to the Northern States, at least, without fear.

A romantic storm broke loose among the New England abolitionists! Douglass had "disappointed" them, "let them down," "stumbled," "violated one of the fundamental principles of the abolition movement," by succumbing to that transaction with a slaveholder, recognizing a fellow creature's "right of property" in him! The abolitionists were simply flabbergasted. Said Elizur Wright, Jr., editor of the *Boston Chronotype*:

> This talented fugitive, now known throughout the civilized world,
> has been a terrible thorn in the side of slavery, for, wherever he has
> gone, he has shown the falsehood of the plea, that the Negroes are
> an inferior race—not really men. But the slaveholders have at last
> gained an advantage over him. He has been guilty of the indiscretion
> and weakness of permitting himself to be bought. . . . It was cause
> enough of indignation when the weak-minded ransomed Latimer, he
> being on the 'free soil' of Massachusetts. But in this case of Douglass,
> there was less excuse. Douglass, while here, may have been in danger,
> but we think not in much fear. He is a courageous man, and would
> have been glad of an attempt at recapture, as another arrow in his
> quiver against the 'abominable institution' from which he had
> escaped. . . . We feel mortified and full of shame that a man like
> Douglass should have cheapened himself to $750 before the slave-
> holders. With thunder-tones he should have forbidden his friends
> thus to disgrace him.[126]

Wright's "mortification" and "shame" at Douglass's "bowing to the slave-holder" found editorial counterparts all over New England during the first months of 1847. The editor of the *Hartford Charter Oak*, for example, after characterizing Douglass as "a man, and a tall man, too, who from his perch across the waters there, can strike back blows at the tyranny here, which make the sparks fly from flinty hearts, and do as certain execution, when well aimed, as if he were on our soil," bemoaned Douglass's "folly," thus:

> We have seen him in the royalty of native manhood, stand up and
> pour his burning eloquence like lava, on the cold heart of the nation,
> and never for once suspected that he needed money to make him
> free. He appeared quite free for the times; freer far than hundreds
> whom he addressed. If there was any clank of the fetter, it was a
> little touch of anti-slavery sectism—a little succumbing to the strong
> master of the early movement; but from this quite unavoidable
> bond, no gold or silver could purchase manumission.

But withal, Frederick Douglass is a man, and by no means a slave; and the act of buying a little ticket with 'Free' written on it, at such an enormous price too, is worse than folly; it is mischievous, and virtually an acknowledgment of the traffic. . . . Was it the market value of the man they cared for, the assassin slaveholders who made his stay in this country dangerous? By no means. It was the terror of his great speech, his free words of scathing and scalding rebuke of oppression. . . . He was free, and will be; he was and will be still a hope to the oppressed. So this idle form of purchase is but a robber claim, to be good in morals and policy.[127]

One Increase S. Smith of Dorchester (who in the opening section of his long "sad" letter to *The Liberator*, dated January 11, 1847, says he would no more think of "mistering Douglass than he would Washington, Bonaparte, Alexander, Plato, or Confucius) thought, with Elizur Wright, that Douglass should have welcomed actual physical battle for his liberty, a valiant martyr to the abolitionists' cause. After wailing over that seven hundred and fifty dollars for quite a while, he asks:

Has he not lost much of that moral power, which he possessed, as the representative of the three millions of his countrymen in chains; taking, as he did, his life in his hands; appearing, wherever he appeared, with all the liabilities, which the law laid upon him, to be returned to stripes, torture, and death? He stood before us, before this transaction, as an impersonation of the moral sublime. He could stand upon his revolutionary principles. He could say, wherever he appeared, I am here in violation of the recognized laws of the land. The laws call me property. The laws require that I shall have free papers before I shall be permitted to walk at large. The only free papers I possess, or will ever accept, is the impress that God has stamped upon me, in creating me a man like yourselves. Judge, brothers, whether these papers are authentic or not. Read for yourselves, in the statute God has given me, in the voice with which I address you, in the thoughts, emotions, and aspirations which warm me to action. If these papers are not authentic, take me up; call me property; put upon my neck the iron collar; and return me, the miserable, degraded beast that I am, to my lawful and rightful owner! This language Douglass could once use with truth. But that time has now passed; and it seems to me that there is no language which he can now use, which will so clearly set forth the injustice of the laws and the wickedness of those who sustain them. . . . I am not alone in these feelings; everyone with whom I have spoken on the subject, has the same feelings that I have. . . . I, and I think I can speak for those, also, with whom I have conversed, am deeply sorry to feel that Douglass has lost aught of the power which he formerly possessed. I have looked forward to his return to this land of tyrants and slaves, with the deepest interest. I have been anxious to see how the threats of recapture, which have been thrown out, would be treated by him. These threats have not been treated as I hoped they would be. I have not lost my faith in the great champion who has, in my opinion, stumbled a little; but I am in the dark as to the causes that made him stumble. That I may receive light, is the object of this communication. Please speak somewhat at large on the subject, at your earliest convenience.[128]

Garrison set about to oblige Increase S. Smith and his unnamed supporters in the only un-Garrisonian prose ever ascribed to him. His forty-three inch editorial, "The Ransom of Douglass," which appeared in *The Liberator* of January 15, 1847, reads like a statement from a clerk of a court session. Careful recapitulation of the articles of complaint of the censorious abolitionists is followed by careful itemization of "circumstances of the case" which satisfied Garrison that Douglass's ransom was "a timely and beneficent act." In conclusion he says, in part:

I will not engage in controversy with any one on a question of probabilities. The transaction may or may not have been judicious, or called for by a wise forecast. On this point, every one must form his own opinion. My judgment is satisfied with what has been done.

It cannot be denied that Douglass was legally a slave, even in Massachusetts. His master, therefore, had a legal right to seize him, wherever found. The Constitution and laws of this State could have given him no protection. He might have been rescued, it is true, but only by violence—by the power of the populace overriding the power of the court. But his safety, on this score, is now rendered certain.[129]

Needless to say, Garrison's explanation did not satisfy the abolitionists. It was probably not the legal facts themselves that had produced Garrison's satisfaction, but rather the salient fact that Douglass was coming back. Students of style should enjoy philosophizing on the "meaning" within Garrison's use of a totally uncharacteristic style in his apologia for his ace figure. Douglass was coming back; whatever made that possible must have been all right with Garrison. But the editor of the *National Anti-Slavery Standard*, Mrs. Child, probably echoed the sentiments of the abolitionist masses, when she came out the following week with the statement:

The Liberator of last week contains two columns in explanation and approval of the purchase of Douglass. The article may convince others of the propriety of the act, but for ourselves, we have the same opinion that we expressed two months ago, that it was unwise and unnecessary.[130]

What Douglass felt about the ransom can be most succinctly gathered in his reply to a letter from Henry C. Wright. Wright had written him on December 12, 1846, asking Douglass to consider it his duty never to use or in any way "recognize" the "hateful" free papers that were then on their way to Douglass. He gave the same general reasons that other abolitionists expressed but phrased them with the more dramatic emphasis of direct appeal to the protagonist in the case. Wright asked Douglass not to abandon his position, which he defined as "a struggle between you and seventeen millions of liberty-loving Republicans":

> Your appeal to mankind is not against the grovelling thief, Thomas Auld, but against the more daring, more impudent and potent thief— the Republic of the United States of America. You will lose the advantages of this truly manly, and, to my view, sublime position; you will be shorn of your strength—you will sink in your own estimation, if you accept that detestable certificate of your freedom, that blasphemous forgery, that accursed Bill of Sale of your body and soul; or, even by silence, acknowledge its validity. . . . I would see your right to freedom, and to a standing on the platform of humanity, openly acknowledged by every human being—not on the testimony of a bit of paper, signed and sealed by an acknowledged thief, but by the declaration of a penitent nation, prostrate at your feet, in tears, suing to you and to God for forgiveness, for the outrages committed against God and man, in your person.[131]

Douglass's reply dwelt upon the necessity of submitting to the requirements set by the constitution and the laws of the country. He thought of his "disputed ransom" as wisdom's only choice. "As to the expediency of other measures," he declared, "different opinions may prevail; but in regard to the principle, I feel it difficult to conceive of two opinions." The generosity of Anna Richardson and the other British abolitionists whose combined gifts had made up the seven hundred and fifty dollars that Wright denounced as an "error in judgment," was considered by Douglass a noble acknowledgment of the power of the law; far from ignoring the free papers sent in exchange for that sum, he intended to use them as a symbol of the need for governmental change. He vowed:

> I will hold up those papers before the world, in proof of the plundering character of the American government. It shall be the brand of infamy, stamping the nation, in whose name the deed was done, as a great aggregation of hypocrites. . . . They declare that all men are

created equal, and have a natural and inalienable right to liberty,
while they rob me of one hundred and fifty pounds, as a condition of
my enjoying this natural and inalienable right. It will be their condemnation, in their own handwriting, and may be held up to the world
as a means of humbling that haughty republic into repentance.[132]

Douglass's hold upon the imaginations of the abolitionists, a possession
scarcely shared by any of the other fugitives as individuals, was owing to his
unprecedented role of the articulate American Negro slave. Even when mo-
mentarily deflected into abolitionists' paths with which he was not entirely
in agreement, it was customary for Douglass to contradict his own time-serv-
ing utterances on subsequent occasions. The focus of his many speeches, by
and large, was the wrong done to the slave and the slaveholder by the institution of slavery. The true spokesman of the slaves, he was able to appreciate
the financial side of the slaveholders' position at the same time that he condemned the sinfulness of a system that exacted the liberty of a race of human
beings as its legal toll. The abolitionist could not understand this view of the
slaveholder, who in his way of thinking had forfeited any such rights by
purchasing men in the first place. But his fellow slaves understood the point.

William Wells Brown tried to take the place of the "fallen leader," Douglass, whom some of the abolitionists accused of deserting "the cause" for a
"handful of silver." Brown apparently aimed to please the abolitionists by
declaring in many of his speeches that he was emphatically opposed to any
kind of monetary settlements with the slaveholder. On one occasion, for
example, Brown told a mammoth audience at Faneuil Hall, in Boston, of a
letter he had received from his owner, Enoch Price, offering to give Brown
his freedom for the sum of three hundred twenty-five dollars so that Brown
might henceforth be free to go anywhere he wanted to go. Brown said that he
was interested not in Price's offer, but in the fact that freedom was also
denied the white Northerner, too, because the latter was obliged by law to
help the slaveholder in his property claims. According to his statement at this
time, he had no intention of ever giving Price a single dollar for his freedom.[133] He soon found it expedient to remove himself to England, however,
from which "safer" distance he told a great audience at the public reception
given him in London, September 27, 1849:

Talk about going to the slaveholders with money! Talk about recognizing their right to property in human beings! What! property in
man! property in God's children! I will not acknowledge that any
man has a right to hold me as property, till he can show his right to
supersede the prerogative of the Creator whose alone I am. (Cheers.)
Just read the letter which you will find in the preface of my narrative, where my own master has very kindly offered to sell me to
myself for half price. (Laughter.) He imagines that the Anti-Slavery

Movement has depreciated his property, and therefore he offers to
take half-price for his runaway property. (Renewed laughter.) My
answer to him was, that he should never receive a single dollar from
me, or any one in my behalf, with my consent. (Cheers.)[134]

It was not long, nevertheless, before William Wells Brown very quietly
dropped this pose and sent the three hundred twenty-five dollars British well-
wishers had collected for the purpose post-haste to Enoch Price, from London to St. Louis, Missouri. Little comment was made in the abolitionist press
beyond brief announcements like the following:

> The friends of Mr. Brown have kindly contributed the amount
> necessary to secure his ransom from bondage, so that he can return
> to his native land without being subjected to the terrible liability of
> being seized as a fugitive, and scourged to death on a Southern
> plantation.[135]

James W. C. Pennington, the "fugitive blacksmith" who had concealed the
fact from everyone but the Quakers who had taken him in and educated him
from the time of his escape from slavery in the early 1830s, took advantage
of the vogue for slave testimony of the 1840s to unburden his soul of its
dread secret. His narrative was published in London in 1849 as one of Gilpin's
popular numbers. Deciding that he, too, would be better off if the money
question attached to him were settled, Pennington asked a friend in Hartford,
Connecticut, to negotiate with his old master, one Frisbie Tilghman of
Hagerstown, Maryland, for a ransom price. Tilghman set the sum at five
hundred dollars, adding in a postscript that "Jim is a first-rate blacksmith,
and well worth $1000." He died, however, before Pennington—whose accom-
plishments as an incognito fugitive included achievement of the degree of
Doctor of Divinity at the University of Heidelberg—raised the sum. Arrangement was then made with the administrator of Tilghman's estate to call the
matter settled for the sum of one hundred and fifty dollars, the bill of sale
having to be made out to Pennington's Hartford friend, John Hooker, as the
administrator had no power of manumission. Hooker's letter to *The Liberator*, dated June 3, 1851 from Hartford, is an amusing commentary on the
attitude of the abolitionist, revealing as it does a certain immaturity of conception of the problem. After reviewing the details of Pennington's life up to
that moment, Hooker writes:

> I have today received the bill of sale making over James Pembroke to
> me as my own property forever, to all intents and purposes whatso-
> ever. I remarked at the opening of my letter, that Dr. Pennington
> was in 'a fair way of becoming a man'. He is not yet completely one.
> The title to him still rests in me, and it remains for me, by deed
> under my hand and seal, to create him a peer of the realm. I shall,

however, defer the execution of this instrument for half an hour, till I
have walked up and down the whole length of Main Street, to see
how it seems to be a slaveholder, especially to own a Doctor of
Divinity. Possibly during the walk I may change my mind, and
think it best to send him to a sugar plantation.[136]

In a postscript, Hooker reports that he was so oppressed by his "ownership
of a human soul" that he hurried back to his home before the half hour was
up and executed the deed of manumission the minute he reached his study,
lest something should happen to him or to his *mind* to prevent him from
"setting Dr. Pennington free"!

A survey of the key members of the antislavery movement by the fugitive
slave longest affiliated with the New England abolitionists appears in William
Wells Brown's chapter on "The Abolitionists," in his *Rising Son: or, The
Antecedents and Advancement of the Colored Race.*[137] Launching his
description from the occasion of a meeting of the executive board of the
American Anti-Slavery Society in Boston in 1859, Brown begins with the
man who first hoisted the banner of "immediate and unconditional emancipation as the right of the slave and the duty of the master": Garrison of the
"high and prominent forehead, piercing eye, and pleasant yet anxious countenance." Round him had rallied men and women who

> . . . fully comprehended the solemn responsibility they were then
> taking and seemed prepared to consecrate the best years of their
> lives to the cause of human freedom. Amid the moral and political
> darkness which then overshadowed the land, the voice of humanity
> was at length faintly heard and soon aroused opposition, for slavery
> was rooted and engrafted in every fibre of American society.

Forty-four of Garrison's associates are named by Brown: the members of
the executive board of 1859, including Wendell Phillips, Edmund Quincy,
Francis Jackson, Maria Weston Chapman, Anne Warren Weston, Samuel May,
Jr., Charles F. Hovey, Eliza Lee Follen, Sydney Howard Gay, William I.
Bowditch, and Charles K. Whipple; then, Lydia Maria Child, James and
Lucretia Mott, Thomas Garrett, Stephen and Abby Kelly Foster, Parker
Pillsbury, Charles L. Remond, Charles C. Burleigh, Cyrus M. Burleigh, Lucy
Stone, Susan B. Anthony, Aaron M. Powell, Andrew T. Foss, Sallie Hollie,
Oliver Johnson, Henry C. Wright, Giles B. Stebbins, James N. Buffum, James
Miller McKim, Mary Grew, Gerrit Smith, Beriah Greene, Nathaniel P. Rogers,
William Goodell, Charles W. Slack, and Thomas Russell; and the Congressional
figures John P. Hale, George W. Julian, Joshua R. Giddings, Henry Wilson,
Thaddeus Stevens, John Quincy Adams, and Charles Sumner. This record of
the men and women who, in the mind of the freedman best qualified to draw
up such a list, were most directly responsible for the crusade ending in the

Act of Emancipation contains citations that worthily register the gratitude
of the slave for the abolitionists.

Brown's omissions are an interesting feature of the chapter. They reveal
the withdrawals from Garrison's band before the late 1840s, when Brown
joined as lecturer, of persons devoted to the cause of freedom for the slave
but unable to keep company with Garrison, who was so given to following
his own convictions that his contemporary, Lowell, spoke of him as a Daniel
Boone moving away as the world crept up to him, considering "every step
a step forward, though it be over the edge of a precipice."[138] Whittier had
left over the issue of Garrison's refusal to consider the power of the vote in
his crusade but had come back at intervals because he agreed with Garrison
so heartily on the basic point. Birney had left in the wake of Garrison's careless words concerning the matter of the preservation of the Union. Others
followed after his childish demonstration with a copy of the Constitution
had angered the Constitutionalists. Douglass is mentioned only as the thorn
provoking the retirement from the ranks of the first Negro abolitionist, freeman Charles Remond. It is a little surprising in view of his disagreement with
the Garrisonians on the free church question, that Gerrit Smith stays on the
roster. Arthur Tappan is conspicuously absent, and so are many others. The
observation of a recent historian comes to mind as Brown's chapter is
checked with the records of the Anti-Slavery Society: speaking of the age in
general, the historian remarks, "No contemporary reform stayed on its own
track; even Abolitionism, with a goal unusually direct, had its difficulties
with a crew of contrary minds."[139]

It was to these men and women, present or absent on the roster of William
Wells Brown, that the slave narrator owed his opportunities in the most
important period of the history of his literary efforts. The Act of Emancipation ended that heyday. There was to be no romantically "repentant
Republic" at his feet. Nor was the tone of the American Negro's story to
change appreciably. Between the *Narrative of the Life of Frederick Douglass,
an American Slave, Written by Himself*, published in 1845, and Richard
Wright's *Black Boy*, published in 1945, there are curious similarities, considering the hundred years' distance in time. Repetition of the popularity
of autobiographies of American Negroes in general recalls a recent critic's
observation that the literary crusade today is "not unlike that conducted by
abolitionist writers in the period between 1830 and 1860."[140] Johnson's
Along This Way (1933), Langston Hughes's *The Big Sea* (1940), DuBois's
Dusk of Dawn (1940), and Redding's *No Day of Triumph* (1942) are enjoying with *Black Boy* a popularity that shows that America is again interested
in the subjective record of the Negro within its bounds.

Chapter 2

The Slave Narrative
Before 1836

Adventure is the chief stock-in-trade of the slave narrative, from the beginning to the end of its history. In the 1830s, after the encouragement of the
Garrisonians led the slave autobiographer to frank denunciation of the structure of a society that denied a considerable proportion of its members the
rights and privileges professed in its avowals, the slave narrative acquired the
character of propaganda. Thereafter all adventure is adroitly heightened, with
emphasis upon social grievances. Before the 1830s, however, the slave narrative tended to minimize class consciousness. The racial identity of one narrator, for example, is disclosed solely in the information given in the title.[1]
In other narratives, chance references to Africa or to Negro kinfold provide
clues to racial identity. The slave status alone was not a sufficiently distinguishing characteristic in the eighteenth century.[2] The slave narratives are
all alike, however, in relating stories of adventure by individuals obliged by
society to be more than usually dependent upon their own gumption to
satisfy the natural craving of the human soul for equality.

The first slave narrative was recorded in the transaction of the Colonial
Society of Massachusetts in Boston, County of Suffolk, on August 3 and
November 2, 1703, under the caption: *Adam Negro's Tryall.*[3] Adam was the
slave of one John Saffin, a prosperous gentleman farmer of Suffolk County,
whose troubles with his slave we first learn of in the tract which Saffin
wrote and printed in Boston in 1701 in response to the recent publication
by Samuel Sewall of the antislavery pamphlet, *The Selling of Joseph.*[4] It
seems that Adam had not only capped a seven-year period of work-dodging
with flat refusal to accompany his master when Saffin was obliged to leave
town; but had taken advantage of Saffin's absence to terminate his indenture-
ship, going to Judge Sewall with a writ of promise Adam had obtained from
Saffin seven years before, to the effect that Saffin would give him his freedom
after seven years of service. A few days after Saffin returned to Boston, Adam
came to the house and informed him that he was to go see "Captain Sewall"
at once. Saffin guessed instantly what Adam had been up to but determined
not to let him have his freedom because he had in no wise fulfilled the conditions of service. Saffin then went to see Sewall. The latter would not let him

touch the paper which Adam had brought him but asked Saffin if he recognized the signature, which Saffin admitted was his own.

Sewall then tried to persuade Saffin to grant Adam his freedom, even though Adam might not have served Saffin as agreed upon. A Mr. Addington, who was with Sewall when Saffin arrived, advised Saffin against using the same standard in judging the behavior of Negroes as he would use on others, saying that there was "much to be allowed to the behaviour of Negroes, who are so ignorant, rude, and brutish, and therefore to be considered as Negroes."5 But Saffin would not give in, because, as he claimed, he had allowed Adam every kind of opportunity during the whole seven years to encourage him to be a good servant to him, and yet Adam had continually behaved "so diametrically contrary to those conditions" he simply would not agree to the manumission. Thereupon Adam provided himself with an attorney, one Thomas Newton, and the matter came to trial before the Court of General Sessions of the Peace for the County of Suffolk on August 3, 1703.

The evidence of the witnesses for John Saffin at the trial, including the various employers to whom Saffin had hired Adam out when he had finally decided that he himself could get nothing but headaches out of Adam, caused the jury to decide in favor of Saffin, ordering Adam's writ of manumission to be rescinded. Adam himself had not been able to refute their charges that he had been continually insolent and quarrelsome; that he would work when he wanted to—making a neat little profit for himself on a piece of "rich ground" which his master Shepard had given him to plant tobacco on for his own use—but would slyly make the others do the rest of the work; and that he would go off when he pleased and stay as long as he liked, returning so "proud and surlie" that no one dared to speak to him when he got back, lest he strike. Adam's reply was that he had not liked the way he had been ordered to do things by the different employers. For example, when one John Griffin of Castle Island had called him "Rascal" in the course of telling him to remove some earth, Adam had replied that he was "No Rascal, no Rogue, and no Thief," and had answered Clark's push with a push of his own, warning him that if he struck Adam, Adam would strike back. Clark then struck him with a stick, which stick Adam promptly broke, and "would have like to have spoilt him" with a shovel had not other laborers come to Clark's aid, carrying Adam off to a "dungeon."

Adam immediately appealed against the jury's decision that he was to remain Saffin's servant, and the appeal was heard at the next Court of Assize. In his appeal, Adam stressed the fact that there was no provision in Saffin's writ of promise whereby he was to forfeit his freedom if he did not serve his master or other employers assigned him by his master as well as they wanted him to. He said that Saffin had not made his promise of freedom subject to any conditions; besides, liberty was too great a privilege to be taken away from a man for anything so trivial or frivolous as the sauciness and laziness reported by Saffin. On November 2, 1703, at Her Majesty's Superiour Court of Judicature, Suffolk County, Judge Sewall presiding, the jury returned a verdict reversing the former judgment of the Court of General Sessions, with the concluding assertion:

> Its therefore Considered by the Court That the sd. Adam and his heirs be at peace and quiet and free with all their Chattles from the sd. John Saffin Esqr and his heirs for Ever.[6]

Though separated by nearly sixty years, in time, the next slave narrative that we have shows a slave who resembles Adam in his flair for mapping out his own destiny without benefit of his master's sanction. A complete outline of the narrative appears in its incredibly long title:

> A Narrative of the Uncommon Sufferings, and Surprizing Deliverance of Briton Hammon, A Negro Man,—Servant to General Winslow, of Marshfield, in New-England; Who Returned to Boston, after Having Been Absent Almost Thirteen Years. Containing An Account of the many Hardships he underwent from the Time he left his Master's House, in the Year 1747, to the Time of his Return to Boston.—How he was cast away in the Capes of Florida;—the horrid Cruelty and inhuman Barbarity of the Indians in murdering the whole Ship's Crew;—the Manner of his being carry'd by them into Captivity. Also, An Account of his being Confined Four Years and Seven Months in a close Dungeon;—And the remarkable Manner in which he met with his good old Master in London; who returned to New-England a Passenger, in the same Ship. (Boston; Printed and Sold by Green and Russell, in Queen-Street, 1760)

The narrative opens with a formal notice "To the Reader," in which Hammon apologizes for any deficiencies in the little book, on the ground that

> As my Capacities and Condition of Life are very low, it cannot be expected that I should make those Remarks on the Sufferings I have met with, or the kind Providence of a good GOD for my Preservation, as one in a higher Station; but shall leave that to the Reader as he goes along, and so I shall only relate Matters of Fact as they occur to my Kind.

It seems likely that the pious note of this opening and the overwhelmingly pious closing page are interpolations of Hammon's scribe, as the body of the narrative is not at all in this tone. Hammon's adventures were self-sought, from the moment on that Christmas Day of 1747 when he decided to leave his master's house for a spree on the first ship he should find ready to set sail from the icy harbor at Plymouth. Teenage readers would enjoy his account of life among cannibalistic Indians off the coast of Florida, who fattened Hammon day by day on corn for the promise of a good big roast on their feast day; of his experiences in shipwrecks; of his long incarceration in a dungeon in Havana by pirates who could not induce him to board their ship; and of later adventures on gunboats. Life had sobered him up a trifle by 1760, so that he was prosaically engaged as ship's cook at the time of his romantic reunion with his master in London, which he describes rather winningly:

> I worked on board Captain Watt's ship almost three months, before she sail'd, and one Day being at work in the Hold, I overheard some Persons on board mention the name of Winslow, at the name of which I was very inquisitive, and having asked what Winslow they were talking about? They told me it was General Winslow; and that he was one of the Passengers. I ask'd them what General Winslow? For I never knew my good Master, by that Title before; but after enquiring more particularly I found it must be Master, and in a few Days Time the Truth was joyfully verify'd by a happy Sight of his Person, which so overcome me, that I could not speak to him for some Time—my good Master was exceeding glad to see me, telling me that I was like one arose from the Dead, for he thought I had been Dead a great many Years, having heard nothing of me for almost Thirteen Years.[7]

Next in order of the slave narratives is *The Life and Dying Speech of Arthur, a Negro Man: Who Was Executed at Worcester, October 20th, 1768. For a Rape Committed on the Body of One Deborah Metcalfe* (Boston: Printed and Sold in Milk Street, 1768). The broadside on which Arthur's story is squeezed presents all the ingredients for a picaresque novel. Arthur himself was a character who would have delighted both a Smollett and a Dickens. He was born a slave in the house of one Richard Godfrey, of Taunton, Connecticut, in 1747, where he lived for fourteen years. He was taught to read and write and was treated kindly by his master. His mistress was so mean to him, however, that he ran away at the age of fourteen, setting out on a career of crime under the tutelage of a company of Indians at Sandwich. He relates:

> At Sandwich, I stole a Shirt, was detected, and settled the Affair, by paying twenty Shillings. My Character now being known, I thought proper to leave the Place; and accordingly shipped myself on board a Whaling Sloop, with Captain Coffin, of Nantucket: We were out eight months, and then returned to Nantucket, from whence we sailed, where I tarried six Weeks. In which Time I broke a Store of Mr. Roach's, from which I stole a Quantity of Rum, a pair of Trow-

sers, a Jacket, and some Calicoe.—The next Day I got drunk, and by
wearing the Jacket, was detected, for which Offence I was whip'd
fifteen Stripes, and committed to Gaol, for the payment of Cost,
etc., from which I escaped in half an Hour, by breaking the Lock.
Being now hardened in my Wickedness, I the next Night broke
another Store in the same Place, from which I took several Articles,
and then shipped myself on board a Vessel bound for Swanzey,
where I was discovered, taken to Shoar, and whip'd sixteen [sic];
being then set at Liberty, I returned to Taunton, after one Year's
absence, where my Master received me kindly, whom I served three
Years: In which time I followed the Seas, sailing from Nantucket
and Newport, to divers parts of the West-Indies, where I whored and
drank to great excess. Being now weary of the Seas, on the 27th of
October, 1764, I came again to live with my master at Taunton,
where I behaved well for six weeks.

Having stood his vagaries longer than was to be expected, Arthur's master
finally sold him to a Dutch gentleman, and after that sale Arthur changed
owners frequently, without giving perceptible service to any. At length his
crimes brought him the sentence which ended his life at the age of twenty-
one. Far from being submerged by sadness at the thought of his approaching
doom, Arthur enjoyed his rake's progress to the end. He tells of starting
out on the last journey with a Mr. Jennison, who had the warrant for him:

On our return to Rutland District, we stop'd at a Tavern in Hard-
wick, where after I had warmed myself, Jennison was Fool enough
to bid me put along, and he would overtake me; accordingly I went
out of the Door, and seeing his Horse stand handily, what should I
do, but mount him, and rode off as fast as I could, leaving Jennison
to pursue me on Foot. I got home before Bed-Time, and took up my
Lodging in my Master's Barn for the Night, where I had a Bottle of
Cherry-Rum (which I found in Mr. Jennison's Baggs) to refresh
myself with.
    On the next day, being the 30th of March, 1767, was discovered,
and committed to Worcestor Gaol, where I continued 'till the 20th
of April following; at which Time I broke out with the late celebrated FRASIER, and a young Lad, who was confined for stealing.
After which, at Worcester, we broke into a Barber's Shop, from
whence we stole a Quantity of Flour, a Comb, and a Razor. We
then set off for Boston. At Shrewsbury, we stole a Goose from Mr.
Samuel Jennison, and from the Widow Kingsley in the same Place,
we stole a Kettle, in which we boiled the Goose, in Westborough
Woods. At Marlborough, we broke into a Distill-House, from whence
we stole some Cyder Brandy. In the same Town we broke into a

Shoe-maker's Shop, and took each of us a pair of Shoes. We likewise broke into Mr. Cip [sic] on Howe's House, in the same Place, from whence [sic] stole some Bread, Meat, and Rum. At Sudbury, we stole each of us a Shirt, and one pair of Stockings. At Weston, we stole some Butter from off a Horse. At Waltham we broke into a House belonging to one Mr. Fisk, from whom we took a small Sum of Money, some Chocolate and Rum. At Watertown we stole a Brass Kettle from one Mrs. White of that Place. My Companions now left me; upon which I went to Mrs. Fisk's in Waltham, who knew me: And having heard of my Escape from Worcester Gaol, immediately secured me, and with the Assistance of another Man, brought me back again, where on the 17th of September following, I was tryed and found guilty. Upon which, by the Advice of my Counsel, I prayed for the Benefit of the Clergy; which after a year's Considera- tion, the Court denied me: And accordingly I was, on the 24th of September last, sentenced to be hanged, which I must confess is but too just a reward for my many notorious Crimes.

With this slave narrative we part company with the rogue and meet the pious Jupiter Hammon, who is credited with being the first American Negro poet by virtue of the publication of his first poem, "An Evening Thought— Salvation by Christ, with Penitential Cries," on Christmas Day, 1760, ten years before the first of Phillis Wheatley's poems appeared.[8] Hammon's autobio- graphical account is included in his *Address to the Negroes in the State of New York*, an impassioned essay written in the hope of helping fellow slaves like Arthur see the folly of their ways.[9] Hammon dedicated this address to the members of the African Society founded in New York City by Prince Hall, a free Negro, in phrases that show the unmistakable social purpose of the work:

Gentlemen,

I take the liberty to dedicate an Address to my poor brethren to you. If you think it is likely to do good among them, I do not doubt but you will take it under your care. You have discovered so much kindness and good-will to those you thought were oppressed, and had no helper, that I am sure you will not despise what I have wrote, if you judge it will be any service to them. I have nothing to add, but only to wish that "the blessing of many ready to perish, may come upon you."[10]

Jupiter Hammon, who was not related to Briton Hammon, was the slave of one John Lloyd of Queens Village, Long Island, and later of Hartford, Con- necticut. Born about 1716, he was humanely treated by his master, receiving the rudiments of learning, intensive religious training, and instruction in various manual skills. He was thankful for being so fortunately situated:

> I have great reason to be thankful that my lot has been so much
> better than most slaves have had. I suppose I have had more advan-
> tages and privileges than the most of you, who are slaves, have
> ever known, and I believe more than many white people have
> enjoyed; for which I desire to bless God, and pray that he may
> bless those who have given them to me.[11]

Religion became the "great business" of Hammon's life, causing any ambition for the things of this world to shrink into insignificance. The attitude of
the seventy-year-old philosopher toward liberty shows understanding:

> Now I acknowledge that liberty is a great thing, and worth seeking
> for, if we can get it honestly; and by our good conduct prevail on
> our masters to set us free: though for my own part I do not wish to
> be free, yet I should be glad if others, especially the young Negroes,
> were to be free; for many of us who are grown up slaves, and have
> always had masters to take care of us, should hardly know how to
> take care of ourselves; and it may be more for our comfort to
> remain as we are. That liberty is a great thing we may know from
> our own feelings, and we may likewise judge so from the conduct of
> the white people in the late war. . . . I must say that I have hoped
> that God would open their eyes, when they were so much engaged
> for liberty, to think of the state of the poor blacks, and pity us. He
> has done it in some measure, and has raised us up many friends; for
> which we have reason to be thankful, and to hope in his mercy. What
> may be done further, he only knows, for known unto God are all his
> ways from the beginning . . . But . . . getting our liberty in this world
> is nothing to our having the liberty of the children of God.[12]

The sole value in knowing how to read, Hammon thought, was the power it
provided human beings to learn the will of God. He advised the illiterate
slave:

> Get those who can read, to learn you; but remember, that what
> you learn for, is to read the Bible. If there was no Bible, it would
> be no matter whether you could read or not. Reading other books
> would do you no good. But the Bible is the word of God, and tells
> you what you must do to please God; it tells you how you may
> escape misery, and be happy for ever.[13]

It pained Hammon that the majority of the slaves added wickedness to
their already lamentable state of being "poor, despised, and miserable" as to
the things of this world. He was only able to "still" his mind by "considering
that it is permitted thus to be, by that God who governs all things, who
setteth up one, and pulleth down another.[14] His answer to the slave's practice

of taking things from the master, a habit first recorded here but referred to again and again throughout the history of the slave narrative, does not condone the practice, as is usually done:

> Though you may try to excuse yourselves by saying that your masters are unjust of you, and though you may try to quiet your consciences in this way, yet if you are honest in owning the truth, you must think of it as wicked, and on some accounts more wicked to steal from your masters, than from others. . . . All that we have to mind, is our own duty. If God has put us in bad circumstances, that is not our own fault, and he will not punish us for it. If any are wicked in keeping up so, we cannot help it; they must answer to God for it. Nothing will serve as an excuse to use for not doing our duty.[15]

Worrying about being slaves in this life would do the slave no good, Hammon believed, as God would set the slave free "in his own time and way." Besides, he reasoned, it did not really matter much, as a mere "forty, fifty, or sixty years" of slavery would seem as nothing compared with the eternity in Heaven that would be the lot of the God-fearing slave, whom nobody in Heaven would "reproach" for "being black, or for being slaves." Therefore he considered slaves like Arthur who elected a course of sinning "the greatest fools," resolved on being slaves not only here, but "slaves for ever." He hoped that the young swashbucklers would think about those things and live as though they believed what he said to be true, whether or not they actually did believe. He concluded by assuring them that if they were to become Christians, they would "have reason to bless God for ever, that you have been brought into a land where you have heard the gospel, though you have been slaves."[16]

Absence of the autobiographic intention is a characteristic of the writings of Phillis Wheatley that has been frequently remarked. She seems to have lived in the world of books, particularly of the Bible and eighteenth-century religious writings, indulged and encouraged by the kindly Wheatleys.[17] The actual fame that came to the frail slave poet in the 1770s attests to the ease with which recognition was won in an age with few writers of poetry. Phillis Wheatley's sickly constitution left her unfit for the routine tasks which occupied everyone in the pioneer days of America. Critics who have expressed disappointment over her lack of interest in the slave's condition should realize that it was probably her isolation from that very condition that saved her name for posterity. Manumitted after Mrs. Wheatley's death by the terms of her will, the poet "graduated" into the world about her, was engulfed by its cares, and wrote no more. The closest we come to an autobiographic note in her writings is a little poem, "On Being Brought from Africa to America,"[18] and a series of six personal letters that she wrote between 1772 and 1774 to her friend Obour Tanner, a slave girl living in Newport, Rhode Island.

These letters, one of the pleasant literary discoveries of 1864 in Boston,[19] were written in Phillis Wheatley's exquisite hand and reveal her preoccupation with spiritual matters along with references to her ill health. The first letter, sent from Boston, May 19, 1772, answers a letter she had received from her friend the preceding February, which tells of Obour Tanner's joy over "the saving change" she had experienced in embracing Christianity. That their friendship began in Africa has been inferred from Phillis Wheatley's exhortation:

> Let us rejoice in and adore the wonders of God's infinite Love in bringing us from a land semblant of darkness itself, and where the divine light of revelation (being obscur'd) is as darkness. Here the knowledge of the true God and eternal life are made manifest; but there, profound ignorance overshadows the land.[20]

Her reference further on in the same letter, however, to her "very great pleasure" in hearing "of so many of my nation, seeking with eagerness the way to true felicity," seems to reduce the inference to no more than the fact that both girls had come from Africa at some time to be sold as slaves in Boston. Her illness during the winter had prevented her from answering the letter sooner, but she expressed the hope that their correspondence might continue, with the "happy effect of improving" their friendship, until they should meet "in the regions of consummate blessedness." The second letter is dated July 19, 1772, at Boston, and reveals even poorer conditions of health. She requests her friend's prayers that, while the "outward man languishes under weakness and pa[in]," the "inward be refresh'd and strenghten'd more abundantly by him who declar'd from heaven that his strength was made perfect in weakness."

Like Jupiter Hammon, Phillis Wheatley's desire was "no longer to be so excessively charm'd with fleeting vanities: but pressing forward to the fix'd mark for the prize." In the second letter she asks her friend to meditate continually on the horror of the snares of the Devil, being mindful of their "high calling" to prepare for "the eternal judgment."[21] Between this letter and the third, written in Boston, October 30, 1773, she made a trip to England, the triumphant nature of which can be learned from many contemporary accounts. Concerning this experience she writes:

> I can't say but my voyage to England has conduced to the recovery (in a great measure) of my health. The friends I found there among the nobility and gentry, their benevolent conduct towards me, the unexpected and unmerited civility and complaisance with which I was treated by all, fills me with astonishment. I can scarcely realize

it. This I humbly hope has the happy effect of lessening me in my
own esteem. Your reflections on the sufferings of the Son of God,
and the inestimable price of our immortal souls, plainly demonstrate
the sensations of a soul united to Jesus. What you observe of Esau is
true of all mankind, who, (left to themselves) would sell their
heavenly birth rights for a few moments of sensual pleasure. . . .
Dear Obour, let us not sell our birthright for a thousand worlds,
which indeed would be as dust upon the balance. The God of the
seas and dry land, has graciously brought me home in safety.

The letter closes with the information that Mrs. Wheatley had been very ill
for the past fourteen weeks. Obour Tanner is also asked to use the copy of
the "Proposals" for Phillis Wheatley's book, enclosed in the letter, "to get
subscriptions, as it is for my benefit."[22] The last letter, dated March 21,
1774, tells of the death of Mrs. Wheatley, whom Phillis Wheatley regarded
as "a parent, sister, or brother, the tenderness of all these were united in
her." The letter reviews the slave girl's happy life with the Wheatleys, from
the time that Mrs. Wheatley had taken her in as "a poor little outcast and a
stranger." "I was treated by her more like her child than her servant," she
recounts; "no opportunity was left unimproved of giving me the best of
advice; but in terms how tender! how engaging!"[23] The *Memoir* which was
published with the edition of Phillis Wheatley's collected poems in Boston in
1834 was written by one Margaretta Matilda Odell, who had known her as a
member of the Wheatley household. Her poems brought her fame in an
unpoetic age, but the tradition of the devout, sensitive refinement that these
rare letters reveal accompanied her name beyond the confines of literary
history, to be stamped today upon the consciousness of hundreds of Negro
girls each year, as they enter "Phillis Wheatley" branches of the Young
Women's Christian Association in many parts of the United States.

The third slave narrator of this period, who also put greater emphasis
upon adventures in the realm of religious experience than upon the affairs
of the everyday world, is the amply named James Albert Ukawsaw Gronniosaw. His autobiography, entitled *A Narrative of the Most Remarkable
Particulars in the Life of James Albert Ukawsaw Gronniosaw, an African
Prince, as Related by Himself*, seems to have been published as early as 1770
at Bath, England. It was published in the United States at Newport, Rhode
Island, in 1774 and went through twelve editions in all by 1814, including a
translation into Celtic in 1779.[24] The narrative has the distinction among the
slave narratives of being the first of only four autobiographies of American
Negro slaves containing accounts of the author's own experiences in Africa.[25]
Inscribed to the "Right Honorable the Countess of Huntingdon," it was
related to a young English woman who committed it to paper for her private
satisfaction but was later prevailed upon to give it to the press on the

grounds that "this little history contains matter well worth the notice and attention of every Christian reader."

Gronniosaw was born about 1710 in Bournou, the chief city of Zaara, Africa. His mother was the eldest daughter of the reigning king of Zaara. His strange interest in mystical questions became noticeable in very early childhood, when he used to annoy his five older brothers and sisters by asking questions they could not answer. They thought him either foolish or insane, and Gronniosaw admits that he himself was somewhat in doubt about his nature:

> 'Twas certain that I was, at times, very unhappy in myself: it being
> strongly impressed on my mind, that there was some GREAT MAN
> of power, which resided above the sun, moon, and stars, the objects
> of our worship. My dear indulgent mother would bear more with
> me than any of my friends beside. I often raised my hands to
> heaven, and asked her who lived there? was much dissatisfied when
> she told me the sun, moon, and stars, being persuaded, in my own
> mind, that there must be some SUPERIOR POWER.—I was fre-
> quently lost in wonder at the works of the creation: was afraid,
> uneasy, and restless, but could not tell for what. I wanted to be
> informed of things that no person could tell me; and was always
> dissatisfied.[26]

The elaborate ritual of sun worship that took place every Saturday, beginning an hour before sunrise in group meetings throughout the city under large palm trees, manifested by remaining on the knees in strict silence and with the hands upheld until the sun had reached a height comparable to about ten or eleven o'clock in the morning, greatly distressed Gronniosaw with an unknown fear. This condition increased until it reached a climax, one Sabbath morning after the "duty" of the sun ritual was over:

> We were all on our way home as usual, when a remarkable black
> cloud arose and covered the sun; then followed very heavy rain, and
> thunder more dreadful than ever I had heard: the heavens roared,
> and the earth trembled at it: I was highly affected and cast down:
> insomuch that I wept sadly; and could not follow my relations and
> friends home. I was obliged to stop, and felt as if my legs were tied,
> they seemed to shake under me: so I stood still, being in great fear
> of the MAN OF POWER, that I was persuaded in myself lived above.
> One of my young companions . . . came back to see for me: he
> asked me why I stood still in such very hard rain? I only said to him
> that my legs were weak, and I could not come faster: he was much
> affected to see me cry, and took me by the hand, and said he would

lead me home, which he did. My mother was greatly alarmed at my tarrying out in such terrible weather; she asked me many questions, such as what I did so for, and if I was well? My dear mother, says I, pray tell me who is the great MAN OF POWER that makes the thunder? She said, there was no power but the sun, moon, and stars; that they made all our country. I then inquired how all our people came? She answered me, from one another; and so carried me to many generations back. Then says I, who made the *first man*? And who made the first cow, and the first lion, and where does the fly come from, as no man can make him? My mother seemed in great trouble; she was apprehensive that my senses were impaired, or that I was foolish. My father came in, and seeing her in grief asked the cause, but when she related our conversation to him, he was exceedingly angry with me, and told me he would punish me severely, if ever I was so troublesome again; so that I resolved never to say anything more to him. But I grew very unhappy in myself.[27]

The strangely unhappy lad, then about fifteen years of age, came to the attention of a merchant who traveled from the Gold Coast to trade in ivory. The man obtained the boy's confidence and offered to cure him of his melancholy by taking Gronniosaw home with him, where he should see such diverting sights as "houses with wings to them walk upon the water" and "white folks." Gronniosaw says that he "seemed sensible of a secret impulse upon my mind, which I could not resist, that seemed to tell me I must go." After his mother had obtained permission for him to pay the merchant a visit, he departed from his father and grandfather and the rest of his relations. His mother rode beside him on a camel for the first three hundred miles of the journey, after which she turned back.

The trip to the Gold Coast was full of excitement. At night the travelers made a circle of fire all around them, keeping well within it with their camels, to protect themselves from the lions and other wild beasts, "that roared terribly as soon as night came on, and continued to do so until morning." Once they passed through a valley of marble of different colors, in pieces of "prodigious length and breadth, but of different sizes and color, and shaped in a variety of forms, in a wonderful manner." As most of the marble was veined with gold, it was an "unspeakably beautiful scene, when the sun shone on the valley."[28] Gronniosaw soon discovered, however, that he was not really among friends. He was even fearful of being murdered by the companions of the merchant who had invited him away from his home, as they were continually grumbling about being hampered by the lad. After journeying about a thousand miles they reached their destination, and he thought that all his "troubles and inquietude would terminate." But how mistaken he was he soon found out:

> I was not suffered long to enjoy this satisfaction, for in the evening
> of the same day, two of the merchant's sons . . . came running to me,
> and told me, that the next day I was to die, for the king intended to
> behead me. I replied, that I was sure it could not be true, for I came
> there to play with them, and to see houses walk upon the water with
> wings to them, and the white folks; but I was soon informed that
> their king imagined I was sent by my father as a spy, and would
> make such discoveries at my return home, as would enable them
> to make wars with greater advantage to ourselves; and for these
> reasons he had resolved I should never return to my native country.
> When I heard this, I suffered misery that cannot be described. I
> wished a thousand times I had never left my friends and country.
> But still the Almighty was pleased to work miracles for me.[29]

The following morning he was washed, his gold ornaments were made
bright and shining, and he was carried up to the palace, where the king was to
behead him himself, as was the custom. The king was seated upon a throne at
the end of a court "as wide and spacious as a large field in England;" and
Gronniosaw proceeded towards him through a "lane of lifeguards," accompanied part of the way by the merchant, who lost courage toward the end
and left Gronniosaw to take the rest of the journey alone. But Gronniosaw
walked on "with an undaunted courage, and it pleased God to melt the heart
of the king, who sat with his cimeter in his hand ready to behead me; yet,
being himself so affected, he dropped it out of his hand, and took me upon
his knees, and wept over me."[30] The outcome of the episode was that Gronniosaw was not to be killed but sold as a slave.

The boy was soon sold to a Dutch captain for two yards of checked cloth.
The captain also took, in the bargain, a quantity of gold made into linked
chains, which Gronniosaw wore round his neck and his arms and legs, and a
large piece "hanging at one ear, almost in the shape of a pear." Concerning
this transaction, Gronniosaw naively added: "I found all this troublesome,
and was glad when my new master took it from me." The captain became
fond of him, and Gronniosaw studied hard to please him, as he believed that
he owed his life to the man's "kind" consent to purchase him. His account of
his first experience with a book is memorable:

> [The master] used to read prayers in public to the ship's crew every
> Sabbath day; and when I first saw him read, I was never so surprised
> in my life, as when I saw the book talk to my master, for I thought
> it did, as I observed him to look upon it, and move his lips. I wished
> it would do so to me. As soon as my master had done reading, I
> followed him to the place where he put the book, being mightily
> delighted with it, and when nobody saw me, I opened it, and put my
> ear down close upon it, in great hopes that it would say something

to me; but I was very sorry, and greatly disappointed when I found it would not speak, this thought immediately presented itself to me, that every body and every thing despised me because I was black.[31]

When he arrived at Barbados, the captain was induced to sell Gronniosaw to a New Yorker named Vanhorn for fifty dollars. Gronniosaw found his new life rather pleasant. An interesting picture of slave life in New York is afforded in this section of his narrative, which reveals the extremes of fortune within a single establishment between the petted slave and the capriciously mistreated:

> My chief business was to wait at table and tea, and clean knives, and I had a very easy place; but the servants used to curse and swear surprisingly; which I learned faster than any thing, it was almost the first English I could speak. . . . One day I had just cleaned the knives for dinner, when one of the maids took one to cut bread and butter with; I was very angry with her, and immediately called upon God to damn her; when [an old black servant] told me I must not say so. I asked him why? He replied that there was a wicked man called the Devil, who lived in hell, and would take all who said these words, and put them into the fire and burn them. This terrified me greatly, and I was entirely broke off swearing. Soon after this, as I was placing the china for tea, my mistress came into the room just as the maid had been cleaning it; the girl had unfortunately sprinkled the wainscot with the mop, at which my mistress was very angry, the girl very foolishly answered her again, which made her worse, and she called upon God to damn her. I was vastly concerned to hear this, as she was a fine young lady, and very good to me, insomuch that I could not help speaking to her; 'Madam," says I, "you must not say so." "Why," said she? "Because there is a black man called the Devil that lives in hell, and he will put you into the fire and burn you, and I shall be very sorry for that." "Who told you this," replied my lady? "Old Ned," says I. "Very well," was all her answer; but she told my master of it, and he ordered that Old Ned should be tied up and whipped, and he was never suffered to come into the kitchen with the rest of the servants afterwards.[32]

Mrs. Vanhorn repeated what Gronniosaw had said to her to many of her acquaintances, including one Mr. Freelandhouse, a minister, who became so much interested in Gronniosaw forthwith that he finally was able to persuade Mr. Vanhorn to sell the lad to him for fifty pounds. His new master and mistress were very good, gracious people and became very fond of Gronniosaw, who thought that their efforts to teach him to pray by kneeling every night and morning, putting his hands together, were "comical, but I liked it well." He was unspeakably delighted to learn that there was one God who had created "all the world, and every person and thing in it, in Ethiopia, Africa, and America, and everywhere." When he heard this, he congratulated himself:

> There, says I, I always thought so when I lived at home! Now if I
> had wings like an eagle, I would fly to tell my dear mother that God
> is greater than the sun, moon, and stars; and that they were made
> by Him.
>   I was exceedingly pleased with this information of my master's,
> because it corresponded so well with my own opinion; I thought
> now if I could but get home, I should be wiser than all my country
> folks, my grandfather, or father, or mother, or any of them.[33]

The progressive stages in Gronniosaw's conversion at home and at the services conducted by his godly master produced reactions of alternate exaltation and depression reminiscent of Bunyan, whose book on "the holy war" his mistress gave Gronniosaw to read when she became aware of his religious quandary. But Gronniosaw did not like Bunyan's book. He gave it back to her, commenting that it concerned a man as wicked as himself and gave him no relief at all, but rather deepened his anxiety. His master handed him Baxter's *Call to the Unconverted* a few days later, but his agonies seemed to increase rather than to diminish:

> [Baxter's book occasioned] as much distress as the other had done
> before, as it invited all to come to Christ; and I found myself so
> wicked and miserable, that I could not come. This consideration
> threw me into agonies that cannot be described: insomuch, that I
> even attempted to put an end to my life. I took one of the large case
> knives and went into the stable, with an intent to destroy myself;
> and as I endeavored with all my strength to force the knife into my
> side, it bent double. . . . I was instantly struck with horror at the
> thoughts of my own rashness, and my conscience told me, that had I
> succeeded in this attempt, I should probably have gone to hell.[34]

With the combined aid of the minister, his wife, and the schoolmaster, a Mr. Vanosdore, Gronniosaw finally achieved the knowledge of personal redemption, with a resulting peace and serenity that filled his mind. "I was now perfectly easy," he relates, "and had hardly a wish to make beyond what I possessed, when my temporal hopes were all blasted by the death of Mr. Freelandhouse." His master left him his freedom by his will and ten pounds. Gronniosaw stayed on with his mistress, however, for the remaining two years of her life. He then lived with her five sons, all ministers, until they all died, within four years of their parents' deaths. Gronniosaw was now resolved to go to Kidderminster, England, to seek out Mr. Baxter, whose *Call* had become a great source of comfort to him. But he was reduced again to slavery by the scheming of one of the friends of the young Freelandhouses, who gave Gronniosaw the loan of some money to pay his debts and then sold him to a seaman when Gronniosaw could not pay it all back at once on sudden notice. After much distress and adventures of a harrowing nature caused by shipwrecks and human perfidy alike, he finally reached England.

On his arrival in England, Gronniosaw made his way straight to Mr. Whitefield's tabernacle at Portsmouth, and the latter undertook to find lodgings for the devout young stranger, paying all of his expenses until he could get started. Gronniosaw made friends with a young widow living in the room above his in Petticoat Lane. As a result of their interest in religion, he joined the church to which she belonged. Discovering before long that he was in love with the earnest young Englishwoman, he was scarcely discouraged by her advice to think no more of it and to go instead to Holland, where friends of his old master had invited him to come. Gronniosaw left "Betty" with the vow that he would return to claim her as his wife, as he believed it was the Lord's will (though "she did not think it at the time"), and was received very graciously in Amsterdam by several ministers to whom he had letters of recommendation.

He spent a year in Amsterdam, where he was welcomed by the friends of his deceased master and was an object of interest to all of the Calvinist ministers of the city as a specimen of the "noble savage" who had achieved conversion. They were eager to hear Gronniosaw tell of his experience, and he was willing:

> So I stood before thirty-eight ministers every Thursday, for seven
> weeks together, and they were all very well satisfied, and persuaded
> I was what I pretended to be. They wrote down my experience as I
> spoke it; and the Lord Almighty was with me at that time in a
> remarkable manner, and gave me words and enabled me to answer
> them; so great was his mercy to take me in hand a poor blind
> heathen.[35]

He accepted the offer of a very rich merchant to enter his household in the capacity of butler, and all would have been very well with him, had he not yearned for the "Betty" he had left in Portsmouth. Against the wishes and advice of all, he left Amsterdam, winning the hand of his beloved, at length, plus her deceased husband's debts and child. Labor troubles upset their dream of financial independence, since it was difficult for a black to get steady work or a living wage. He became afraid to let his wife work after the weavers commenced their picketing, "lest they should insist on my being one of the rioters, which I could not think of, and possibly, if I had refused to do so, they would have knocked me in the head."[36] His small wages as handyman or carpenter barely kept a roof over their heads and food for a growing family, but always when they seemed about to perish, "it pleased God to alter my situation," as Gronniosaw expressed it. The narrative ends:

> Such is our situation; my wife by hard labor at the loom, does every thing that can be expected from her, towards the maintenance of our family; and God is pleased to incline his people to yield us their charitable assistance, being myself through age and infirmities able to contribute but little to their support. And as poor pilgrims, we are traveling through many difficulties, waiting patiently for the gracious call, when the Lord shall deliver us out of the evils of this present world, and bring us to the everlasting glories of the world to come.[37]

Though copies of Gronniosaw's narrative are exceedingly scarce today,[38] the work enjoyed a wide popularity among the English abolitionists during the last quarter of the eighteenth century and went through two American editions in that time. Even more popular, however, was *The Interesting Narrative of the Life of Olaudah Equiano, or Gustavus Vassa, the African, Written by Himself*, published in London in 1789. It went through thirty-six editions in English, Dutch, and German between that year and 1857.[39] This narrative was issued at first in a handsome two-volume format and became one of the chief vehicles for the spread of abolitionist propaganda at the turn of the century. Variously listed as "Olaudah Equiano" or as Gustavus Vassa," the author of this account of slave life in Africa, the West Indies, Georgia, Pennsylvania, and on board war ships off the Spanish coast is given high praise by the historian of American Negro literature.[40]

As we learn from the footnotes given, the first twenty pages of Equiano's autobiography are a compilation by some other hand of facts culled from handbooks on the history of Guinea, along with trite observations on the difficulties involved in writing one's memoirs. The information provides an interesting background for the appreciation of native African customs that suddenly become real as the personality of Equiano emerges from the introduction of his helper, and he begins to relive the story of his eventful life.

Equiano's recollection of the religious habits of his people provides his first noteworthy passage. Their belief in the presence of the spirits of deceased kinfolk had induced the habit of reserving a small portion of meat and drink for the dead and of making ablutions of the blood of beasts or fowl at their graves. Of the latter practice, Equiano recalls:

> I was very fond of my mother, and almost constantly with her. When she went to make these oblations at her mother's tomb, which was a kind of small solitary thatched house, I sometimes attended her. There she made her libations, and spent most of the night in cries and lamentations. I have been often extremely terrified on

these occasions. The loneliness of the place, the darkness of the
night, and the ceremony of libation, naturally awful and gloomy,
were heightened by my mother's lamentations; and these concurring
with the doleful cries of birds, by which these places were frequented, gave an inexpressible terror to the scene.[41]

The youngest of his mother's seven sons, Equiano was the son of the tribal
chief, born about 1745 among the Eboue tribe in Guinea. He had one sister,
his devoted playmate. One day, as they were guarding the houses while the
grown people in the neighborhood had gone beyond the walls to labor in the
fields, the two children were kidnapped by members of an enemy tribe. This
was in Equiano's eleventh year. The brother and sister spent the first night
of their captivity together, "bathing each other with our tears," but the next
day they were separated. After many days' journey, Equiano was sold to
another chieftain, then sold again to a slave coffle going toward the coast.
One of the unforgettable moments in the narrative happens shortly after the
slave gang started west:

In this manner I had been travelling for a considerable time, when
one evening to my great surprise, whom should I see brought to the
house where I was but my dear sister! As soon as she saw me she
gave a loud shriek, and ran into my arms—I was quite overpowered:
neither of us could speak; but, for a considerable time, clung to each
other in mutual embraces, unable to do anything but weep. Our
meeting affected all who saw us; and indeed I must acknowledge, in
honour of those sable destroyers of human rights, that I never met
with any ill treatment, or saw any offered to their slaves, except
tying them, when necessary, to keep them from running away. When
these people knew we were brother and sister, they indulged us to be
together; and the man, to whom I supposed we belonged, lay with
us, he in the middle, while she and I held one another by the hands
across his breast all night; and thus for a while we forgot our misfortunes in the joy of being together; but even this small comfort
was soon to have an end; for scarcely had the fatal morning
appeared when she was again torn from me for ever![42]

Sold again to a plantation owner, Equiano enjoyed such a comfortable
status as the slave companion of a lad of his own age that for a while he had
almost ceased to lament his fate. But he was whisked away very early one
morning by slave traders while the household was still asleep and taken to the
sea coast. Equiano describes his first acquaintance with a slave ship:

The first object which saluted my eyes when I arrived on the coast
was the sea, and a slave ship, which was then riding at anchor, and
waiting for its cargo. These filled me with astonishment, which was

soon converted into terror when I was carried on board. I was immediately handled, and tossed up to see if I were sound, by some of the
crew; and I was now persuaded that I had gotten into a world of bad
spirits, and that they were going to kill me. Their complexions too
differing so much from ours, their long hair, and the language they
spoke . . . united to confirm me in this belief. . . . When I looked
round the ship, too, and saw a large furnace or copper boiling, and a
multitude of black people of every description chained together,
every one of their countenances expressing dejection and sorrow, I no
longer doubted of my fate; and, quite overpowered with horror and
anguish, I fell motionless on the deck and fainted. When I recovered a
little I found some black people about me, who I believed were some
of those who had brought me on board, and had been receiving their
pay; they talked to me in order to cheer me, but all in vain. I asked
them if we were not to be eaten by those white men with horrible
looks, red faces, and long hair. They told me I was not.[43]

The horrors of the middle passage included the loathsome stench below
deck, the pitiful crying of the outraged slaves, and severe floggings of Equiano
across the windlass for his refusal to eat. He tried to commit suicide by
jumping over board, but was prevented by deckwatchers on the lookout for
such attempts. The slaves were not the only ones treated brutally. He saw
one white man, "when we were permitted to be on deck, flogged so unmerci-
fully with a large rope near the foremast, that he died in consequence of it;
and they tossed him over the side as they would have done a brute."[44] His
spirits were a little revived, however, when, "a little time after, amongst the
poor chained men, I found some of my own nation." He was therefore able
to ask them what was to be done with them; and when they told him that
they were "to be carried to these white people's country to work for them,"
he was somewhat relieved, even though he was still fearful of being put to
death, since the white people looked and acted "in so savage a manner." He
became ill during the voyage, so that it was thought necessary to keep him
almost always on deck. Many of the slaves died from want of fresh air and
sanitation. A few days after the arrival of the slaver at the West Indies, he was
shipped off on a sloop bound for Virginia.
  Equiano was bought by an invalided Virginian planter, and although his
work weeding grass and gathering stones was not too arduous, the fact that
he was without anyone at all to talk to made him exceedingly miserable. He
was "constantly grieving and pining, and wished for death rather than anything else." One day the planter sent for him to come to the house to fan him
while he slept. Equiano relates:

When I came into the room where he was I was very much affrighted
at some things I saw, and the more so as I had seen a black woman

slave as I came through the house, who was cooking the dinner, and the poor creature was cruelly loaded with various kinds of iron machines; she had one particularly on her head, which locked her mouth so fast that she could scarcely speak; and could not eat nor drink. I was much astonished and shocked at this contrivance, which I afterwards learned was called the iron muzzle. Soon after I had a fan put into my hand, to fan the gentleman while he slept; and so I did indeed with great fear. While he was fast asleep I indulged myself a great deal in looking about the room, which to me appeared very fine and curious. The first object that engaged my attention was a watch which hung on the chimney, and was going. I was quite surprised at the noise it made, and was afraid it would tell the gentleman any thing I might do amiss: and when I immediately after observed a picture hanging in the room, which appeared constantly to look at me, I was still more affrighted, having never seen such things as these before. At one time I thought it was something relative to magic; and not seeing it move I thought it might be some way the whites had to keep their great men when they died, and offer them libations as we used to do our friendly spirits.[45]

Dejected and forlorn by his burdensome solitude, Equiano was overjoyed when the captain of a merchant ship, on a visit to the Virginian, took a liking to him and purchased him from his master for "thirty or forty pounds sterling," intending to send him "for a present to some of his friends in England." It was this master, one Lieutenant Paschal, who gave him the name "Gustavus Vassa":

While I was on board this ship, my captain and master named me *Gustavus Vassa*. I at that time began to understand him a little, and refused to be called so, and told him as well as I could that I would be called Jacob; but he said I should not, and still called me Gustavus: and when I refused to answer to my new name, which at first I did, it gained me many a cuff; so at length I submitted, and by which I have been known ever since.[46]

During the two-year period that he was on board this ship, Equiano experienced the greatest formative influence in his life in the close friendship that developed between him and an American lad four or five years older than he, who had never been to sea before. This boy, one Richard Baker, took an instant liking to Equiano and during their two years together was his constant companion and instructor, teaching him patiently and skilfully how to speak, read, and write the English language. Like Gronniosaw, Equiano's first acquaintance with books made him curious to "talk" to a book and then put his ear to it, "when alone, in hopes it would answer me; and I have been very much concerned when I found it remained silent."[47]

Equiano, together with his friend Dick, was placed to board for a time at Guernsey with the wife and family of one of the mates on his master's ship. He tells of the dawning of an inferiority complex because of his color:

> This mate had a little daughter, aged about five or six years, with
> whom I used to be much delighted. I had often observed that when
> her mother washed her face it looked very rosy; but when she
> washed mine it did not look so: I therefore tried oftentimes myself
> if I could not by washing make my face of the same colour as my
> little playmate [Mary], but it was all in vain; and I now began to
> be mortified at the difference in our complexions.[48]

While still at Guernsey, he happened one day to pass a field in which he saw "a black boy about my own size," who ran out of the house to meet Equiano, "transported at the sight of one of his countrymen." Equiano says that he "turned a little out of his way at first," not knowing what the boy was about:

> But to no purpose: he soon came close to me and caught hold of
> me in his arms as if I had been his brother, though we had never seen
> each other before; and after we had talked together for some time
> he took me to his master's house, where I was treated very kindly.
> This benevolent boy and I were very happy in frequently seeing each
> other till about the month of March, 1761, when our ship had orders
> to fit out again for another expedition.[49]

In addition to his friendship with young Richard Baker, Equiano acquired a staunch friend in the person of the captain's clerk, who taught him figuring. He also won the atttachment of a forty-year-old messmate named Daniel, a deeply religious man who brought about Equiano's conversion and who brooded over him with the affection of a father for his son. All of his friends on board the ship believed that Equiano would be given his freedom when the ship hands were paid off, as they had "heard great talk about a peace" and were ordered up to London at the beginning of December, 1762, to receive their wages and "prize money," for their services during the warfare at sea. Equiano thought now of "nothing but being freed, and working for myself, and thereby getting money to enable me to get a good education." He had no inkling that the end of his life as a slave was not at hand:

> My heart burned within me, while I thought the time long till I
> obtained my freedom. For though my master had not promised it to
> me, besides the assurance I had received that he had no right to
> detain me, he always treated me with the greatest kindness, and

reposed in me an unbounded confidence; he even paid attention to my morals and would never suffer me to deceive him, or tell lies, of which he used to tell me the consequences; and that if I did so God would not love me; so that from all this tenderness, I never once supposed, in all my dreams of freedom, that he would think of detaining me longer than I wished.[50]

Nevertheless, Equiano was doomed for disappointment. When the ship cast anchor on the Thames on December 10, just at high water, his master suddenly thrust him from the ship into a barge that he had ordered manned, saying that he knew Equiano had planned to leave him, but that he would take care that he should not. At first, the lad, who was now seventeen years old, was so stunned that he could not speak out, but when his wits returned to him, "plucking up courage," he told his master that by law he was now free, as he had served him faithfully throughout the war. This only enraged the man, who sprang from the barge into the ship, forced the unwilling seamen to pull alongside the ship, and made arrangements to sell him with the captain of the first vessel they met that was bound for the West Indies. Equiano was soon sent for to go to the captain of the *Charming Sally*:

> When I came there Captain Doran asked me if I knew him: I answered that I did not. "Then," said he, "you are now my slave." I told him my master could not sell me to him, nor to any one else. "Why," said he, "did not your master buy you?" I confessed he did. "But I have served him," said I, "many years, and he has taken all my wages and prize money, for I had only got one sixpence during the war; besides this I have been baptized; and by the laws of the land no man has a right to sell me." And I added that I had heard a lawyer and others at different times tell my master so. They both then said that those people who told me so were not my friends. But I replied, "It was very extraordinary that other people did not know the law as well as they." Upon this Captain Doran said I talked too much English; and if I did not behave myself well, and be quiet, he had a method on board to make me. I was too well convinced of his power over me to doubt what he said; and my former sufferings in the slave-ship presenting themselves to my mind, the recollection of them made me shudder. However, before I retired I told them that as I could not get any right among men here I hoped I should hereafter in Heaven; and I immediately left the cabin, filled with resentment and sorrow.[51]

Equiano's shipmates felt great sympathy for him and assured him that as soon as they could get their pay, they would try to find him and help him. But he was not to know freedom soon.

After his first agony of weeping subsided, he began to reflect that perhaps the Lord was punishing him thus severely for something he had done that was displeasing:

> This filled me with painful reflections on my past conduct; I recollected that on the morning of our arrival at Deptford I had rashly sworn that as soon as we reached London I would spend the day in gambling and sport. My conscience smote me for this unguarded expression: I felt that the Lord was able to disappoint me in all things, and immediately considered my present situation as a judgment of Heaven on account of my presumption in swearing: I therefore, with contrition of heart, acknowledged my transgression to God, and poured out my soul before him with unfeigned repentance, and with earnest supplications I besought him not to abandon me in my distress, nor cast me away from his mercy for ever.[52]

When the *Charming Sally* docked at Montferrat, the captain sold Equiano to a Mr. King, a Quaker living in Philadelphia, who was interested in purchasing him because of his knowledge of arithmetic and his splendid references. Equiano's former master, Captain Paschal, had requested Doran to get him the best master that could be found when they arrived at the West Indies, as Equiano was "a very deserving boy." Mr. King, who was connected with a "great mercantile house in that city," planned to send him to school in Philadelphia and train him for a clerk. Because of Equiano's knowledge of the rudiments of seamanship, however, he was soon put to work pulling and managing shore boats at Montferrat, and he finally became captain's mate on vessels belonging to Mr. King which plied between the West Indies and Philadelphia. The way in which he prepared himself for this unusual advancement shows the workings of a determined soul:

> I determined to make every exertion to obtain my freedom, and to return to Old England. For this purpose I thought a knowledge of navigation might be of use to me; for, though I did not intend to run away unless I should be ill used; yet, in such a case, if I understood navigation, I might attempt my escape in our sloop, which was one of the swiftest sailing vessels in the West Indies, and I could be at no loss for hands to join me. . . . I therefore employed the mate of our vessel to teach me navigation, for which I agreed to give him twenty-four dollars, and actually paid him part of the money down. . . . However, my progress in this useful art was much retarded by the constancy of our work. Had I wished to run away I did not want opportunities, which frequently presented themselves; and particularly at one time after this. When we were at the island of Guadeloupe there was a large fleet of merchantmen bound for Old France;

and, seamen being then very scarce, they gave from fifteen to twenty
pounds a man for the run. Our mate, and all the white sailors, left
our vessel on this account, and went on board of the French ships.
They would have had me also go with them, for they regarded me;
and swore to protect me, if I would go: and, as the fleet was to sail
the next day, I really believe I could have got safe to Europe at that
time. However, as my master was kind, I would not attempt to leave
him. . . . My captain was much afraid of my leaving him and the
vessel at that time, as I had so fair an opportunity: but, I thank God,
this fidelity of mine turned out much to my advantage hereafter.[53]

The captain now began to teach him navigation himself and persuaded his
master to leave Equiano entirely to him, though Mr. King missed having
with him so competent a manager of the slave crews manning the boats that
unloaded ships at the harbor at Montferrat. At times, some of the passengers
complained to the captain that "it was a very dangerous thing to let a Negro
know navigation" when they observed him teaching Equiano. But this did not
change the captain's attitude.

On the first day Equiano had come to him, Mr. King had agreed to let him
have an opportunity to earn money to purchase his freedom. Equiano had
worked with alacrity to make and save money for that purpose, though often
he had to submit to imposition and cheating from white merchants who
would not pay him for goods he had sold them, knowing that a slave could
obtain no judgment against them no matter what wrongs they made him
suffer. The price agreed upon for his freedom was forty pounds sterling, the
same price Mr. King had paid Captain Doran for him, though Mr. King could
have sold Equiano "for a hundred guineas any day, in the West Indies."
Equiano was highly regarded by the planters as a slave who had shrewd
ability in overseeing other slaves, who was liked by the slaves, and who was
nevertheless a trustworthy servant to his master. Mr. King would allow him a
tierce of rum and a tierce of sugar on credit to take on board as his own
goods and sell as he could in the ports of Savannah, Charleston, or Philadelphia. We visit Charleston with him on an historic occasion in Colonial
history:

> After our vessel was discharged, we soon got her ready, and took in,
> as usual, some of the poor oppressed natives of Africa, and other
> Negroes; we then set off again for Georgia and Charlestown. We
> arrived at Georgia, and, having landed part of our cargo, proceeded
> to Charlestown with the remainder. While we were there I saw the
> town illuminated; the guns were fired, and bonfired and other
> demonstrations of joy shown, on account of the repeal of the stamp
> act. Here I disposed of some goods on my own account; the white
> men buying them with smooth promises and fair words, giving me,

however, but very indifferent payment. There was one gentleman
particularly who bought a puncheon of rum of me, which gave me
a great deal of trouble; and, although I used the interest of my
friendly captain, I could not obtain any thing for it; for, being a
Negro man, I could not oblige him to pay me. This vexed me much,
not knowing how to act; and I lost some time in seeking after this
Christian; and though, when the sabbath came (which the Negroes
usually make their holiday) I was much inclined to go to public
worship, I was obliged to hire some black men to help to pull a
boat across the water to go in quest of this gentleman. When I found
him, after much entreaty, both from myself and my worthy captain,
he at last paid me in dollars; some of them, however, were copper,
and of consequence no value; but he took adavantage of my being a
poor Negro man, and obliged me to put up with those or none,
although I objected to them. Immediately after, as I was trying to
pass them in the market, amongst other white men, I was abused for
offering to pass bad coin; and, though I showed them the man I got
them from, I was within one minute of being tied up and flogged
without either judge or jury; however, by the help of a good pair of
heels, I ran off.[54]

Equiano had many such adventures in the ports of the Southern Colonies,
including one in Savannah that nearly cost him his life. One Sunday night,
when he was visiting some slaves in their master's yard,

It happened that their master, one Doctor Perkins, who was a very
severe and cruel man, came in drunk; and not liking to see any
strange Negroes in his yard, he and a ruffian of a white man, he had
in his service, beset me in an instant, and both of them struck me
with the first weapons they could get hold of. . . . Though I gave a
good account of myself, and he knew my captain, who lodged hard
by him, it was to no purpose. They beat and mangled me in a
shameful manner, leaving me near dead. I lost so much blood from
the wounds I received, that I lay quite motionless, and was so
benumbed that I could not feel any thing for many hours. Early in
the morning, they took me away to jail. As I did not return to the
ship all night, my captain, not knowing where I was, and being
uneasy that I did not make my appearance, he made enquiry after
me; and having found where I was, immediately came to me. As
soon as the good man saw me so cut and mangled, he could not
forbear weeping. He soon got me out of jail to his lodgings, and
immediately sent for the best doctors in the place, who at first
declared it as their opinion that I could not recover. My captain on
this went to all the lawyers in the town for their advice, but they

told him they could do nothing for me as I was a Negro. . . . However, by the skilfulness of one Doctor Brady of that place, I began
at last to amend; but, although I was so sore and bad with the
wounds I had all over me that I could not rest in any posture, yet
I was in more pain on account of the captain's uneasiness about me
than I otherwise should have been. The worthy man nursed and
watched me all the hours of the night; and I was able . . . to get out
of bed in about sixteen or eighteen days. All this time I was very
much wanted on board, as I used frequently to go up and down the
river for rafts, and other parts of our cargo, and stow them. . . . In
about four weeks I was able to go on duty.[55]

Equiano's experience as a merchant seaman in Philadelphia was much
happier. When their ship was bound for this port, he would "lay in as large
a cargo as I could, trusting to God's providence to prosper my undertaking."
Once in the city, he would sell his goods "chiefly to the Quakers: they always
appeared to be a very honest, discreet sort of people, and never attempted to
impose on me; I therefore liked them, and ever after chose to deal with
them in preference to any others."[56] One of the most interesting of the
sights that he saw was an evangelistic meeting in that city:

I came to a church crowded with people; the churchyard was full
likewise, and a number of people were even mounted on ladders
looking in at the window. I thought this a strange sight, as I had
never seen churches, either in England or the West-Indies, crowded
in this manner before. I therefore made bold to ask some people the
meaning of all this, and they told me the Rev. George Whitefield
was preaching. . . . I now therefore resolved to gratify myself with
the sight, and pressed in amidst the multitude. When I got into the
church I saw this pious man exhorting the people with the greatest
fervour and earnestness, and sweating as much as I ever did while in
slavery on Montferrat Beach. I was very much struck and impressed
with this.[57]

By July of 1766, after numerous cheatings and losses but without ever losing faith that God would grant him deliverance from slavery at last, Equiano
had got together the money needed for his purchase. Realizing that the transaction would depend entirely upon Mr. King's good-heartedness, he asked the
captain for advice as to how to go about offering his master the money for
his freedom. The captain advised him to appear on a certain morning, when
he and Mr. King would be at breakfast together. Accordingly, Equiano went:

When I went in I made my obeisance to my master, and with my
money in my hand, and many fears in my heart, I prayed him to be
as good as his offer to me, when he was pleased to promise me my

freedom as soon as I could purchase it. This speech seemed to con-
found him; he began to recoil; and my heart that instant sunk
within me. "What," said he, "Give you your freedom? Why, where did
you get the money? Have you got forty pounds sterling?" "Yes, sir,"
I answered. "How did you get it?" replied he. I told him, very
honestly. The Captain then said he knew I got the money very
honestly and with much industry, and that I was particularly careful.
On which my master replied, I got money much faster than he did;
and said he would not have made me the promise he did if he had
thought I should have got the money so soon. "Come, come," said
my worthy captain, clapping my master on the back, "Come,
Robert, (which was his name) I think you must let him have his
freedom;—you have laid your money out very well; you have
received good interest for it all of this time, and here is now the
principal at last. I know Gustavus has earned you more than a
hundred a year, and he will still save you money, as he will not leave
you:—Come, Robert, take the money."[58]

Declaring then that he would not be "worse than his promise," Mr. King
took the money and told Equiano to go to the Secretary of the Register
Office to get the manumission papers drawn up. Equiano was so filled with
gratitude that he was unable to speak, but he "bowed most reverently," and
left with tears of joy raining down his cheeks. He flew to the registry, telling
every one he met of his happiness and blazing about the virtues of his master
and the captain. Even the secretary congratulated him and said he would
draw up the papers "for half price, which was a guinea." When Mr. King had
signed the papers making him a free man at the age of twenty-one, Equiano
was so happy that he gave a dance and believed that he "cut no indifferent
appearance" in the "superfine blue clothes from Georgia" that he put on for
the occasion. Some of "the sable females, who formerly stood aloof, now
began to relax and appear less coy" than it seems they must have during the
days when Equiano was but a slave, but for all his good fortune, his heart
was fixed on London and a sight of his old master, Captain Paschal. For, as he
reflected, he still loved that master of his boyhood, "notwithstanding his
usage of me, and pleased myself with thinking of what he would say when he
saw what the Lord had done for me in so short a time, instead of being, as he
might perhaps suppose, under the cruel yoke of some planter."[59]

For a year after his manumission, however, Equiano remained in his
former master's service, becoming first mate and then, upon the captain's
death, captain of his ship. His determination to return to England could not
be shaken at the end of that period, though Mr. King tried to persuade him,
if he would not remain in his service as captain, to become a planter with
slaves of his own. Equiano thus left Montferrat on January 26, 1767, with a

splendid letter of reference from Mr. King, whom he "begged to excuse" him for not desiring to remain with him longer.

But life in England as a freedman was not so joyous as Equiano had anticipated. Captain Paschal met his eager return with a sarcasm that caused him to change his mind about the man, so that Equiano even reached the point of reproaching his former master for having used him very ill.[60] Although the women in the households where he had been boarded as Paschal's slave were as kind to him as formerly, they were unable to help him obtain work better than barbering or butler's service. He had expected to enjoy full freedom as a human being but found instead that this was denied him solely because he was "a black." His chief relief from this disappointment was the good that he learned he could do in joining the abolitionists in the cause of freedom for those still enslaved. It is in the capacity of lecturer and author in this cause that we last hear of him in the pages of his long and captivating narrative.

Our next slave narrator, Venture Smith, was spared the disillusionment that dimmed the hopes of Gronniosaw, Equiano, and unnumbered more freedmen during the "Age of Enlightenment" who reached the land of the English abolitionists only to discover that a few humanitarians cannot by themselves make a new world. Venture Smith was an uncommonly sensible man. The editor's preface to his narrative, highly tinctured though it is with cliches from the ideology of the primitivists in vogue in the 1790s, proves to be a sound characterization of the stalwart slave whose progress is recorded in the pages of *A Narrative of the Life and Adventures of Venture, a Native of Africa; But Resident above Sixty Years in the United States of America.*[61] In the words of this preface:

> The reader is here presented with an account, not of a renowned politician or warrior, but of an untutored slave, brought into this Christian country at eight years of age, wholly destitute of all education but what he received in common with other domesticated animals, enjoying no advantages that could lead him to suppose himself superior to his beasts, his fellow servants. . . . It may perhaps be not unpleasing to see the efforts of a great mind, wholly uncultivated, enfeebled and oppressed by slavery, and struggling under every disadvantage. The reader may here see a Franklin and a Washington, in a state of nature, or rather in a state of slavery. Destitute as he is of all education, and broken by hardships and infirmities of age, he still exhibits striking traces of native ingenuity and good sense.[62]

Venture (whose surname "Smith" was an acceptance by courtesy, in recognition of his willingness to be bought by his third master, a Colonel Smith, when Venture was already thirty-one years of age) was born in Dukandara, Guinea, about 1729, the son of a prince of that tribe by the first of his three wives. His earliest memory was of leaving his father at the age of five with two younger children on the occasion of a rupture between his parents over his father's having married the third wife without the consent of his first and eldest, contrary to the custom of the country. The mother left without any means of sustenance, carrying one child on her back and the other in her arms, with Venture trudging by her side. After five days of travel through a desert she left Venture with a sheep farmer and returned home. Here he remained for a year, very kindly treated, until his father sent a man and horse after him. The sojourn proved very costly to his family, however, as it obligated his father to go to the rescue of the sheep farmer within six weeks of Venture's return, as the farmer had been attacked by an enemy nation and had no war equipment. Before the matter was ended, the domain of Venture's father had also been attacked, and though the prince fought valiantly, the whole community was forced to surrender. Men, women, and children were bound, put into a castle, and parceled out in groups for the slave market. Venture was only six-and-a-half at the time but was very large for his age. He was sold to the steward of "a vessel belonging to Rhode Island," one Robertson Mumford, for "four gallons of rum, and a piece of calico, and called VENTURE, on account of his having purchased me with his own private venture."

The habit of strict obedience to orders, which Venture first acquired during the year he spent on the sheep farm, entrusted with watching the sheep, earned him the high regard of his master. Venture guarded the latter's belongings even when threatend with punishment by Mumford's father if he did not hand over the keys which his master had told him to give to no one. His master commended Venture for his faithfulness and declared that he should not fear to trust him with his whole fortune, for the boy "had been in his native place so habituated to keeping his word, that he would sacrifice even his life to maintain it,[63] Mumford exacted hard tasks of the husky little slave. Until he was eight years old his chief business was employment in the house carding wool and doing other household tasks. But soon he was required to "pound four bushels of corn every night in a barrel for the poultry, or be rigorously punished," or card wool until a very late hour, in addition to the long day's work. Further distress came from the problem of how to serve two masters. His master's son began to give him orders that he had to obey or be whipped, and at the same time he had a full program of orders from his master to carry out. Venture recounts one such occurrence in detail:

> One day in particular, the authority which my master's son had set up, had like to have produced melancholy effects. For my master having set me off my business to perform that day and then left me to perform it, his son came up to me in the course of the day, big

with authority, and commanded me very arrogantly to quit my
present business and go directly about what he should order me. I
replied to him that my master had given me so much to perform
that day, and that I must faithfully complete it in that time. He then
broke out into a great rage, snatched a pitchfork and went to lay me
over the head therewith; but as soon I got another and defended
myself with it; or otherwise he might have murdered me in his outrage. He immediately called some people who were within hearing
at work for him, and ordered them to take his hair rope and come
and bind me with it. They all tried to bind me but in vain, though
there were three assistants in number. My upstart master then
desisted, put his pocket handkerchief before his eyes and went home
with a design to tell his mother of the struggle with young Venture.
He told that their young Venture had become so stubborn that he
could not control him, and asked her what he should do with him.
In the mean time I recovered my temper, voluntarily caused myself
to be bound by the same men who tried in vain before, and carried
before my young master, that he might do what he pleased with me.
He took me to a gallows made for the purpose of hanging cattle on,
and suspended me on it. Afterwards he ordered one of his hands to
go to the peach orchard and cut him three dozen of whips to punish
me with. These were brought to him, and that was all that was
done with them, as I was released and went to work after hanging
on the gallows about an hour.[64]

When he was about twenty-two years old, having lived with his master
thirteen years, Venture married Meg, another of Mumford's slaves. They were
separated a year later when Mumford sold Venture because of the latter's
share in the attempt of three other servants of Mumford's, including an
indentured Irishman named Heddy, to strike out for the Mississippi River
and freedom. Venture's new master, one Thomas Stanton of Stonington
Point, Connecticut, purchased Venture's wife and infant daughter a year-and-
a-half later for "seven hundred pounds old tenor." But though things went
well for a while, his mistress and his wife did not get along, and when Venture
came into the house one day while his wife was being beaten, he was so angry
that he took the horsewhip from his mistress's hand and threw it into the fire.
His master said nothing at all to him for several days after being informed of
the happening; then he suddenly struck Venture on the crown of his head
with "a club two feet long and as large round as a chair post" as he was
putting a log in the fireplace. Venture grabbed the club and, after further
scuffling, carried it to a neighboring justice of the peace, complaining of his
master. The justice listened to him and finally advised him to return to his
master, live peaceably with him until again abused, and then complain.

Venture relates what changed his mind about doing this:

> Before I set out for my master's, up he come and his brother Robert
> after me. The Justice improved this opportunity to caution my
> master. He asked him for what he treated his slave thus hastily and
> unjustly, and told him what would be the consequence if he con-
> tinued the same treatment towards me. After the Justice had ended
> his discourse with my master, he and his brother set out with me for
> home, one before and the other behind me. When they had come to
> a bye place, they both dismounted their respective horses, and fell to
> beating me with great violence. I became enraged at this and imme-
> diately turned them both under me, laid one of them across the
> other, and stamped them both with my feet what I would.[65]

The two men got a constable and two other men, and with such aid were
able to get Venture to a blacksmith's shop, where handcuffs were forged on
him, to the great joy of his mistress. His master then locked an ox chain
about his legs with two padlocks, which Venture wore "peaceably for two or
three days." He was then asked whether it would not be better for him to be
freed from his chains and go to work. Venture relates:

> I answered him, No. Well then, said he, I will send you to the West
> Indies or banish you, for I am resolved not to keep you. I answered
> him, I crossed the waters to come here, and I am willing to cross
> them to return.[66]

At least part of the reason for the ill will toward Venture of his master's
brother Robert seems attributable to the fact that soon after Stanton had
bought Venture, Robert borrowed the sum of "near twenty pounds York
currency" from Venture and had no intention of paying it back. Venture had
earned the money while a slave of Mumford "by cleaning musk-rats and
minks, raising potatoes and carrots, and by fishing in the night, and at odd
spells."[67] Five pounds of the amount belonged to his wife Meg. Robert
Stanton had given his note to Venture for the "hire" of the money. This
note, however, he had recovered and destroyed by breaking open Venture's
chest during the time the latter was chained.

Realizing that he was in imminent danger of being sold to the West Indies,
Venture now buried a sum of money that he had got together a second time
at a certain spot on the high road. He was sold to a slave speculator for "fifty-
six pounds lawful," but the latter was unable to find a purchaser for him, as
Venture was very insolent in his replies to the queries of prospective purchasers. Finally, the speculator, Hempstead Miner, "pawned" Venture to
Daniel Edwards of Hartford for ten pounds.

Mr. Edwards became interested in buying Venture after the latter had
proved to be not only extraordinarily strong and capable as a laborer but

also completely honest. Miner, however, had given one Colonel Smith a bill for Venture in the meantime. Since Smith promised Venture that he would allow him to purchase his freedom, Venture decided in favor of belonging to Smith rather than to Edwards. He immediately unburied the money he had hidden in the highroad and offered it as part of the purchase fund. Venture was at this time thirty-one years old. He gives evidence of his clear-headedness in describing this deal:

> The money which I had some time since buried . . . I took out of the earth and tendered to my master, having previously engaged a free Negro man to take his security for it, as I was the property of my master, and therefore could not safely take his obligation myself. What was wanting in redeeming myself, my master agreed to wait on me for, until I could procure it for him.[68]

Venture set about earning the balance of his purchase money with great zeal. The interest continually accruing on his master's note to the Negro friend was applied to his nest egg, which was growing steadily from profits made by fishing and by cultivation of a plot of ground which he had bought while still a slave at Stanton's. In two years he had laid up ten pounds, which his friend tendered to his master for him in exchange for Colonel Smith's note. To speed up the earning process, Venture made arrangements with Smith whereby he might hire out his time the following winter, on condition that Smith receive one-quarter of his earnings. On these terms he worked the next winter, earning "four pounds and sixteen shillings, one quarter of which went to my master for the privilege, and the rest was paid him on my own account." After that season, he struck an agreement with his master to hire out all of his time, paying Smith two pounds a month for the privilege. His account of the process of making up the sum for his redemption shows how his focus was riveted on the project to obtain his liberty:

> I hired myself at Fisher's Island, earning twenty pounds; thirteen pounds six shillings of which my master drew for the privilege, and the remainder I paid for my freedom. This made fifty one pounds two shillings which I paid him. In October following I went and wrought six months at Long Island. In that six months' time I cut and corded four hundred cords of wood, besides threshing out seventy-five bushels of grain, and received of my wages down only twenty pounds, which left remaining a larger sum. Whilst I was out at this time, I took up on my wages only one pair of shoes. At night I lay on the hearth, with one coverlet over and one under me. I returned to my master and gave him what I received of my six months' labor. This left only thirteen pounds eighteen shillings to make up the full sum of my redemption. My master liberated me,

saying that I might pay what was behind, if I could make it convenient, otherwise it would be well. The amount of money which I had paid to my master towards redeeming my time, was seventy-one pounds two shillings. The reason of my master for asking such an unreasonable price, was, he said, to secure himself in case I should ever come to want. Being thirty-six years old, I left Colonel Smith once for all. I had already been sold three different times, had made considerable money with seemingly nothing to derive it from, had been cheated out of a large sum of money, lost much by misfortune, and paid an enormous sum for my freedom.[69]

He had yet, however, to purchase his wife and three children from Stanton. The first thirty-eight pounds that he piled up for this purpose, in the form of paper currency stored in his chest, Venture lost by fire. Undaunted, he sold his property at Stonington and went to Long Island, laying aside there two hundred pounds ten shillings in four years of "singular and wonderful labors." For the benefit of any curious to know how he lived so penuriously, Venture itemizes:

Perhaps some may enquire what maintained me all the time I was laying up money. I would inform them that I bought nothing which I did not absolutely want. All fine clothes I despised in comparison with my interest, and never kept but just what clothes were comfortable for common days, and perhaps I would have a garment or two which I did not have on at all times, but as for superfluous finery I never thought it to be compared with a decent homespun dress, a good supply of money and prudence. Expensive gatherings of my mates I commonly shunned, and all kinds of luxuries I was perfectly a stranger to; and during the time I was employed in cutting the aforementioned quantity of wood [several thousand cords], I never was at the expense of six-pence worth of spirits.[70]

By his fortieth year Venture was able to purchase his sons Solomon and Cuff, for two hundred dollars each. Counting on Solomon, his oldest son, to help with the labor of redeeming the rest of their family, Venture was stunned when the boy was sent out to sea on a whaling voyage by a Rhode Island man to whom Venture had hired the seventeen-year-old lad, on "consideration of his giving him twelve pounds and an opportunity of acquiring some learning." As fate would have it, the boy contracted scurvy and died at sea, with much cause for lament for Venture. He had lost Solomon all his "hope and dependence for help" besides the loss of his life, and the seventy-five pounds he had just paid to redeem him from slavery. In addition, the man who had bound him out on the whaling voyage without Venture's knowledge, one Charles Church, never paid the father "the least of his wages."

Still undaunted, however, Venture chartered a sloop of "about thirty tons burthen" and hired men to assist in navigating her, employing the vessel mainly to bring wood from Long Island to Rhode Island, from which project he cleared "above one hundred dollars with her in better than one year." He seems somewhat jubilant over being able to purchase his wife Meg when he did for forty pounds, because he avoided "having another child to buy, as she was then pregnant." He tried every honest means he could conceive to raise the funds still needed to complete the redemption of his family. One project of raising watermelons netted him nearly five hundred dollars, despite the loss of a large number "with the thievishness of the sailors." He often went fishing at night with nets and pots for eels and lobsters, and for a period of seven months he went on a whaling voyage with his former master, Colonel Smith. In his forty-sixth year he purchased his oldest child, a daughter Hannah, for forty-four pounds, thus ending his undertaking to free himself and all his family.

Able now to turn his abilities to the pursuits of human beings with only normal cares, Venture soon acquired a farm of seventy-six acres at Haddam Neck, Connecticut, and built a substantial dwelling on it. He became a slave-holder himself, literally upon the request of one Negro, as he relates:

> I purchased a Negro man, for no other reason than to oblige him,
> and gave for him sixty pounds. But in a short time after he run
> away from me, and I thereby lost all that I gave for him, except
> twenty pounds which he paid me previous to his absconding.[71]

Another time he purchased a slave for four hundred dollars, but because the slave subsequently developed "an inclination to return to his old master, I therefore let him go." His third venture in slaveholding was equally short-lived: "Shortly after I purchased another Negro man for twenty-five pounds whom I parted with shortly after." He seemed to be better satisfied with hiring Negro laborers, for his whaling and trafficking business and farm work. He had his share of troubles from all of them, however. He was cheated continually but sometimes went out of his way to try to exact his due, as in the following instance:

> Having reached my fifty-fourth year, I hired two Negro men, one
> named William Jacklin, and the other Mingo. Mingo lived with me
> one year, and having received his wages, run in debt to me eight
> dollars, for which he gave me his note. Presently after he tried to run
> away from me without troubling himself to pay up his note, I pro-
> cured a warrant, took him, and requested him to go to Justice
> Throop's of his own accord, but he refusing, I took him on my
> shoulders, and carried him there, distant about two miles. The
> justice asking me if I had my prisoner's note with me, and replying

that I had not, he told me that I must return with him and get it. Accordingly I carried Mingo back on my shoulders, but before we arrived at my dwelling, he complained of being hurt, and asked me if this was not a hard way of treating our fellow creatures. He then told me that if I would let him off my shoulders, he had a pair of silver buckles, one shirt and a pocket handkerchief, which he would turn out to me. I agreed, and let him return home with me on foot; but the very following night he slipped from me, stole my horse and has never paid me even his note. The other Negro man, Jacklin, being a comb-maker by trade, he requested me to set him up, and promised to reward me well with his labor. Accordingly I bought tools for making combs, and procured him stock. He worked at my house about one year, and then run away from me with all his combs, and owed me for all his board.[72]

Apparently expecting a comparable diligence to duty from his children, Venture closes his absorbing narrative with several pages of lamentation over the fact that his sons had not "walked in the way of their father," adding, "But a father's lips are closed in silence and grief!—Vanity of vanities, all is vanity." His children quietly dropped the last pages from the edition reprinted in 1835 from the 1798 edition, for reasons easy to imagine. At his death in 1805 at the age of seventy-seven, Venture left a farm of more than a hundred acres of land and three "habitable dwelling houses." The town of East Haddam, Connecticut, erected a brownstone memorial to this ex-slave who had obliged the community to accept his presence as an industrious, thriving, and finally prosperous landowner.

The spread of evangelicism throughout the British Isles and America as part of the Romantic Movement was instrumental in the turning out of a flood of religious tracts, of which a considerable number bore on their paper covers the picture of a kneeling slave in chains, with his hands outstretched toward the caption: AM I NOT A MAN AND A BROTHER? These chapbooks were written by evangelists eager to relate to larger audiences than could be reached by the pulpit narratives of the wondrous power of the gospel as manifested in the lives of even the humblest members of human society, the slaves. The books were distributed to Sunday schools and at revival meetings by the thousands.[73] One of the most widely circulated of these little books seems to have been the tract entitled *The Negro Servant*, concerning which the rest of the title-page conveys the information that it is "an authentic narrative of a young Negro, showing how he was made a slave in Africa; and carried to Jamaica, where he was sold to a captain in His Majesty's navy, and taken to America, where he became a Christian; and afterwards brought to England, and baptised." It was printed for the Religious Tract Society in London, sometime during the latter part of the eighteenth century, as one of a series of real-life accounts of conversions among servants of different races by a Reverend Richmond Legh of Chelsea.[74] Its publication history shows steady reprinting until 1841, as a single work or in combination with other "Annals of the Poor," by the Religious Tract Societies of England and Scotland and by the American Tract Society.[75]

The Negro Servant is a good representative of this group of slave narratives, which may be considered an offshoot of the propagandist literature of the English abolitionists as well as religious propaganda. It is written in the form of the colloquy popular during the period, with an awkward attempt at realism through the use of a kind of dialect. The Reverend Mr. Legh had made the acquaintance of William through the latter's master, "Captain W—," who had sent for the minister to baptize William after such a period of preparation as should be needed. The slave had been bought by this master three years before, and during the first year had manifested a very "unruly and deceitful character." But upon being taken to church when the captain moved to America, William suddenly changed, becoming as honest and as civil a fellow "as ever came aboard a ship, or lived in a house." William impressed the minister as a "very young-looking man, with a sensible, lively, and pleasing turn of countenance." He answered the minister's question as to why he wished baptism by saying that he wished to go to heaven when he died, having had that wish ever since he heard a minister preach two years before. Swiftly reviewing the outward facts of his life, William told his questioner:

> Me left father and mother one day at home [in Africa] to go get shells by the sea shore; and, as I was stooping down to gather them, some white sailors came out of a boat, and took me away. Me never see father nor mother again . . . Me was put into ship, and brought to Jamaica, and sold to a master, who keep me in his house to serve him some years; when, about three years ago, Captain W—, my master that spoke to you, bought me to be his servant; he gave me my liberty, and me live with him ever since.[76]

Before he heard the American minister, William had known nothing at all about his soul, but his naive certainty that the minister was speaking directly to him caused the message to register indelibly in his mind. In the words of the dialogue:

> "And what did the minister say?"
> "He said, me was a great sinner."
> "What, did he speak to you in particular?"
> "Yes, me think so: for there was great many to hear him, but he tell them all about me."
> "What did he say?"

"He say, about all the things in my heart . . . My sin, my ignorance, my know nothing . . . He sometimes look me in the face, and say Jesus Christ came to die for sinners, poor black sinners, as well as white sinners. Me thought this was very goot indeed, to do so for a wicked sinner.

William's master let him go to hear the minister three times, and each time he felt the urge to turn to Jesus and to avoid being turned into hell fire. But he did not know how to do it, and that reduced him to tears. Asked how he had learned to read, he replied:

God teach me to read . . . God give me desire to read, and that make reading easy. Master give me a Bible, and one sailor show me the letters, and so me learn to read by myself, with God's goot help . . . Me read all about Jesus Christ, and how he loved sinners, and wicked men kill him, and he died, and came again from the grave, and all this for poor Negro . . . Some wicked people that do not love Jesus, call me great fool, and Negro dog, and black hypocrite. That make me sometime feel angry; but then me remember Christian must not be angry for that; Jesus Christ was called ugly black names, and he was quiet as a lamb; and so then me remember Jesus Christ, and me say nothing . . . Me believe that Jesus Christ came into the world to save sinners; and though me be chief of sinners, yet Jesus will save me though me be only poor black Negro . . . Me love Jesus Christ, because he love me. Me love all men, black men and white men too; for God made them all. Me love all goot Christian people, because Jesus love them, and they love Jesus.[77]

On a later occasion, when the Reverend Mr. Legh had come upon William reading his Bible in a lonely, rocky spot, he learned of the peculiar isolation of the pious young Negro, whose fellow servants detested him; though, as far as William was concerned, it was to be borne philosophically:

Me love my fellow servants, though, as I tell you before, they not much love me, and I pray God to bless them. And when they say bat things, and try to make me angry, then me tink, if Jesus Christ were in poor Negro's place, he would not revile and answer again with bat words and temper, but he say little and pray much. And so then, me say nothing at all, but pray God to forgive them.[78]

His favorite prayer was the one spoken by the man on the cross to Jesus: "Lord, remember me," to which he sometimes added the words, "a poor Negro sinner." The clergymen was very shortly convinced of the sincerity of William's conversion, and the final pages of the twenty-four-page tract concern William's "triumphal entry" into the church.

The influence of such narratives as William's upon the lives of other slaves is revealed in the foreword, "To the Reader," of the slave narrative of George White.[79] White says:

> As reading the accounts of the lives and religious experiences of others, has often quickened and comforted my own soul, and encouraged me in the way to heaven, I feel it my duty to present the friends of Jesus with a short detail of the dealings of God towards me; in my conversion, temptations, religious conflicts, call to preach, and sufferings therein; hoping to administer some of those benefits to them, which I have derived from the writings of others on the same subject.

George White was born in 1764 to a slave on an estate in Accomack, Virginia. He was sold away from his mother at the age of a year-and-a-half and sold again at the age of six to a master in "Sommerset County," Maryland. There he "received much better treatment than is usual for Africans to meet with, in this land of oppression and barbarity."[80] But he was again sold at the age of fifteen and sent to Suffolk, where he experienced "all the severities of the most abject slavery" until providentially delivered at the age of twenty-six. His yearning to see the mother from whom he had been taken as a baby became an obsession with him until his wish was granted, as he relates:

> My frequent inquiries about, and earnest entreaties to visit [my parents], though very offensive to my master, yet at length prevailed with him, to give me permission to return to the place of my nativity, to see my mother, who, as I was informed by one of her acquaintance, was yet living.
>   As my mother knew not what had become of me, the reader will easily imagine the affecting nature and circumstances of the scene of the first meeting, of a parent lost, and a child unknown; and both in a state of the most cruel bondage, without the means, or even hope of relief. But our joyful interview of mingling anguish, was of but short duration; for my condition, as a slave, would not permit of my prolonging the visit beyond the day appointed for my return; there we were obliged to undergo the painful sensations, occasioned by a second parting; and I, to return to my former servitude.[81]

White, however, had the wonderful good fortune, at the age of twenty-six, of manumission upon the death of his master, even though for a while it seemed doubtful that he would be able to get his freedom, for, as he reports, "It was with great difficulty that I saved myself from the renewal of my thraldom, which was attempted by the heirs to his estate."[82]

Like the slave narratives before his, White's story reveals the conditions of vice and immorality among the slaves as the usual reaction to the degrading and oppressive state in which they were forced to exist. Deprived "by their inhuman masters and overseers of almost every privilege and enjoyment," White explains, the young men slaves "in their absence, without much restraint or reserve, fall into those practices, which are contrary to the well-being of society, and repugnant to the will of God, whenever opportunity offers." Consequently, when the great fortune of manumission fell suddenly upon some slaves who had abandoned themselves to sinful practices as their antidote for the sufferings of the slave status, it also often brought the slave a sudden frantic desire to repent for his past actions. Therefore, after White had eventually obtained the liberty that his master was "so far humanized" in his heart to grant him at death, he considered it his greatest duty to seek from the God who had delivered him from temporal bondage, "deliverance from the slavery of sin." He tried attending services in churches of different denominations, without "any sufficient evidence of being benefited thereby" until he happened upon a quarterly meeting of the Methodists, at Annimissick, where he became "considerably alarmed with a sense of my sins, and enabled to form resolutions for life, very different from those I had before." He was now anxious to become acquainted with more Christian people and thus made up his mind to leave the South because as he explains:

> Hearing that the Africans were treated with less severity and contempt in the Northern than in the Southern states, I resolve to evade these scenes of brutal barbarity, which I had so long witnessed in my native land, and so set off for the city of New York: which place, however, I did not reach till about three years after; finding good employ in the interim at Philadelphia, and in the state of New-Jersey, which induced me to tarry at those places.[83]

He ultimately became a Methodist preacher, and we return to the final paragraph of his opening words to the reader for the statement of his purpose in telling the story of his life and enclosing a sample of his sermons:

> When I consider the station in which I am placed, and the obligations I am under, especially to my African brethren, I rejoice at every opportunity of facilitating their spiritual welfare and happiness. And should the present undertaking prove conducive thereto, the reader will do me the pleasure, to ascribe the honour and glory to God, while he enjoys the proposed benefit.

The swashbuckling slave did not always enjoy a successful career as a minister, however. Another narrative, *The Address of Abraham Johnstone, a Black Man, Who Was Hanged at Woodbury, in the County of Glocester, and State of New Jersey, etc.*, relates a very different outcome.[84] Johnstone was born a slave in the state of Delaware. Although he had five masters in all, he says that he was never treated "as rigidly or as cruelly as thousands have been to my own knowledge, yet God knows I have suffered incredible and innumerable hardships." In reviewing the events of his life for the benefit of the "people of colour" to whom he addressed his narrative, Johnstone tried to show how the condition of the Negro was gradually improving with the help of "wholesome" laws and a growing disposition among the citizens toward more liberal treatment of the race. His advice to his fellow slaves reveals a sensible appreciation of the interracial problem:

> Consider, my dear friends, that it is but a very few years since any body could be found that had courage enough to step out of the common road of thinking and object to the insufficient, unsatis- factory, and unsubstantial arguments used against us, and though some probably might have thought on the subject, and could have used weighty and substantial ones in our favor, yet they were deterred, possibly by private considerations and interested motives, and probably by a fear of encountering popular and vulgar prejudice, from saying anything on a subject that required to be treated with so much circumspection and caution; but thank God in this en- lightened age there will not be wanting men of genius, spirit and candour, who will have courage enough to step out of the common road of thinking.[85]

Johnstone claimed to be guiltless of the crime for which he was being hanged, but instead of blaming that tragic fortune upon the country and its machinery of justice, he blamed himself for having lived for years in such a manner that the reputation he had acquired contributed to his sentence of condemnation. Therefore he besought members of his race to try by their "irreproachable conduct to ripen that good disposition" towards them into esteem, not only in order to build up for themselves the protection of a respectable reputation, but also to help bring about "the relief of the rest of our brethren, as yet in thraldom." Toward the close of Johnstone's narra- tive, the sentences become increasingly incoherent, even hysterical, as he fearfully contemplates his approaching doom. The letter to his "ever dear, ever beloved and adored Wife!" that is appended to the narrative is an excep- tional example, painful to read, of emotional hysteria. Johnstone was exe- cuted on the eighth of July, 1797.

In the pages of the annual report of the American Historical Society Asso- ciation for 1894 we find the next slave narrative, "The First Fugitive Slave Case of Record in Ohio." It is the case of Jane, a slave of one Joseph Tomlin- son, Jr., of Charlestown, Brooke County, Virginia, as discovered by the historian William Henry Smith.[86] Jane had been tried before the Virginia court for "entering the premises of a merchant one night, and stealing goods valuing four dollars." Although the value her owner claimed for her was three hundred and fifty dollars, the court sentenced her to be "hanged by the neck until she be dead" on October 22, 1808. An appeal was made to the governor, but while his decision was being awaited, Jane walked through the unlocked door of the jail where she had spent eighteen days. She stayed in the town for two days but was unmolested, "as it was felt the law had been too severe." Then she left, crossing the Ohio River and finding work as a domestic servant in the home of Abner Lord in Marietta, Ohio. In the following year she married a free Negro living in Marietta, and they settled down in a home of their own. Shortly after a child was born to them, an heir of Joseph Tomlinson, Jacob Beeson, appeared in Marietta with a writ of habeas corpus for the two "slaves," claiming on the basis of the fugitive slave law enacted in 1793. Jane and her husband fought for a year for her release from Beeson's claims of property rights in Jane and her baby. It was to no avail, however. Finally, in June of 1810, the reclaimed Jane plus the little child succumbed to the decision of the court and "disappeared in the Cimmerian darkness of slavery."[87]

The fugitive slave William Grimes had a like call back to slavery that threatened an equally tragic end six years after his escape from Virginia to Connecticut in 1814. But better fortune attended his efforts to thwart attempts of recapture. By selling all of his possessions and turning the money thus obtained, together with all of his savings, to his master's agents, Grimes was able to purchase the freedom he had assumed, though the purchase reduced him in one minute from the position of a propertied resident to a beggar in the streets. In order to obtain help in the heartbreaking task of starting life "all over again," Grimes wrote and found a publisher for the narrative of his life, entitled *Life of William Grimes, the Runaway Slave, Written by Himself.*[88] In his opening appeal "To the Public," Grimes solicits buyers of his little book:

> To those who still think the book promises no entertainment, he
> begs leave to suggest another motive why they should purchase it.
> To him who has feeling, the condition of a slave, under any possible
> circumstances, is painful and unfortunate, and will excite the sym-
> pathy of all who have any. Such was my condition for more than
> thirty years, and in circumstances not only painful, but often
> intolerable. But after having tasted the sweets of liberty, (em-
> bittered, indeed, with constant apprehension,) and after having, by
> eight years' labor and exertion, accumulated about a thousand
> dollars, then to be stripped of all these hard earnings and turned
> pennyless upon the world with a family, and to purchase freedom,
> this gives me a claim upon charity, which, I presume, few possess,
> and I think, none will deny.

Grimes is the first of the mulatto slave narrators. He was born in King George's County, Virginia, to a slave belonging to a Dr. Steward, his father

being known to be "one of the most wealthy planters in Virginia." His childhood was a miserable one, consisting chiefly of hunger, whippings, and grief
over the brutal treatment of his mother and other slaves dear to him. At the
age of ten he was sold for sixty-five pounds to a Colonel Thornton of Culpepper County, Virginia. Recalling the transaction, Grimes writes:

> I then started with my new master for Savannah, with a carriage and
> four horses; we traveled about four miles the first day. I was dis-
> satisfied with him before I had got two miles. We traveled the next
> day twenty-five miles, as far as Petersburgh. I was so much dissatis-
> fied with him, that I offered a black man at that place, two silver
> dollars to take an axe and break my leg, in order that I could not go
> on to Savannah; but he refused, saying he could tell me a better
> way. I asked him how? He said run away. I told him I would not run
> away unless I was sure of gaining my freedom by it.[89]

Grimes and his owner went farther and farther into the South, and the
boy's "dissatisfaction" was greater than ever. One night when they had put
up at an inn, he therefore decided to take matters into his own hands:

> I then attempted to break my leg myself. Accordingly, I took up an
> axe, and laying my leg on a log, I struck at it several times with an
> axe, endeavoring to break it. At the same time I put up my fervent
> prayers to God to be my guide, saying, "if it be thy will that I break
> my leg in order that I may not go on to Georgia, grant that my blows
> may take effect; but thy will not mine be done." Finding I could
> not hit my leg after a number of fruitless attempts, I was convinced
> by my feelings then, that God had not left me in my sixth trouble,
> and would be with me in the seventh. Accordingly I tried no more to
> destroy myself.[90]

Fear of slavery in Georgia was added to Grimes' dislike of his new master.
From his earliest childhood his old master and mistress in Virginia had used
the threat of selling him "to the Negro buyer from Georgia" whenever Grimes
offended them. He had also been told frequently that the slaves in Georgia
had only cotton seeds and indigo to eat. Because he was unable to conquer
this fear, the lad prayed constantly for the strength to "go willingly" to
Georgia if it be God's will that he go. Colonel Thornton sensed his unwilling-
ness to go South but was determined to prevent any attempt Grimes might
make to run away. Therefore, Grimes was not allowed to leave the yard when
they stopped at inns on their journey, except for the purpose of exercising
the horses. Even with this restriction, however, Grimes managed to seek a
little information that he wanted:

> At such times, I would often go to the fortune-teller, and by paying
> her twenty-five cents, she would tell me what she said my fortune
> would be. She told me I should eventually get away, but that it
> would be attended with a great deal of trouble; and truly, I ex-
> perienced a vast deal of trouble before I could get away.[90]

A gruelling experience with an old black female slave named Frankie, who
had the reputation of being an actual witch and certainly impressed Grimes as
a genuine specimen, hastened his determination to escape from the South and
from slavery while he still possessed his native wits. Therefore he set out
bravely one night, and had the good fortune of experiencing nothing more
than physical hardships and deprivations on the dangerous journey. Everything went well with him, in fact, for six years. He obtained work at once in
Connecticut, married happily, and was happily providing for his growing
family. One day, however, friends of Colonel Thornton spied him on the
streets of New Haven, recognized him as the slave who had run away, and
brought down upon William Grimes' head one of the blackest loads to be
imagined: the choice of penury in the midst of dependent loved ones or living
death in the depths of slavery.

In the same year that William Grimes staked his hopes on the sale of his
narrative for recovering a measure of the material respectability his family
had known before all of his possessions had been snatched away at one
stroke, a London minister published in England the narrative of another
slave who had made his escape from slavery in the South, entitled *Narrative
of Some Remarkable Incidents in the Life of Solomon Bayley, formerly a
Slave, in the State of Delaware, North America; Written by Himself, and
Published for His Benefit; to Which are Prefixed, a Few Remarks by Robert
Hurnard.*[91] An earlier version of Bayley's narrative had appeared in 1820,
concerning which Hurnard writes in the preface to the 1825 edition that he
had "met with the piece containing the account of [Solomon Bayley's]
escape from slavery, with the mental and bodily trials he underwent, resulting
from that step," during the early part of Hurnard's resident in Wilmington,
Delaware, in 1820. Hurnard's sympathies were so "deeply excited" by
Bayley's lyrical recital of his sufferings and wrongs, especially since he had
"long felt a warm interest towards the descendants of Africa generally," that
he sought out Bayley. He found him living at a distance of fifty miles from
Wilmington, rather inform with age but still able to follow the vocation of
preaching which he had felt the call to obey somewhat past middle life.
Hurnard urged the former slave to complete the narrative from the point
where he had left off. Hurnard acquaints us with the difficulty with which
Bayley was persuaded to take up the writing of his life story again:

> I wished to possess it in his own simple, unvarnished style; but
> Solomon being a self-taught penman, and ignorant of orthography,

though willing to oblige me if he could, made many objections on the ground of his incapacity and the advanced period of his life; he was, however, at length induced to comply with my request, and in a while forwarded me such parts as I had particularly requested. I cannot but regret that the manuscript is so disjointed and incomplete, being written and forwarded to me at different times; but imperfect as it is, it appeared too interesting and valuable, to be restricted to the circle of my own acquaintance; and I offer it to a candid public, presuming that every indulgence on this score will be granted to a man, whose life has been chiefly spent in slavery and servitude.[92]

An active abolitionist, Hurnard found a publisher for Bayley's manuscript as soon as he returned to England, and when Bayley had at length sent him the last of three instalments added to the initial section, it was published, the proceeds from the sale being for the benefit of "the aged Solomon and his wife." Hurnard also expressed the hope that "the friends of humanity, generally, will, for this purpose, assist in promoting an extensive circulation of the tract; by so doing, they will also contribute to place SLAVERY in a new and appalling light."[93]

Solomon Bayley was born a slave in Delaware and chafed early at the restrictions of slavery upon the slave. After he had reached manhood and had acquired a wife and children, he was sold to a planter near Richmond. He brooded so bitterly upon the trip down to his new owner that quite suddenly he decided to do something about it. His description of the events that followed is unique:

On the third day [in the wagon on the road South] my distress was bitter, and I cried out in my heart, "I am past all hope": and the moment I said I was past all hope, it pleased the father of all mercy to look on me, and he sent a strengthening thought into my heart, which was this: that he that made the heavens and the earth, was able to deliver me. I looked up to the sky, and then to the trees and ground, and I believed in a moment, that if he could make all these, he was able to deliver me. . . . I then made haste and got out of the waggon, and went into the bushes; I squatted down to see what would follow. . . . They soon missed me, and took out one of the horses and rode back, and were gone about three-quarters of an hour, and then returned, and put the horse in the waggon again, and went on their way; and that was the last I ever saw or heard of them.[94]

Solomon Bayley remained hidden until night and then started walking northward, but he was beset by dogs at the very house where he had heard a man tell the waggoner during the day that a runaway had been picked up three days previously. "But it pleased the highest," reported he, "to send out a dreadful wind, with thunder and lightning, and rain; which was the means by which I escaped, as I then thought, as I travelled." He took sick along the way to Richmond and also suffered the misfortune of betrayal by a free black man in that city, who pretended friendship at the same time that he sent word to slave-catchers to come find him. But "the Maker of heaven and earth" heard his cry to save him, "and he did so." He met with many difficulties before he reached Dover. The most remarkable of these occurred at a place called Anderson's Cross-Roads, where Bayley's pursuers finally caught up with him:

> I lay down and slept till about nine o'clock, and then waked; and
> when I awoke, I felt very strange. I said to myself, I never felt so
> in all my distress: I said something was going to happen to me to-day.
> So I studied about my feelings until I fell to sleep, and when I awoke
> there had come two birds near to me; and seeing the little strange-
> looking birds, it roused up all my senses; and a thought came quick
> into my mind that these birds were sent to caution me to be away
> out of this naked place; that there was danger at hand. And as I
> was about to start, it came into my mind with great energy and
> force, "If you move out of this circle this day you will be taken;"
> for I saw the birds went all round me: I asked myself what this
> meant, and the impression grew stronger, that I must stay in the
> circle which the birds made. At the same time a sight of my faults
> came before me, and a scanty sight of the highness and holiness of
> the great Creator of all things.[95]

As Bayley raised his head to look about him, he saw one of the young men who had questioned him that morning in a boat as he was crossing a ford. Walking along beside him was an old man with a surveyor's rod. Both of them were observing the rod very carefully. We read:

> The old man kept on away past me about sixty yards, and then
> stopped; and I heard him say, "He hasn't gone this way." Then he
> took his stick and threw it over his shoulder, and pointed this way
> and that way, until he got it right towards me; and then I heard him
> say, "Come let us go this way." Then he turned his course and came
> right towards me: then I trembled, and cried in my heart to the
> Lord, and said, What shall I do? What shall I do? and it was im-
> pressed on my mind immediately, "Stand still and see the salvation
> of the Lord;" the word that was spoken to the children of Israel
> when at the Red Sea. And I said in my heart, Bless the Lord, O my
> soul; I will try the Lord this time. Here they came; and still that

word sounded in my heart; "Stand still and see the salvation of the Lord." They came not quite so near as the circle the birds had made, when the old man sheered off, and went by me; but the young man stopped and looked right down on me, as I thought, and I looked right up into his eyes; and then he stood and looked right into my eyes, and when he turned away, he ran after the old man, and I thought he saw me; but when he overtook the old man, he kept on, and then I knew he had not seen me . . . I thought I must jump and shout; but another thought struck my mind, that it was not a right time to shout; I therefore refrained. But my heart was overwhelmed at the sight of the goodness and the power of God. . . . I now believed if everybody in the world was engaged against me, that he was able to deliver me out of their hands.[96]

The second installment of Bayley's story concerns the purchase of his freedom. Not long after the escape from his pursuers related above, his master came the "three or four hundred miles" from central Virginia to Camden, Delaware, in search of him. Bayley hired a lawyer in preparation for suing his master for his freedom under the laws of the state of Delaware. The meeting between slave and slaveholder is graphically presented:

Upon first sight he asked me what I was going to do? I says, how, master? he asked me, how did I think I was going to get free, by running and dodging about in that manner? I said, why, master, I have suffered a great deal, and seen a great deal of trouble. I think you might let me go for a little or nothing: he said, I won't do that, but I will give you the same chance I gave you before I sent you away; give me forty pounds bond and security, and you may be free: but I replied, I work hard at nights to get a little money to fee my lawyers, and if it had been right for me to be free, I ought to have been free without so much trouble; he asked me who I blamed for my trouble? I answered, I did not consider that I was to blame. Ah! said he, my wrongs don't make yours right, and that word put me to silence; but I thought where the laws of the land made liberty the right of any man, he could not be wrong in trying to recover it: but finally he sold me my time for eighty dollars and I dropped the lawsuit. I went to work, and worked it out in a shorter time than he gave me, and then I was free from man.[97]

The third and fourth installments of the narrative deal with a recital of the shameful practices he had engaged in as a young, unregenerate slave and Bayley's call to the ministry, the result of his last "great warfare and strife" as he found himself beset "first, with man-fear, and a man-pleasing spirit, then with shame, desire of praise, and a good name. . . ."[98] The pages of his autobiography are saturated with the phraseology and spirit of the books of the Prophets and of Paul, especially in the final section, which matches the Pauline tone of the opening lines of the first section much more closely than the exciting passages recording his escape: "Solomon Bayley, unto all people, and nations, and languages, grace be unto you, and peace from God our Father, and from the Lord Jesus Christ."

Robert Voorhis, the "Hermit of Massachusetts," is the next slave narrator to be considered. For fourteen years he lived in a cave near Providence, Rhode Island. Although many were curious to know his story, no one was successful in obtaining it from the solitary creature until one Henry Trumbull gained his confidence and the narrative, which he took down from Voorhis' own lips and published in 1829 under the title *Life and Adventures of Robert Voorhis, the Hermit of Massachusetts, Who Has Lived Fourteen Years in a Cave, Secluded from Human Society, etc.*[99]

Voorhis was born a slave in Princeton, New Jersey, about 1769. His father, his mother told him, was an eminent Englishman. When he was four years old he was taken to Georgetown, District of Columbia. An attempt to make a shoemaker out of him was made when he was about fifteen, but he did not do well in that trade so he was returned to the plantation. In time he married another slave, Alley Pennington. Seeing how devoted Voorhis was to his wife and growing family, an acquaintance of Voorhis' master, James Bevens, interested Voorhis in having his ownership transferred to Bevens for the sum of fifty pounds from the latter, with the understanding that Bevens would give Voorhis full opportunity to work and earn the fifty pounds to buy his freedom. It proved to be a rascally trick. Bevens only purchased Voorhis in order to sell him farther South for a larger sum. Voorhis was dragged away in the middle of the night from his terrified wife and little ones, bound with riveted irons, and hurried secretly on board a schooner bound for Charleston, South Carolina. Four days later, however, he managed to escape from his enslavers and reached Philadelphia by stowing away on a sloop. Seeking aid among the Quakers, he was sheltered for a time, but before long was recaptured and sent back to Charleston, where he was purchased by a kindly doctor of considerable wealth. Having nothing on his mind, however, but the desire for freedom and his own family, Voorhis could not brook even the mild form of slavery he experienced in the home of Dr. Fersue. He soon managed to stow himself in the hold of a brig bound direct for Boston.

Very close to death from thirst, he finally made his presence known to the crew as a desperate last resort. Voorhis was nursed back to health by the compassionate captain and his crew when they had learned his story. They advised him of what to do when they arrived at Boston in order to avoid recapture. Realizing that it would be impossible for him to reach his beloved little family for a while at least, Voorhis signed up as a sailor, making three trips to India and one to China. After the second trip he undertook a second marriage in Salem, but set off again shortly after. The woman finally left him on his return from the fourth trip.

Twenty years after his escape from slavery, Voorhis went down to Baltimore on a sloop and searched about until he obtained information concerning the wife and children from whom he had been so ruthlessly sold. They had all died of grief and deprivation not long after he had been taken away from them. It was at this point that Voorhis decided the world contained no attractions for him. He declares:

> I then felt but little desire to live, as there was nothing then remaining to attach me to this world—and it was at that moment that I formed the determination to retire from it—to become a recluse, and mingle thereafter as little as possible with human society. With this determination I returned direct to Rhode Island, and soon after selected a retired spot well suited to my purpose. . . . There I built me a hut. . . . Here in solitude I have dwelt more than six years— once or twice a week and sometimes oftener I leave my recess, cross over the bridge into Providence, converse a little and return again well satisfied to my peaceable dwelling.[100]

A well-formed man of about sixty years, with regular features in a tan-colored face and a long jet-black beard, the "Hermit of Massachusetts" whiled away his days growing plants to feed the cattle that hovered round his cell and brooded still over the breakup of the proud dreams of the young slave husband and father by a shyster member of the society of slaveholders.

One of the most curious proofs of the appeal of the slave narrative was the publication in Baltimore in December, 1831, of an edition of fity thousand copies of *The Confessions of Nat Turner, the Leader of the Late Insurrection in Southampton, Virginia, etc.*[101] As an editorial in *The Liberator* observed directly after the appearance of the reportorial scoop by Thomas R. Gray: "We advise the Grand Juries in several slave States to indict Mr. Gray and the printers of the pamphlet forthwith; and the legislative bodies at the South to offer a large reward for their apprehension." Certainly it should have been clear to all that the distribution of such a record of adventurous living would "only serve to rouse up other leaders and cause other insurrections, by creating among the blacks admiration for the character of Nat, and a deep, undying sympathy for his fate."[102]

Nat Turner was born on the second of October, 1800, the slave of one Benjamin Turner. He was twice sold, once as a child to a Putnam Moore, then as a young man to Joseph Travis. From early childhood he had been accustomed to hearing his mother and others say that he would surely be a prophet, "as the Lord had shown him things that had happened before his birth." He had learned to read so easily that he had no recollection whatever of learning the alphabet. His fellow slaves revered him, and white neighbors used to shake their heads and say that Nat Turner was too smart to raise as a slave. He was never known to have a dollar in his life, or to steal, or to swear an oath, or to drink a drop of "spirits," and he was given to hours of fasting and prayer. On one such occasion of mystical devotion, he had a vision in which he saw white spirits and black spirits engaged in battle. The sun was darkened, the thunder rolled in the heavens, blood flowed in streams, and he heard a voice saying: "Such is your luck, such you are called to see, and let it come rough or smooth, you must bear it." One day soon after, while at work in the field, he discovered "drops of blood on the corn, as though it were dew from heaven," and he found on the leaves in the woods "characters and numbers, with the forms of men sketched in blood." So we are told.[103]

Descriptions of Nat Turner present him as a short, stout, powerfully built person of tawny complexion and strongly marked African features, his face full of animation and resolution.[104] Though he claimed that his three masters were all kind, he was described in Governor Floyd's proclamation "as having a scar on one of his temples, also one on the back of his neck, and a large knot on one of the bones of his right arm, produced by a blow."[105] According to traditions among the Virginia slaves, their "Prophet Nat" had long been engaged in figuring out plans for the "deliverance" of his people. If caught with lime and lampblack in his hand, "conning over a half-finished county map on the barn door," he was "planning what to do if he were blind." When poor whites came eavesdropping to learn what he was saying in the meetings he frequently held, he changed the subject to gossip about what the master was planning to do about "Mr. Jones' fence" or "Mr. Smith's pigs." The report that he was once a Baptist preacher is unfounded, but he did pretend on one occasion that he was one, in order to "manage" a wily white man named Brantley.

The actual words of Nat Turner's recital of their night of murder have the soundless clarity of the candid camera flash. We can be certain that he was not sane as we read:

> I saluted them on coming up, and asked Will how came he there: he answered, his life was worth no more than others, and his liberty as dear to him. I asked him if he thought to obtain it? He said he would, or lose his life. This was enough to put him in full confidence. . . . It was quickly agreed we should commence at home (Mr. J. Travis) on that night, and until we had armed and equipped ourselves, and gathered sufficient force, neither age nor sex was to be spared, (which was invariably adhered to). We remained at the feast, until about two hours in the night, when we went to the house and found Austin; they all went to the cider press and drank, except myself. On returning to the house, Hark went to the door with an axe, for the purpose of breaking it open, as we knew we were strong

enough to murder the family, if they were awaked by the noise; but
reflecting that it might create an alarm in the neighborhood, we
determined to enter the house secretly, and murder them whilst
sleeping. Hark got a ladder and set it against the chimney, on which I
ascended, and hoisting a window, entered and came downstairs, un-
barred the door, and removed the guns from their places. It was then
observed that I must spill the first blood. On which, armed with a
hatchet, and accompanied by Will, I entered my master's chamber;
it being dark, I could not give a death blow; the hatchet glanced
from his head, he sprang from the bed and called his wife; it was his
last word. Will laid him dead, with a blow of his axe, and Mrs. Travis
shared the same fate, as she lay in bed. The murder of this family,
five in number, was the work of a moment, not one of them awoke;
there was a little infant sleeping in a cradle, that was forgotten,
until we had left the house and gone some distance, when Henry
and Will returned and killed it; we got here, four guns that would
shoot, and several old muskets, with a pound or two of powder.
We remained some time, at the barn, where we paraded. I formed
them in a line as soldiers, and after carrying them through all the
maneuvres I was master of, marched them off to Mr. Salathiel
Francis', about six hundred yards distant. Sam and Will went to the
door and knocked. Mr. Francis asked who was there? Sam replied it
was him, and he had a letter for him, on which he got up, and came
to the door. They immediately seized him, and dragging him out a
little from the door, he was despatched by repeated blows on the
head. There was no other white person in the family. We started
from there to Mrs. Reese's, maintaining the most perfect silence on
our march, where finding the door unlocked, we entered, and
murdered Mrs. Reese in her bed, while sleeping; her son awoke, but
it was only to sleep the sleep of death; he had only time to say who
is that, and he was no more. From Mrs. Reese's we went to Mrs.
Turner's, a mile distant, which we reached about sunrise, on Monday
morning. Henry, Austin, and Sam went to the still, where, finding
Mr. Peebles, Austin shot him, and the rest of us went to the house;
as we approached, the family discovered us, and shut the door. Vain
hope! Will, with one stroke of his axe, opened it, and we entered
and found Mrs. Turner and Mrs. Newsome in the middle of a
room, almost frightened to death. Will immediately killed Mrs.
Turner, with one blow of his axe. I took Mrs. Newsome by the
hand, and with the sword I had when I was apprehended, I struck
her several blows over the head, but not being able to kill her,
as the sword was dull. Will turning around, and discovering it,
despatched her also.

The horror continues, as Nat Turner counts off one after the other of the victims of axe and shotgun and blunt sword on that mad foray. By mid-morning, after the alarm was spread, the killings were speeded up somewhat, Turner becoming more of a checking clerk than actual participant. The narrative turns, after the last of the murders, to a recital of his various shifts to avoid capture, his sallies forth from the cave that served as his headquarters, and his capture.

As a representative of the narrative of the insurrectionist, Nat Turner's is most important, since his insurrection actually took place, whereas the narratives of slaves captured before the projected plans could be carried out lack the finality of Turner's.[106] The shudder is reserved exclusively for this one. Leaving aside all speculation as to the why or the wherefore, we have here the revelation of the subversive power of slavery, at its nadir.

What Nat Turner and his associates lacked was faith in a higher power than man. The slave narrator Thomas Cooper, whose life story was published in New York a few months after Turner's *Confessions*, was able to declare in triumph over the hardships of his slave experience—the very hard labor, scanty food and clothing, drafty open hut—that although his body was held in cruel bondage, his mind was free, and he could send up his prayers in secret, to God, for deliverance from his sufferings. He believed unswervingly that "all are the work of the Almighty hand, who hath placed them in various situations, and that he was disposed to extend equally his care and protection to all."[107]

Thomas Cooper was born in Maryland about 1775, a slave on the estate of a Mr. Notly. In 1800 he ran away from his hard life, changed his name to John Smith, and hired himself out to lumberyard employers in Philadelphia. He married and had children. After a number of years, however, his master learned where he was to be found, and despite the entreaties of Smith's employers to accept a large sum of money for him, that he might continue working for them, Smith was dragged back down to slavery by his master. In the presence of his wife and children he was handcuffed. A rope was fastened to each arm across his back and another fastened to it, one end of which the master held in his hand. Mounting his horse, the latter rode off, "driving John before him." By the time they reached Washington, however, John Smith managed to escape before his master was able to get him onto the slave block for sale to Georgia traders. After a perilous journey by night on foot, he got back to Philadelphia. He dared not remain under his own roof, so he found shelter in the home of a friendly Quaker.[108] A slave hunter disguised as a Quaker tried to ferret out his hiding place, but his wife had the wisdom of fear for her husband's safety, and he was warned to flee. Eight miles from home, he found employment on a New Jersey farm, saved money, and bought a small farm on which he established his family.

Again his master tracked him down, and he had to flee with his family to Boston, leaving all of his possessions, and even changing his name again, this time becoming Thomas Cooper.[109] Again he hired out to a lumber merchant, but, feeling the call to preach, soon became so popular in that capacity that his days as a lumberman ended. He was sent to the West Indies as visiting preacher, and after that experience was invited to go to London, with his family. For about a year and a half, Cooper was the pastor of a church in London, during which period he prepared a hymnal, which was published there in 1820.[110] His constant desire to go to Africa led finally to arrangements for him to go to Sierra Leone. After a farewell sermon before several thousand persons in Brown's Lane, Spitalfields, on November 5, 1818, he departed for Africa. He fell victim to the climate three years later. His wife and children returned first to London and then to Philadelphia.

The narrative of "Good Bishop Allen," the founder of the African Methodist Episcopal Church, was not published until the year after his death, by his request, though he had prepared it for printing years earlier.[111] One of the most helpful of the leaders of the Negro race, the Right Reverend Richard Allen had learned the gospel of self-help which became the keystone of the enterprise he established while yet a slave. The doctrine of racial pride based upon self-respect and business acumen that he taught to slaves and freemen alike remains the distinguishing characteristic of the network of African Methodist Episcopal churches, schools, colleges, and missions that had developed into the chief enterprise "owned, operated, and controlled by Negroes" in Allen's own day—an enterprise that still thrives.

Richard Allen was born in 1760, the slave of one Benjamin Chew of Philadelphia. At an early age, he was sold along with the rest of his family to a Mr. Stokely, a Delaware planter. For a number of years the slave family was together, but when financial difficulties beset Mr. Stokeley, a kindly man whom Allen characterized in his narrative as "more like a father to his slaves than anything else," he found himself unable to finish paying for Allen's family and was obliged to sell Allen's mother and her three youngest children. Richard Allen remained with him, together with an older brother and sister. All three of them turned to religion in their need for comfort after the loss of their parents and other sisters and brother, and they were grateful for their master's cooperation with their desire to attend services. As Allen describes it:

> Our neighbors, seeing that our master indulged us with the privilege
> of attending meeting once in two weeks, said that Stokeley's
> Negroes would soon ruin him; and so my brother and myself held a
> council together, that we would attend more faithfully to our
> master's business, so that it should not be said that religion made us
> worse servants; we would work night and day to get our crops
> forward, so that they should be disappointed. We frequently went
> to meeting on every other Thursday; but if we were likely to be

backward with our crops we would refrain from going to meeting. . . .
So we always continued to keep our crops more forward than our
neighbors, and we would attend public meeting once in two weeks,
and class meeting once a week. At length, our master said he was
convinced that religion made slaves better and not worse, and often
boasted of his slaves for their honesty and industry. Some time
after, I asked him if I might ask the preacher to come and preach at
his house.[112]

Mr. Stokeley and his wife permitted Methodist preachers to come regularly
to their house to preach and always attended the services. This continued
for months. At length, a preacher with the suggestive name of Freeborn
Garrison delivered a sermon on the text: "Thou art weighed in the balance,
and art found wanting." From that evening, Mr. Stokeley brooded over
the belief that the preacher had pointed to him, in the course of showing
how the slaveholders fell short of the weight needed for salavation, even
though he had always tried to be a good master. Since he could not afford
to free his slaves, as he was old and infirm and in poor circumstances, he
proposed to Richard Allen and his brother that they "buy" their time. He
was convinced that slaveholding was wrong and could no longer be satisfied
to hold slaves. The price agreed upon was "sixty pounds gold and silver, or
two thousand dollars Continental money."

Allen and his brother thereupon left Mr. Stokeley's house to find work
whereby they might pay him for their freedom. They left on the understanding that they could return at any time when they were out of a place
or sick, and Allen writes that "it was like leaving a father's house; for he was
a kind, affectionate and tender-hearted master." But with what joy they set
about their project we learn in his next words:

> I had it often impressed upon my mind that I should one day enjoy
> freedom; for slavery is a bitter pill, notwithstanding we had a good
> master. But when we would think that our day's work was never
> done, we often thought that after our master's death we were liable
> to be sold to the highest bidder, as he was much in debt; and thus
> my troubles were increased, and I was often brought to weep
> between the porch and the altar. But I have reason to bless my dear
> Lord that a door was opened unexpectedly for me to buy my time
> and enjoy my liberty.[113]

When they left the plantation, the two young slaves did not know at first
what to do, as they had not been used to working outside of the farm. Allen
found a job cutting cord wood, but by the end of the first day his hands were
so blistered and sore that it was with difficulty that he opened or shut them.
He turned to the only help he knew:

> I kneeled down upon my knees and prayed that the Lord would
> open some way for me to get my living. In a few days, my hands
> recovered and became accustomed to cutting of wood and other
> hardships; so I soon became able to cut my cord and a half or two
> cords a day.[114]

The woodcutting job giving out, he next obtained work at a brickyard for a wage of fifty dollars a month, "Continental money." When that work ended, he turned to day's work. Sundays were reserved for worship, as he "did not forget to serve my dear Lord." By the year 1777, both brothers were able to comply with Mr. Stokeley's proposal and were free. Richard Allen was then seventeen years old.

Allen was so devout a Christian and such a dependable individual that, despite his youth, he soon became affiliated with the Methodists as an assisting preacher on the circuit south of Wilmington. After he became free he devoted an increasingly large proportion of his time to preaching to those who were still slaves. He was employed cutting wood or driving wagons or the like during the day and preached nights and on Sundays. To what lengths he went in order to help his enslaved people, we learn from such passages as the following:

> I received nothing from the Methodist connection. My usual method
> was, when I would get bare of clothes, to stop travelling and go to
> work, so that no men could say I was chargeable to the connection.
> My hands administered to my necessities. . . . The autumn of 1785 I
> returned again to Radnor. I stopped at George Giger's, a man of
> God, and went to work. His family were all kind and affectionate to
> me. I killed seven beeves and supplied the neighbors with meat; got
> myself pretty well clad through my own industry—thank God—and
> preached occasionally. The elder in charge in Philadelphia frequently
> sent for me to come to the city. February, 1786, I came to Philadel-
> phia. Preaching was given out for me at 5 o'clock in the morning at
> St. George's church. I strove to preach as well as I could, but it was a
> great cross to me; but the Lord was with me. We had a good time and
> several souls were awakened, and were earnestly seeking redemption
> in the blood of Christ. . . . I soon saw a large field open in seeking and
> instructing my African brethren, who had been a long forgotten
> people, and few of them attended public worship. I preached in the
> Commons, in Southwark, Northern Liberties, and wherever I could
> find an opening. I frequently preached twice a day, at 5 o'clock in
> the morning and in the evening, and it was not uncommon for me to
> preach from four to five times a day. I established prayer meetings; I
> raised a society in 1786 of forty-two members. I saw the necessity
> of erecting a place of worship for the colored people.[115]

Thwarted in his plans for establishing a church in which his own people, including himself when he was not in the pulpit, would not be subject to ejection at the caprice of both the free Negroes and the whites, Allen persisted until he was successful in opening the doors of the "Bethel Church" in Philadelphia in 1793. With his own hands plus the labor of volunteers, he converted a dilapidated old blacksmith shop for that purpose. His reasons for not founding a separate sect, but rather a segregated division of the Methodist Episcopal connection to which he was all his life devoted, show his deep desire to help strengthen the Negro:

> I was confident that there was no religious sect or denomination
> would suit the capacity of the colored people as well as the Metho-
> dist; for the plain and simple gospel suits best for my people; for
> the unlearned can understand, and the learned are sure to under-
> stand; and the reason that the Methodist is so successful in the
> awakening and conversion of the colored people . . . is its having a
> good discipline. . . . We are beholden to the Methodists, under God,
> for the light of the Gospel we enjoy; for all other denominations
> preached so high-flown that we were not able to comprehend their
> doctrine.[116]

Inspired by Allen's beginnings, unnumbered slaves labored in their garden patches and cut extra cords of wood to contribute to the support of the African Methodist Church thus founded in a blacksmith shop. With its expansion grew the roster of freedmen who had purchased their liberty by their own extra labor and dogged thrift. Allen's doctrine of self-help became the rudder of many a slave who might otherwise have fallen by the wayside, like Arthur, or poor Abraham Johnstone.

Looking down the list of the slave narratives published before 1836, the reader finds a striking variety of human personalities represented there, yet with one characteristic in common in addition to race and "condition of servitude." The personalities include such divergent types as the frail, bookish Phillis Wheatley and the hoyden Jane Tomlinson; the sentimental James Albert Ukawsaw Gronniosaw and the practical Venture Smith; the recluse Robert Voorhis and the Christian-socialist Richard Allen; the sage Jupiter Hammon and the warped Nat Turner; the rascally Arthur and the dependable William; the intrepid Briton Hammon and the fearful Abraham Johnstone; the impatient William Grimes and the trusting Solomon Bayley; the opportunistic Adam and the idealist Equiano. The characteristic common to all, in addition to their being Negroes and slaves, can be best described, possibly, as *stage presence*.

The slave narrator's concept of the world as a stage and of his role as the "bad part" assigned him to play is the most distinct, single impression left upon the reader by the slave narratives before 1836. Except in notably few instances, the slave's consciousness of the Director is evident. The play will end well or not according to his submission to *that* Master's will.

Chapter 3

The Slave Narrative
After 1836

A new day dawned for the slave narrative with the rise of abolitionism in New England. Though the new ideology spread slowly at first, the intense conviction of that small central band of Garrisonians that it was the first duty of society to restore human rights to the American Negro slave brought about a revolution in the attitude of the slave towards himself as one of its earliest results. It transferred the stigma traditionally associated with slavery from the slave to the slaveholder. Instead of having to consider one's slave status a humiliating secret to be fearfully guarded, the fugitive slave began to find the fact an actual asset in some respects by the 1840s. In fact, overtures to the slave in some quarters reached such proportions that, according to contemporary records, it was not long before free Negroes were pretending to be fugitive slaves.[1] The ability to make friends had always been the good fortune of the slave, and these friends could be counted upon to support any literary enterprise one might undertake. But the horizon widened to include a public now beginning to become interested in the slave on the ground of general principles, which ushered in a new day indeed.

By 1836, the antislavery press was avid for slave narratives. There were by that year twelve different abolitionist journals: the *American Anti-Slavery Almanac*,[2] the *Chronotype*,[3] and *The Liberator*,[4] in Boston; the *American Anti-Slavery Record*,[5] the *Anti-Slavery Examiner*,[6] the *Anti-Slavery Record*,[7] *The Emancipator*,[8] *Human Rights*,[9] the *Quarterly Anti-Slavery Magazine*,[10] and the *Slave's Friend*,[11] in New York; the *National Enquirer*[12] in Philadelphia; and the *Observer*[13] in St. Louis. For a while there were reprintings of narratives that were originally published as religious tracts and summaries of longer narratives that had appeared in book form.[14] Southern newspapers were culled for data on the lives of the slaves. Soon it was possible to include testimonials taken down from the lips of fugitive slaves whose arrivals were ceasing to be secret.

The prospectus for the first book-length slave narrative published under the aegis of the abolitionists, *Slavery in the United States: A Narrative of the Life and Adventures of Charles Ball, a Black Man*,[15] stressed the value of the book as a revelation of social wrongs:

These pages ... will present ... a faithful view of the opinions and
feelings of the colored population, constituting so large a portion of
the people [in the South]. [The reader] will here see portrayed in
the language of truth, by an eye witness and a slave, the sufferings,
the hardships, and the evils which are inflicted upon the millions of
human beings, in the name of the law of the land and of the Constitution of the United States. ... Every American must read with concern, that part of this narrative, in which the author states the incidents of the war in the waters of the Chesapeake, on the western
shore of Maryland, and near the City of Washington; nor is it easy
to suppress the feelings of regret which naturally arise in the bosom,
when we learn that one of the men who fought at Bladensburg in
defense of the Capitol, under the orders and eye of Barney, was
afterwards driven in slavery and in chains over the very ground
where he had seen his commander fall.[16]

The identities of Charles Ball and of the "Mr. Fisher" to whom the narrative
was related were never made clear. At the end of a very popular year of circulation, a controversy grew up concerning its authenticity that checked the
sales of this exciting book for twenty years.[17] No such uncertainty attended
the publication of the narrative of Moses Roper, however. Roper was the
slave narrator with the distinction of being the first person to achieve publicity as a fugitive who fled all the way to England from the Southern States in
search of safety.

Moses Roper had fled from a particularly harassing experience as a slave in
North and South Carolina and in Georgia in 1834. He traveled in the arduous
manner peculiar to the journeying of slaves upwards from slavery for a distance of five hundred miles until he reached New York in August of that
year. Thence he went to Vermont, where, as the people seemed opposed to
slavery, he admitted that he was a runaway slave. Learning that his master had
found out where he was, he left Vermont for Boston, where he resided for
several months and had the amusing experience of being taken for a white
person by the city officials, of being duly warned to train in the militia during
his stay there, and of actually performing military duty "without any person
suspecting that he had African blood in his veins."[18] Learning that his master
was again upon his trail, he fled to New York, where he remained in hiding
until he obtained passage on a ship, the *Napoleon*. On November 11, 1835, he
sailed for England, carrying with him letters of recommendation from New
England abolitionists to abolitionists in the British Isles and bearing in his
breast a newly discovered knowledge of his "sinfulness and need of a Saviour,"
which had come to him by way of his attendance at several places of worship
during his months in New England. In England, upon presenting his letters of
introduction, he became the house guest, successively, of the abolitionists

Dr. Morison, Dr. T. Price, and Mr. F. A. Cox. Dr. Morison encouraged Roper to write his autobiography in the course of the period of two years that Roper spent with him.

Moses Roper's *Narrative of the Adventures and Escape of Moses Roper from American Slavery* was published in London in 1837 in an edition of fifty-one pages. New editions appeared in 1838, 1839, and 1840 in London and in Philadelphia, with the pagination gradually swelling to one hundred pages plus an appendix. It was translated into Celtic in 1841 and appeared in ten editions in all by 1856.[19] The editor's preface to the first edition, written by Dr. Price in the illness of the actual editor, Dr. Morison, tells of the splendid impression Roper had made upon them as an "excellent young man" possessing "uncommon intelligence, sincere piety, and a strong desire to preach the gospel." During the two years of his residence with them, Roper had been learning how to read and write in order to be "qualified for usefulness among his own people" as a missionary in the West Indies. Dr. Price declared, "The progress he has already made justifies the belief, that if the means of education can be secured for a short time longer, he will be eminently qualified to instruct the children of Africa in the truths of the gospel of Christ." Partly, therefore, with the hope of obtaining funds from the sale of his narrative for furthering his education, and partly to "engage the sympathies of our countrymen on behalf of his oppressed brethren," Roper's book was being boosted by the English abolitionists. According to Dr. Price:

> We feel quite sure that the religious public in general, and the Anti-Slavery public in particular, will show their sympathy with the author independent of eleemosynary support, and that none of our readers, who can possibly spare two shillings, will permit the brief outline of the poor fellow's 'eventful history,' which we purpose to subjoin, to prevent them from purchasing at least one copy of the little volume . . . for we feel that the honor of the British name is at stake, when a fugitive slave publishes the story of his successful flight with the manly and benevolent desire of realising thereby the means of educating his own emancipated mind, that he may become the instrument of emancipating the minds of his 'kinsmen according to the flesh.'[20]

In his own preface to the first edition of his narrative, Roper begins by stating that "the determination of laying this little narrative before the public, did not arise from any desire to make myself conspicuous, but with the view of exposing the cruel system of slavery . . . from the urgent calls of nearly all the friends to whom I had related any part of my story, and also from the recommendation of anti-slavery meetings, which I have attended, through the suggestion of many warm friends of the cause of the oppressed."

Though he is aware that many of the things his readers will find in his pages will seem to them "somewhat at variance with the dictates of humanity," he advises them that it is possible for them to "be put in possession of facts respecting this system which equal in cruelty my own narrative." In addition, since "the slaveholder, the colonizationist, and even Mr. Gooch himself" will soon be able to possess a copy of his book, it should be interesting to await the reactions of those individuals to his accusations, and to see how they "set me down as the tool of a party." His earnest wish to give an "impartial statement of facts" in developing his narrative brings with it the obligation to recount "some part of my conduct, which I now deeply deplore," for which Roper wishes to be pardoned. His explanation echoes the explanation now grown familiar from earlier slave narratives: "The ignorance in which the poor slaves are kept by their masters, precludes almost the possibility of their being alive to any moral duties."[21]

Roper's opening passage presents a phase of the experience of the mulatto slave that is frequently attested to in the course of the slave narratives, but does not seem to be generally appreciated. Far from enjoying a favored position in the slaveholder's household, in recognition of his mixed blood, the lot of the mulatto slave was usually harder than that of the other slaves on the plantation if he was a male. If a female, the early years might be spent pleasantly in the company of the members of the slaveholder's household, but the usual outlook for the mulatto slave woman, especially if she possessed striking beauty, which many of them did, was sale, sometimes at prices ranging from twelve hundred to as high as *eight thousand* dollars, for licentious purposes that were the heartbreak of the helpless girl and her saddened family.[22] Roper tells of the birth of his troubles on this account:

> I was born in North Carolina, in Caswell County, I am not able to
> tell in what month or year. What I shall now relate, is what was told
> me by my mother and grandmother. A few months before I was
> born, my father married my mother's young mistress. As soon as my
> father's wife heard of my birth, she sent one of my mother's sisters
> to see whether I was white or black, and when my aunt had seen me,
> she returned back as soon as she could, and told her mistress that I
> was white, and resembled Mr. Roper very much. Mr. Roper's wife
> not being pleased with this report, she got a large club-stick and
> knife, and hastened to the place in which my mother was confined.
> She went into my mother's room with a full intention to murder me
> with her knife and club, but as she was going to stick the knife into
> me, my grandmother happening to come in, caught the knife and
> saved my life. But as well as I can recollect from what my mother
> told me, my father sold her and myself, soon after her confine-
> ment. . . . I am not sure whether he exchanged me for another slave

or not, but think it very likely he did exchange me with one of his wife's brothers or sisters, because I remember when my mother's old master died, I was living with my father's wife's brother-in-law, whose name was Mr. Durham. My mother was drawn with the other slaves. . . . The way they divide their slaves is this: they write the names of different slaves on a small piece of paper, and put it into a box, and let them all draw. I think that Mr. Durham drew my mother, and Mr. Fowler drew me, we were separated a considerable distance, I cannot say how far. My resembling my father so much, and being whiter than the other slaves, caused me to be soon sold to what they call a Negro trader, who took me to the Southern States of America, several hundred miles from my mother. As well as I can recollect I was then about six years old. The trader, Mr. Mitchell, after travelling several hundred miles, and selling a good many of his slaves, found he could not sell me very well (as I was so much whiter than other slaves were) for he had been trying several months—left me with a Mr. Sneed, who kept a large boarding house, who took me to wait at table, and sell me if he could. I think I stayed with Mr. Sneed about a year, but he could not sell me. When Mr. Mitchell had sold his slaves, he went to the North, and brought up another drove, and returned to the South with them, and sent his son-in-law into Washington, Georgia, after me; so he came and took me from Mr. Sneed, and met his father-in-law with me, in a town called Lancaster, with his drove of slaves. We stayed in Lancaster a week, because it was court week, and there were a great many people there, and it was a good opportunity for selling the slaves; and there he was enabled to sell me to a gentleman, Dr. Jones, who was both a Doctor and a Cotton Planter. He took me into his shop to beat up and mix medicines, which was not a very hard employment, but I did not keep it long, as the Doctor soon sent me to his cotton plantation, that I might be burnt darker by the sun.[23]

Roper was sold soon after this to a Mr. Allen, who exchanged him for "a female slave to please his wife," with a pair of slave traders named Cooper and Lindsey, who finally "swopt" Roper "for a boy, that was blacker than me," out of sheer disgust at not being able to sell him, "people objecting to my being rather white." His new master was a Mr. Smith, with whom he lived for a year. He was then sold to a Mr. Hodge, a slave trader, and thence to a Mr. Gooch, of Cashaw County, South Carolina, when he was about thirteen years of age. It was with Mr. Gooch that Moses Roper's spectacular hardships were to begin and end. His name became a popular symbol for the notorious slaveholder during the remainder of the antislavery crusade, sharing "honors" with Douglass' "Mr. Gore" in the next decade.

Mr. Gooch had bought Roper to serve as field hand for his son-in-law on a farm with but two other slaves. Discovering that the boy had never worked as a regular field hand, however, he set him to work under overseers and, receiving a very poor report as to the progress young Roper was making, Mr. Gooch "flogged me nearly every day, and very severely." After a time, though still not satisfied that the boy had been sufficiently "trained," Mr. Gooch took him to his son-in-laws' plantation about five miles away. The work was very hard, and he was always flogged for not accomplishing enough. One day Roper ran away into the woods, half-starved and half-naked. He was found by a slaveholder and landed in Lancaster Gaol, to await his master's claim. A severe flogging of one hundred lashes welcomed the return of the fourteen-year-old slave. But, "having determined from my youth to gain my freedom," Roper writes, "I made several attempts, was caught, and got a severe flogging of one hundred lashes, each time: Mr. Hammans was a very severe and cruel master, and his wife still worse; she used to tie me up and flog me while naked."[24] After Mr. Hammans saw that the boy was determined "to die in the woods" rather than live with him, he exchanged him with Mr. Gooch for a piece of farm land. Mr. Gooch received him with macabre delight:

> [Knowing that I was averse to going back to him,] he chained me
> by the neck to his chaise. In this manner he took me to his home at
> McDaniels Ferry, in the County of Chester, a distance of fifteen
> miles. After which, he put me into a swamp to cut trees, the heaviest
> work, which men of twenty-five or thirty years of age have to do, I
> being but sixteen. Here I was on a very short allowance of food, and
> having heavy work, was too weak to fulfill my tasks. For this, I got
> many severe floggings: and, after I had got my irons off, I made
> another attempt at running away. He took my irons off, in the full
> anticipation that I could never get across the Catarba River, even
> when at liberty. On this, I procured a small Indian canoe, which was
> tied to a tree, and ultimately got across the river in it. I then
> wandered through the wilderness for several days without any food,
> and but a drop of water to allay my thirst, till I became so starved,
> that I was obliged to go to a house to beg for something to eat, then
> I was captured and again imprisoned.[25]

Mr. Gooch soon arrived, obtained the assistance of another slaveholder in tying him up and giving him a beating with a cowhide, and then "put a log chain, weighing twenty-five pounds, round my neck, and sent me into a field, into which he followed me with a cow-hide, intending to set his slaves to flog me again." Dread of suffering again in this way gave Roper the power to "give him the slip" when Mr. Gooch stopped to speak with some other slaveholders.

A series of escapes and recaptures follows, Mr. Gooch's ingenuity at discovering unusual methods of punishing Roper never seeming to fail him. He tied his wrists together, placed the wrists over his knees, placed a stick under the knees and over the arms—and flogged him. He chained him in a log-pen with a forty-pound chain, making him lie on the damp earth all night, and then in the morning, without giving him any breakfast, tied him to a heavy harrow and made him drag it to the cotton field in place of a horse. He chained him for a week with a forty-pound chain to a female slave who could not keep up with her task work, repeatedly flogging them both while thus chained together and forcing them to keep up with the other slaves, though retarded by the weight of the chain. He poured tar over his face and head and ignited it because he would not divulge the name of the slave who helped him get off his irons.

Again Roper escaped, this time making his way from central Georgia to Milton, North Carolina, the place from which he had been taken at the age of six. He tells of how he made his way back to his mother:

> I wandered about a long time, not knowing which way to go and
> find my mother. After some time, I took the road leading over Ikeo
> Creek. I shortly came up with a little girl, about six years old, and
> asked her where she was going; she said, to her mother's, pointing to
> a house on a hill, half a mile off. She had been at the overseer's
> house, and was returning to her mother. I then felt some emotions
> arising in my breast, which I cannot describe. . . . I told her I was
> very thirsty, and would go with her to get something to drink. On
> our way I asked her several questions, such as her name, that of her
> mother; she said hers was Maria, and that of her mother was Nancy.
> I inquired, if her mother had any more children besides herself? She
> said five besides herself, and that they had been sold, that one had
> been sold when a little boy. I then asked the name of this child? she
> said it was Moses. . . . At last I got to my mother's house! my
> mother was at home. I asked her if she knew me? she said, no. Her
> master was having a house built close by, and as the men were dig-
> ging, he supposed that I was one of the diggers. I told her, I knew
> her very well, and thought that if she looked at me a little, she would
> know me, but this had no effect. I then asked her if she had any
> sons? she said, yes; but none so large as me. I then waited a few
> minutes, and narrated some circumstances to her, attending my
> being sold into slavery, and how she grieved at my loss. Here the
> mother's dire feelings on that occasion . . . rushed to her mind; she
> saw her own son before her, for whom she had so often wept; and,
> in an instant, we were clasped in each other's arms, amidst the
> ardent interchange of caresses and tears of joy. Ten years had elapsed
> since I had seen my dear mother.[26]

That night there was joy in the little house on the hill, in the reunion with his mother and her husband, a blacksmith whom she had married when Roper was a baby. His stepfather, upon arriving home at night from work on the plantation of a Mr. Jefferson, to whom he belonged, kissed him affectionately when he found out who he was. Roper met also his little brothers and sisters, who had heard of him all their lives as the oldest of their family and the first to be sold. He wanted to leave that night to continue his journey up to the free states but succumbed to their pleas to stay with them a short while. He stayed for about a week, hiding in the woods by day and sleeping there at night. About midnight on the following Sunday, however, he was suddenly awakened, and "found my bed surrounded by twelve slaveholders with pistols in hand, who took me away (not allowing me to bid farewell to those I loved so dearly) to the Red House, where they confined me in a room the rest of the night, and in the morning lodged me in the gaol of Caswell Court House."[27]

He never saw his relatives again. Mr. Gooch did not hear of his being in the gaol for thirty days, but then sent his son-in-law, a Mr. Anderson, after him in a horse and chaise, with orders to have a smithy rivet an iron collar around his neck, with a heavy chain attached, before they set off for "home." Even with that precaution, Roper gave Anderson much cause for unhappiness on the trip. Anderson almost shot him before they arrived at Mr. Gooch's outstretched lash. His welcome is graphically described:

> My master gave me a hearty dinner, the best he ever did give me; but it was to keep me from dying before he had given me all the flogging he intended. After dinner he took me to a log-house, stripped me quite naked, fastened a rail up very high, tied my hands to the rail, fastened my feet together, put a rail between my feet, and stood on one end of it to hold me down; the two sons then gave me fifty lashes each, the son-in-law another fifty, and Mr. Gooch himself fifty more.
>
> While doing this his wife came out, and begged him not to kill me, the first act of sympathy I ever noticed in her. When I called for water, they brought a pail-full and threw it over my back ploughed up by the lashes. After this, they took me to the blacksmith's shop, got two large bars of iron, which they bent round my feet, each bar weighing twenty pounds, and put a heavy log-chain on my neck.[28]

Moses Roper lived, somehow, to tell his tale, which included still more escapes and recaptures. The punishments were later administered with the aid of a "screw box," which Mr. Gooch had acquired in his long absence, and several other "torture chambers." We return from the shudders of Roper's pages to Dr. Price's preface to nod inwardly in agreement with his words:

We trust the deeply interesting and clearly written narrative . . . will
meet with rapid and extensive sale. It contains many very interesting
facts and details . . . but the grounds on which we would urge our
readers to purchase it are, that by so doing, they would lend a helping hand to the extinction of that monstrous system which spoils all
that is good in America.[29]

The antislavery journals during September and October of 1838 kept
their readers supplied with the progress of a dreadful case at Warm Springs,
Georgia, from reports in the Southern press. The slave narrative that can be
pieced together from the resulting data offers prime material for a gothic
ballad. It tells of Sally, an aged slave belonging to Judge Mayes of Virginia.
Her reason had gradually become unhinged from seeing her slave children
beaten and sold South. The last of her children left to her was Jane, a girl
of fourteen. Sally had threatened the judge, who later testified that Sally
had told him, once when he finished lecturing her for "such talk," that "no
child of the Judge's should live to horsewhip a child of hers." Public knowledge of the sorrows that soon befell the Judge and his wife in the murder of
six of their seven children came in connection with the fourth and fifth
murders of a child of four and another of eight. The slave girl Jane had been
in the habit of taking the two children to a school in the vicinity. When, one
Friday, they did not return as usual, the recently bereaved parents became
frantic. A search was made, with Jane in the party, and the children's bodies
were found at dusk, in a blackberry patch. Jane had exclaimed, when they
were still about thirty feet away from the bodies, "Here they are with their
throats cut!" So suspicion at once fell upon her, and she was placed in jail.
At length she revealed that on that fatal Friday, her mother, Sally, had told
her to bring the children home by way of the blackberry patch when school
was out. When she arrived there, the old woman seized the youngest child
and cut its throat. Then Andy, a young slave who had become desperate from
many beatings, had rushed from the bushes and cut the throat of the other
child. They then wanted to murder the infant of Judge Mayes, which Jane
held in her arms. Jane fled, however, saving the baby. Reasoning backwards
from that dreadful scene, the distraught parents came finally to the conclusion that the sudden deaths of four of their children in one day some time
before had probably been brought about by the poisoning of their food by
Sally. On the twenty-fourth of September, it was recorded at Warm Springs
that one Lucinda and one Andrew, slaves of judge and Mrs. Mayes, were
hanged.[30]

John Greenleaf Whittier was one of a number of abolitionists who were by
nature disinclined toward repeated stories "of torturing slaves by whipping
and then tearing with the claws of a cat" and the like, as too dreadful for
human credibility. But after he had made the acquaintance and heard the

story of a slave who had escaped from slavery in Virginia and in Alabama, one James Williams, Whittier changed his mind and took down Williams' story from dictation. Misfortune befell the book, which seemed destined for great popularity, judging from the sales during the two months in which it was offered to the public by the American Anti-Slavery Society.[31] The details of the controversy as to whether the narrative was or was not authentic are given elsewhere in this study,[32] so that it must suffice here to report that the abolitionists saw fit to accept the advice to withdraw the book from circulation. There were probably many, however, who had already read the book and privately concurred with the sentiments expressed by the editor of a recently established antislavery paper, *The Herald of Freedom*:[33]

> The *Vermont Chronicle* is quite complacently announcing the discovery, that James Williams' story is not true. . . . We wished it had not been true all the while we were reading it, and guess James wished so, and Big Harry, and all of them. It is true that there was a James Williams who told the story, or at least that there was a John Greenleaf Whittier, who said he told it. . . . He says a colored man, who seemed to be a fugitive, and to have a strong bump for the North Star, told him the facts he writ down in that narrative. Now if he invented them all, he is a dabster at invention, for an 'inferior race,' and in time will be sharp enough for freedom, if he keeps on. But how could he have invented all that story out of whole cloth? We are inclined to reckon there must be something down South, pretty much resembling slavery, that the creature had undergone, and that he hatched up names and maybe places and times, and put them in shape and told them to 'the Poet,' as the *Chronicle* calls Friend Whittier. . . . We shall believe the story substantially false when we find out that Negroes have more genius and invention than everybody else; and that there is no slaveholding in the country.[34]

It was in the pages of *The Herald of Freedom*, in 1839, that the narrative of the slave Robert first appeared, serially, being copied subsequently in other antislavery journals.[35] Concerning the narrative, the editor announces in the same jaunty vein:

> We give an account of the recent fugitive slave who passed through here to Canada. Whether it is all true or all false we can't vouch. We saw him. He was black, looked like a slave and acted like a fugitive, and looked as if he felt pursued and hunted. Some of his story strikes us as unnatural though there can't be much *nature* in slavery or slaveholders.[36]

Robert was born in Maysville, Kentucky, the slave of a Mr. Dudley, a kind man who did not whip his slaves. But Robert's luck changed when his master gave him as a wedding present to his daughter on her marriage to a young lawyer whose first show of authority over his newly acquired property took the form of an attempt to horsewhip Robert for not being able to catch a horse as ordered. Robert snatched the whip from the new master's hand, threw it into the fire, and escaped to the woods, where he hid for a week. His master recaptured him and sold him to a trader bound for New Orleans who put him on a slave chain with sixty other men and forty women. Robert was not allowed to bid good-bye to his wife and children, who lived about four miles away, but it happened that the slave chain passed by their house, and he saw his wife at the window. He was not allowed to speak to her, however, or to see his children. Frantic with grief, he went on with the forlorn coffle, and never again saw any of his dear ones.

He found life in New Orleans very different from life in Kentucky. The slaves were forced to go to church, but the only kind of sermons they heard were about how the better they served their masters, the brighter they would shine in heaven. He had never heard of abolitionists while in Kentucky, but in New Orleans he was told that abolitionists were dreadful creatures from the North who came South to steal slaves to make fur collars out of their scalps to wear on their coats. The slaves believed that, as they saw that the Southerners did not have black fur collars like the Northerners who came to New Orleans; therefore, "when they saw a man with such a collar, they thought it must be an abolitionist, and would run for their lives."

His mistress in New Orleans looked after the punishment of the house servants, which she generally managed with the aid of a "steel instrument with a swell at both ends, with which she keeps knocking their heads till they are full of bumps." He added: "And we must stand it, you know—I had rather be whipped." The woman seemed to have a disposition resembling the slaveholders told about by Crevecoeur and Timothy Dwight and the Grimke sisters. She had made a hole with hot tongs in one of Robert's cheeks because, when she had ordered him to carry her thirteen-year-old daughter across a muddy street, he had replied that he thought a girl that old "might go without being carried." Another scar across the back of his neck had come from her during one of her dinner parties, when he had accidentally touched her elbow, causing a little tea to be spilled on her dress. Thereupon she had caught up the big carving knife and cut his neck "so that the blood run a stream." His master gave her a scolding, but that did him no good, Robert said. Although he had come to overlook the other things his mistress did to him, he said he could never forget that event and repeated: "No, I couldn't forget that."

Robert's escape was made possible when he accompanied his master and mistress on a trip to New York. In order to make a fine impression for his owners, he was dressed in ruffled linen shirts and an eight-dollar hat and treated by his master with great kindness in public. His master left him in charge of a barkeeper at Utica while he went to a "great bank meeting" in Albany. Through the efforts of Alvan Stewart and Gerrit Smith, Robert became convinced that the only master he had was in Heaven, so he stripped off his fine clothes, gave them to a poor colored man to whose house the abolitionists had taken him, put on some poorer ones, and left for Boston with fifteen dollars from Gerrit Smith and a letter to Garrison. Robert got a job as coachman for the mayor of Salem, to begin on a Monday. The very day he was to start work, he ran into his master. An exciting race ensued in and out of Salem, Brookline, and Boston. Some abolitionists whisked him away to Dunbarton, where he told his story at an antislavery meeting. He was given money to defray his traveling expenses to Canada.

The next morning he was conveyed to Concord, where he was prevailed upon to relate his experiences in the office of the *Herald of Freedom*. Asked by the reporter, when he had finished his story, whether the slaves would come north if they were freed, Robert answered emphatically in the negative: "O no, I would rather work there for six dollars a month than for twelve dollars here; I would go right back if I could be free—don't like this climate." Asked further whether the slaves if liberated would injure their masters— "cut their throats?," he replied, "No, I would rather kneel down and pray for my master than to injure him." But, when asked how he felt when his master was knocked down by a colored man in Salem, to allow Robert time to escape, Robert paused a moment before his answer came: "Well, I will tell the truth—I was glad he was knocked down, for that give me a chance to cut; but I did not want him hurt."[37]

The narrative of James Curry, widely printed in antislavery periodicals in 1840, first saw publication as the entire front page, in small print, on *The Liberator's* vast sheet, January 10, 1840. It is an absorbing account of slave life on the plantation of a man who was both a planter and a slave trader in Person County, North Carolina. According to the editor's note in *The Liberator*:

> It is a real case, and no fiction, as written down from the lips of the self-emancipated bondman by a talented female who will accept our thanks for the favor she has done in communicating it for publication in *The Liberator*.[38]

Although the narrative is of great interest throughout, since it presents vividly practically every conceivable phase of the slave experience,[39] its most important contribution to the literature of the slave narrative is, perhaps, James Curry's portrait of his mother. She was given to the mother of Curry's master as a wedding present, together with her brother, when they were both very little children. As both the new master and mistress were drunkards, and as they possessed very little property besides those two little slaves, the children had a very hard life. His mother was treated so outrageously when she came into her teens that, said Curry, "it is not proper to be written; but the treatment of females in slavery is very dreadful." When she was about fifteen she tried to run away, staying in the home of a poor white woman for three weeks while she tried to get word to her mother, "giving her intelligence of herself," but a white man saw her who knew her and returned her to her master. Soon afterward she married a slave in the neighborhood. Many slave narratives attest to the slave's ways of maintaining standards of decency, such as the following:

> Her mistress did not provide her with clothes, and her husband
> obtained for her a wheel, which she kept in her hut, for the purpose
> of spinning in the night, after her day's work for her cruel mistress
> was done. This her mistress endeavored to prevent, by keeping her
> spinning in the house until twelve or one o'clock at night. But she
> would then go home, and, fixing her wheel in a place made in the
> floor to prevent its making a noise, she would spin for herself, in
> order that she might be decently clad in the daytime.

Her mistress treated her so badly that she, with her sister, who was the slave of her mistress's sister, concocted a plan for running away, persuading their husbands to join them. But "not knowing any better, they went directly South"! After they had traveled three nights, they thought that they were in the North and should be able to travel safely by the day. They walked on in broad daylight instead of seeking a hiding place in the woods. They were promptly stopped and examined for passes. They had got some person to write them out "free papers" before leaving home, and showed the papers to the man who stopped them on the road and later to the magistrate to whom he took them. The magistrate examined the papers, declaring that they would not do for the men but that the girls could go. Thereupon their husbands were marched off to jail and the girls decided to go to jail with them rather than risk parting with them forever. Their presence in the jail was advertised in the usual way in the Southern papers, and soon their masters came after them. "This ended my mother's running away," Curry concluded. "Having young children soon, it tied her to slavery." Two or three years afterward, she was separated from her husband "by the removal of his master to the South," concerning which tragedy Curry observed: "The separation of the slaves in this way is little thought of. A few masters regard their union as sacred, but where one does, a hundred care nothing about it."

Sometime after this, Curry's mother was married to a free colored man named Peter Burnet, who became Curry's father. About two years after their marriage, he traveled South with a white man, as his servant, and was sold by him into slavery. Curry's mother never heard from him again. After a few years she married a slave belonging to her master and bore him six children. At this point in his recital Curry paused for a special encomium for his mother:

She gave to each of her children two names, but we were only called
by one. It is not common for slaves to have more than one name,
but my mother was a proud-spirited woman, and she gave her children two. She was a very good and tender mother. She never made a
public profession of her religion, but she always tried to do right,
and taught her children to know right from wrong. When I was a
little child she taught me to know my Maker, and that we should all
die, and if we were good, we should be happy.

When his master's oldest son, who was six months older than he, began to
attend day school, Curry wanted to learn to read, and his mother procured
a "blue-back speller" for him. Curry prevailed upon the boy to teach him
what he was learning and got along very well until his master forbade his sons
to teach him any more.

His mistress died very shortly after beating a young girl to death, which
the slaves interpreted as "being called by her Maker to her account," and life
on the plantation became less bearable after she was gone. His master provided them with no clothes, but by working nights upon little patches of
ground which he allowed them for raising tobacco and food for the hogs
which they were allowed to keep, they "thus obtained clothes" for themselves. The patches of ground were "little spots, they were allowed to clear
in the woods, or cultivate upon the barrens, and after they got them nicely
cleared, and under good cultivation, the master took them away, and the
next year they must take other uncultivated spots for themselves." Curry's
stepfather felled trees in the woods and built his family a commodious log
house. Curry shows how mother and father tried to make life bearable for
their children:

With my mother's assistance, it was furnished with two comfortable
beds, chairs, and some other articles of furniture. His children were
always comfortably and decently clothed. I knew him, at one time,
to purchase for my mother a cloak, and a gown, a frock for each of
my two sisters, two coats for two brothers younger than myself, and
each of them a hat, all new and good, and all with money earned in
the time allowed him for sleep. My mother was cook in the house
for about twenty-two years. She cooked for from twenty-five to
thirty-five, taking the family and the slaves together. The slaves ate
in the kitchen. After my mistress' death, my mother was the only
woman kept in the house. She took care of my master's children,
some of whom were then quite small, and brought them up.

One of the most trying experiences Curry was ever to pass through
occurred one day when one of the master's children struck his mother in the
face "for some trifle about the dinner." "I would have laid down my life to

protect her if I had dared," Curry said. His mother pushed the girl away, and she fell to the floor. When her father came home, which was while the slaves were eating in the kitchen, the girl told him about it. Curry continues:

> He came down, and called my mother out, and with a hickory rod, he beat her fifteen or twenty strokes, and then called his daughter and told her to take her satisfaction of her, and she did beat her until she was satisfied. Oh! it was dreadful, to see the girl whom my poor mother had taken care of from her childhood, thus beating her, and I must stand there, and did not care to crook my finger in her defense.

"My mother's labor was very hard," her son laments. He gives proof that he does not exaggerate:

> She would go to the house in the morning, take her pail upon her head, and go away to the cow-pen, and milk fourteen cows. She then put on the bread for the family breakfast, and got the cream ready for churning, and set a little child to churn it, she having the care of from ten to fifteen children, whose mothers worked in the field. After clearing away the family breakfast, she got breakfast for the slaves, which consisted of warm corn bread and buttermilk, and was taken at twelve o'clock. In the meantime, she had beds to make, rooms to sweep, etc. Then she cooked the family dinner, which was simply plain meat, vegetables and bread. Then the slaves' dinner was to be ready at from eight to nine o'clock in the evening. It consisted of corn bread, or potatoes, and the meat which remained of the master's dinner, or one herring apiece. At night she had the cows to milk again. There was little ceremony about the master's supper, unless there was company. This was her work day by day. Then in the course of the week, she had the washing and ironing to do for her master's family (who, however, were clothed very simply), and for her husband, seven children, and herself.
>
> She would not get through to go to her log cabin until nine or ten o'clock at night. She would then be so tired, that she could scarcely stand; but she would find one boy with his knee out, and another with his elbow out, a patch wanting here, and a stitch there, and she would sit down by her lightwood fire, and sew and sleep alternately, often till the light began to streak in the east; and then lying down, she would snatch a nap, and hasten to the toil of the day.

Nor was this yet her whole duty. Among the dozen or more children committed to her care while their mothers were at work in the field were three little orphans, whose mothers had left them to her when they died. One of them was a baby. When reproached for doing so much for those children not her own in the midst of all the labors she could not escape performing, she responded, Curry says, with the argument:

> She took them and treated them as her own. The master took no care about them. She always took a share of the cloth she had provided for her own children, to cover these little friendless ones. She would sometimes ask the master to procure them some clothes, but he would curse them and refuse to do it. We would sometimes tell her, that we would let the master clothe them, for she had enough to do for her own children. She replied, "Their master will not clothe them, and I cannot see them go naked; *I* have children, and I do not know where their lot may be cast. I may die and leave them, and I desire to do by these little orphans, as I should wish mine to be done by."

We learn that Curry's mother's first name was Lucy. He tells of a visit to the plantation of his master's uncle, who took hold of Curry when told that he was "one of Lucy's boys" and remarked, "Well, his father was a free man, and perhaps when he gets to be a man, he'll be wanting to be free too." Curry's comments upon the remark:

> Thinks I to myself, indeed I shall. But if he had asked me if I wanted to be free, I should have answered him, 'No, sir.' Of course no slave would dare to say, in the presence of a white man, that he wished for freedom. But among themselves, it is their constant theme. No slaves think they were made to be slaves. Let them keep them ever so ignorant, it is impossible to beat it into them that they were made to be slaves. I have heard some of the most ignorant I ever saw, say, 'It will not always be so, God *will* bring them to an account.'

The last we see of Curry's mother is at the whipping post, where she is being whipped along with her son for allowing him to take out a small piece of his own pig which he had fattened. His master had given Curry the runt pig because he had thought it was worthless, but ordered Curry to kill it and give it to him when it proved to be "ready to bursting for the table." The whipping determined Curry's future: he would run away from the terrible degradation of slavery. Many of the cruelties manifested in his story do not bear directly on experiences connected with his mother and have not been touched upon. Though we are not told so, we know that his mother rejoiced at his going, agonized with him in his recapture and torture, prayed for the recovery that sent him on the fugitive's path again, and had faith that he would at last find freedom.

A narrative of a slave with a rascal's nature that calls the eighteenth-century Arthur to mind is that of the slave Madison, whose owner was a notorious rascal and slave trader by the name of Blakeley. The narrative appeared first in the *St. Louis Gazette* in June 1841.[40] The slave and his master are "birds of one feather" in this odyssey of two rogues. Blakeley made that interesting discovery soon after he purchased Madison at some slave auction. Madison soon had the full confidence of Blakeley and became adept at telling false tales to slaves whom Blakeley wanted to lure from plantations in Maryland into the far South, for sale at New Orleans and elsewhere, without benefit of a purchase price. Madison would go in among the slaves to tell them of the kind "Northerner" who had come down to help the slaves and who was ready to take them with him up to Canada, out of the reach of their masters. He would tell some of the women and girls a different story, luring some with "the prospect of marrying rich white men, and of living in style and splendor." In this way, the two collected about one hundred slaves and went with them by land to New Orleans.

They were as adept at spending their ill-got wealth as at getting it and soon returned to Washington with rather empty pockets and another scheme afoot: a plan by which Madison's master was to sell him as often as he could, after which Madison was to run away and return to him. Thus, Madision was sold for thirteen hundred dollars to a Mr. Clay in Washington and rejoined his master in Baltimore. Then, for one thousand dollars, he was sold in Virginia, returning soon after. Together they robbed vaults and people. At length they returned to New Orleans. Blakeley sold Madison to a Mr. Blanchard for nine hundred dollars, Madison ran away from Blanchard and back to Blakeley, and Blakeley presented him with the nine hundred dollars as a sort of splitting-up present! Left to his own devices, Madison entered upon a series of forgeries, robbed stores, and engaged in similar practices as the thought came to him. He was finally caught trying to cash a check which he had changed from $200 to $2700. As charges piled up against him, his career abruptly came to a close upon the scaffold.

The first slave narrative to be published in book form after the controversy over the *Narrative of James Williams* was the *Narrative of Lunceford Lane*, published by himself in Boston in 1842. In its third edition of 1845, a note by the printers Hews and Watson states: "The rapidity with which the first and second editions of this work has [*sic*] been sold, renders it necessary to put another edition to press, without any enlargement or material alteration."[41] In his opening words "To the Reader," Lane gives as his reason for reporting the story of his life, "the solicitation of very many friends," coupled with the desire that he might "realize something from the sale of my work towards the support of a numerous family." He believes that the narrative will prove to be "most interesting and instructive to readers generally," and also that the facts presented "will . . . cast some light upon the policy of a slave-holding community, and the effort on the minds of the more enlightened, the more humane, and the Christian portion of the Southern people, of holding and trading in the bodies and souls of men."

Lunceford Lane considered his slave experience a "comparatively happy, indeed a highly favored one." He writes:

> To this circumstance is it owing that I have been able to come up from bondage and relate the story to the public; and that my wife, my mother, and my seven children, are here with me this day. If for anything this side the invisible world I bless Heaven, it is that I was not born a plantation slave, nor even a house servant under what is termed a hard and cruel master.[42]

Born a slave on a plantation of about two hundred and fifty slaves near Raleigh, North Carolina, Lane had a fairly pleasant childhood. His mother was a house servant, and he had playmates among the master's children. But by the time he reached his tenth or eleventh year, when his master's children began to go to school and he was put to work, he became conscious of the difference between his lot in life and the lot of his former playfellows, "who began to order me about, and were told to do so by my master and mistress." His master set him, at this age, to cutting wood in the winter and working in the garden in the summer. At the age of fifteen he was put in charge of the pleasure horses and became his master's carriage driver. He describes his day's routine:

> Early in the morning, I used to take his three horses to the plantation and turn them into the pasture to graze, and myself into the cotton or cornfield, with a hoe in my hand, to work through the day; and after sunset I would take these horses back to the city, a distance of three miles, feed them, and then tend to any other business my master or any of his family had for me to do, until bed time, when, with my blanket in my hand. I would go into the dining-room to rest through the night. The next day the same round of labor would be repeated, unless some of the family wished to ride out, in which case I must be on hand with the horses to wait upon them, and in the meantime to work about the yard. On Sunday I had to drive to church twice, which, with other things necessary to be done, took the whole day. So my life went wearily on from day to day, from night to night, and from week to week.[43]

From the time that he realized that others were destined to go to school and to command him while he was apparently doomed to labor and to take orders, Lane brooded over the fact:

I was not permitted to have a book in my hand. To be in possession of anything written or printed, was regarded as an offense. And then there was the fear that I might be sold away from those who were dear to me, and conveyed to the far South. I had learned, that, being a slave, I was subject to this worst (to us) of all calamities; and I knew of others in similar situations to myself, thus sold away. My friends were not numerous; but in proportion as they were few they were dear; and the thought that I might be separated from them forever, was like that of having the heart torn from the socket; while the idea of being conveyed to the far South seemed infinitely worse than the terrors of death. To know, also, that I was never to consult my own will, but was, while I lived, to be entirely under the control of another, was another state of mind hard for me to bear. Indeed, all things now made me feel, what I had before known only in words, that I was a slave. Deep was this feeling, and it preyed upon my heart like a never-dying worm. I saw no prospect that my condition would ever be changed. Yet I used to plan in my mind from day to day, and from night to night, how I might be free.[44]

One day, while he was brooding over the problem as usual, Lane's father gave him a small basket of peaches, which he sold for thirty cents, "the first money I ever had in my life," he records. As time went on, he was able to add to this little sum sixty cents from sale of some marbles he had won, a dollar tip from a visitor from Fayetteville, a dollar-and-a-half tip from two visitors from Orange County. An idea gripped his mind:

These sums, and the hope that then entered my mind of purchasing at some future time my freedom, made me long for money; and plans for money-making took the principal possession of my thoughts. At night I would steal away with my axe, get a load of wood to cut for twenty-five cents, and the next morning hardly escape a whipping for the offense. But I persevered until I had obtained twenty dollars. Now I began to think seriously of becoming able to buy myself; and cheered by this hope, I went on from one thing to another, laboring "at dead of night" after the long weary day's toil for my master was over, till I found I had collected one hundred dollars. This sum I kept hid, first in one place and then in another, as I dare not put it out, for fear I should lose it.[45]

With his father's help, Lane invented a new method for mixing pipe tobacco, resulting in "the double advantage of giving the tobacco a peculiarly pleasant flavor, and of enabling me to manufacture a good article out of a very indifferent material." He put up this product in quarter-pound packages, to sell at fifteen cents. Also, he learned how to construct a pipe out of a reed that grew plentifully in that region making a passage through the reed with a wire and attaching a clay bowl to the end, "so that the smoke should be cooled in flowing through the stem, like whiskey or rum in passing from the boiler through the worm of the still." These pipes he priced at ten cents. As the Legislature sat in Raleigh every year, he had a considerable sale for these articles among the members. He sold his tobacco and pipes in "the early part of the night" and manufactured them "in the latter part." Soon he became known, "not only in the city, but in many parts of the State, as a tobacconist."

Perceiving that he was "getting along well," slave though he was, Lunceford Lane began "to think about taking a wife." His first choice was a Miss Lucy Williams, the slave of one "Thomas Devereaux, Esq., an eminent lawyer in the place." Failure in that undertaking caused him to believe that he "never would marry," but at the end of two or three years his resolution "began to slide away, till finding I could not keep it longer, I set out once more in pursuit of a wife." He reports success this time:

> So I fell in with her to whom I am now united, Miss Martha Curtis, and the bargain between us was completed. I next went to her master, Mr. Boylan, and asked him, according to custom, if I might "marry his woman." His reply was, "Yes, if you will behave yourself." I told him I would. "And make her behave herself?" To this I also assented: and then proceeded to ask the approbation of my master, which was granted. So in May, 1828, I was bound as fast in wedlock as a slave can be. God may at any time sunder that bond in a freeman; either master may do the same at pleasure in a slave. The bond is not recognized in law. But in my case it has never been broken.[46]

At first it seemed that their married life was going to be idyllic, as far as such was possible for slaves. Their masters were both naturally kind individuals and provided for them decently. Within two years' time a son and daughter were born to them. Soon after, however, Lane's wife was sold to a Mr. Smith, an exceedingly stingy man. Although they had cause to be thankful that they were not to be separated, as Mr. Smith also lived in the neighborhood, the necessity for providing for his wife and children the essentials of living, which Mr. Smith was supposed to furnish "his property" but refused to, reduced Lane's money hoard. Thus he found himself, before he realized it almost, with only five dollars of the considerable sum he had put aside from his earnings by night labor; and this last five dollars he "lost one day in going to the plantation"! Lane tells of that dark hour:

> My light of hope now went out. My prop seemed to have given way from under me. Sunk in the very night of despair respecting my

> freedom, I discovered myself, as though I had never known it before,
> a husband, the father of two children, a family looking up to me for
> bread, and I a slave, penniless, and well watched by my master, his
> wife, and his children, lest I should, perchance, catch the friendly
> light of the stars to make something in order to supply the cravings
> of nature in those with whom my soul was bound up; or lest some
> plan of freedom might lead me to trim the light of diligence after
> the day's labor was over, while the rest of the world were enjoying
> the hours in pleasure or sleep.[47]

Just as life seemed too full of burdens for hope, however, an event occurred which, "while it cast a cloud over the prospects of some of my fellow slaves," as Lane observed, "was a rainbow over mine": the death of his master. His widow, in order to meet payments on a "debt of twenty thousand dollars presented by the bank," was obliged to sell some of her slaves, and hire out others, Lane falling in this latter group. This opportunity of hiring out one's time, for which Lane paid his mistress a price "varying from one hundred dollars to one hundred and twenty dollars per year," was contrary to the laws of North Carolina at that time but, Lane remarks, "in Raleigh it is sometimes winked at." "This was a privilege which comparatively few slaves at the South enjoy," he adds, "and in this I felt truly blessed."[48]

Thenceforth "on his own", providing nothing happened to change his mistress' mind about allowing him to continue that arrangement, Lane became a manufacturer and merchant of pipes and tobacco on a large scale, with a store in Raleigh and agencies in various parts of the state—Fayetteville, Chapel Hill, Salisbury, and elsewhere. In six or eight years, besides supporting his family and paying his mistress, he had saved one thousand dollars. We are reminded of Venture Smith, in his story of how he managed such a feat:

> During this time I had found it politic to go shabbily dressed, and
> to appear to be very poor, but to pay my mistress for my services
> promptly. I kept my money hid, never venturing to put out a penny,
> nor to let anybody but my wife know that I was making any. The
> thousand dollars was what I supposed my mistress would ask for me,
> and so I determined now what I would do.[49]

Also like Venture Smith, and many other foresighted slaves, Lunceford Lane was careful not to be rash in handing over his money to his owner for his own purchase:

> I went to my mistress and inquired what was her price for me. She
> said a thousand dollars. I then told her that I wanted to be free, and
> asked her if she would sell me to be made free. She said she would;
> and accordingly I arranged with her, and with the master of my wife,

Mr. Smith, already spoken of, for the latter to take my money and buy of her my freedom, as I could not legally purchase it, and as the laws forbid emancipation, except for "meritorious services." This done, Mr. Smith endeavored to emancipate me formally, and to get my manumission recorded. I tried also; but the court judged that I had done nothing "meritorious"; and so I remained, nominally only, the slave of Mr. Smith for one year; when, feeling unsafe in that relation, I accompanied him to New York, whither he was going to purchase goods, and was there regularly and formally made a freeman, and there my manumission was recorded.[50]

This was in 1838. By 1842, Lane had also purchased his wife and his seven children. Conditions for a free Negro in the South were becoming increasingly hazardous, so he left with them for Boston to start the business of making a livelihood anew.

Moses Grandy was as ambitious to work unsparingly and purchase his way out of slavery as Lunceford Lane but was less fortunate as to the character of his masters. Obliged to pay for his freedom three times over before he was formally recognized as "free," he finally made his way to England in the hope of better opportunities for completing the task of purchasing his family. His wife and two children had been bought, but three children still remained in captivity. The distinguished abolitionist George Thompson became personally interested in Grandy and arranged for his appearance at antislavery meetings, where generous offerings to help ransom the rest of his family were always taken up for him. Thompson also served as editor and sponsor for Grandy's story of his life.

The Narrative of the Life of Moses Grandy, Late a Slave in the United States of America, as Related to George Thompson. Sold for the Benefit of His Relations Still in Slavery was published in London in 1843 and in Boston in 1844. In his introduction to the little book, Thompson says:

Considering his narrative calculated to promote a more extensive knowledge of the workings of American slavery, and that its sale might contribute to the object which engages so entirely the mind of Moses, namely, the redemption of those who are in bonds, belonging to his family, I resolved to commit it to the press, as nearly as possible in the language of Moses himself. I have carefully abstained from casting a single reflection or animadversion of my own. I have the touching story of the self-liberated captive to speak for itself, and the wish of my heart will be gratified, and my humble effort on his behalf be richly rewarded, if this little book is the means of obtaining for my colored brother the assistance which he seeks, or of increasing the zeal of those who are associated for the purpose of 'breaking every yoke and setting the oppressed free.'[51]

Moses Grandy was born about 1796 in Camden, North Carolina. His earliest memory was of being frightened at seeing his mother beaten until she lost consciousness, for "carrying on" because he had been sold away from her. His childhood years were uneventful rounds of hunger, nakedness, and long seasons of suffering from the cold. Whippings were normal, as the poor slaves were too hungry to have the strength to accomplish the task work set for them by the overseers. At length, when he was about fifteen, Grandy made up his mind to tell his master, at the earliest opportunity, that they could not do their work because they were not fed. He tells us the result:

> One day he came into the field, and asked why no more work was done. . . . I said . . . we were so hungry, we could not work. He went home and told his mistress to give us plenty to eat, and at dinner time we had plenty. . . . We came out shouting for joy, and went to work with delight. From that time, we had food enough, and he soon found that he had a great deal of work done. The field was quite active with people striving who should do most.[52]

Grandy had been given to one of his master's sons when the latter was a child. When the younger master came of age, he took all the slaves his father had given him to start his own establishment, hiring his slaves out at various jobs and making them pay most of what they earned so that they had very little left upon which to maintain themselves. Having grown up with Grandy's superior industry and perseverance, the young master made Grandy pay him almost twice as much for his time as Grandy had previously paid in the short period he had been released from field labor for freighting. Grandy had to pay him one half of all that he received for freight. Out of the other half he had to "victual and man the boats" besides maintaining himself. But even under such terms, he was getting along fairly.

It was not long after this that Grandy experienced the deepest sorrow of his life. The story of that sorrow common to hundreds of loving slave couples is epitomized in Grandy's terse sentences:

> It was some time after this that I married a slave belonging to Mr. Enoch Sawyer, who had been so hard a master to me. I left her at home (that is, at his house) on Thursday morning, when we had been married about eight months . . . she was well, and seemed likely to be so: we were nicely getting together our little necessaries. On the Friday, as I was at work as usual with the boats, I heard a noise behind me, on the road which ran by the side of the canal. I turned to look, and saw a gang of slaves coming. When they came up to me, one of them cried out, "Moses, my dear!" I wonder who among them should know me, and found it was my wife. She cried out to me, "I am gone!" I was struck with consternation. Mr. Rogersons was

with them, on his horse, armed with pistols. I said to him, "For
God's sake, have you bought my wife?" He said he had. When I
asked him what she had done, he said she had done nothing, but that
her master wanted money. He drew out a pistol, and said that if I
went near the wagon on which she was, he would shoot me. I asked
for leave to shake hands with her, which he refused, but said I might
stand at a distance and talk with her. My heart was so full, that I
could say very little. I asked leave to give her a dram: he told Mr.
Burgess, the man who was with him, to get down and carry it to
her. I gave her the little money I had in my pocket, and bid her
farewell. I have never seen or heard of her from that day to this. I
loved her as I loved my life.[53]

Although years were to elapse, and much unfairness and trickery were to
be borne before Grandy could realize his determination to make his way out
of slavery, he never forgot that vow that he made as he followed with aching
eyes the wagon that was bearing away forever the person who meant all the
world to him. His experience as a slave carried him from North Carolina to
Louisiana, where he again married a slave. Five children were borne to them.
It is amazing to follow his path, full of disappointments and mistreatments,
and to watch him bound up again after each setback to forge ahead on the
road to freedom. In the course of it all, he paid $1850 for himself, $300 for
his second wife, $450 for one son, $400 for a grandchild, and $60 to ransom
a kidnapped child. The story of his life went through two English and two
American editions in two years. It is the story of an indefatigable pursuer of
freedom for himself and his loved ones.

The month of May, 1845, saw publication in Boston of the narratives of
the two most popular fugitive slave lecturers of the day, Frederick Douglass
and Lewis Clarke. Attuned to the interests of the abolitionist audience from
their years of lecturing for the American Anti-Slavery Society, the narrators
resemble each other in the new flavor of their stories. Subsequent revisions
of Douglass's narrative diluted this flavor.[54] On the other hand, the second
edition of Clarke's story, published the next year, uses it in even stronger
doses. Although there is no appreciable heightening of the power of their
data to reveal the evils of slavery, in comparison with some of the earlier slave
narratives both Douglass and Clarke seem intent, in 1845, upon injecting their
material with vitriol. They started a fad that persisted, in some measure,
through the rest of the 1840s and the 1850s. The slave narratives of this
period are generally distinguishable, consequently, from those of other years
by virtue of this vogue for rhetorical vindictiveness. As though anything besides an inkling of the facts could be needed to declare the nature of slavery!

The abolitionist Joseph C. Lovejoy was the scribe for the *Narrative of the
Sufferings of Lewis Clarke, during a Captivity of More than Twenty-Five*

Years among the Algerines of Kentucky. Dictated by Himself.[55] Clarke was a mulatto slave whose mother was a handsome quadroon, given in marriage by her master—who was also her father—to a free white man, a Scotsman "with the express understanding that she and her children were to be free." Notwithstanding this agreement, when her husband died, Clarke's mother was brought back with her nine children as slaves in her father's house. Life in the household of Mr. Campbell was just "slavery as usual," until the days came when the members of Lewis Clarke's family were separated, one by one, by "gift," sale, or exchange. One of his sisters, the fifth of his mother's children, died in childhood. One became the slave of a Dr. Richardson, a very kindly man with whom she had an easy time. One sister, Christiana, remained in the Campbell household as a domestic, experiencing tragedy when her master sent away the free colored man whom she had married and who was the father of her three children, because Mr. Campbell "did not like the connection." His oldest brother became the slave of a Mr. Archy, who allowed him time to earn money to purchase his freedom for six hundred dollars. That brother died not long afterwards, leaving a wife and four or five children in bondage. Another brother, Dennis, also purchased his freedom, assisted by a Mr. Stevenson and his sister. He remained in Kentucky as a business man. A sister, Manda, died when about fifteen or sixteen years old, having suffered a good deal from the mistreatment of her mistress, a Mrs. Logan. Deliah, the family beauty, "was considered a great prize for the guilty passions of the slaveholders." She died in New Orleans after "a most bitter and tragical history." Milton, Cyrus, and Lewis finally escaped from various brands of misery to the North. Both Milton and Lewis became anti-slavery lecturers.

Lewis Clarke's portrait of his mistress, the incomparable shrew, Mrs. Banton, is the high point of his narrative from a literary standpoint. She was the daughter of Mr. Campbell and apparently had been the dread of the family from an early age. Clarke's acquaintance with her dated from the day when she arrived at the plantation to demand from her father another slave in exchange for the one she had been given, whom she had reduced by abuse "to a state of idiocy" and whom she was now returning on the grounds that the child was good for nothing. The boy Lewis struck her fancy. We learn of the transaction that followed:

> Mr. Campbell . . . offered her Moses . . . but objections and claims
> of every kind were swept away by the wild passion and shrilltoned
> voice of Mrs. B. Me she would have, and none else. Mr. Campbell
> went out to hunt, and drive away bad thoughts; the old lady
> became quiet, for she was sure none of her blood run in my veins,
> and, if there was any of her husband's there, it was no fault of hers.
> Slave-holding women are always revengeful toward the children of

slaves that have any of the blood of their husbands in them. I was too young—only seven years of age—to understand what was going on. But my poor and affectionate mother understood and appreciated it all. When she left the kitchen of the mansion-house, where she was employed as cook, and came home to her own little cottage, the tear of anguish was in her eye, and the image of sorrow upon every feature of her face. She knew the female Nero whose rod was now to be over me. That night sleep departed from her eyes. With the youngest child clasped firmly to her bosom, she spent the night in walking the floor, coming ever and anon to lift up the clothes and look at me and my poor brother, who lay sleeping together. *Sleeping*, I said. Brother slept, but not I. I saw my mother when she first came to me, and I could not sleep. The vision of that night—its deep, ineffaceable impression—is now before my mind with all the distinctness of yesterday. In the morning I was put into the carriage with Mrs. B. and her children, and my weary pilgrimage of suffering was fairly begun.[56]

In ferociousness Lewis Clarke's "Mrs. B." even eclipsed the "wife of Master George" of the suppressed *Narrative of James Williams*. Both women, along with the slave Robert's mistress in New Orleans and a number of other such women described in the slave narratives represent the scarcely human monstrosities that evolved from sharp-tempered women unfortunately invested with absolute power. Mrs. B.'s method of "training" the little slave Lewis can be illustrated by the following:

A very trivial offense was sufficient to call forth a great burst of indignation from this woman of ungoverned passions. In my simplicity, I put my lips to the same vessel, and drank out of it, from which her children were accustomed to drink. She expressed her utter abhorrence of such an act by throwing my head violently back, and dashing into my face two dippers of water. The shower of water was followed by a heavier shower of *kicks*; but the words, bitter and cutting, that followed, were like a storm of hail upon my young heart. "She would teach me better manners than that; she would let me know I was to be brought up to her hand; she would have one slave that knew his place; if I wanted water, go to the spring, and not drink there in the house." This was new times for me; for some days I was completely benumbed with sorrow.[57]

Mrs. B. kept him busy until late at night with rocking the baby or spinning flax. If he did not waken at her first call in the morning, such severe beatings would follow that the dread of them caused the little fellow nightmares:

> Such horror has seized me, lest I might not hear the first shrill call,
> that I have often in dreams fancied I heard that unwelcome voice,
> and have leaped from my couch and walked through the house and
> out of it before I awoke. I have gone and called the other slaves, in
> my sleep, and asked them if they did not hear mistress call. Never,
> while I live, will the remembrance of those long, bitter nights of fear
> pass from my mind.[58]

Although his mistress lived only thirty miles from her father's home, where Clarke's mother was, she allowed him to see his mother only three times "in ten long, lonely years of childhood." Sometimes his mother found a chance to send him a little token, concerning which Clarke recalls:

> My mother occasionally found an opportunity to send me some
> token of remembrance and affection—a sugar-plum or an apple; but
> I scarcely ever ate them; they were laid up, and handled and wept
> over, till they wasted away in my hand. My thoughts continually by
> day, and my dreams by night, were of mother and home; and the
> horror experienced in the morning, when I awoke and behold it was
> a dream, is beyond the power of language to describe.[59]

Before long, as the boy grew into the adolescent, he pondered over his wrongs and the conflicting stories he was hearing as to a slave's chances for escape to a land of freedom. He made up his mind to take the risk and strike out for the North when he learned one day that he was slated to be sold in New Orleans. His flight was successful. He reached Cincinnati without any interference, though he found his way slowly, being afraid to ask questions of anyone. According to Mrs. Stowe, "soon after his escape from slavery, he was received into the family of a sister-in-law of the author, and there educated. His conduct during this time was such as to win for him uncommon affection and respect, and the author has frequently heard him spoken of in the highest terms by all who knew him."[60]

The narrative of Lewis Clarke's brother Milton was added to the second edition of his book, together with an appendix containing various addenda of interest to antislavery audiences. The new edition appeared in 1846 under the title *Narrative of the Sufferings of Lewis and Milton Clarke, Sons of a Soldier of the Revolution; during a Captivity of More than Twenty Years among the Slaveholders of Kentucky, One of the So-Called Christian States of North America.* Milton was also a popular antislavery lecturer, and their joint autobiography added greatly to their popularity, becoming one of the "best sellers" in this period of the blossoming of the slave narrative.

The fugitive slave Leonard Black, who had escaped from slavery years before, married and became the father of four children in Boston. He is representative of a number of slaves who "came out of hiding" as opportunities arose to capitalize on their condition. His *Life and Sufferings of Leonard Black, A Fugitive from Slavery, Written by Himself* was published in New Bedford in 1847. The extent to which the phrase "Written by Himself" was to be taken seriously is explained in a "Notice" to the reader by one A. M. Macy of Nantucket:

> This book was written substantially by Mr. Black himself, but, in consequence of his deficiency of education—growing out of the fact that his childhood and youth were spent in slavery—it needed considerable correction to fit it for the press. The work was kindly performed, gratuitously, by a friend of the author, who was, however, very careful to preserve the narrative as nearly unchanged as possible—confining himself mostly to punctuation, correcting the orthography, striking out unnecessary words and sentences, etc., etc.[61]

In his introduction to his narrative, Black describes as his purpose the apparently recent determination to obtain funds to meet the expenses of fitting himself for the ministry, to which end he had written this "account of my life and sufferings, with the hope that I might realize a sufficient sum from its sale, to enable me to procure a greater degree of education, thereby increasing my usefulness as a minister." The little book possesses no literary merit, except for the slight contribution to slave literature of his song of discontent over his food as a slave.[62]

The publications of the year, however, in the field of the slave narrative, were *The Life and Adventures of Zamba, an African Negro King, and His Experiences of Slavery in South Carolina, Written by Himself*[63] and the *Narrative of William Wells Brown, a Fugitive Slave, Written by Himself.*[64] Both of these slave narratives became immediately popular and enjoyed wide circulation on both sides of the Atlantic for a decade and a half.[65]

Zamba's narrative was obviously dependent upon its editor, Peter Neilson, of Kirkintilloch, North Britain, for molding it into shape. There are passages containing analogous instances added from published histories of slavery to amplify Zamba's accounts, and there are statistical amplifications for Zamba's conceivably original plan for the gradual emancipation of the slaves that certainly claim the editor as author. But the pith of the book is Zamba's. Concerning his authorship, Mr. Neilson writes in the editor's preface:

> I could not comply with the request of the Publishers of the work, that I would afford them an opportunity of communicating directly with Zamba; for . . . a letter addressed to a coloured person in Charleston by his proper name, would be opened at the post-office of that city, and in such a case as the present, Zamba's life would not be worth an hour's purchase.

> I therefore do not hesitate to declare, that I was personally
> acquainted with the African Negro named Zamba, whose history is
> here related; and that, during a residence of several years in Charles-
> ton, I heard from his own lips the leading incidents of his life. I
> have therefore no doubt of the truth of the statements contained in
> this narrative; indeed, as regards the occurrences in Charleston,
> some anecdotes are too well known in that city to be controverted.
> . . . The inherent evidences of its authenticity will be recognized
> and felt by the reader; for I can truly state, that in all essential
> points this narrative is genuine and authentic.[66]

The "Author's Preface" follows Neilson's and gives as Zamba's purpose for
writing his autobiography the ambition "to add fuel to the heavenly fire of
humane and Christian feeling which already exists in the hearts of Britain's
free-born sons towards the oppressed slave." He admits having had many
misgivings in regard to his attempt at composition but entertains the hope
that, as the production of an African Negro, it will excite in Christian England considerable interest. The vogue for slave testimonials is referred to as a
reason for his expectation of success:

> Even a larger share of interest and sympathy than were it the pro-
> duction of an educated white man; for Negro authors are, no doubt,
> scarce in the world; but I am aware that I must not be too sanguine
> on this point. It is my conviction, however, that in this city of
> Charleston, there are many of my oppressed and vilified race, who
> could produce a book, not only equal, but superior to this; had they
> only enjoyed the same opportunities of education and information
> as have fallen to my lot.[67]

He hopes that fifty or more copies of his narrative will find their way to
Charleston, so that the slaveholders there can fret and fume over the contents:

> They will offer rewards of dollars by the hundreds (he opines), and
> perhaps by the thousand, to discover who Zamba is; but I calculate,
> as the Yankees express it, that Zamba is beyond the reach of their
> malice and fury. I feel thus far sanguine, because I am convinced that
> ere another generation pass away, American slavery will be on its
> last legs.[68]

Zamba was born in 1780 in a village consisting of ninety huts and a king's
palace on the south bank of the Congo. His father, Zembola, was the chief or
king. Zamba gives an entertaining description of their ceremonial customs and
of his father's exploits, including his exciting encounter with a lion, which his
father killed and had stripped. Upon his father's death Zamba became king

and soon married a lovely young captive named Zillah, daughter of the king who happened to have slain Zembola in battle. Zamba became converted to the Christian faith as a result of the efforts of one Captain Winton, a representative of a type of slave trader that was quite successful in decoying slaves under the pretense of having converts accompany them to a "church" some distance away for the purpose of "baptism." Zamba left the Congo with thirty-two of his men in October of 1800, to be taken somewhere by Captain Winton for this holy purpose, only to realize, when they had at last been ushered on board a ship where there were already more than four hundred other Africans in shackles, that they had been kidnapped. In the words of Zamba's account:

> [Winton said to him] Really, King Zamba, I must charge you for all the lessons I have given you for these some years past, and I cannot charge you less than a doubloon per hour. I could positively have picked up many a good boat-load of niggers during the time I spent in hammering lessons into your head; and besides this, it is not every day that the poor master of a slave-ship falls in with a king for a pupil. We shall talk of this again, however, and settle our accounts at the end of the voyage.[69]

Although Winton laughed heartily as he said this, and Zamba at first thought that he meant it for a joke when he claimed that Zamba was indebted to him for "twenty thousand dollars' worth of good English and sound religion," Zamba became uneasy as the voyage progressed. When they landed at Charleston, his fears were realized, as Winton sold him to a Mr. Naylor of that city for six hundred dollars.

The fears expressed by Mr. Neilson for Zamba's personal safety, should Charlestonians ever learn his identity, were doubtless felt in connection with Zamba's accounts of cruelties practiced by neighboring slaveholders, since he himself experienced very little harshness. He felt keenly the sufferings of slaves he saw tortured. The punishment of one slave girl who had had the misfortune to burn her mistress' muslin gown, for example, was so fiendish as to make him ill.[70] But his personal treatment was not bad. Mr. Naylor was a merchant and placed Zamba under the personal supervision of the manager of his store, a Scotsman named Mr. Thomson, whose natural humaneness deepened into an attitude of great kindness toward Zamba after the latter had saved him from drowning. Mr. Naylor allowed Mr. Thomson to teach Zamba to read, although to do so was contrary to the laws of the state (as Winton reminded him on a later trip to Charleston with more slaves). Zamba had the opportunity of working in the store, where he was alertly observant of all that went on. He felt that if only he could have his wife with him, he could be content in his situations. In this connection he says:

> After I had been about two years in Charleston, I asked Mr. Thomson whether or not he thought Mr. Naylor would allow me to embark in some slave ship for Africa, and arrange matters so as to return with my wife to Charleston. I had felt so much of the benefits of civilization, and of the sublime hopes and ideas with which Christianity inspired me, that I had no wish to return to Africa as a permanent residence. I was now a close and attentive hearer of the Gospel; and humbly hope [sic] that without any prospect of future personal freedom, I should on no account have foregone the advantages which I weekly, or oftener, derived from the preaching of the Gospel.[71]

This yearning for his wife was unexpectedly gratified a year later, when Zillah was brought to the Charleston port in a slave ship, having been captured easily by Winton. She had gone to the African coast looking for Zamba when she learned that he had been taken to "Charleston." Zamba induced Mr. Thomson to persuade Mr. Naylor to purchase Zillah, which he did for three hundred and fifty dollars.

The narrative's credibility begins to strain as romantic good luck continues for Zamba. His brother-in-law, Pouldamah, is credited with smuggling him a nugget of pure gold from Africa, concealed in a jar of honey. This gold is turned over to Mr. Naylor, who in due time has free papers made out for Zillah and Zamba, though they continue to live with him until his removal to another state in 1819. After he leaves, Zamba takes a small shop and carries on "a limited trade" for a number of years, "more for the sake of keeping myself in employment than for the sake of gain." He retires from business about 1827, however, devoting the last twenty years to "alleviating the distresses of others" and in "perusing the works of the 'mighty dead.'"[72]

The editor of the German edition of Zamba's narrative, which was published in Stuttgart in 1853,[73] provides an introduction of singular importance, because it reveals an active interest among Germans in the American slave's quest for liberty. He praises especially the plan for the gradual amelioration of the slave's condition and emancipation, which Zamba gives in the twelfth chapter of his book. Zamba's plan, no doubt formulated with the aid of Mr. Neilson as has been suggested earlier, was as follows:

> Congress cannot interfere with the individual laws of any particular state of the Union; but it can pass a law, imposing a tax. Now, a tax of five dollars per head, annually, on every coloured person in America, whether bond or free, would effect this happy change in twenty-one years; or, a tax of only three dollars, would bring it about in thirty years. At the rate of five dollars per head, allowing the money to yield 6%, and calculating compound interest (and there is no doubt but that in a thriving, enterprising, and rapidly

increasing country, as America undoubtedly is, money can be safely
invested, so as to make my calculations good,) a five dollar poll-tax
on Negroes, would produce in twenty-one years, $670,000,000. But
to make the tax easier to the planters, who must pay for their slaves,
and to give more time for the gradual amelioration of the Negro's
moral condition, I shall go upon the three dollar tax. . . . Independent of all extraneous aid, . . . I calculate that three dollars per head
per annum would, in the first year, yield about ten millions of
dollars, at 6%, and compound interest on this sum, and on ten
millions additional every year, for thirty years, would at the end of
that period amount altogether to $845,000,000; or $253 per head,
compensation money, for each Negro slave—man, woman, and
child—in the whole of the United States of America.[74]

The German editor endorses the plan enthusiastically, declaring:

Zamba's Plan, der freilich hinsichtlich der Vorbereitung der Sklaven
zum wurdigen Gebrauch der Freiheit grossere Sichersheit gabe, ist
dem ungeduldigen Charakter unserer Zeit viel zu weitausehend. Er
wird aber auch durch die Ereignisse uberflussig werden, die so
manchen Plan zu Schanden machen.[75]

One of the most popular sections of the narrative for discussion purposes,
Zamba's plan concludes with suggestions for the education of the slaves
awaiting manumission. His ambition for them to be taught how to read suggests Jupiter Hammon's ideal rather than Zamba's own declared practice of
"perusing the works of the 'mighty dead'":

I have no ambition to make my fellow-blacks learned men: only
enable them to read the Bible, and the blessing of Heaven will
second your endeavors. Let emissaries, or missionaries, be sent
among the slaves . . . and being thus civilized and instructed by
degrees, there will be few, indeed, in a state of ignorance, at the end
of thirty years. I would answer for my brethren that their industry,
and their gratitude, will be developed in proportion as they become
enlightened.[76]

The narrative closes with an address "to the inhabitants of the only truly
free country upon earth—Great Britain," appealing to them to stretch forth
their hands and assist in alleviating the condition of the slave. He asks them
for their sympathy and their prayers, as individuals and as associations, and
for as much aid in the form of remonstrance as they could manage, although,
Zamba ingenuously submits, "we cannot ask you to interpose directly in our
behalf, by interfering with the Government of America.[77]

The narrative of William Wells Brown ranked second only to Douglass's narrative in popularity during its day. According to the publisher's note to the third edition, issued less than a year and a half after the first edition of 1847, "no anti-slavery work has met with a more rapid sale in the United States than this narrative."[78] The English publisher Charles Gilpin seemed to feel the same way, as the eleven thousand copies he published in 1849 were soon sold. Before the year had ended, a fourth edition was sent forth from the press of the Boston publishers with a new publisher's note, which called the narrative

> one of the most interesting and valuable publications which the
> Anti-Slavery reform has given to the world. . . . An additional chap-
> ter (the 12th) is given with this edition, containing an account of a
> daring attempt by some Tennessee slaveholders to seize certain fugi-
> tives in Canada with the intent of taking them back to slavery—of
> their partial success—of their being pursued and overtaken—the
> rescue of the slaves and, after a desperate contest, their restoration
> to the free soil of Canada. In an appendix is a valuable abstract of
> the Slave Laws of the Southern States, and some specimens of
> slave-advertisements.[79]

For the literary historian, one of the most interesting features of this fourth American edition is the inclusion in the preface by Edmund Quincy, the editor, of a letter to Quincy from Mr. Enoch Price, the owner of William Wells Brown. Brown had sent Mr. Price a copy of his narrative as soon as it was published in July of 1847. Quincy's letter from Mr. Price was sent from St. Louis, January 10, 1848. It begins with the blunt assertion, "Now I see many things in his book that are not true, and a part of it is as near true as a man could recollect after so long a time." He said that he had purchased Brown, whom he called "Sandford," from a Mr. S. Willi, in September of 1833, for six hundred dollars. He was later offered two thousand dollars for him in New Orleans and fifteen hundred dollars in Louisville. But, says he:

> I would not sell him. I was told that he was going to run away, the
> day before he ran away, but I did not believe the man, for I had so
> much confidence in Sandford. I want you to see him, and see if what
> I say is not the truth. I do not want him as a slave, but I think that
> his friends, who sustain him and give him the right hand of fellow-
> ship, or he himself, could offer to pay my agent in Boston three
> hundred and twenty-five dollars, and I will give him free papers. . . .
> just half what I paid for him.[80]

Brown's note to the reader, in connection with Mr. Price's letter, directs attention to the fact that he had lived with his last owner only three months, requiring only six of the 110 pages of his narrative to describe, so that it could not be expected that Mr. Price would know anything about the truth of his autobiography except in regard to that part dealing with himself and his family. But in admitting "that a part of it is true," Mr. Price had provided Brown with evidence that he considered of value.

Brown was a mulatto slave, born in Lexington, Kentucky, March 15, 1815. He starts his narrative "with full abolitionist flavor":

> The man who stole me as soon as I was born, recorded the births of all the infants which he claimed to be born his property, in a book which he kept for that purpose. My mother's name was Elizabeth. She had seven children viz: Solomon, Leander, Benjamin, Joseph, Millford, Elizabeth, and myself. No two of us were children of the same father. My father's name, as I learned from my mother, was George Higgins. He was a white man, a relative of my master, and connected with some of the first families of Kentucky.[81]

While William was still a baby, his master, Dr. John Young—half brother of George Higgins, as we are told later in Josephine Brown's biography of her father[82]—took him with his mother to a plantation in Missouri, about sixty miles above St. Louis. Life on the plantation under the cruel overseers was "heartrending," as Brown explains:

> Experience has taught me that nothing can be more heartrending than for one to see a dear and beloved mother or sister tortured, and to hear their cries, and not be able to render them assistance.[83]

He was made assistant overseer when he reached manhood, then hired out to proprietors of the steamer "Enterprise," with the duty of preparing the slaves for market at New Orleans. By his twenty-first year he had resolved upon flight. We go with him on that perilous venture:

> I had long since made up my mind that I would not trust myself in the hands of any man, white or colored. The slave is brought up to look upon every white man as an enemy to him and his race; and twenty-one years of slavery had taught me that there were traitors, even among colored people. After dark, I emerged from the woods into a narrow path, which led me into the main-travelled road. . . .
> I looked in vain for the North Star; a heavy cloud hid it from view. I walked up and down the road until near midnight, when the clouds disappeared, and I welcomed the sight of my friend—the North Star!
> As soon as I saw it, I knew my course, and before daylight I travelled twenty or twenty-five miles. It being in the winter, I suffered intensely from the cold; being without an overcoat, and my other clothes rather thin for the season. I was provided with a tinder

box, so that I could make up a fire when necessary. And but for this, I should certainly have frozen to death; for I was determined not to go to any house for shelter. . . . I travelled at night, and lay by during the day.

On the fourth day my provisions gave out, and then what to do I could not tell. Have something to eat I must; but how to get it was the question. On the first night after my food was gone, I went to a barn on the roadside and there found some ears of corn. I took ten or twelve of them, and kept on my journey. During the next day, while in the woods, I roasted my corn and feasted upon it, thanking God that I was so well provided for.[84]

Feeling confident that his escape was certain, now that his stomach was full, the fleeing slave bent his thoughts to the "prospects of the future." He wondered what he would find to do and what his name should be. His mother had given him the name "William," but his master had changed it to "Sandford" when the latter's nephew by the same name had come to live on his plantation. William mused as he ran:

I resolved on adopting my old name of William, and let Sandford go by the board, for I always hated it . . . because it had been forced upon me. . . . Travelling along the road, I would sometimes speak to myself, sounding my name over, by way of getting used to it, before I should arrive among civilized human beings. On the fifth or sixth day, it rained very fast, and froze about as fast as it fell, so that my clothes were one glare of ice. I travelled on at night until I became so chilled and benumbed—the wind blowing in my face—that I found it impossible to go any further, and accordingly took shelter in a barn, where I was obliged to walk about to keep from freezing. . . . Nothing but the providence of God, and that old barn, saved me from freezing to death. I received a very severe cold, which settled upon my lungs, and from time to time my feet had been frostbitten, so that it was with difficulty I could walk. In this situation I travelled two days, when I found that I must seek shelter somewhere, or die. . . . I secured myself behind some logs and brush, intending to wait there until some one should pass by; for I thought it probable that I might see some colored person, or if not, some one who was not a slaveholder; for I had an idea that I should know a slaveholder as far as I could see him.

The first person that passed was a man in a buggy-wagon. He looked too genteel for me to hail him. Very soon another passed by on horseback. I attempted to speak to him, but fear made my voice fail me. As he passed, I left my hidingplace, and was approaching the road, when I observed an old man walking towards me, leading a white horse. He had on a broad-brimmed hat and a very long coat, and was evidently walking for exercise. As soon as I saw him, and observed his dress, I thought to myself, "You are the man that I have been looking for!" Nor was I mistaken. He was the very man![85]

When the man approached Brown, he asked him if he were not a slave. Brown looked at him for some time, without replying, and then asked the man if he knew of anyone who would help him, as he was sick. The man said that he would help him and asked him again if he was not a slave. When Brown answered that he was, the man told him that he was in "a very pro-slavery neighborhood," so that he would have to wait there until he could go home and return in a covered wagon for him. Brown said that he would remain, but after the man had mounted his horse and disappeared from sight, he grew apprehensive, lest he had mistaken the man—lest he had gone for someone to arrest him instead of a wagon to take him to shelter. He decided to remain:

> I finally concluded to remain until he should return, removing some few rods to watch his movements. After a suspense of an hour and a half or more, he returned with a two-horse covered wagon, such as are usually seen under the shed of a Quaker meeting house on Sundays and Thursdays: for the old man proved to be a Quaker of the George Fox stamp.
>
> He took me to his house, but it was some time before I could be induced to enter it; not until the old lady came out, did I venture into the house. I thought I saw something in the old lady's cap that told me I was not only safe, but welcome, in her house. I was not, however, prepared to receive their hospitalities. The only fault I found with them was their being too kind.

As he had never "had a white man to treat me as an equal," Brown was very uncomfortable at first, especially at being waited upon by a white woman. Although the table was loaded with food, he could not eat, wishing that they would allow him "the privilege of eating in the kitchen," by himself.

> Finding that I could not eat, the old lady, who was a "Thompsonian," made me a cup of "composition," or "number six," but it was so strong and hot, that I called it "number seven!"

This helped soothe his nerves, and soon he was feeling at home among these good people. It was found that his feet were quite frozen, however, and he was soon seized with a fever, through which Mr. and Mrs. Wells Brown nursed him tenderly, so that he recovered by the end of two weeks. In the meantime Mrs. Brown had made him some clothing, and Mr. Brown had bought him a pair of boots. He now learned that he was in the free state of Ohio, about fifty miles from Dayton and about two hundred miles from Cleveland, the city he wanted to reach in order to catch a steamer on Lake Erie bound for Canada. Before leaving the Browns, he gave Mr. Brown "the privilege of naming" him, as he was "the first white man to extend the hand of friendship" to him. The old man's reply endears him even further to the reader:

> "If I name thee," said he, "I shall call thee Wells Brown, after myself. "But," said I, "I am not willing to lose my name of William.
> As it was taken from me once against my will, I am not willing to part with it again upon any terms."
> "Then," said he, "I will call thee William Wells Brown."[86]

As Brown walked away, in the direction of Canada with the warm clothes the Browns had given him on his body and a little money to help buy his needs in his pocket, he wished that his mother and his sister could see him walking the road to freedom; he wished that he could see Mr. Price to tell him he and Mrs. Price would have to get another coachman; and he wished, above all, to see Eliza, the girl he had left behind.

How Brown happened to choose Edmund Quincy as his editor we do not know. It was a happy choice, and we learn Quincy's first impression upon reading Brown's manuscript from his letter to Brown from Dedham, Massachusetts, dated July 1, 1847, in which he says:

> I heartily thank you for the privilege of reading the manuscript of your narrative. I have read it with deep and strong emotion. I am much mistaken if it be not greatly successful and eminently useful. It presents a different phase of the infernal slave-system from that portrayed in the admirable story of Mr. Douglass. . . .
>   Your opportunities of observing the workings of this accursed system have been singularly great. Your experiences in the Field, in the House, and especially on the River in the service of the slave-trader, have such as few individuals have had,—no one, certainly, who has been competent to describe them. What I have admired, and marvelled at, in your narrative, is the simplicity and calmness with which you describe scenes and actions which might very well move the very stones to rise and mutiny against the National Institution which makes them possible.
>   You will perceive that I have made very sparing use of your flattering permission to alter what you had written. To correct a few errors, committed in the hurry of composition, under unfavorable circumstances, and to suggest a few curtailments, is all that I have ventured to do. I should be a bold man as well as a vain one, if I

should attempt to improve your descriptions of what you have seen and suffered. Some of the scenes are not unworthy of De Foe himself.[87]

The fall from grace of the "ranking" fugitive slave lecturer, Frederick Douglass, because he had seen fit to choose "compromise with the slave-holder" in the form of purchasing his freedom from his claimant rather than indulge the abolitionists' fetish of no payments on any count, had left the position of top antislavery attraction conspicuously unoccupied for the first six months of 1847. Abolitionist publicity centering upon Brown's narrative in July, however, ostensibly marked his succession to Douglass's place. Though he was never actually to supplant Douglass as the popular idol in the antislavery movement, Brown did become the official slave-spokesman for the American Anti-Slavery Society in the summer of 1847. But Brown was a different type of man altogether from Douglass and was still to rank second in the public mind even after six years of grooming as the top-ranking slave lecturer. We read in the Hereford (England) *Times* for December 17, 1853:

The name of Mr. William Wells Brown, the fugitive from American slavery, has become so well known through his lectures on that infamous system, during the last four years, in various parts of this country, that anything from his pen possesses an *a priori* claim to attention. As a man of color, whose public addresses have given another signal refutation to the slaveholder's calumny, that the Negro race are incapable of anything above forced toil, Mr. Brown occupies a position in public esteem only second to that of his powerful-minded compatriot, Frederick Douglass. Without Mr. Douglass, vivid imagination, deep pathos, and wealth of language, Mr. Brown has achieved not less honor, by the clearness of his state-ments, his generally happy choice of language, and the calm power of his appeals to the reason of his auditors. When we add that the men who have thus nobly vindicated the capacity for, as well as the right of their injured race to freedom, are self-educated—Douglass having only begun to cultivate his great natural powers when a man, at his escape from slavery; and Brown having been ignorant even of the alphabet up to twenty years of age—we need say no more to justify their high place in the esteem and the sympathy of all true lovers of freedom and progress. As a specimen of Mr. Brown's power of public address, we may point to his lucid and powerful lecture on Monday night (reprinted on our sixth page), while the neat little book before us is not less pleasing evidence that he knows how to wield the pen of a ready writer.[88]

The "neat little book" was *Clotel; or, The President's Daughter,*[89] Brown's fourth publication in England after he had become an exile from the United States in 1849 in the wake of his defiant announcement from the abolitionist platform and press that he would never pay his claimant Mr. Enoch Price one dollar in "purchase" of his freedom or allow anyone else to do so for him. These books, which were all based on his life in slavery or as a fugitive slave, were published by the enterprising Charles Gilpin in London, at the same time that he was turning out edition after edition of Brown's *Narrative.* They included: *A Description of William Wells Brown's Original Panoramic Views of the Scenes in the Life of an American Slave, from His Birth in Slavery to His Death or His Escape to His First Home of Freedom on British Soil;*[90] *An Illustrated Edition of the Life and Escape of William Wells Brown;*[91] *Three Years in Europe;*[92] and *Clotel.*

The antislavery public's unprecedented interest in *Uncle Tom's Cabin* from 1852 on led Brown into the field of the novel for the thin cloaking of autobiographical experiences we find in *Clotel.* Using as a framework the widely known gossip concerning the slave daughter of a late president of the United States, Brown's "novel" is a convenient vehicle for his expansion of the theme developed in the early pages of his *Narrative,* in which he records the nefarious practices of the uncle who was also his owner. The book provoked heated discussions, a typical reaction to its message being represented in the following review:

> *Clotel* is a tale, made up (as we learn from the preface) chiefly from
> incidents in which Mr. Brown was either an actor or an eye-witness.
> . . . In the case of Mr. Brown, himself, his uncle was the 'master' who
> sold him, his sisters, and his mother; while every hour, American
> fathers pollute that sacred title by selling their own children like
> cattle. . . . The large infusion of Anglo-Saxon blood among the
> slaves, has made them all the more difficult to keep down. As Mr.
> Brown remarks, it is that element which has produced the insurrec-
> tionary movements of late years; and we do not doubt that a half-
> breed Tell will some day avenge the wrongs of his maternal ancestors
> upon their corruptors and oppressors. . . . The writer has touched
> lightly upon his dreadful subject, yet, writing upon a matter of which
> he has had such painful experience, he could hardly fail to be inter-
> esting. His portraitures of character, especially the slaveholding
> parson, his excellent daughter, and Carleton, disgusted with religion
> because it is perverted by hypocrites to sanction slavery, are each
> graphically drawn. Some of his sketches are drily humorous—witness
> the stage-coach discussion between the Massachusetts clergyman and
> his Louisiana friend.[93]

Brown's *Three Years in Europe*, published in the same year as *Clotel*, was a work of even greater interest for abolitionists equipped with a sense of humor: a volume of foreign travels by an American slave! The book enjoyed a considerable sale in the British Isles and in America, where it appeared in an enlarged edition in 1854 under the title *Places and People Abroad*.[94] It was again enlarged and published in 1855, under the title *The American Fugitive in Europe; Sketches of Places and People Abroad, with a Memoir by the Author*.[95] The reviews in the English quarterlies and journals compared Brown's *Three Years in Europe* with other contemporary travel books, without disparagement to Brown's book. He was criticized in some quarters for his unfavorable portrait of Carlyle, whom he had met in a railway coach and whose natural irascibility had seemed rather unnatural to Brown.[96] None of the other portraits of persons with whom Brown had talked during his travels over more than twenty thousand miles through the British empire provoked any adverse comments. He had addressed one thousand public meetings in the course of his tour, including lectures before twenty-three mechanics' associations and literary institutions. A reviewer in the Providence *Tribune* called his account "the most readable book of travels that we have read in several years."[97] Charles Dickens, Bulwer-Lytton, Tennyson, Beranger, Harriet Martineau, and George Thompson are among the authors whom Brown has sketched. From the point of view of literary history, this book of travels has the distinction of being one of the very few books that have been written by the American Negro that do not have racial discrimination as their theme.[98] Contemporary reviews frequently drew the reader's attention to the urbane charm of its descriptions. One critic declared: "The Author is always a philosopher, save when he steps aside to become a humorist, or to give language to a soul-ennobling sentiment."[99]

Exile from America finally became irksome to Brown, however, so that he did not hesitate to do as Douglass had done: he accepted the money proferred by British friends for his ransom in 1854. His daughter includes a copy of his "Bill of Sale" in her biography of her father, published the following year.[100] It reads:

Deed of Emancipation

Know all men by these presents, that I, Enoch Price, of the city and county of St. Louis, and State of Missouri, for and in consideration of the sum of three hundred dollars, to be paid to Joseph Greely, my agent in Boston, Massachusetts, by Miss Ellen Richardson, or her agent, on the delivery of this paper, do emancipate, set free, and liberate from slavery, a mulatto man named Sandford HIggins, *alias* William Wells Brown, that I purchased of Samuel Willi on the 2d of October, 1833. Said Brown is now in the fortieth year of his age, and I do acknowledge that no other person holds any claim on him as a slave but myself. In witness whereof, I hereunto set my hand and seal, this 24th day of April, 1854.[101]

The abolition movement was so vast, by 1854, that no perceptible agitation met the news that Brown was now to be numbered among the manumitted. He returned to America with no noticeable loss of rank in the American Anti-Slavery Society and was soon adding "dramas" to his literary record. He became more popular than ever at antislavery affairs for his dramatic readings. One notice in *The Liberator*, in 1856, advised the public that Brown was "so swamped with calls for his readings, twenty engagements already booked, that he has had to stop everything else."[102] The published plays included: *Experience: or, How to Give a Northern Man a Backbone*;[103] *Escape: or, A Leap for Freedom*; and *Jeremiah Adderson*.[104] Brown's *Black Man*, the first history of the Negro in America,[105] *My Southern Home*,[106] and *The Rising Son*[107] constitute the chief writings of this talented ex-slave after his return from his profitable exile.

The fugitive slave Henry Watson was one of hundreds whose escape from slavery had been engineered by abolitionists visiting in Southern states. He prepared the story of his life as a slave while in the midst of a busy life as a lecturer in Rhode Island, a career into which he was launched as soon as he arrived on free soil, as he said. In a letter to Garrison announcing the fact that his narrative was about to issue from the press in February of 1848, Watson tells of his activities in the "cause":

At the request of a few tried friends of the slave, I still remain in this busy little State, delivering addresses, distributing books, and calling public attention to "the sum of all villainies," in every proper manner. During the last two months, I have spoken before nearly fifty different audiences, the most of which were large, and all of them very kind and attentive. I am now in this active, pleasant corner of the land of Roger Williams, expecting to lecture this evening, and although the Seventh Day Baptists are now active, and are holding a protracted meeting here, I have the prospect of a full attendance. Our faithful friend, Charles Perry, whose hospitality I am now enjoying, has been very active in giving notice, and in making preparations.[108]

Watson was born a slave in Virginia, about 1813, on the Bibb plantation, about thirteen miles from Fredericksburg. His mother, Letty, was sold away from him, to the South, when he was a little child. He was brought up as a house servant and valet to his master, a mean man, but was turned out into the fields as part of his punishment for not telling his master which slave had stolen a pig that was missing. The work in the field was naturally hard for him, as he was unaccustomed to it and the overseer was cruel. Soon his master sold him to his brother, a man who would have been all right, Watson believed, had he had a better wife. The new master was "turned into a mere automaton," moving at the will of the mistress, who was so evil, according to Watson, that she made torture her pastime and "inspired every one about her with terror."[109] Watson traveled with them to Louisiana, Mississippi, and Tennessee. In the latter state he was hired out by his owners to the proprietor of a large hotel, where he met the Bostonian to whose tutelage he owed his subsequent change of fortune.

Apparently an experienced trainer in the art of escape, the Bostonian soon had Watson learning by rote the answers to questions he could expect to be asked if apprehended on board ship for Boston, which he was henceforth to call "home." He was to tell them that he lived in the North End, on Ann Street; that Ann Street ran "parallel with Commercial Street;" then "take a step forward and turn away from the captain with a laugh, telling him he needs no information about the streets of Boston, as he knows as well as you do of their situation."[110] Watson's Northern friend drilled and drilled him in those replies until he considered it safe for him to be put on board ship. The Bostonian had made arrangements with the steward of a certain ship, who came forward to greet Watson as an old acquaintance, though Watson had never seen him before. The captain asked him all the questions that had been anticipated, so that Watson was able to utilize his training, even to the stage directions of the step forward and the laugh. But his heart sank when he learned that he needed fifteen dollars more than he had to complete the fare the captain charged him. At this point, however, the steward came forward, kindly offered to "stand for" the amount, and told the captain he needed someone to assist him. Pretending that Watson was taken sick, the steward whisked Watson into his cabin, until they should leave the dock, so that Watson would be out of sight in the event that his master should come on board for any reason and see him. When he arrived in Boston, he made his way to Garrison, as he had been advised. Garrison counselled him to go to England, which he did. After staying a few months there, he returned to New England and busied himself as a lecturer.

The Narrative of the Life and Adventures of Henry Bibb, an American Slave, Written by Himself was the first of a series of popular slave narratives that appeared in 1849.[111] We have been acquainted with the name of Henry Bibb in the pages of the antislavery journals of two years earlier. As early as May, 1847, at a meeting held at Belknap Street Church, Boston, to welcome Douglass after his twenty months abroad, one reporter observed: "Henry Bibb, the eloquent fugitive, came forward . . . and offered a brief exposition of his feelings—rejoicing in the success of his brother Douglass, etc."[112] Again, in 1848, a notice was printed concerning a set of resolutions offered by Henry Bibb in a meeting of colored citizens of Boston, recommending the support of the Canada Colony in preference to Liberia as a settlement for fugitive slaves. He congratulated all fugitives on their escape and advocated resistance against recapture by slaveholders or their agents "to the sacrifice of human life, in self-defence, if necessary, and to suffer the penalty of the law, which would be far better than to be taken back in hopeless bondage."[113] An irate article entitled "Another Douglass" was reprinted by *The Liberator* from the Richmond *Whig*, giving an insight into the Southerners' view of the heyday of the fugitive slave:

> The free Negroes at the North are about to speculate on John Bull's sympathies. Seeing that Frederick Douglass had been so highly honored, by the aristocracy of England—invited as the most distinguished guest to dinners and suppers, mounted upon the rostrum with Lords and Dukes and Right Reverends, and placed in the chief seats of the synagogue among the scribes and pharisees—and all because he was a runaway slave—(pity that some of the white slaves in their factories and fields can't run away!)—seeing all this, one Henry Bibb, a greasy denizen perhaps of the Five Points, but professing to be a self-emancipated wooly-head from Kentucky, is about to follow in Douglass' footsteps! He is to go as a CABIN PASSENGER in one of the Cunard Steamers . . . doubtless with the expectation of eliciting from British aristocrats, who are revelling in splendor upon the toil of their own more abject and in all respects worse-conditioned slaves, a portion of that sympathy and cash by which Frederick Dougalss has been rendered immortal in the calendar of Abolitionism, and in his own estimation! Should Bibb make a successful spec [*sic*], we may expect to see the steamers crowded with free Negroes, pretending to be runaway slaves, eager to avail themselves of the tide before it ebbs.[114]

The front matter of Bibb's *Narrative* contains a variety of interesting data establishing the narrative. There is a report from a committee appointed by the "Detroit Liberty Association" to investigate the truth of the narrative, including copies of letters from Southerners who knew Bibb and who verified many of his statements in the process of trying to disprove others.[115] There is an introduction by Bibb's editor, Lucius Matlack, bearing directly upon his function as editor as he exercised it:

> To many, the elevated style, purity of diction, and easy flow of language, frequently exhibited, will appear unaccountable and contradictory, in view of his want of early mental culture. But to the thousands who have listened with delight to his speeches on anniversary and other occasions, these same traits will be noted as unequivocal evidence of originality. Very few men present in their written

composition, so perfect a transcript of their style as is exhibited by
Mr. Bibb. . . . The entire manuscript I have examined and prepared
for the press. Many of the closing pages of it were written by Mr.
Bibb in my office. And the whole is preserved for inspection now.
An examination of it will show that no alteration of sentiment,
language, or style, was necessary to make it what it now is, in the
hands of the reader. The work of preparation for the press was that
of orthography and punctuation merely, an arrangement of the
chapters, and a table of contents—little more than falls to the lot
of publishers generally.[116]

In his "Author's Preface," Bibb says that the writing of his narrative was
done during irregular intervals while he was traveling and "laboring for the
emancipation of my enslaved countrymen." Anticipating questions as to why
he should write the story of his life as a slave "when there has been so much
already written and published of the same character from other fugitives,"
and "after having told it publicly all through New England and the Western
States to multiplied thousands," he explains:

In no place have I given orally the detail of my narrative; and some
of the most interesting events of my life have never reached the
public ear. Moreover, it was at the request of many friends of down-
trodden humanity, that I have undertaken to write the following
sketch, that light and truth might be spread on the sin and evils of
slavery as far as possible.[117]

His deep wish is to reach the slave, however possible. He forecasts the message
of the magazine he soon founded and edited, *The Voice of the Fugitive,*[118]
when he writes.

To be changed from a chattel to a human being, is no light matter,
though the process with myself practically was very simple. And if I
could reach the ears of every slave today, throughout the whole
continent of America, I would teach the same lesson, I would sound
it in the ears of every hereditary bondman, "break your chains and
fly for freedom!"[119]

Bibb was a mulatto slave, born on a plantation near Louisville, Kentucky.
He endured the usual hardships and became determined to bring about an end
to his slavery after he had become the husband of a slave and a father. The
cruelties which he could stand when they were inflicted on him became
intolerable when they fell upon the body of his beloved Malinda. As they
looked upon their little Mary Frances, they both prayed that she might
somehow be spared the lot they feared was in store for her. So, after a tearful parting, Bibb made his escape and reached Canada safely. The story of his

struggles to take his family to freedom is one of the outstanding records of human devotion in the literature of the slave.

Bibb was caught by slave hunters upon his return from Canada to get his wife and child but managed to escape from them when practically back on his master's plantation. He made his way back to the village, where a friend concealed him. In time, he was able to get a message relayed to Malinda by way of the wonderful "grapevine" of the slaves, requesting her to meet him on a certain day at a certain spot near his master's plantation at Bedford. Malinda came to him at the appointed time:

> We met under the most fearful apprehensions, for my pursuers had returned from Louisville, with the lamentable story that I was gone, and yet they were compelled to pay the three hundred dollars to the Cincinnati slave catchers for re-capturing me there. Daniel Lane's account of my escape from him, looked so unreasonable to slave-holders, that many of them charged him with selling me and keeping the money; while others believed that I had got away from him, and was then in the neighborhood, trying to take off my wife and child, which was true. Lane declared that in less than five mintues after I had run out of the stable in Louisville, he had over twenty men running and looking in every direction; but all without success. They could hear nothing of me. They had turned over several tons of hay in a large loft, in search, and I was not to be found there. Dan imputed my escape to my godliness! He said that I must have gone up in a chariot of fire, for I went off by flying; and that he should never again have anything to do with a praying Negro.[120]

While the frail, trembling little wife was relating these facts to her husband, the whole town of Bedford was excitedly looking for him. Both of them realized that she should get back at once to her mother's cabin. Bibb was hidden for several days in the house of a friend in the village. They waited anxiously for a chance to get together, but Malinda was watched day and night in the hope that Bibb might be caught:

> They knew well that my little family was the only object of attrac-tion that ever had or ever would induce me to come back and risk my liberty over the threshold of slavery—therefore this point was well guarded by the watch dogs of slavery.[121]

She managed to come to him one morning about two o'clock, when they made quick plans to separate until the excitement attending his capture and escape had blown over. She was then to meet him at a certain place in Ohio. Bibb took leave of her, which "was almost like tearing off the limbs from my body," and went on up to Canada. He waited for them three months. When he returned a second time, he was captured by a mob as he was planning with

Malinda's mother how to get away. Bibb was put in irons and flung into a damp dungeon, where he narrowly escaped death by illness and cruel treatment. Malinda was not allowed to enter the dungeon, but could see him through the prison grates. Bibb implored her to bear up for his sake:

> With manacled limbs; with wounded spirit; with sympathizing tears
> and with bleeding heart, I intreated Malinda to weep not for me, for
> it only added to my grief, which was greater than I could bear.[122]

To add to his torment, his master, after trying without success to assault his wife, tied her up and lashed her two days in succession, told her that he had sent her child away to be sold, and finally "drove Malinda before him to the workhouse swearing by his Maker that she would submit to him or die."[123] She lived through it all, and several weeks later the little family of three was unexpectedly reunited—bound in a coffle chain with other slaves for sale in New Orleans. They were allowed to remain together, Bibb reasons, because

> Garrison was not so much afraid of my running away from him
> while he held on to my family, for he knew from the great sacrifices
> which I had made to rescue them from slavery, that my attachment
> was too strong to run off and leave them in his hands, while there
> was the least hope of ever getting them away with me.[124]

Arrived in New Orleans at the slave market, Bibb had the surprising experience of being mistaken for a slave trader when he was actually trying to pick out some master he thought looked bearable. When he told Malinda about it, she became fearful. As he tells us:

> She thought that in addition to my light complexion, my being
> dressed up in Garrison's old slave-trading clothes might have caused
> the man to think that I was a slave trader, and she was afraid that we
> should yet be separated if I should not succeed in finding somebody
> to buy us.
>   Every day to us was a day of trouble, and every night brought
> new and fearful apprehensions that the golden link which binds
> together husband and wife might be broken by the heartless tyrant
> before the light of another day.
>   Deep has been the anguish of my soul when looking over my little
> family during the silent hours of the night, knowing the great danger
> of our being sold off at auction the next day and parted for ever.
> That this might not come to pass, many have been the tears and
> prayers which I have offered up to the God of Israel that we might
> be preserved.[125]

They were finally bought as one family by a pious-looking "Baptist-deacon cotton planter" named Francis Whitfield, who paid twelve hundred dollars for Bibb and one thousnad dollars for Malinda and Mary Frances together. They were unspeakably grateful for the fortune of remaining together and hoped for the best from their new master on the plantation to which they were taken up the Red River, about fifty miles from New Orleans. But they found their hopes blasted—the plantation was what was known among slaves as "mean": very meagre food rations of one pack of corn for each grown person plus one pound of pork and perhaps a quart of molasses for a week; brutal treatment employed to extract labor; and insufficient clothing and shelter. As for Whitfield's pious face:

> I afterwards found him to be one of the basest hypocrites that I ever saw. He looked like a saint—and talked like the best of slave-holding Christians, and acted at home like the devil.[126]

Bibb managed to make an escape, alone, and returned to take his family. They seemed about to get away, hiding by day and forging ahead at night, when they were set upon by a pack of wolves, barely escaping with their lives. Then they ran into their pursuers.[127] They were separated now by sale: Malinda and Mary Frances were bought by gamblers and Bibb was sold to Indians. He escaped from them before long, and for three long, dangerous years he hovered in and around the plantations looking for his family until at length he found Malinda. She had been sold "for adulterous purposes at a high price" and was beyond his reach.[128] Bibb then made his way sadly to the North. By 1845, he was resolved to spend his life in the cause of helping the fugitive. In 1848 he was married to "one Mary E. Miles, of Boston," eight years after losing Malinda and his daughter.

The abolitionists probably believed that they had met every conceivable kind and condition of fugitive slave by 1849, until they were suddenly stunned by the news that the Reverend James W. C. Pennington, pastor of a Presbyterian church in New York City and for many years an earnest supporter of the antislavery crusade, an educated person with the degree of doctor of philosophy from the University of Heidelberg, was in reality a fugitive slave from the state of Maryland. Dr. Pennington had fled to England on the eve of making known his identity, a secret that had been burning his heart for many years.[129]

Pennington's narrative was published by Gilpin in London in 1840. The first edition was exhausted in a few weeks. The newly declared slave author expresses his surprise and gratification over the sale of that long-suppressed story in the letter to Gilpin that appears in the second edition, published in October of 1849:[130]

The information just communicated to me by you that another
edition of my little book, "The Fugitive Blacksmith," is called for,
has agreeably surprised me. The British public has laid me under
renewed obligations by this mark of liberality, which I hasten to
acknowledge. I would avail myself of this moment also, to acknowledge the kindness of the gentlemen of the newspaper press for the
many favourable reviews which my little book has received. It is to
them I am indebted, in no small degree, for the success with which
I have been favored in getting the book before the notice of the
public.[131]

Like William Wells Brown, Pennington owed his start upward in life to a
Quaker, whose letter to Pennington on the eve of the publication of *The
Fugitive Blacksmith* is an interesting feature of the preface. Asked by Pennington for permisstion to use his name in the narrative, Friend "W.W."
writes:

I know thee so well, James, that I am not afraid of thy making a
bad use of it, nor am I afraid or ashamed to have it known that I
took thee in and gave thee aid, when I found thee travelling alone
and in want. . . . Understand me, James, that thee is at full liberty
to use my name in any way thee wishes in thy narrative. We have
a man here from the eastern shore of thy state. He is trying to
learn as fast as thee did when here.[132]

Pennington was born in Maryland to slaves belonging to different owners.
He was apprenticed to a stone mason from age nine to eleven, after which
time he was apprenticed to a blacksmith. Soon he was known as a first-rate
blacksmith," continuing in this trade for nine years until he was twenty-one.
In 1828 he was sold to a Methodist for seven hundred dollars. When the man
offered him for sale again because he could not keep him busy, his old master
repurchased him and proposed that he take up the carpentering business.
Pennington had worked at this trade for six months with a white partner
when a series of fresh abuses at the hands of his master compelled him to
fly. He relates these causes:

Three or four of our farm hands had their wives and families on
other plantations. In such cases, it is the custom in Maryland to
allow the men to go on Saturday evening to see their families, stay
over the Sabbath, and return on Monday morning, not later than
"half an hour by sun." To overstay their time is a grave fault, for
which, especially at busy seasons, they are punished.
    One Monday morning, two of these men had not been so fortu-
nate as to get home at the required time: one of them was an uncle

of mine. Besides these, two young men who had no families, and for whom no such provision of time was made, having gone somewhere to spend the Sabbath, were absent. My master was greatly irritated, and had resolved to have, as he said, "a general whipping-match among them." . . . [He declared] "By the Eternal, I'll make them know their hour. The fact is, I have too many of you; my people are getting to be the most careless, lazy, and worthless in the country."[133]

Hearing his master say this, Pennington's father, who seems to have been a very gentle-souled old man with a quiet dignity, gave the reply that if the master wanted to sell them, he could sell them. The master turned all of his fury on the old slave for his daring to answer back, and with insolent words reined savage stripes upon his back within sight of his son, who recalls:

This act created an open rupture with our family—each member felt the deep insult that had been inflicted upon our head; the spirit of the whole family was roused; we talked of it in our nightly gatherings, and showed it in our melancholy aspect. The oppressor saw this, and with the heartlessness that was in perfect keeping with the first insult, commenced a series of tauntings, threatenings, and insinuations, with a view to crush the spirit of the whole family. . . .

Although it was sometime after this event before I took the decisive step, yet in my mind and spirit, I never was a *Slave* after it.

Whenever I thought of the great contrast between my father's employment on that memorable Monday morning, [feeding the little lamb] and the barbarous conduct of my master, I could not help cordially despising the proud abuser of my sire; and I believe he discovered it, for he seemed to have diligently sought an occasion against me.[134]

The occasion came not long after, in the shop yard one day, when Pennington was shoeing a horse. The description is graphic:

I had been stooping for some time under the weight of the horse, which was large, and was very tired; meanwhile, my master had taken his position on a little hill just in front of me, and stood leaning back on his cane, with his hat drawn over his eyes. I put down the horse's foot, and straightened myself up to rest a moment, and without knowing that he was there, my eye caught his. This threw him into a panic of rage; he would have it that I was watching him. "What are you rolling your white eyes at me for, you lazy rascal?" He came down upon me with his cane, and laid on over my shoulders, arms, and legs, about a dozen severe blows, so that my limbs and flesh were sore for several weeks; and then after several offensive epithets, left me.

This affair my mother saw from her cottage, which was near. I being one of the oldest sons of my parents, our family was now mortified to the lowest degree. I had always aimed to be trustworthy; and feeling a high degree of mechanical pride, I had aimed to do my work with dispatch and skill, my blacksmith's pride was one thing that had reconciled me so long to remain a slave. . . . Besides, I used to assist my father at night in making straw hats and willow-baskets, by which means we supplied our family with little articles of food, clothing, and luxury, which slaves in the mildest form of the system never get from the master; but after this, I found that my mechanic's pleasure and pride were gone. I thought of nothing but the family disgrace under which we were smarting, and how to get out of it.[135]

Pennington frequently interrupts his narrative to discuss slavery and the evil influence upon the slaveholder of the temptations of irresponsible power, in very much the same fashion, we can imagine, that he was wont to discourse in from the pulpit. But when he leaves the expository mood, and lets his memory carry him directly back to the experiences riveted into his soul, there is no cluttering of the page with rhetoric. The account of his journey of escape is unforgettable:

The day dawned upon me when I was near a small house and barn, situate close to the road side. The barn was too near the road, and too small to afford secure shelter for the day; but as I cast my eye around by the dim light, I could see no wood, and no larger barn. It seemed to be an open country, to a wide extent. The sun was travelling so rapidly from his eastern chamber, that ten or fifteen minutes would spread broad daylight over my track. Whether *my* deed was evil, *you* may judge, but I freely confess that I did *then* prefer darkness rather than light; I therefore took to the mow of the little barn at a great risk, as the events of the day will show. It so happened that the barn was filled with corn fodder, newly cured and lately gotten in. You are aware that however quietly one may crawl into such a bed, he's compelled to make much more noise than if it were hay or straw. Besides inflicting upon my own exciting imagination the belief that I made noise enough to be heard by the inmates of the house who were likely to be rising at the time, I had the misfortune to attract the notice of a little house-dog, such as we call in that part of the world a "fice," on account of its being not only the smallest species of the canine race, but also, because it is the most saucy, noisy, and teasing of all dogs. This little creature commenced a fierce barking. I had at once great fears that the mischievous little thing would betray me; I fully apprehended that as soon as the man of the house arose, he would come and make search in the barn. It now being entirely daylight, it was too late to retreat from this shelter, even if I could have found another; I, therefore, bedded myself down into the fodder as best I could, and entered upon the annoyances of the day, with the frail hope to sustain my mind.[136]

It was a Thursday morning, and the sun rose very bright and clear. He did not hear any movements in the yard for about an hour, and careful listening to the sounds that were then audible convinced him that they were being made by one man and that he was evidently preparing to "go some distance to work for the day." In the "busy movements about the yard, and especially the active preparations in the house for breakfast," the continuous barking of the little "fice" was drowned out. But the little animal kept barking, at intermissions, throughout the day, making "regular sallies from the house to the barn, and after smelling about," flying back to the house, trying as hard as he could to alarm his mistress. There seemed to be only the woman of the house and one or two children with her. Pennington began to feel the gnawing pains of his empty stomach after the fear of immediate discovery abated. He had had nothing to eat since Sunday except for a hurried bite snatched the day before in the midst of great agitation. At one moment during the day, believing he could not stand the pains any longer, he had nearly resolved upon throwing himself upon the mercy of the woman and asking for food. But fearing the results might be fatal, he made up his mind "to suffer the day out." It was a day of complete discomfort, as we see:

> The wind sprang up fresh and cool; the barn being small and the crevices large, my wet clothes were dried by it, and chilled me through and through.
>   I cannot now, with pen or tongue, give a correct idea of the feeling of wretchedness I experienced; every nerve in my system quivered so that not a particle of my flesh was at rest. . . . About the middle of the afternoon . . . there seemed to be an unusual stir about the public road, which passed close by the barn. Men seemed to be passing in parties on horseback, and talking anxiously. From a word which I now and then overheard, I had not a shadow of a doubt that they were in search of me. . . . All this while the little fice was mingling his voice with those of the horsemen, and the noise of the horses' feet. I listened and trembled.
>   Just before the setting of the sun, the labouring man of the house returned, and commenced his evening duties about the horse and barn; chopping wood, getting up his cow, feeding his pigs, etc.,

attended by the little brute, who continued barking at short intervals. He came several times into the barn below. While matters were passing thus, I heard the approach of horses again, and as they came up nearer, I was led to believe that all I had heard pass, were returning in one party. They passed the barn and halted at the house, when I recognized the voice of my old captor; addressing the labourer, he asked, "Have you seen a runaway nigger pass here today?"

Laborer—No, I have not been at home since early this morning. Where did he come from?

Captor—I caught him down below here yesterday morning. I had him all day and just at night he fooled me and got away. A party of us have been after him all day; we have been up to the line, but can't hear or see anything of him. He is a blacksmith, and a stiff reward is out for him, two hundred dollars.

Labourer—He is worth looking for.

Captor—I reckon so. If I get my clutches on him again, I'll mosey him down to ___ before I eat or sleep.

Reader, you may if you can, imagine what the state of my mind was at this moment. . . . To my great relief, however, the party rode off, and the labourer after finishing his work went into the house. Hope seemed now to dawn for me once more; darkness was rapidly approaching, but the moments of twilight seemed much longer than they did the evening before. . . . About eight o'clock, I ventured to descend from the mow of the barn into the road. The little dog the while began a furious bit of barking. . . . I quickly crossed the road, and got into an open field opposite. After stepping lightly about two hundred yards, I halted, and on listening,I heard the door open. Feeling about on the ground, I picked up two stones, and one in each hand I made off as fast as I could, but I heard nothing more that indicated pursuit, and after going some distance I discharged my encumbrance, as from the reduced state of my bodily strength, I could not afford to carry ballast.[137]

Josiah Henson was a fugitive from slavery in Kentucky whose rocketing to worldwide notice in the late 1850s thereafter pinned attention upon the features of a versatile personality that paralleled the characteristics of "Uncle Tom," whose prototype he was claimed to be.[138] He was well known a decade earlier than that period as one of the leaders among the fugitive slaves colonizing in Canada. Arriving there with his slave family in 1830, he was a pioneer in the project undertaken by the fugitives to secure a tract of wild land between Lake Erie and St. Clair and become a colony of independent farmers instead of clinging to the large Canadian towns and living a hand-to-mouth existence as "fringe" laborers. Henson frequently went down to

Boston in the interest of soliciting support for his colony and won not only the financial support but also the personal concern of Samuel A. Eliot of that city. Eliot encouraged him to narrate the story of his life, which Eliot took down from Henson's dictation. The narrative appeared in July of 1849, entitled *Life of Josiah Henson, Formerly a Slave, Now an Inhabitant of Canada, as Related by Himself*, and was as fortunate in its reception by the public as the narratives of Bibb and Pennington in the same season.

Like the narrative of James Curry, Henson's account of his experiences presents detailed descriptions of a wide range of subjects connected with the slave's life. We can suspect the guiding influence of his scribe's questions in passages of the factual value of the following:

> The every-day life of a slave on one of our Southern plantations, however frequently it may have been described, is generally little known at the North; and must be mentioned as a necessary illustration of the character and habits of the slave and the slave-holder, created and perpetuated by their relative position. The principal food of those upon my master's plantations consisted of corn meal, and salt herrings; to which was added in summer a little buttermilk, and the few vegetables which each might raise for himself and his family, on the little piece of ground which was assigned to him, for the purpose, called a truck patch. The meals were two, daily. The first, or breakfast, was taken at twelve o'clock, after laboring from daylight; and the other when the work of the remainder of the day was over. The only dress was of tow cloth, which for the young, and often even for those who had passed the period of childhood, consisted of a single garment, something like a shirt, but longer, reaching to the ancles [*sic*]; and for the older, a pair of pantaloons, or a gown, according to the sex; while some kind of round jacket, or overcoat, might be added in winter, a wool hat once in two or three years, for the males, and a pair of coarse shoes once a year. Our lodging was in log huts, of a single small room, with no other floor than the trodden earth, in which ten or a dozen persons—men, women, and children—might sleep, but which could not protect them from dampness and cold, nor permit the existence of the common decencies of life. There were neither beds, nor furniture of any description—a blanket being the only addition to the dress of the day for protection from the chillness of the air or the earth. In these hovels were we penned at night, and fed by day; here were the children born, and the sick neglected. Such were the provisions for the daily toil of the slave.
>
> Notwithstanding this system of management, however, I grew to be a robust and vigorous lad, and at fifteen years of age, there were

few who could compete with me in work, or in sport—for not even the condition of a slave can altogether repress the animal spirits of the young Negro.[139]

According to the "advertisement" accompanying the first edition of Henson's narrative, the method by which the book was composed was well designed to develop clear treatment of his material, the facts of which are verified hundreds of times over in the mass record of the slave narratives. The "advertisement" states:

> The following memoir was written from the dictation of Josiah Henson. A portion of the story was told, which, when written, was read to him, that any errors of statement might be corrected. The substance of it, therefore, the facts, the reflections, and very often the words, are his; and little more than the structure of the sentences belongs to another. The narrative in this form, necessarily loses the attraction derived from the earnest manner, the natural eloquence of a man who tells a story in which he is deeply interested; but it is hoped that enough remains to repay perusals, and that the character of the man, and the striking nature of the events of his life will be thought to justify the endeavor to make them more extensively known.

Henson was born June 15, 1789, on the plantation of Francis Henson, near Port Tobacco, in Charles County, Maryland. His very first memory was the appearance of his father, head bloody with the cutting off of his right ear and back lacerated with a hundred lashes for having beaten the overseer for a brutal assault on his wife. Before this, Henson learned from his mother, his father had been an amiable man, but that outrage changed his whole nature. He became "morose, moody, and intractable," and his master sold him South as "a bad nigger" to Alabama. Neither his wife nor his child ever heard of him again. His mother had been hired out to the owner of his father by her master out of a kindly desire to allow the slave couple to live together. After that dreadful event, however, her master took her back home, and Henson enjoyed several years of comparative comfort with his mother, three sisters, and two brothers. This master was kind-hearted and jolly and never allowed a slave to be struck. But when he died, the slaves were sold. Henson's mother, he recalls, was brutally kicked for begging her new owner to buy him too so that they could be together. The man refused, but as Henson fell sick and seemed likely to die, another slaveholder who had purchased him offered him to his mother's owner for a "pittance," so that the two were reunited by that stroke of providence. The new master was "coarse, vulgar, and cruel," and "brutality was the order of the day." Henson spent more than thirty years as the slave of that man.

We are reminded of the early promise showed by Nat Turner as we read Henson's glowing account of his own prowess:

> I was competent to all the work that was done upon the farm, and could run faster and farther, wrestle longer, and jump higher, than anybody about me. My master and my fellow slaves used to look upon me, and speak of me, as a wonderfully smart fellow, and prophecy the great things I should do when I became a man. A casual word of this sort, sometimes overheard, would fill me with a pride and ambition which some would think impossible in a Negro slave, degraded, starved, and abused as I was, and had been, from my earliest recollection. But the love of superiority is not confined to kings and emperors; and it is a positive fact, that pride and ambition were as active in my soul as probably they ever were in that of the greatest statesman. . . . The objects I pursued, I admit, were not just the same as theirs. Mine were to be first in the field, whether we were hoeing, mowing, or reaping; to surpass those of my own age, or indeed any age, in athletic exercises; and to obtain, if possible, the favorable regard of the petty despot who ruled over us. This last was an exercise of the understanding rather than of the affections; and I was guided in it more by what I supposed would be effectual, than by a nice judgment of the propriety of the means I used.[140]

It is very important for the reader to make a mental note of the above passage in order not to be misled concerning the motives of this fascinating character in activities at various times later on in his colorful career. Henson's story is yet "to be done up round" by the novelist or biographer. His stereotyping as "Uncle Tom" was an afterthought and a publicity stunt, as is proved in another chapter.[141] As a black "Elmer Gantry," Josiah Henson offers some writer a very ripe prospect. We watch the budding leader of men as he works himself up to the role of plantation supervisor:

> I have toiled, and induced others to toil, many an extra hour, in order to show my master what an excellent day's work had been accomplished, and to win a kind word, or a benevolent deed from his callous heart. In general, indifference, or a cool calculation of my value to him, were my reward, chilling those hopes of an improvement in my condition, which was the ultimate object of my efforts. I was much more easily moved to compassion and sympathy than he was; and one of the means I took to gain the good-will of my fellow sufferers, was by taking from him some things that he did not give, in part payment of my extra labor. The condition of the male slave is bad enough, Heaven knows; but that of the female, compelled to perform unfit labor, sick, suffering, and bearing the burdens of

her own sex unpitied and unaided, as well as the toils which belong to the other, has often oppressed me with a load of sympathy. And sometimes, when I have seen them starved, and miserable, and unable to help themselves, I have helped them to some of the comforts which they were denied by him who owned them, and which my companions had not the wit or the daring to procure. Meat was not a part of our regular food; but my master had plenty of sheep and pigs, and sometimes I have picked out the best one I could find in the flock, or the drove, carried it a mile or two into the woods, slaughtered it, cut it up, and distributed it among the poor creatures, to whom it was at once food, luxury, and medicine.[142]

By means of this kindness to them, Henson acquired great influence among his fellow slaves, which led directly to his promotion, as we see:

By means of the influence thus acquired, the increased amount of work done upon the farm, and by the detection of the knavery of the overseer, who plundered his employer for more selfish ends, and through my watchfulness was caught in the act and dismissed, I was promoted to be superintendent of the farm work, and managed to raise more than double the crops, with more cheerful and willing labor, than was ever seen on the estate before.[143]

One of the most graphic of Hanson's descriptions, one which most profoundly impressed his first literary critic and through him impressed Mrs. Stowe,[144] is his account of his conversion to the Christian faith. Preachers were "somewhat rare at that period" in his neighborhood, but when his mother learned one day that a man noted thereabouts for his godly character was to preach the following Sunday at a place four or five miles distant from their plantation, she persuaded Henson to ask his master's leave to go to hear him. Henson tells of his success:

Although such permission was not freely given or often, yet his favor to me was shown for this once by allowing me to go, without much scolding, but not without a pretty distinct intimation of what would befall me, if I did not return immediately after the close of the service. I hurried off, pleased with the opportunity, but without any definite expectations of benefit or amusement; for up to this period of my life, and I was then eighteen years old, I had never heard a sermon, nor any discourse or conversation whatever, upon religious topics, except what had been impressed upon me by my mother, of the responsibility of all to a Supreme Being. When I arrived at the place of meeting . . . the speaker was just beginning his discourse, from the text, *Hebrew* ii,9, "That he, by the grace of God, should taste of death for every man." This was the first text of the

Bible to which I had ever listened, knowing it to be such. I have never forgotten it, and scarce a day has passed since, in which I have not recalled it, and the sermon that was preached from it. . . . I was wonderfully impressed, with the use which the preacher made of the last words of the text, "*for every man.*" He said the death of Christ was not designed for a select few only, but for the salvation of the world, for the bond as well as the free; and he dwelt on the glad tidings of the Gospel to the poor, the persecuted, and the distressed, its deliverance to the captive, and the liberty wherewith Christ has made us free, till my heart burned within me, and I was in a state of the greatest excitement at the thought that such a being as Jesus Christ had been described should have died for me. . . . I imme-diately determined to find out something more about Christ and his being crucified, and revolving the things which I had heard in my mind as I went home, I became so excited that I turned aside from the road into the woods, and prayed to God for light and for aid with an earnestness . . . which the subsequent course of my life has led me to imagine might not have been unacceptable to Him who heareth prayer.[145]

From that day forward, Henson was so deeply convinced of the "superior importance to everything else" of religious matters that he "used every means and opportunity of inquiry" to learn more about them. The result comes soon:

I could not help talking much on these subjects with those about me; and it was not long before I began to pray with them, and exhort them, and to impart to the poor slaves those little glimmer-ings of light from another world, which had reached my own eye. In a few years I became quite an esteemed preacher among them, and I will not believe it is vanity which leads me to think I was useful to some.[146]

At this time, Henson entered into an arrangement with his master, where-by he might purchase his freedom for the sum of four hundred fifty dollars, as he was able to earn money enough by preaching to save up towards this sum. Unfortunately for him, however, his master exchanged him and some other slaves with his brother, a slaveholder near Louisville, Kentucky. In the process of returning to Maryland to obtain his papers of manumission "in due form of law" in March of 1829, Henson suffered cruel trickery at his master's hands. Henson had paid him $350 in cash, plus a note for the remaining hundred dollars, and had taken his master's advice about not traveling with his free papers in his pocket, letting his master enclose them in a letter to his brother instead. He was tricked into remaining a slave as he reached the Kentucky plantation:

> It so happened that the boat which took me down from Louisville, landed me about dark, and my walk of five miles brought me to the plantation at bedtime. I went directly to my own cabin, where I found my wife and little ones well; and of course, we had a good deal to communicate to each other. Letters had reached the "great house," as the master's was always called, long before I had arrived, telling them what I had been doing, and the children of the family had been eager to communicate the great news to my wife—how I had been preaching, and raising money, and making a bargain for my freedom. It was not long before Charlotte began to tell me with much excitement what she had heard, and to question me about how I had raised the money I had paid, and how I expected to get the remainder, of the thousand dollars, I was to give for my freedom. I could scarcely believe my ears; but before telling her how the case exactly was, I questioned her again and again as to what she had heard. . . . I began to perceive the trick that had been played upon me, and to see the management by which Isaac R. had contrived that the only evidence of my freedom should be kept from every eye but that of his brother Amos, who was instructed to retain it till I had made up six hundred and fifty dollars, the balance I was reported to have agreed to pay. Indignation is a faint word to express my deep sense of such villainy. I was without the means of setting myself right. The only witness to the truth was my friend Frank, who was a thousand miles off; and I could neither write to him, nor get any one else to do it.[147]

Sad as was Henson's heart at this discovery that freedom was thus to be stolen from him, it was soon to know even deeper distress. His master Amos, troubled by the sight of the man whom both he and his brother had tricked, sent Henson down to New Orleans to be sold, although they did not tell him so when he left Louisville. But his master was taken deathly ill of a stomach disorder in New Orleans the night before Henson was to be placed on the auction block. We find Henson arriving back in Louisville twelve days later:

> By eight o'clock in the morning he was utterly prostrate; his head was on my lap, and he was begging me to help him, to do something for him, to save him. The tables were turned. He was now rather more dependent on me than I had been upon him the day before. He entreated me to dispatch matters, to sell the flat boat, in which we two had been living by ourselves for some days, and to get him and

his trunk, containing the proceeds of the trip, on board the steamer as quick as possible, and especially not to desert him so long as he lived, nor to suffer his body, if he died, to be thrown into the river.[148]

Henson nursed his master night and day, as the boat went up the river; and when they arrived at the dock, which was five miles from the house, he fitted up a stretcher and got a "party of slaves belonging to the estate to form relays for the purpose" of carrying it home. The arrival has its full share of irony:

> As we approached the house, the surprise at seeing me back again, and the perplexity to imagine what I was bringing along, with such a party, were extreme; but the discovery was soon made which explained the strange appearance; and the grief of father and mother, and brothers and sisters, made itself seen and heard. Loud and long were the lamentations over poor Amos; and when the family came a little to themselves, great were the commendations bestowed upon me, for my care of him and of the property.
>
> We arrived home about the tenth of July, but it was not till the middle of August that Amos was well enough to move out of his chamber, though he had been convalescent all the while. As soon as he could speak, he told all I had done for him, and said, "If I had sold him, I should have died;" but it never seemed to occur to him or the rest of the family that they were under any, the slightest obligation to me on that account. I had done well as a slave, and to have it acknowledged, and to be praised for it, was compensation enough for me. My merits . . . seemed only to enhance my money value to them.[149]

A plan whereby he might make his escape from slavery now occupied Henson's whole thought, as he realized that he had nothing to hope for from his master but sale "in the highest market." When he had fully devised the plan, he told it to his wife, who at first was "too much terrified by the dangers of the attempt" to do anything but try to dissuade him from his purpose. Henson explained and explained the matter to her, but she could not agree to the wisdom of the plan. We watch him win the argument:

> I explained to her the liability we were in of being separated from our children as well as from each other; and presented every argument which had weighed with my own mind, and had at last decided me. She had not gone through my trials, and female timidity overcame her sense of the evils she had experienced. I argued the matter with her . . . till I was satisfied that argument alone would not prevail; and then I said to her, very deliberately, that though it was a cruel thing for me to part with her, yet I would do it, and take all

the children with me but the youngest, rather than run the risk of
forcible separation from them all, and of a much worse captivity
besides, which we were constantly exposed to here. She wept and
entreated, but found I was resolute, and after a whole night spent in
talking over the matter, I left her to go to my work for the day. I
had not gone far when I heard her voice calling me;—I waited till
she came up to me, and then, finding me as determined as ever, she
said, at last, she would go with me. It was an immense relief to my
nerves, and my tears flowed as fast as hers had done before. I rode
off with a heart a good deal lighter.[150]

As Henson was overseer on the plantation, he was riding about every day
from one part to another of the five square miles of the plantation. His cabin
was situated close by the boat landing and all of his family were there with
the mother except their oldest son, who was houseboy for Master Amos.
Charlotte had given her consent to her husband to go with him on a Thursday
morning. Henson planned to leave on the coming Saturday night, as it would
then be several days before he would be missed, and they could thereby get
a good start. There is nothing in literature quite like the story of their escape:

Some time previously I had got my wife to make me a large knap-
sack, big enough to hold the two smallest children; and I had
arranged it that she should lead the second boy, while the oldest was
stout enough to go by himself, and to help me carry the necessary
food. I used to pack the little ones on my back, of an evening, and
trot round the cabin with them, and go some little distance from it,
in order to accustom both them and myself to the task before us.

At length the eventful night came, I went up to the house to ask
leave to take Tom home with me, that he might have his clothes
mended. No objection was made, and I bade Master Amos "good
night" for the last time. It was about the middle of September, and
by nine o'clock in the evening all was ready. It was a dark, moonless
night, and we got into the little skiff in which I had induced a
fellow-slave to take us across the river. It was an agitating and
solemn moment. The good fellow who was rowing us over, said this
affair might end in this death; "but," said he, "you will not be
brought back alive, will you?" "Not if I can help it," I answered.
"And if you are overpowered and return," he asked, "will you conceal my part of the business?" "That I will do, so help me God," I
replied. "Then I am easy," he answered, "and wish you success."
We landed on the Indiana shore, and I began to feel that I was my
own master. But in what circumstances of fear and misery still! We
were to travel by night, and rest by day, in the woods and bushes.[151]

About a month later, on the twenty-eighth of October, 1830, the doughty little family reached Canada, weary from the strain and rigors of the fearful trip, afraid at every moment that pursuers would pounce upon them, but with the thrilling hope that God would see them through their trials to safety in a land of freedom. Soon they were settled, Tom and a younger child were put in school, and Henson alternately preached and worked at day labor, to make their living. There is an amusing account of Tom's attempt to teach his father to read, the twelve-year-old and the forty-two-year-old having extreme difficulty over the pedagogical method to be used. Henson refused to be taught by means of anything but the pages of the Bible. Finally, Tom had to give in to his persuasive father's determination, in spite of the almost insurmountable difficulty of teaching him to read by this dubious method.[152] Fugitive slaves kept coming from all parts of the southern Canadian boundary, and for a person of the leadership qualitites of Henson there was much to do. In June of 1838, the slaves held a convention in London, Upper Canada, to discuss the disposition of a sum of fifteen hundred dollars raised in England for their relief. Henson soon began making periodic trips to Boston in quest of additional funds for the fugitives. It was the beginning of twenty years of identification with the needs of the fugitive, to be crowned by fame and happy fortune during the last twenty years of Josiah Henson's very long and exceptionally eventful life.

As entertaining as the other strikingly popular slave narratives published in 1849 is *The Narrative of Henry Box Brown, Who Escaped from Slavery Enclosed in a Box Three Feet Long, Two Feet Wide, and Two-and-a-Half Feet High, Written from a Statement of Facts Made by Himself.*[153] The new brand of excitement which "Box" Brown introduced into abolitionist circles with his odyssey through New England and the British Isles is related elsewhere in this study.[154] His narrative was taken down by the publisher Charles Stearns in Boston, and it is easy to separate the passages literally the product of dictation from the passages helped out generously by Northern inspiration, such as the opening sentences of the first chapter:

> I entered the world a slave—in the midst of a country where most
> honoured writings declare that all men have a right to liberty—but
> had imprinted upon my body no mark which could be made to
> signify that my destiny was to be that of a bondman. Neither was
> there any angel stood by, at the hour of my birth, to hand my body
> over, by the authority of heaven, to be the property of a fellow-
> man; no, but I was a slave because my countrymen had made it
> lawful, in utter contempt of the declared will of heaven, for the
> strong to lay hold of the weak and to buy and to sell them as mar-
> ketable goods.[155]

There is no literary swelling when "Box" Brown speaks forth on the subject of his plan for his escape from slavery. The account of that escape is one of the treasures of the literature of the slave.

"Box" Brown, whose identity is linked in abolitionist history with the spectacular means of his escape, was born in 1815 on a plantation belonging to a Mr. Barut, near Richmond, Virginia. His master was a kind enough man, but his advanced age made it necessary for him to have overseers to superintend his slaves, and the overseers were often cruel. His brother had become so convinced that slaveholding was a sin that he had emancipated forty slaves, paying their expenses to a free state. Mr. Barut died, and "Box" Brown and his mother were hopeful of being freed. Instead, however, "Box" Brown was left to his master's son, William, to serve as a plough boy. They moved to Richmond about eighteen months before the Nat Turner insurrection, the effect of which upon the treatment of the Negroes, slave and free, was felt by the lad, who says:

> I did not know then precisely what was the cause of this excitement,
> for I could get no satisfactory information from my master, only
> he said that some of the slaves had plotted to kill their owners. . . .
> Many slaves were whipped, hung, and cut down with the swords in
> the streets; and some that were found away from their quarters
> after dark, were shot; the whole city was in the utmost excitement,
> and the whites seemed terrified beyond measure.[156]

A slave could not expect even normal sympathy for his condition. After the Turner incident, however, "Box" Brown ventured to trust a Richmond storekeeper with his desire to make his escape from slavery, which had become unbearable to him ever since his wife had been sold South five months before. He had got together a little money, and he wanted advice as to what he could do. The storekeeper did not disappoint the "favorable opinion of his integrity" that "Box" Brown had already made of him in the course of purchasing provisions from him over a considerable period of time. He was surprised, however, that "Box" Brown should trust him so. We read:

> The man asked me if I was not afraid to speak that way to him; I
> said no, for I imagined he believed that every man had a right to
> liberty. He said I was quite right, and asked me how much money
> I would give him if he would assist me to get away. I told him that I
> had one hundred and sixty-six dollars and that I would give him the
> half: so we ultimately agreed that I should have his service in the
> attempt for eighty-six dollars. Now I only wanted to fix upon a
> plan.[157]

One day while he was at work in his tobacconist business his thought "eagerly feasting upon the idea of freedom," the idea suddenly flashed across his mind of shutting himself up in a box and getting himself conveyed "as dry goods to a free state." Advised by the storekeeper to obtain permission to be absent from his work for a few days in order to keep down suspicion until he had "fairly started on the road to liberty," "Box" Brown went to the overseer with the complaint that he had "a gathered finger" that was paining him so that he could not work. The overseer, a Mr. Allen, looked at the finger and decided it was not serious enough to warrant his stopping work. Thereupon "Box" Brown enlisted the aid of a Dr. Smith, another friend who was interested in his plans, and procured from him some oil of vitriol to aggravate the condition of the infected finger. We sympathize with him, in his nervous hurry:

> In my hurry I dropped rather much and made it worse than there
> was any occasion for, in fact it was very soon eaten in to the bone,
> and on presenting it again to Mr. Allen, I obtained the permission
> required, with the advice that I should go home and get a poultice
> of flax-meal to it, and keep it well poulticed until it got better.[158]

The box which he had obtained measured 3 feet 1 inch by 2 feet 6 inches by 2 feet. The journey in that box, in that unprecedented quest for freedom, begins:

> On the morning of the twenty-ninth day of March, 1849, I went into
> the box—having previously bored three gimlet holes opposite my
> face, for air, and provided myself with a bladder of water, both for
> the purpose of quenching my thirst and for wetting my face, should
> I feel getting faint. I took the gimlet also with me, in order that I
> might bore more holes if I found I had not sufficient air. Being thus
> equipped for the battle of liberty, my friends nailed down the lid
> and had me conveyed to the Express Office, which was about a mile
> distant from the place where I was packed. I had no sooner arrived
> at the office than I was turned heels up, while some person nailed
> something on the lid of the box. I was then put upon a waggon and
> driven off to the depot with my head down, and I had no sooner
> arrived at the depot, than the man who drove the waggon tumbled
> me roughly into the baggage car, where, however, I happened to
> fall on my right side.
>   The next place we arrived at was Potomac Creek, where the bag-
> gage had to be removed from the cars, to be put on board the
> steamer; where I was again placed with my head down, and in this
> dreadful position had to remain nearly an hour and a half, which,
> from the sufferings I had thus to endure, seemed like an age to me.

I felt my eyes swelling as if they would burst from their sockets; and the veins on my temples were dreadfully distended with pressure of blood upon my head. In this position I attempted to lift my hand to my face but I had no power to move it; I felt a cold sweat coming over me which seemed to be a warning that death was about to terminate my earthly miseries, but as I feared even that less than slavery, I resolved to submit to the will of God, and, under the influence of that impression, I lifted up my soul in prayer to God, who alone was able to deliver me. My cry was soon heard, for I could hear a man saying to another, that he had travelled a long way and had been standing there two hours, and he would like to get something to sit down; so perceiving my box, standing on end, he threw it down and then two sat upon it. I was relieved from a state of agony which may be more easily imagined than described. I could now listen to the men talking, and heard one of them asking the other what he supposed the box contained; his companion replied he guessed it was "THE MAIL." I too thought it was a mail but not such a mail as he supposed it to be.[159]

Washington was the next stop for the "Box," which was carried by wagon from the steamboat to the depot, this time "right side up with care." The instructions, however, did not save him from being thrown from the wagon onto the platform by the driver's helper, who replied to the driver's warning that he might break something if he slung it off carelessly, "That it did not matter if he broke all that was in it, the railway company [was] able enough to pay for it." So he threw the "Box" onto the platform! We continue to read:

No sooner were these words spoken than I began to tumble from the waggon, and falling on the end where my head was, I could hear my neck give a crack, as if it had been snapped asunder, and I was knocked completely insensible. The first thing I heard, after that, was some person saying, "There is no room for that box, it will have to remain and be sent through to-morrow with the luggage train; but the Lord had not quite forsaken me, for in answer to my earnest prayer He so ordered affairs that I should not be left behind; and I now heard a man say that the box had come with the express, and it must be sent on. I was then tumbled into the car with my head downwards again, but the car had not proceeded far before, more luggage having to be taken in, my box got shifted about and so happened to turn upon its right side; and in this position I remained till I got to Philadelphia.[160]

The "Box" lay in the luggage depot in Philadelphia until seven in the evening, at which time "Box" Brown heard someone inquire for such a box as his, and he was then placed in a wagon and conveyed to the house where his friend in Richmond had made arrangements for him to be received. We read of the journey's end:

> A number of persons soon collected round the box after it was taken into the house, but as I did not know what was going on I kept myself quiet. I heard a man say, "Let us rap upon the box and see if he is alive;" and immediately a rap ensued and a voice said, tremblingly, "Is all right within?" to which I replied—"All right." The joy of the friends was very great; when they heard that I was alive they soon managed to break open the box, and then came my resurrection from the grave of slavery. I rose a freeman, but I was too weak, by reason of my long confinement in that box, to be able to stand; so I immediately swooned away.[161]

Original as "Box" Brown's plan seemed to all who heard it, the very same plan had been used, though unsuccessfully, four years earlier. We read in *The Liberator* of July 25, 1845, of the ill-fated venture of a slave in Memphis, who had hoped to reach Cincinnati by way of a steamship and the "Box" formula. The slave, who belonged to a Mr. Job Lewis and was hired out in Memphis, had followed the suggestion of a free Negro, John Bennet of Louisville, that he let Bennet box him up and ship him on the first boat bound for Cleveland. But Bennet had forgot to put any water in the box, so that after about two hours, unable to stand it any longer, the slave had called out from the box, "Open the door!" Though the boat was thrown into consternation, the box was finally opened, and out fell "a great strapping Negro, steaming like the escape pipe of a steamboat." The box had contained air holes, a quantity of moss, a few dozen crackers, and some plates, but for want of some water, the venture was lost. The slave was not only recaptured, but forced to give the name of his helper, who was arrested and probably reduced to slavery.[162]

Need for water also caused failure in the case of the slave discovered packed in a box on the steamship *Roanoke*, arriving in New York from Virginia, October 5, 1856. The slave forced the lid, as he was nearly suffocated. He was sent back to Virginia.[163] The fourth occurrence of the "Box" formula was reported by Mrs. Child in 1860. A slave girl of eighteen, betrothed to a free black man in Baltimore who wanted to marry her in a land of freedom, was packed into a small box lined with hay for the train trip from Baltimore to Philadelphia. The girl almost suffocated. Hay got into her eyes and nose, making it almost impossible to avoid choking, and she was in addition terrified for fear that they should decide to examine the box out of curiosity over its weight. At the end of the two-hour ride, when her fiance rushed to rescue her, he found that she had developed a terrible brain fever. Though she lived to recover, her face aged ten years, and her hair turned gray.[164] Whether there was a germinal connection between any of these attempts and Henry "Box" Brown's story will never be known. As the representative of one method of escape that was doubtless tried more times than are here recorded, his breath-taking narrative is a valuable contribution.

Although scores of short accounts of the kidnapping of free Negroes and their wretched lives as slaves appear in the antislavery journals throughout the period of their existence, no book-length narrative of a kidnapped Negro appeared until 1853, when Solomon Northup's *Twelve Years a Slave* was published.[165] The book became popular over night. It appeared simultaneously in Auburn and Buffalo, and in London scarcely a week later. The first issues at each publishing house were speedily exhausted. The book was dedicated to Mrs. Stowe, and it undoubtedly owed much of its initial success to the publicity given by the reviewers to the fact that the enforced slavery of Northup took place in the same Red River section of Louisiana that hundreds of thousands of readers were becoming acquainted with in the pages of *Uncle Tom's Cabin*. But the fact that there was really a fundamental difference between the experience of Solomon Northup and the experience of any of the other slave narrators was soon sufficient reason in itself for *Twelve Years a Slave* to continue to be ranked among the best-sellers. All of the other slave narrators had been born slaves, but Solomon Northup had been stolen and sold into slavery.

One of the earliest emphases of Garrison in the pages of *The Liberator* had been upon the danger to the rights of the entire Negro population in the United States from the rapidly increasing practice of kidnapping and selling free Negroes into slavery. This evil practice had been going on since the beginning of the slave trade and had included the kidnapping and enslaving of other races as well as Africans. In fact, two very popular publications of the eighteenth century, erroneously listed as narratives by Americn Negro slaves, were accounts of the kidnapping and selling into slavery of a British peer and a Scotsman, respectively, in Virginia and in Pennsylvania![166] It required long, tedious litigation, ending finally in victory through the decree of the Supreme Court of Louisiana, before one Salome Muller, a German girl brought to this country with her parents in 1818 at the age of five and kidnapped and sold as a slave in Louisiana, could obtain her release from her status "as an African slave for more than twenty-five years." The case is disclosed in the "Suit for Freedom of Salome Muller vs. Louis Belmonti and John Fitzmiller . . . Decided by the Final Decree of the Supreme Court of Louisiana, June 23, 1845."[167] Probably unknown hundreds of free American Negroes disappeared into slavery in this way after suppression of the African slave trade in the United States by law in 1808. This does not take into account the reducing of free Negro vagrants or other persons unfortunately brought under arrest in Southern states and sold as slaves to pay their bill for room and board in jail. Kidnapping was a separate racket aimed at the same goal: swelling the ranks of slave laborers. The reader may recall James Curry's loss of his father in this way.[168]

Many such cases are recorded in the antislavery journals. There was the case of the free colored woman living in Westchester, hired by a visiting clergyman from Richmond to go to Virginia with him as his servant. She spent the rest of her life as a slave, unable to make contact with her people in order to be rescued.[169] There was the Boston free Negro, employed on a ship bound for South Carolina and Georgia and kidnapped in Virginia. He was sold as a slave to a Mississippi trader and spent thirty years as s slave before he could escape.[170] The whole town of Poughkeepsie participated in collecting the sum of one hundred dollars to post as a reward for the return of an eleven-year-old free Negro lad, kidnapped by a Kentucky trader in horses and Negroes. The boy was finally found and brought back after having been sold in Louisville.[171] One John Williams of New Jersey was seized as a boy and sold into slavery in New Orleans but later was rescued by a Newport captain when he was about twenty-eight years of age.[172] A free Negro woman, recently widowed in Maryland, was seized with her infant daughter and sold into slavery in Georgia, despite her violent efforts to regain her freedom.[173] One young free Negro visiting in New Orleans was kidnapped and sold into slavery. He was handcuffed and chained for about five months for attempting to communicate with his people by writing a note with a stick and blood drawn from his own veins.[174] The abolitionist Henry B. Stanton could never forget the pathetic little family of a "widow" and four small children whom he visited in Cincinnati upon learning that the father of the family had been kidnapped. "Papa stole," the little children kept wailing.[175] And we must not forget to include in this record of infamy the experience that almost befell the newly free Olaudah Equiano in Georgia back in the 1780s:

> One day [relates Equiano], while I was a little way out of the town of Savannah, I was beset by two white men, who meant to play their usual tricks with me in the way of kidnapping. As soon as these men accosted me, one of them said to the other, "This is the very fellow we were looking for, that you lost." And the other swore immediately that I was the identical person. On this they made up to me, and were about to handle me; but I told them to be still; and keep off; for I had seen those kind [sic] of tricks played upon other free blacks, and they must not think to serve me so. At this they paused a little, and one said to the other—it will not do; and the other answered that I talked two [sic] good English. I replied, I believed I did; and I had also with me a revengeful stick equal to the occasion; and my mind was likewise good. Happily however it was not used; and, after we had talked together a little in this manner, the rogues left me.[175]

Solomon Northup's experience was ideal for a slave narrative thriller. He was born to free Negroes living in Essex County, New York, about 1808. In 1829 he married and, in the winter of 1841, moved his wife and children to Saratoga Springs. Two men approached him with the offer of a job driving a team South for a dollar a day. Northup accepted the offer, not being averse to seeing more of the country than his own state, which he had never left before, and took out free papers when he got as far as New York City to show that he was not a slave. He then drove the team on down to Washington City, putting up for the night at Gadsby's Hotel. This was on April 2, 1841.

Taken sick with severe pains in the stomach soon after arriving at the hotel, Northup went to bed. When some persons came into his room with some medicine they were offering to ease his pain, he took it. This was the last thing he had any recollection of until he discovered himself lying hand-cuffed and chained to the floor of a slave pen run by a Mr. Williams in Washington City. A few hours after he had made this unbelievable discovery, a slave dealer named James Burch came in. Northup asked him why the irons had been put on him and told Burch that he wanted them off. He was told he had no business to ask questions. Northup answered that he was a free man, born in New York State. Burch then called in a man by the name of Ebenezer Rodbury. The two men stripped Northup and then administered a severe beating of more than a hundred lashes. Burch swore that he would kill him if he were ever to tell anyone that he was a free man. He remained in the slave pen about ten days, while it was being filled with others like himself. Then they were all taken away by night, handcuffed and shackled, down to Richmond by riverboat. At Richmond he was loaded, with forty-eight others, onto the brig *Orleans*, bound for the city of New Orleans. Before the brig docked at that city, they were unloaded by one Theophilus Freeman, a former partner with Burch, and whisked away to a slave pen. Northup was taken sick with smallpox and sent to a hospital, where he remained two or three weeks. He was sold soon after he left the hospital to a Mr. Ford of Rapides Parish, Louisiana. He lived with Mr. Ford for about a year, working in his business as a carpenter, and was fairly well treated. But Ford encountered financial difficulties and had to sell Northup. A Mr. Tibaut became his second owner. Tibaut sold him in a short time to the "Mr. Gooch" of Northup's narrative. His real name was Mr. Edwin Eppes, of Bayou Beouf, Louisiana, the owner of a cotton plantation about one hundred and thirty miles from the mouth of Red River. There Northup was to spend nine harrowing years in a "perpetual nightmare" of slave life.

It was a plantation on the same order as Francis Whitfield's in Henry Bibb's narrative, with the same type of accommodations for the workers as we have found the slaves "enjoying" where Grandy lived, and Henson, and Curry, and many, many others: no floor, no chair, no bed, no mattress, no clothes, and almost no food. The slaves were driven from sunup to sundown, beaten fiendishly to extract labor from them, no matter how hungry or how sick they were, and punished even more dreadfully for any manifestations of normal desires for social contacts—visiting one's mother on an adjoining plantation or going to prayer meeting. Northup "worked up to" the position of overseer, which proved more revolting to him than his position in the ranks, as he was forced by Eppes to beat the slaves "to order," their bodies tied and hung up or stretched taut between stakes or worse. He had tried, whenever possible, to get word to Northern friends to tell them where he was, but he had no luck. One letter, however, finally made its way out of the dangerous labyrinth in which he was confined. Sent from Bayou Beouf in August, 1842, it told of his plight:

> Mr. William Penny, or Mr. Lewis Parker.
>   Gentlemen: It having been a long time since I have seen or heard from you, and not knowing that you are living, it is with uncertainty that I write to you; but the necessity of the case must be my excuse. Having been born free just across the river from you, I am certain you know me; and I am here now a slave. I wish you to obtain free papers for me, and forward them to me at Marksville, Louisiana, Parish of Avovelles . . .[176]

His friends received the letter and straightway set about applying to Governor Hunt of New York State for permission to send an agent to Louisiana for the purpose of procuring Solomon Northup's freedom. That freedom was finally obtained when the case was tried before the court in Washington, D.C. Northup's story of his experience was written at once in order to take advantage of the publicity that had come to the case through reports in the New York *Times* and other public journals, as well as in the antislavery press. Then began Northup's tour of the Northern States as a lecturer on his experience. A typical reaction to the tour can be found in a letter to Garrison two years after the first appearance of *Twelve Years a Slave*:

> *Twelve Years a Slave* has been widely read in New England, and no narrative of man's experience as a slave . . . is more touching, or better calculated to expose the true character and designs of slaveholders. But it is far more potent to see the man, and hear him, in his clear, manly, straightforward way, speak of slavery as he experienced it, and as he saw it in others. Those who have read his Narrative can scarce fail to desire to see the man . . . and to hear his story from his own lips.[177]

Three years after the appearance of Northup's narrative, the second book-length account of the experience of being kidnapped into slavery was published under the title, *The Kidnapped and the Ransomed, Being the Personal Recollections of Peter Still and His Wife "Vina," after Forty Years of*

Slavery.[178] Three editions were exhausted during the first year of publication, and the book continued to enjoy good sales, despite the competition with a veritable avalanche of "slave novels" descending upon the public.

After promising the "lovers of exciting adventure very much in the ensuing volume to gratify their taste," the Reverend Samuel J. May, in his introduction to *The Kidnapped and the Ransomed*, called special attention to its human interest qualitites, saying:

> In this narrative will also be found, incidentally, but very clearly given, intimations of many excellences that are latent, as well as lively sketches of some that are patent, in the Negro variety of our race—indeed, all the qualities of our common, and of our uncommon humanity—persistence in the pursuit of a desired object; ingenuity in the device of plans for its attainment; self-possession and self-command that can long keep a cherished purpose unrevealed; a deep, instinctive faith in God; and patience under hardship and hope deferred, which never dies; and, withal, a joyousness which, like a life-preserver, bears one above the dark waves of unparalleled trouble.[179]

We venture the opinion that it was on the strength of this sound appreciation of the slave narrative that this particular narrative was recently chosen for reprinting as the first in a projected series of publications that promote racial understanding.[180] The statement is the best we have found to characterize the slave narrative in general. But *The Kidnapped and the Ransomed* is by no means the best representative of the genre to be found.

The role of Mrs. Kate E. R. Pickard in connection with Peter Still's story is the same as that held by other scribes and editors of slave narratives, though the position of her name in the author's place is a little confusing. With the rapid development of literacy among fugitive slaves in the 1850s, it became more and more possible for the slave to prepare his own manuscript. Because there were enough Negro authors represented in the book stalls for the abolitionists' purpose of showing the world what the Negro slave could do, the "ghost writers" could be named on the front cover if they so chose. Mrs. Pickard herself is an interesting character. Her acquaintance with Peter Still dated back to the years when she was a teacher in a select "Female Seminary" in Tuscumbia, Alabama, where Still was the slave porter. The fact that she never at that time "suspected his hunger for liberty" renders all the more remarkable the sensitiveness to the problems of the slave that she later developed. The volume was dedicated:

> To the memory of Levin Still, and of all the unransomed, who like him have fallen even while panting to be free, and who now lie in nameless unsought graves, the victims of American slavery.[181]

It was completed four years after Peter Still's "ransom," and its object in part was to help him purchase the remainder of his family. Kidnapped in early childhood from the doorstep of his home in New Jersey, he had spent more than forty years as a slave in Kentucky and Alabama, with all the usual experiences of heartache and cruelty. Mr. May's description lingers in the mind:

> Within the last four years, many hundreds, probably thousands, of persons in our nominally free States, have seen Peter Still, a neat, staid black man, going from city to city, town to town, house to house, asking assistance to enable him to purchase the freedom of his wife and children. He has always been grateful for the smallest favors, and never morose when utterly denied.[182]

Faced with thousands of pages of the slave narratives of the last ten years before Emancipation, the atrocities of that worst of systems, human slavery, form an unmistakable pattern, a network of bull whips and iron chains and auction blocks and slave coffles and empty stomachs and broken hearts. The atrocities are not all the story. Good masters do exist, and good food, and good times. But they do not fit the dominant pattern. The finest passages in the slave narratives tell of the direst times.

The Experience and Personal Narrative of Uncle Tom Jones, Who Was for Forty Years a Slave, published first in New York in 1854,[183] contains a series of vignettes to trim the general story of slavery. The slave family is all together in one of the early pictures, as the young daughter, Sarah, is being whipped by their master, tied up in the smoke house, entirely naked:

> I stood by my mother, who was wringing her hands in an agony of grief, at the cruelties which her tender child was enduring. I do not know what my sister had then done for which she was then whipped: but I remember that her body was marked and scarred for weeks after that terrible scourging, and that our parents always after *seemed* to hold their breath when they spoke of it. Sarah was the last of the family who was sold; and my poor mother never looked up after this final act of cruelty was accomplished.[184]

We see a devoted father and mother:

> Father and mother tried to make it a happy place for their dear children. They worked late into the night many and many a time to get a little simple furniture for their home . . . and they spent many hours of willing toil to stop up the chinks between the logs of their poor hut, that they and their children might be protected from the storm and the cold. I can testify, from my own painful experience, to the deep and fond affection which the slave cherishes in his heart for its home and its dear ones. We have no other tie to link us to the

human family, but our fervent love for those who are with us and
of us in relations of sympathy and devotedness, in wrongs and
wretchedness. My dear parents were conscious of the desperate and
incurable woe of their position and destiny; and of the lot of inevitable suffering in store for their beloved children. They talked
about our coming misery, and they lifted up their voices and wept
aloud, as they spoke of our being torn from them and sold off to the
dreaded slave-trader, perhaps never again to see them or hear from
them a word of fond love. I have heard them speak of their willingness to bear their own sorrows without complaint, if only we, their
dear children, could be safe from the wretchedness before us. And I
remember, and *now* fully understand, as I did not then, the sad and
tearful look they would fix upon us when we were gathered round
them and running on with our foolish prattle.[185]

The boy Thomas was sold to a Mr. Jones of Wilmington, North Carolina,
about forty-five miles away from the plantation where his parents were. His
leave-taking from his mother was marked by her master's order to stop
bawling and his striking her cruelly as he sent her into the house. Thomas's
job in his new "home" was chiefly to tend his master's store. A friendship
developed between him and a little white boy named Hiram Bricket, which
started him on the road to literacy. The little boy was forbidden to teach
him as soon as his elders discovered that he was doing so. Young Jones then
had to forge ahead the best he could, alone, with no beginning but a knowledge of the alphabet. We watch him "slip to learn":

After I was deprived of my kind little teacher, I plodded on the best
way I could, and in this way I got into words of five syllables. I got
some little time to study by daylight in the morning, before any of
my master's family had risen. I got a moment's opportunity at noon,
and sometimes at night. During the day I was in the back store a
good deal, and whenever I thought I could have five minutes to myself, I would take my book and try to learn a little in reading and
spelling. If I heard James, or master Jones, or any customer coming
in, I would drop my book among the barrels, and pretend to be very
busy shovelling the salt or doing some other work. Several times I
came very near being detected. My master suspected something,
because I was so still in the back room, and a number of times he
came very slily to see what I was about. But at such times I was
always so fortunate as to hear his tread or see his shadow on the wall
in time to hide away my book.[186]

Not *always* so fortunate, though, as we soon find in a passage without
peer in the literature of the struggle for education:

I was at the store early one morning, and, thinking I was safe from all danger for a few minutes, had seated myself in the back store, on one of the barrels, to study in my precious spelling-book. While I was absorbed in this happy enterprise, my master came in, much earlier than usual, and I did not hear him. He came directly into the back store. I saw his shadow on the wall, just in time to throw my book over in among the barrels, before he could see what it was, although he saw that I had thrown something quickly away. His suspicion was aroused. He said that I had been stealing something out of the store, and fiercely ordered me to get what I threw away just as he was coming in at the door. Without a moment's hesitation, I determined to save my precious book and my future opportunities to learn out of it. I knew if my book was discovered that all was lost, and I felt prepared for any hazard or suffering rather than give up my book and my hopes of improvement. So I replied at once to his questions, that I had not thrown anything away; that I had not stolen anything from the store; that I did not have anything in my hands which I could throw away when he came in. My master declared in a high passion, that I was lying, and ordered me to begin and roll away the barrels. This I did; but managed to keep the book slipping along so that he could not see it, as he stood in the door-way. He charged me again with stealing and throwing something away, and I again denied the charge. In a great rage, he got down his long, heavy cow-hide, and ordered me to strip off my jacket and shirt, saying, with an oath, "I will make you tell me what it was you had when I came." I stripped myself, and came forward, according to his directions, at the same time denying his charge with great earnestness of tone, and look, and manner. He cut me on my naked back, perhaps thirty times, with great severity, making the blood flow freely. He then stopped, and asked me what I had thrown away as he came in. I answered again that I had thrown nothing away. He swore terribly, said he was certain I was lying, and declared he would kill me if I did not tell him the truth. He whipped me the second time with a greater severity, and at greater length, than before. He then repeated his question, and I answered again as before. I was determined to die, if I could possibly bear the pain, rather than give up my dear book. He whipped me the third time, with the same result as before, and then seizing hold of my shoulders, turned me round as though he would inflict on my quivering flesh still another scourging, but he saw the deep gashes he had already made, and the blood already flowing under his cruel infliction; and his stern purpose failed him. He said, "Why, Tom, I didn't think I had cut you so bad," and saying that, he stopped, and told me to put on my shirt

again. I did as he bade me, though my coarse shirt touching my raw
back put me to a cruel pain. He then went out, and I got my book
and hid it safely away before he came in again.[187]

His first wife was a talented seamstress named Lucilla, the slave of a Mrs.
Moore on a nearby plantation. They lived happily together for a few years,
and became the parents of two daughters and a son. When the son was still
a baby, however, Mrs. Moore moved away with them. We read of the loss of
his family:

> My dear wife and my precious children were seventy-four miles
> distant from me, carried away from me in utter scorn of my
> beseeching words. I was tempted to put an end to my wretched
> life. . . . A deep despair was in my heart, such as no one is called to
> bear in such cruel, crushing power as the poor slave, severed forever
> from the objects of his love by the cupidity of his brother. But that
> dark time of despair passed away, and I saw once more my wife and
> children. Mrs. Moore left Newbern for Tuscaloosa, Alabama, and
> passing through Wilmington on her journey, she spent one night in
> her old home. That night I passed with my wife and children. Lucilla
> had pined away under the agony of our separation even more than
> I had done. That night she wept on my bosom, and we mingled
> bitter tears together. Our dear children were baptized in the tears
> of agony that were wrung from our breaking hearts. The just God
> will remember that night in the last award that we and our oppres-
> sors are to receive.
>   The next morning Mrs. Moore embarked on board the packet. I
> followed my wife and children to the boat and parted from them
> without a word of farewell. Our sobs and tears were our only adieu.
> Our hearts were too full of anguish for any other expression of our
> hopeless woe. I have never seen that dear family since, nor have I
> heard from them.[188]

In the course of years, when he had been given the opportunity of hiring
out his time from his master on payment of one hundred and fifty dollars a
year, Jones married a slave who was hiring her time from her master for forty-
eight dollars a year. Three children were born to them. Fearful always of
repetition of the fate that befell his first family, he bought this second wife
for three hundred and fifty dollars. He sent her to Brooklyn, New York,
with their children when advised that they were in danger of reenslavement.
Then he himself ran away on board a turpentine brig. He had a perilous
journey, but "that, too, passed away," and he was reunited with his family.
    Herman Melville and the slave narrator John Thompson probably never
met, but they went whaling at the same time and were in the same ocean

together. *The Life of John Thompson, a Fugitive Slave; Containing His History of Twenty-Five Years in Bondage; and His Providential Escape, Written by Himself*[189] is a narrative of uncommon interest. Thompson wrote the book and found a printer for it himself, without benefit of editor or other advisory aid. The recital of the turbulent course of his life, from his birth in Maryland in 1812 as the slave of a she-devil named Mrs. Wagar to his audacious passage on board a whaler, was soon fascinating the abolitionist reading public. Like Tom Jones, he acquired the rudiments of learning while still a slave. A review of the narrative in a contemporary journal comments:

> The unusual opportunities which John Thompson enjoyed of acquiring an education by stealth have enabled him to tell his story in a clear, connected, and interesting manner. He seems to have belonged to a comparatively favored class of slaves, but yet suffered enough to drive him to the fearful risks which must always accompany flight from such slave States to free States. . . . We trust the Worcester people have the power as well as the will to protect him from further dangers.[190]

In the interest of parallel study with Tom Jones' sufferings in the cause of learning, we present John Thompson's experience when caught with a book:

> I spared no exertions to learn to read and write, both of which I could now do tolerably well; and although I spent all my Sundays in study, still, master did not know that I could do either. One day he sent me with a note to a gentleman, requiring an answer by the bearer. The answer I put into my pocket with some writing of my own, one of which was the copy of a pass I had received from my master long before, to go to visit a friend. This copy I accidentally handed him, instead of the answering note, not perceiving my mistake until he exclaimed, "What is this?" Immediately I discovered my mistake, and handed him the right paper. He kept both. At the time he said no more to me, but soon communicated the fact to his sister [Thompson's owner, who had hired him out to her brother], pressing her to sell me, which she at length consented to do, empowering him to transact the business in reference to the sale. The next morning, while I was preparing feed for the horses in the stables, he, with four other white men, armed with bludgeons and pistols, came upon me. . . . My hands were at once tied, after which I was taken to another part of the barn, where they commenced whipping me; but the switches proving brittle, two of them were broken at once. This so enraged my master, that he cursed the switches, and swore he had something that would not break. This was a cowhide, which he went and brought from the house, I mean-

while, hanging suspended between the heavens and the earth, for no crime save what he himself was guilty of, namely, education. He finally concluded, however, not to whip me, lest it might injure my sale, and therefore ordered one of the other slaves to take me down, and prepared to go to Alexandria.[191]

At the last moment, as they were setting out for the auction sale, a message came from his owner to her brother, saying that she had changed her mind about selling him.

One of the best of the descriptions of the helplessness of the slave girl is Thompson's account of his sister:

One day, during his wife's absence on a visit to her friends, being, as he thought, a good opportunity, [her master] tried to force my sister to submit to his wishes. This she defeated by a resistance so obstinate that he, becoming enraged, ordered two of his men to take her to the barn, where he generally whipped his slaves; there to strip off her clothes and whip her, which was done, until the blood stood in puddles under her feet.

Upon his wife's return, Mr. Thomas told her that my sister had been whipped for neglect of duty. Of this Mrs. Thomas did not complain, as she had no objection to necessary floggings. But similar scenes occurring quite often, our mistress began to suspect that sister was not in fault, especially as in her presence she never neglected her business, and these complaints only came in her absence. . . . Accordingly, she began to question her maid concerning her offences, who, fearing to tell her plainly, knowing it would be certain death to her, answered in low and trembling terms, "I must not tell you, but you may know what it is all for. If I have done anything, Madam, contrary to your wishes, and do not suit you, please sell me, but do not kill me without cause. Old Mistress, your mother, who is dead, and I trust in heaven, took great pains to bring me up a virtuous girl, and I will die before I will depart from her dying counsel, given, as you well know, while we were standing by her dying bed."

These words so affected Mrs. Thomas, that she fainted and was carried to her bed. To which she was confined by illness five or six weeks. Her husband's conduct still persisted in, finally caused her death, which occurred four years after.[192]

Thompson was finally warned by his uncle, a free Negro living nearby, that constables were on the lookout for him on the accusation of some slaveholders that he had been writing passes for fugitive slaves. A reward of three hundred dollars had been posted, and the uncle begged him to flee for his life at once, ere it be too late. Thompson had a premonition of some such turn of affairs, and the way in which he reacted to his uncle's frantic pleas to hurry away reveals the strange beauty as well as power of many a slave's belief in God:

> Now my morning feelings were fully explained. I knew it was the hand of God, working in my behalf; it was his voice warning me to escape from the danger towards which I was hastening. . . . I felt renewed confidence and faith, for I believed that God was in my favor, and now was the time to test the matter. About two rods from Uncle Harry's house I fell upon my knees, and with hands uplifted to high heaven, related all the late circumstances to the Great King, saying that the whole world was against me without a cause, besought his protection, and solemnly promised to serve him all the days of my life. I received a spiritual answer of approval; a voice like thunder seeming to enter my soul, saying, I am your God and am with you; though the whole world be against you, I am more than the world; though wicked men hunt you, trust in me, for I am the Rock of your Defence.
>
> Had my pursuers then been near, they must have heard me, for I praised God at the top of my voice. I was determined to take him at his word, and risk the consequences.[193]

Thompson would not leave the district until he could see or hear from his mother. So, despite his uncle's worried pleading, he remained hidden in the nearby woods until the next night, when he returned to his uncle's house. We read:

> I found her there waiting for me. She had brought food in her pocket for me. . . . My mother appeared almost heart-broken. She did not wish me to go away, and had been to Master Richard about me, who had promised to inquire into the accusations against me, and if there was not sufficient proof to substantiate them, they could not injure me. But he recommended that I should keep out of sight for the present, and if he could do nothing else in my favor, he would so manage, that when he was ready to go South, I could be off with him. I thought this was a very wise plan, too, in case I desired to go South; but I had fully resolved to go North.[194]

Shortly after this episode we were surprised to find Thompson on board a whaler, booked as ship's steward! As we might expect, the first thing that befalls him is seasickness. The story of the "working of the hand of God" in connection with this intrepid adventure to escape recapture into slavery brings into the general picture of slavery a representative of a group of men frequently appearing in the slave narratives, notably as aides in time of dire need to Robert Voorhis and Tom Jones: the friendly sea captain. The "old salt" in Thompson's case is quite angry when we first meet him:

> The captain . . . came into the cabin very angry, and said to me, "What is the matter with you," I told him I was sick. "Have you ever been at sea before," he asked. I told him I never had, upon which he asked how I came to ship as a steward, I answered, "I am a fugitive slave from Maryland, and have a family in Philadelphia; but fearing to remain there any longer, I thought I would go a whaling voyage, as being the place where I stood least chance of being arrested by slave hunters. I had become somewhat experienced in cooking by working in hotels, insomuch that I thought I could fill the place of steward."
>
> This narrative seemed to touch his heart, for his countenance at once assumed a pleasing expression. Thus God stood between me and him, and worked in my defence.
>
> He told me that, had circumstances been different, he should have flogged me for my imposition; but now bade me to go on deck, where I could inhale the fresh air, and I should soon be well. I did so and soon recovered.
>
> The captain became as kind as a father to me, often going with me to the cabin, and when no one was present, teaching me to make pastries and sea messes. He had a cook-book, from which I gained much valuable information.[195]

The crew captured a sperm whale before the voyage ended. Thompson stayed on for a number of years, voyaging around Africa and visiting New Zealand before returning to the States, where the decision to identify himself with the abolitionists' crusade for his fellow men soon dwarfed other interests.

Slave Life in Georgia: A Narrative of the Life, Sufferings, and Escape of John Brown, a Fugitive Slave, Now in England (1855)[196] contrasts with John Thompson's narrative in being very heavily edited by its sponsor, L. A. Chamerovzow, the secretary of the British and Foreign Anti-Slavery Society. The book went into its second edition the same year it appeared. Four years hence, the name of "John Brown" was being used in many circles to designate an individual who could not have "hit upon" a change of name better able to drown his identity in the public mind. Chamerovzow, in his "Editor's Preface" to the narrative, declared that the twofold object in preparing the volume for the press had been "to advance the anti-slavery cause by the diffusion of information; and to promote the success of the project John Brown has formed, to advance himself by his own exertions, and to set an example to others of his 'race.'" He disclaimed doing more than conveying "as nearly as possible in the language of the subject of it, and written under his dictation" the story of this fugitive.

There is an authentic ring, substantiated by the mass of records, in John Brown's portraits of his mistress and master. It shows the power of his material, at times, to control the natural tendency of his scribe toward rhetoric. We meet the old mistress:

> Our mistress Betty Moore was an old, big woman, about seventy, who wore spectacles and took snuff. I remember her very well, for she used to call us children up to the big house every morning and give us a dose of garlic and rue to keep us "wholesome," as she said, and make us "grow likely" for the market. After swallowing our dose, she would make us run round a great sycamore tree in the yard, and if we did not run fast enough to please her, she used to make us nimbler by laying about us with a cow-hide. She always carried this instrument dangling at her side, like ladies in this country wear their scissors. It was painted blue, and we used to call it the "blue lizard." She used to like to see her people constantly employed, and would make us all set to work at night, after our day's labour was over, picking the seed out of cotton. We had a hard time of it with the old lady.[197]

The old master was not much better, except that when the mistress was mean she seemed to be more consistently and devilishly mean than the general run of mean masters. We find John Brown's master fearful of dying because of what he seems to understand is due to him:

> Ever so many times before he really did die, he thought his time had come. But though he made a mistake on all these occasions, and recovered from his illnesses, in his frights he sent for us all and asked us to forgive him. Many a time he would exclaim that he wished he'd "never seen a nigger." I remember his calling old Aunt Sally to him, and begging and praying of her to get the devil away from behind the door, and such like. It is a common belief amongst us that all the masters die in an awful fright, for it is usual for the slaves to be called up on such occasions to say they forgive them for what they have done. So we come to think their minds must be dreadfully uneasy about holding slaves, and therefore there cannot be any good in it. . . . When the masters die, we cannot but feel that somebody is stronger than they are. . . . When we see them sick, and hear them cry out with pain and fear on their death-bed, just like we do when we are flogged . . . we come at last to learn that they are only poor human creatures like ourselves.[198]

The high point of John Brown's narrative is his account of his first meal after his flight from slavery, in the home of Quakers as closely akin to the

Wells Browns, as Mistress Betty is akin to Lewis Clarke's Mistress Banton. We recall William Wells Brown's difficulty in starting off with the eating process, as we read:

> I was introduced by two sturdy young men to their father, as "another of the travellers bound to the North Star." The old man laid a hand upon my shoulder, and taking my other hand in his, gave me a welcome, and then conducting me into the parlour, introduced me to his wife. It was now past sun-rise, and they were about going to breakfast. I was, however, taken to an upper room, where I had a good wash, in a white basin, and where clean linen and a complete suit of clothes were brought to me. After refreshing myself by this wholesome change, I was re-conducted to the parlour, and seated at the table.
>
> It was the first time in my life I had found myself in such grand company. I was so completely abashed, and felt so out of my element, that I had no eyes, no ears, no understanding. I was quite bewildered. As to eating, it was out of the question.
>
> "Come, friend John Brown, thee must eat," said the kind old lady, heaping my plate with fried ham and eggs. "Thee needn't be afraid of eating."
>
> "I'm sure thee must be hungry," added the old gentleman, handing me a great chunk of bread. "Eat away, and don't thee be afraid. We have plenty more in the house."
>
> But it was all of no use, and though an hour or even half an hour before, I had felt that I could devour anything, the smoking coffee, ham, eggs, and sausages, and the nice white bread could not tempt me. For a good hour this continued: they pressing me to eat, and I quite unable to do so. At last I began, and picked a bit now and then, receiving encouragement as my courage seemed to increase. My appetite came with my courage, and then—oh! how I did eat!
>
> I fear my readers may think I exaggerate when I tell them that I ate straight on for an entire hour, quite steady. I demolished all the ham and eggs and sausages they placed before me, with their due accompaniment of bread, and then a round of cold salt beef was brought up, from which I was helped abundantly. I could not but notice the looks of my new friends. The old gentleman would cough and wipe his eyes now and then, and the younger folks keep exchanging glances with one another. The old lady, fearing I should do myself an injury, made several ineffectual attempts to draw my attention off.
>
> "Friend John Brown, we wish to talk with thee, as soon as thou can," she said; "we want to hear all about thee."

"Yes, ma'am," I answered, without leaving off: "you can go on, ma'am; I can talk and eat too."

I dare not say how long I might have gone on. I had not eaten a meal for so long, that now it seemed as though I never could satisfy my craving. At last the old lady said, decidedly:

"Friend John Brown, thee mustn't take it unkindly, but thee mustn't eat any more now. Thou canst have some more in the daytime if thou like; but thou wilt make thyself ill, if thou take more now."

And so I was obliged to give in.

A chapter from the Scriptures was read after breakfast, which, including my "spell" at the table, had lasted two hours from the time we sat down.[199]

Two other slave narratives were published in the same season that John Brown's narrative appeared. They were destined at once for popularity as the "inside stories" of two fugitive slaves who had become very prominent in the 1850s as Negro abolitionists. These were the Reverend Peter Randolph's *Sketches of Slave Life: or, Illustrations of the "Peculiar Institution," by Reverend Peter Randolph, an Emancipated Slave,*[200] which went through the first edition and appeared in a second edition, enlarged, in the year of its first printing; and the Reverend Samuel Ringgold Ward's *Autobiography of a Fugitive Negro: His Anti-Slavery Labours in the United States, Canada, and England.*[201]

Randolph was the leader of a group of sixty-six slaves, ranging in age from twelve months to seventy-five years at the time of their departure from Prince George County in Virginia. They were set free by the terms of their master's will at his death in 1844 and went up from Virginia to Boston as a group. Slightly resembling Josiah Henson in character, Randolph was the leading spirit in winning the three-year fight before the Virginia courts to obtain the freedom which their master had given them but which his heirs were determined not to let those eighty valuable slaves have. The number to be manumitted had dwindled from eighty to sixty-six slaves as a result of the litigation, and the inheritance of fifty dollars that had been willed to each was cut to less than fifteen dollars each. But Randolph marshalled the band to "the stronghold of righteousness, Boston," and was able to prove to the citizens of that city that it was possible for ex-slaves to take care of themselves respectably, "without slave-driving." It was a social experiment that greatly interested experimenters in social living like the Fourierites in Massachusetts. It also provided the abolitionists with a "living proof" of their assertion that the slave was as capable of self-government as anybody.

The first edition of Randolph's narrative was a modest description of the odyssey of Edloe's slaves for the purpose of "increasing the sympathy now so widely felt for the poor, crushed, and perishing slaves in this land." In a few months' time, public interest demanded an edition more than double the first one in size. The new edition contained greater particulars concerning the fight in Virginia over the emancipation. In the preface, Samuel May, Jr. of Boston points out the value of Randolph's experiment in connection with programs being projected throughout the North for the uplift of former slaves. Recognition of the friction caused by the abolitionists' work on behalf of the slaves is given in Randolph's opening passage:

> The good Anti-Slavery men have very much to contend with, in their exertions for the cause of freedom. Many people will not believe their statements; call them unreasonable and fanatical. Some call them ignorant deceivers, who have never been out of their own home, and yet pretend to a knowledge of what is going on a thousand miles from them. Many call them dangerous members of society, sowing discord and distrust where there should be nought but peace and brotherly love.[202]

He wishes to disprove such critics by showing that even though he himself has been "no stranger to the *beauties* of slavery or the *generosity* of the slaveholder," yet when it comes to portraying "the half of the woes and horrors of slavery," even as he has known it, his "feeble pencil" will not be able to fulfil the task. Among many thought-provoking statements concerning the relationship between master and slave, his answer to the popular fallacy that the slaveholder would not deliberately harm "property" into which he had put so much money is noteworthy:

> The argument so often brought forward that it would be for the interest of the owner to treat his slaves well, and of course he would not injure his own interests . . . when does the angry tyrant reflect upon what, in the end, will be the best for him? To gratify his passion for the moment, to wreak out his vengeance upon a helpless menial, is, at the time of the excitement, his interest, and he will serve it well.[203]

The qualities of fairness and justice that were outstanding characteristics of Randolph's criticisms of the slaveholder and slavery were the qualities most conspicuously missing from the eloquent criticisms of Samuel Ringgold Ward, even though he was always far from being blind. His four-hundred-twelve-page autobiography was published in London in the same year as Randolph's. Critics in that day, and also in this, resented Ward's bitter sarcasm and caustic tirades. A contemporary critic spoke of the deficiency in respect to the qualities in which Randolph excelled.[204] A recent literary historian becomes heated, as well as inaccurate, in his estimate:

> Upon some of [the slave narrators] Abolitionists showered more
> attention than was sensible, and unhappily enough spoiled their
> proteges—of whom a particularly unlovely example was Samuel
> Ringgold Ward. Ward had never been a slave; he was a "fugitive"
> from justice in the United States. . . . In England, where he was feted
> and feasted like a Roman hero, he shortly began not only to talk
> familiarly of his new friends in the British nobility, but to complain
> that the United States still harbored people who would not greet
> him as peer and brother. Almost every page he wrote is marred by
> excessive egotism, so that although his writing is forcible, it has
> scarcely any other commendable quality. If Henson and Northup
> and Ball did their race honor, Ward disgraced it—but he would have
> been a disgrace to any race.[205]

In fairness to Ward, it must be stated that he *was* born a slave in Maryland, escaping to New Jersey with his parents as a small child. He left the United States for Canada and crossed to England as an abolitionist preacher and lecturer, not as a fugitive from justice. It is true, though, that his identifying himself with the fugitive slave was a charlatan's claims, for he really had no memory of the actual experience of slavery. A handsome, eloquent, "pure black" man, with fine features, Ward is our best example of the opportunist's use of the popular interest in the fugitive slave in the 1840s and 1850s. Only the first thirty-four pages of his book deal with scenes connected with slavery in his early years. But the book itself is a remarkable compendium of facts on slavery and stories of the activities of bona fide fugitives in the Northern States, Canada, and the British Isles.

According to his preface, Ward's first plan had been to write a series of articles in the form of letters to a newspaper, recounting his travels as an abolitionist lecturer. British friends persuaded him, however, to prepare "a volume which might remain as a parting memorial of my visit to England, and serve to embody and perpetuate the opinions and arguments I had often employed to promote the work of emancipation." A publisher stepped forward with a generous offer of "every faculty for rendering the proposal practicable." Ward expresses his "warmest obligations for the promptitude and elegance with which the volume has been prepared." In view of the criticisms which he received, the reader should find the following apology to the point:

> I do not think the gentlemen who advised it were quite correct in
> anticipating that so much would be acceptable, in a Book from
> me. . . . The work is not a literary one, for it is not written by a
> literary man; it is no more than its humble title indicates—the
> Autobiography of a Fugitive Negro. In what sense I am a fugitive,
> will appear on perusal of my personal and family history.[206]

Ward was associated with Josiah Henson in the project of the fugitive slaves to colonize in Canada. He seems to have obtained the position of official agent to England from the Anti-Slavery Society of Canada that Henson was ambitious to obtain. Henson was much the abler and finer man, but both had the ability to play up to the public. Success, too, came to each on their own terms.

A curiosity among the slave narratives is the story of Ralph Roberts, written down by his *owner*, who had it printed in *Putnam's Monthly* in June of 1857 but was not brave enough to append his name to the account.[207] In the letter to the editor accompanying the unusual manuscript, the anonymous slaveholder gives his reasons for having written it:

> The slave question is becoming more and more prominent, and I have thought it well to give a simple, faithful narrative of a slave's experiences and views. The sketch has not been gotten up for effect, but has been written as an authentic illustration of the results, moral and physical, of the system. Though the owner of slaves, I have always advocated some plan of gradual emancipation, *by our own state*, and, therefore have no motive for concealing anything in relation to the effects of slavery. I have given, exactly, Ralph's narrative—many facts in which I could myself establish, and verify others by unquestionable evidence.[208]

The narrative sounds genuine, in no respect resembling the fictionalized stories of slaves continually appearing in the literary magazines of the day. It tells of Roberts's life from the time of his birth as a slave, about 1794, on a large plantation about thirty miles from Richmond, up to 1857. Though his experiences were not so bitter as the experiences of most of the slaves, they were bad enough—about like those Randolph had known. The author neither glosses over the cruelties nor excuses them. He probably could not have afforded revelation of his identity. One might keep him in mind, however, when generalizations about the slaveholders are made.

In the same year that Ralph Roberts's story was published, there appeared the narrative of Austin Steward, a prominent abolitionist who had been very active in the cause of the fugitive slave from the time he himself arrived "upward," about 1820. As early as March, 1833, we find him writing to Garrison and Knapp from the Wilberforce Colony in London, Canada West, of which colony he had become president. He reported duplicities in connection with the management of funds that had been sent to the colony but had not been directed to the proper persons.[209] After spending a quarter of a century in efforts to "elevate [fugitive slaves] in manners and morals," he decided to write his own story. The book was published in Rochester in 1857, under the title: *Twenty-Two Years a Slave, and Forty Years a Freeman;*

Embracing a Correspondence of Several Years, While President of Wilber-
force Colony, London Canada West.[210]

In a letter from Edwin Scranton included in the front matter of Austin
Steward's narrative, Scranton recommends:

> Let its plain, unvarnished tale be sent out, and the story of Slavery
> and its abominations again be told by some one who has felt in his
> own person its scorpion lash, and the weight of its grinding heel. . . .
> Your book may be humble and your descriptions tame, yet truth is
> always mighty; and you may furnish the sword for some modern
> Sampson, who shall shout over more slain than his ancient
> prototype.[211]

The preface is written in the third person but was probably written by
Steward himself, as he had no editor. Though the two letters given are credited to Scranton and to Governor Hall of New York, respectively, there is no
name appended to the preface. The preface speaks of American slavery as
"now the great question before the American People," for both political and
moral reasons. It expresses the belief that Steward's experiences, "by faithful
exposition of stubborn facts," will help reveal the nature of slavery, that
Steward fully intended presenting the public with a very intimate record of
his life as a slave, as we see in his announcement:

> In his old age he sends out this history—presenting as it were his own
> body, with the marks and scars of the tender mercies of slave drivers
> upon it, and asking that these may plead in the name of Justice,
> Humanity, and Mercy, that those who have the power, may have the
> magnanimity to strike off the chains from the enslaved, and bid him
> stand up, a Freeman and a Brother.[212]

The book became one of the top-ranking antislavery publications, reaching a
second edition in 1858 and a third in 1861.

Austin Steward was born a slave on the plantation of Captain William
Helm in Prince William County, Virginia. His recital of his experiences reveals
the usual round of the overseer-managed plantation—sunrise meant work
would begin in the field, thirty minutes after the "conch shell blew." Breakfast for the slaves was earlier than on most plantations, at the "almost decent"
hour of 9:30, instead of the usual noon. Discovered in a sugar bush by his
master's son-in-law as he was trying to learn to read, he was of course flogged.
His reaction to this was exactly the same as that of Thomas Jones' and many
many others: "Even then, with my back bleeding and smarting from the
punishment I had received, I determined to learn to read and write, at all
hazards, if my life was only spared."[213]

The regret that we find expressed in the narratives of many slaves for their
"bad ways" as young men is described by Steward in connection with the

determination that he made, as he lay on what he thought was to be his deathbed, to mend his ways if he should ever recover. We attend that solemn moment:

> I really thought my time had come to die; and when I had strength to talk, I tried to arrange the few little business affairs I had, and give my father direction concerning them. And then I began to examine my own condition before God, and to determine how the case stood between Him and my poor soul. And "there was the rub." I had often excused myself, for frequent derelictions of duty, and often wild and passionate outbreaks, on account of the harshness of my lot, and the injustice with which I was treated, even in my best endeavors to do as well as I knew how. But now, with death staring me in the face, I could see that though I was a friendless "slave-boy," I had *not* always done as well as I knew how; that I had *not* served God as I knew I ought, nor had I always set a good example before my fellow-slaves, nor warned them as well as I might, "to flee the wrath to come." Then I prayed my Heavenly Father to spare me a little longer, that I might serve Him better; and in His mercy and gracious goodness, He did so.[214]

How profoundly his religious belief permeated his being, we learn from an episode that his master had expected to provide him with amusement:

> On the day of the total eclipse of the sun, it entered [my master's] head that it would be fine sport, knowing my ignorance and superstition, to send me, just as the darkness was coming on, to return the borrowed wagon. I accordingly hitched the ox-team to it and started. As I proceeded through the wood, I saw, with astonishment and some alarm, that it was growing very dark, and thought it singular at that hour of the day. When I reached the place of my destination it was almost total darkness, and some persons, ignorant as myself, were running about wringing their hands, and declaring that they believed the Day of Judgment had come, and such like expressions.
>
> The effect of all this was, however, very different from what my master had expected. I thought, of course, if the Judgment Day had come, I should be no longer a slave in the power of a heartless tyrant. I recollect well of thinking, that if indeed all things earthly were coming to an end, I should be free from [my master's] brutal force, and as to meeting my Creator, I felt far less dread of that than of meeting my cross, unmerciful master. I felt that, sinful as I had been, and unworthy as I was, I should be far better off than I then was; driven to labor all day, without compensation; half starved

and poorly clad, and above all, subjected to the whims and caprices of any heartless tyrant to whom my master might give the power to rule over me. But I had not much time for reflection. I hurried home, my mind filled with the calm anticipation that the end of all things was at hand; which greatly disappointed my expectant master, who was looking for me to return in a great fright, making some ludicrous demonstration of fear and alarm.[215]

A phase of the ideology of a certain type of slave, generally stereotyped as the "contented slave" and usually thought of as "not knowing any better," is well presented by Austin Steward in a passage that should not be cited without careful inclusion of the fact that the author of the passage is not intending to indicate that *all* slaves were so inclined, for he is himself a slave (in terms of his recollection) and yet does not include himself among those possessors of "a foolish pride":

It must be confessed that among the poor, degraded and ignorant slaves there exists a foolish pride, which loves to boast of their master's wealth and influence. A white person, too poor to own slaves, is often looked upon with as much disdain by the miserable slave as by his wealthy owner. This disposition seems to be instilled into the mind of every slave at the South, and indeed, I have heard slaves object to being sent in very small companies to labor in the field, lest that some passer-by should think that they belonged to a poor man, who was unable to keep a large gang. Nor is this ridiculous sentiment maintained by the slaves only; the rich planter feels such a contempt for all white persons without slaves, that he does not want them for his neighbors. I know of many instances where such persons have been under the necessity of buying or hiring slaves, just to preserve their reputation and keep up appearances; and even among a class of people who profess to be opposed to Slavery, have I known instances of the same kind, and have heard them apologize for their conduct by saying that "when in Rome, we must do as the Romans do."

Uncle Aaron Bristol was one of Captain Helm's slaves who had a large amount of this miserable pride; and for him to be associated with a white man in the same humble occupation, seemed to give him ideas of great superiority, and full liberty to treat him with all the scorn and sarcasm he was capable of, in which my uncle was by no means deficient.

At this time the Captain owned a fine and valuable horse, by the name of *Speculator*. This horse, groomed by Uncle Aaron, stood sometimes at Bath and sometimes at Geneva; and at the latter village another horse was kept, groomed by a white man. The white

groom was not very well pleased with Aaron's continual disparagement of the clumsy animal which my uncle called "a great awkward
plowhorse;" and then he would fling out some of his proud nonsense
about "poor white people who were obliged to groom their own old
dumpy horses."[216]

The moment when the slave made up his mind to put an end to his slavery,
through purchase of himself or through flight, marked the end of the enslave-
ment of his spirit, as we learn from narrative after narrative of fugitive or
manumitted slave alike. Austin Steward's determination to end his slavery
came in the winter of 1814 at the age of twenty-two. His master had taken
him to Canandaigua, New York, on a trip. While they were there, Steward
received permission to visit some people in that city with whom he had
made passing acquaintance. One of the persons was a Mr. James Moore, one
of the directors of a manumission society. While there, Stewart talked with
Mr. Moore about the possibility of leaving his master. His reasons for wanting
to escape from slavery had long been clear in his mind, as he reports:

> There is no one, I care not how favorable his condition, who desires
> to be a slave, to labor for nothing all his life for the benefit of
> others. I have often heard fugitives say, that it was not so much the
> cruel beatings and floggings that they received which induced them
> to leave the South, as the idea of dragging out a whole life of un-
> requited toil to enrich their masters. Everywhere that Slavery exists,
> it is nothing but *slavery*.[217]

Mr. Moore advised him to return to the plantation with Captain Helm and go
on with his work as usual until March, saying nothing to anyone about his
plans to make his way out of slavery at that time. From the moment that he
made up his mind *when* he was going to strike out for himself, says Steward,
his "heart [was] so light, that I could not realize that my bonds were not yet
broken, nor the yoke removed from off my neck: I was already free in spirit,
and I silently breathed in the bright prospect of liberty."[218] In March he did
make his escape. He was hunted for a time but eluded his pursuers. Arriving
at Canandaigua, he hired out at farm labor until his natural abilities for the
position led him into the field of social service for the fugitive.

Another fugitive slave who became prominently identified with the efforts
to aid the fugitives, directing the activities of the Underground Railroad at
Syracuse for many years, published the narrative of his experiences in 1859
under the title: *The Reverend J. W. Loguen, as a Slave and as a Freeman.*[219]
Although this narrative contains material of value for a study of the anti-
slavery movement in New York State or for a detailed picture of the atrocities of the slave system, particularly in Tennessee, it is not of distinct
importance as a slave narrative. The book is frankly a biography rather than

an attempt to take down its subject's words from dictation. According to the preface by the editor, whose name is not given, "the features" in the life of Reverend Jermain Wesley Loguen were accurately given, and then he "filled up the picture." We learn further from this candid biographer:

> Not a fact relating to his, or his mother's, or brother's or sister's experience with slavery, is stated, that is not literally or substantially true. Those facts were history before they were written. . . . We have adopted the popular form or style in our narrative, in respect to popular taste; and, as aforesaid, occasionally supplied vacancies in his southern life from our own fancy; but in every case that we have done so, the picture is outside Mr. Loguen's experience with slavery—and . . . all we have given as his slave life will remain true.[220]

Recent social historians have turned to Loguen's narrative as one of the few slave narratives useful for obtaining "the inmost thoughts of the slaves," doubtless because the narrative is to be found somewhat more easily than the majority of the slave narratives. The actual worth of the Loguen narrative should therefore be understood.[221] In this connection, it is valuable to consider the letter that Loguen received from his old mistress, sent by her to his publisher in Syracuse on February 20, 1860, from Maury County, Tennessee, after she had found out about his narrative. (There is no reference in the letter to the narrative, nor does Loguen refer to the book in his reply to her letter, which he sent from Syracuse, March 28, 1860. But the fact that she had found out where to send a letter to him, and that she evidently believed him to be in affluent circumstances, leads us to infer that the narrative was known to her.) Mrs. Loguen substantiates many of the facts given in the narrative, as she writes "Jarm" of his mother, whom she calls "Cherry"; of the "situation" he put them in by "running away and stealing Old Rock our fine Mare;" and of the land they were forced to sell, along with his brother Abe and his sister Ann, because he had taken off with his own, more valuable self. She says that she has had an offer for him, "but did not see fit to take it;" and proposed, instead, that he send her one thousand dollars and pay for the old mare, in which event she will send him a bill of sale for himself and give up all further claim to him. The end of the letter must have angered Loguen as he read. It is provocative enough to a stranger:

> If you do not comply with my request I will sell you to someone else and you may rest assured that the time is not far distant when things will be changed with you. . . . You had better comply with my request.
>   I understand that you are a preacher. As the Southern people are so bad, you had better come and preach to your old acquaintances. I would like to know if you read your Bible. If so, can you tell what

will become of the thief if he does not repent and, if the blind lead the blind, what will the consequence be? ... A Word to the wise is sufficient. ... You know that we reared you as we reared our own children; that you was never abused, and that shortly before you ran away, when your master asked you if you would like to be sold, you said you would not leave him to go with anybody.[222]

Loguen's answer is a much more satisfying record of the man's personality than can be found in the biography. He thanks Mrs. Loguen for her letter, particularly for the welcome news that the mother he has not heard from in so long "is yet alive, and, as you say, 'as well as common.'" The letter continues:

I wish you had said more about her. ... You sold my brother and sister, Abe and Ann, and twelve acres of land, you say, because I ran away. How you have the unutterable meanness to ask me to return and be your miserable chattel, or, in lieu thereof, send you $1000 to enable you to redeem the *land*, but not to redeem my poor brother and sister! If I were to send you money, it would be to get my brother and sister, and not that you should get land. ... You say you are a *cripple*, and doubtless you say it to stir my pity, for you knew I was susceptible in that direction. I do pity you from the bottom of my heart. Nevertheless, I am indignant beyond the power of words to express, that you should be so sunken and cruel as to tear the hearts I love so much all in pieces; that you should be willing to impale and crucify us all, out of compassion for your poor *foot* or *leg*. Wretched woman! Be it known to you that I value my freedom, to say nothing of my mother, brothers, and sisters, more than your whole body; more, indeed, than my whole life; more than all the lives of all the slaveholders and tyrants under heaven.

You say you have offers to buy me, and that you shall sell me if I do not send you $1000, and in the same breath and almost in the same sentence you say, "You know we raised you as we did our own children." Woman, did you raise your *own children* for the market? Did you raise them for the whipping post? Did you raise them to be driven off, bound to a coffle in chains? Where are my poor bleeding brothers and sisters? Can you tell? ... You say I am a thief, because I took the old mare along with me. Have you got to learn that I had a better right to the old mare ... than Mannasseth Loguen had to me?[223]

Unnamed editor of Loguen's narrative had accurate statements of facts to build his book from, judging from the sequel to the book that is furnished by these two letters, which should be reprinted with the original text if the narrative is ever reprinted. The conclusion of his preface is arresting:

This is not only a reading age, but it is a new age, and it is well to occupy our youth with its philosophy and facts. . . . Society is in process of incubation and . . . we should keep an eye on the formative elements, to see what portion is combining to form the substance and life of the coming age. The African element contributes largely to the causes that agitate mankind, and must have its place in the product. . . . We have come, therefore, to consider and honor a new element in the social state, and for that reason a man like Mr. Loguen becomes a subject of speculative and philosophical enquiry. At such a time, colored men are Divine instrumentalities for Divine ends.[224]

Where *The Reverend J. W. Loguen as a Slave and as a Freeman* is practically without value as a personal record, the *Narrative of the Life of Reverend Noah Davis, a Colored Man* derives much of its worth from its refreshingly unedited genuineness.[225] It is unique among the slave narratives of all periods as the only one to be published below the Mason–Dixon Line not connected with a criminal record, and in 1859, when the slavery controversy was at its peak. The narrative does reveal the slaveholder at his kindliest, as might be expected. The fact, therefore, that the great emphasis of Noah Davis is upon his determined effort to achieve freedom for himself and his family from slavery enables his narrative to reveal even more clearly than the narratives of Lunceford Lane and Peter Randolph—the only other slave authors able to record any measure of fairmindedness in their treatment by their owners— the evils of slavery inherent in the system. For Noah Davis's master was good to him.

Davis was born in 1804, a slave on the estate of a wealthy merchant and mill owner, Robert Patten, of Fredericksburg, Virginia. His father was head miller at the mill on "Crooked Run," located on a stream running between Madison and Culpepper counties, and enjoyed many privileges. Davis comments: "Mr. Patten was always considered one of the best of masters, allowing his servants many privileges; but my father enjoyed more than many others."[226] He was allowed to keep his children with him "until they were old enough to put out to such trades as they might choose." Both parents were "pious members of a Baptist church;" and it was the father's custom, "on those Sabbaths when we remained at home . . . to spend his time in instructing his children or the neighboring servants, out of a New Testament, sent him from Fredericksburg by one of his older sons." When Noah Davis was about fourteen, their owner sold the mill and set his parents free, allowing them to maintain themselves by cultivating as much ground on the farm as they needed. Davis was sent into Fredericksburg to become apprenticed in the trade he had chosen, that of "boot and shoe-making." He tells of his feelings on the important occasion:

In December, 1818, for the first time in my life, I left my parents, to go a distance from home; and I was sad at the thought of parting with those whom I loved and reverenced more than any persons on earth. But the expectation of seeing Fredericksburg, a place which, from all I had then learned, I supposed must be the greatest place in the world, reconciled me somewhat with the necessity of saying Good-bye to the dear ones at home. I arrived at Fredericksburg, after a day and a half's travel, in a wagon—a distance of some fifty miles. Having arrived in town, a boy green from the country, I was astonished and delighted at what appeared to me the splendor and beauty of the place. I spent a merry Christmas at my old master's stately mansion, along with my older brother, and for a while forgot the home on the farm.[227]

Davis's master selected the home of "Mr. Thomas Wright, a man of sterling integrity, who was considered the best workman in the whole town," as the place for his apprenticeship until he reached the age of twenty-one. Davis had an older brother who was already apprenticed to Mr. Wright, so he was not unhappy to join the household, even though the first year of his service was not to be spent in the shop, as we see:

Upon entering with Mr. Wright, I learned that the colored boys had to serve one year with Mrs. Wright, in the house and kitchen. The object of this was to train them for future usefulness, when called from the shop, to serve as waiters and cooks. Mrs. Wright was a good manager, and a very particular housekeeper. I used to think she was too particular. But I have learned better since. I have often wished, when I had been seeking homes for my children, that I could find one like Mrs. Wright. She would spare no pains to teach her servants how she wanted her work done; and then she would spare no pains to make them do it. I have often looked back, with feelings of gratitude and veneration, to that pious lady, for her untiring perseverance in training me up in the way I should go. But she is gone, I trust, to receive the reward of righteousness, in a better world.

After I had been under Mrs. Wright's special charge the first year, she could leave me to cook a dinner, or clean the house, or do anything she might set me at, without her being present. I was now considered fit to take my seat among the hands in the shop.[228]

A very different mode of living now began for young Davis, as a fledgling apprentice among the shoemakers who, "at that time, in Fredericksburg, were considered the most intemperate of any class of men in the place." They soon trained him to bring them liquor "with such secrecy as to prevent the boss, who had forbidden it to come on the premises, from knowing it;" and Davis obliged them, "in order to get along pleasantly with them." Soon he had acquired "the habit of drinking, along with every vile habit to which my companions were addicted." Despite his condemnation of his habits at this period, however, we can assume that he was "bad" only in having fallen from the previous standard to which he had always kept; for he continued to enjoy the good favor of Mr. and Mrs. Wright. Concerning their trust in him, he says:

> Mr. Wright readily gave me a recommendation for honesty, truthfulness, and goodness of character. In fact, he felt such confidence in me, that he would often leave his store in my care, when he would have to go to the north, for a supply of stock. And I can truly say, that I never deceived him, when he thus trusted me. Nothing would mortify me as much, as to hear it said, "A Negro can't be trusted." This saying would always nerve me with a determination *to be trustworthy.*—If I was trusted, to deserve to be trusted. I wanted to show that principle was not confined to color. But I have been led to look at it since, and have thought that perhaps it was more pride than principle in me, at that time, for I was a wicked sinner.[229]

He experienced no discouragement, albeit no aid, in his efforts to learn to write. His description of his method of learning joins the record of other slaves concerning this very important key to civilization:

> The first idea I ever got of writing, was from trying to imitate my employer, who used to write the names of his customers on the lining of the boots and shoes, as he gave them out to be made. So I tried to make letters, and soon succeeded in writing my name, and then the word Fredericksburg, and so on. My father had previously taught me the alphabet, in the spelling book, before I had left the mill. After I became religious, I would carry my father's New Testament to church, and always try to get to meeting in time to hear the preacher read a chapter before sermon. If he named the chapter before reading it, I would soon find it. In this way, I gathered much information in pronouncing many hard words in the Scriptures. It was a long time before I learned the meaning of the numeral letters put in the Bible over the chapters. I had often seen them in the spelling book running alongside a column of figures; but no one ever told me that they were put there for the same use as the figures.[230]

There is a quality definitely reminiscent of Bunyan in Noah Davis' account of his conversion, which came about as a result of his engaging in the normal habit of going out with the girls in the evening in Fredericksburg. Prayer meeting was the frequent choice of these young people, and Davis was in the habit of going to any one of the four churches in the city that had "apartments for worship with the white people"—Methodist, Presbyterian, Episcopalian, and Baptist. As he says, he had "no particular preference for any one of these denominations, more than another; but, went wherever my favorites went." It happened to be at a Methodist church, one evening, that he decided that "now was the time to begin to pray," having always purposed in his mind, as a result of his parental training, to become religious before he died. He would not try to pray in the church, for fear that the girls would laugh at him. He left the house, intending to find some place where he could pray, but was beset with distress and fears because of his unworthiness in God's sight. His consternation reminds us of Bunyan's:

> I now said to myself, "It is of no use for me to pray.—If God has seen all my wickedness, as I feel that He has, then there is no mercy for me."
>
> So I ran to my lodging-place, and tried to hide myself in a dark room. But this was useless; for it appeared that God could see me in the dark, as well as in the light.
>
> I now felt constrained to beg for mercy, and spent the time in trying to obtain pardon for my sins. But the morning came, and the hour drew near for the hands to go to work and I was still unhappy. . . .
>
> Up to this time, I was not fully convinced that God knew all about me. So I began to study about the matter. As I sat upon the shoe-bench, I picked up a bunch of bristles, and selecting one of the smallest, I began to wonder, if God could see an object so small as that. No sooner had this inquiry arose [sic] in my heart, than it appeared to me, that the Lord could not only see the bristle, but that He beheld me, as plainly as I saw the little object in my hand; and not only so, but that God was then looking through me, just as I would hold up a tumbler of clear water to the sun and look through it.
>
> But it really seemed, that the more I prayed the less hope there was for me. Still I could not stop praying; for I felt that God was angry with me. I had sinned against his holy laws; and now, if He should cut me off, and send me to hell, it was but right. At length, one day, while sitting on my shoe bench, I felt that my time had come when I must die. What troubled me most, was that I should have to appear before God, in all my sins;—O, what horror filled my soul at the thought![231]

Noah Davis's agony was prolonged for several weeks, during which he alternately felt convinced of his conversion and despair because of his unworthiness. At length, however, after having made a promise to God in prayer to devote his life to the service of preaching, he believed that he was truly converted and was baptized in the Baptist church of Fredericksburg with about twenty others. An attachment grew up between Davis and another slave who was baptized at the same time that he was. He had been acquainted with the girl for several years but had not particularly noticed her until that day. Several points of interest are to be found in Davis's account of this matter:

> We were both slaves, and of course had to get the consent of our
> owner before we went further. My wife belonged to the late Carter
> L. Stephenson, Esq., who was a brother to Hon. Andrew Stephen-
> son, of Virginia. My wife's master was quite indulgent to the servants
> about the house. He never restrained visitors from coming on his
> premises to visit his domestics. It was said he had the likeliest set
> of servant girls in the town; and though I cannot say I got the
> prettiest, yet I think I got the best one among them. We have lived
> happily together, as husband and wife, for the last twenty-eight
> years. We have had nine children—seven born in slavery, and two
> since my wife's freedom. Five out of the seven in slavery I have
> bought—two are still in bondage.[232]

Embarrassment over not being able to read a chapter in the Bible cor-rectly led Davis, after much prayer, to ask his owner, Dr. F. Patten, not only to let him purchase his freedom, but also to take time from his work to travel in the northern cities to find friends who would give him the money to meet his master's price for him, which was five hundred dollars. After hearing his wishes fully, Dr. Patten consented to let him try his luck at traveling, telling him that when he was ready to go, he would be given a pass to go where he pleased. Davis accordingly set forth, June 1, 1845, for Philadelphia, New York, Boston, and other points, after paying his master the one hundred and fifty dollars which he was able to raise in Fredericksburg on his "debt."

The four-month tour in the North only netted him another one hundred and fifty dollars, however, and Davis returned home "greatly disheartened." His interpretation of the cause of his failure is characteristically honest:

> The cause of my failure to raise all the money, I believe, was that I
> was unaccustomed to addressing large congregations of strangers;
> and often, when I was favored with an opportunity of presenting my
> case to the people, I would feel such embarrassment that I could
> scarcely say anything. And I met another obstacle, which discour-
> aged me very much; which was, that some persons would tell me
> they sympathized with me, in my efforts to get free; but they said it
> was against their principles to give money, to buy slaves. I confess,

this was new to me, and would cut me down much in my spirits—
still I found generous and noble-hearted friends, who treated me
with every mark of kindness.[233]

Davis paid his master what money he could, reserving enough to open up a
shop of his own with his "old boss" during his apprenticeship days. Mr.
Wright was his "protector, so that I might carry on my business lawfully." He
was not very successful in this venture but was not destined to remain engaged in the business long. He soon received the call from Baltimore that
changed the course of his life. Through the pastor of the church to which he
belonged in Fredericksburg, he was sent a letter from a group of white
Baptists in Baltimore, informing him that if he would come to that city they
would secure for him an appointment as missionary to the colored people
there, under the Domestic Board of the Southern Baptist Convention, and
would also assist him in raising the balance of the money due upon himself.
We find Davis at first unfavorably disposed toward the offer:

> This was indeed an unexpected, and to me an undesired call. I began
> to think how can I leave my wife and seven small children, to go to
> Baltimore to live, a distance of more than a hundred miles from
> them. This, I thought, could not be. I thought my children would
> need my watchful care, more now than at any other time. It is
> true, they were all slaves, belonging to a rich widow lady. But
> she had always given me the entire control of my family. Now, if
> I should leave them at their tender age, mischief might befall them.
> Still, as the letter from Baltimore was from gentlemen of the best
> standing, it became me to give them an answer. This I could not
> do, without first consulting my master. I did so, and after giving
> the matter careful consideration, he thought I had better go and
> see those gentlemen—he was perfectly willing to leave the matter
> to me.
>
> The result was, that I accepted the offer of the brethren in Balti-
> more; and by them I was enabled to pay the debt I owed; and I
> have never had cause to repent it—though I had misgivings some-
> times, when I would get into trouble.[234]

At first there were all kinds of discouragements in his new vocation. For
one thing, there were fewer Negroes of Baptist faith in Baltimore than of any
other denomination. The city had "some ten or eleven colored Methodist
churches, one Episcopalian, one Presbyterian, and one little Baptist church,
located upon the outskirts." The people themselves were not friendly towards
him, standing aloof and seeming "to look upon all my movements with dis-
trust and suspicion, and opposed to all I was trying to do for the moral and
spiritual benefit of our degraded race." But his gravest problem was his keen

realization that he "was far behind the people" in education. As he admitted, this "did not appear well in a preacher, [and] I felt very small, when comparing my abilities with others of a superior stamp." He describes his dilemma:

> I had never had a day's schooling; and coming to one of the first cities in the Union, where the colored people had the advantage of schools, and where their pulpits were occupied, Sabbath after Sabbath, by comparatively intelligent colored ministers—what could I expect, but that the people would turn away from one who was trying to preach in the room of a private house, some fifteen by twenty feet? Yet, there was no turning back: God had called me to the work, and it was His cause I was advocating.
>
> I found that to preach, like other preachers, I must improve my mind, by reading the Bible and other good books, and by studying my own language. I started afresh—I got a small stock of books, and the white brethren loaned and gave me other useful volumes, to which they added a word of instruction and encouragement, whenever an opportunity offered; and the ministers cordially invited me to attend their Monday ministerial conference meeting, which was very useful to me.[235]

At the end of the first year, plans were made with his wife's mistress for the purchase of his wife and two youngest children. The owner fixed their price at eight hundred dollars and gave him twelve months in which to raise the money. When the year passed with but half the sum raised by means of subscriptions, she raised the price one hundred dollars, as it was considered that the value of the children had increased in the interim, and gave him six weeks in which to consummate the deal. Mr. Wright promised to give him endorsement on a bond for three hundred dollars, and a friend in Baltimore loaned him two hundred dollars to make up the amount still needed after he had obtained what he could from well-wishers in Fredericksburg, Baltimore, Washington, and Philadelphia. Thus he was able to redeem his wife and two children, arriving with them in Baltimore on November 5, 1851. It was a joyful occasion, and augured success in the future, though it was to come with difficulty as we see:

> This year was a joyful one to me—my little church increasing, and the Sabbath school flourishing. . . . My wife and little ones were also with me, both the church and Sabbath school. I was a happy man, and felt more than ever inclined to give thanks to God, and serve Him to the best of my ability.
>
> My salary was only three hundred dollars a year; but with hard exertion and close economy, together with my wife's taking in washing and going out at day's work, we were enabled by the first

of the year, to pay the two hundred dollars our dear friend had loaned us, in raising the six hundred dollars, before spoken of. But the bond for three hundred dollars was now due, and how must this be met? I studied out a plan; which was to get some gentlemen who might want a little servant girl, to take my child, and advance me three hundred dollars for the purpose of paying the note, which was now due in Virginia. In this plan I succeeded; and had my own life insured for seven years for five hundred dollars, and made it over to this gentleman, as security; until I ultimately paid him the whole amount; though I was several years in paying it.[236]

Noah Davis had two big problems confronting him: the constant need to strengthen the membership of his church and its facilities, and the fear lest his five children remaining in bondage be sold South before he could purchase them. In order to provide for the former, he made plans and entered into arrangements for the building of a suitable chapel on Saratoga Street in Baltimore. If this had been the only project in hand, his program would have been full but not uncomfortable. As to the second problem, three times, between the beginning of 1852 and December of 1858, he received the harassing news that a child was about to be sold South at auction. The story of how this dauntless preacher, with his trust in God and his feet hurrying everywhere, was able to raise twenty-seven hundred and fifty dollars within that seven-year period is one of the most stirring in slave literature. Two daughters and three sons were still in slavery, and his oldest daughter was about to be sold. With "great difficulty and the help of friends," he raised eight hundred and fifty dollars, and "got her on to Baltimore." Not long after this, his oldest son was about to be sold. We learn:

Entirely unexpected, I received the painful news that my boy was in one of the traders' jails in Richmond, and for sale. The dealer knew me, and was disposed to let me have him, if I could get any one to purchase him. I was, of course, deeply anxious to help my boy; but I began to think that I had already drawn so heavily on the liberality of all my friends, that to appeal to them again seemed out of the question. I immediately wrote to the owners of my son, and received an answer—that his price was fixed at seven hundred dollars.

The fact is, God had already done so much more for me and my family than we had ever expected, that we could not tell what further help He might give us, until we had asked Him for it; and we could but pray over this trying affair. I hardly knew what else to do, but pray. The boy was twenty years old, and had been accustomed to waiting in the house, for the most respectable families. It occurred to me, that I might perhaps get him a home near me, where we might see him and use our parental influence over him. I thought it was possible, that I might find three hundred persons among my friends in Baltimore, who would contribute one dollar each to save my son, and that I might then obtain some friend in Baltimore to advance four hundred dollars, and let my son work it out with him: and give this friend a life insurance policy on the boy, as a security. This plan seemed practical, and I wrote to his owners, asking for ten days to raise the money; which they granted me.[237]

The case was made known to the different colored congregations in the city, with the result that Davis obtained three hundred dollars in this manner. He was also able to find a person who advanced the four hundred dollars. Thus, within ten days, his son was purchased and brought to Baltimore, where he at once began to work to pay in service the money advanced on him. With the death in 1856 of the owner of the three children still in slavery, however, Davis's needs again became acute. His two sons were sold at auction. The one who had just entered his twenty-first year brought five hundred and sixty dollars, and the seventeen-year-older brought five hundred and seventy. The bidding for his daughter reached the sum of eleven hundred dollars, but two friends of Noah Davis gave their joint bond for the amount, and Davis was allowed one year in which to redeem her.

Able to raise only one hundred and fifty dollars on the bond in six months, Davis obtained permission from the Mission Board to travel for the purpose of soliciting funds. Once again, as he says, "I started . . . on this painful business of begging money, to purchase my fifth child out of slavery." He obtained two hundred dollars from churches in Philadelphia and about four hundred dollars from "friends in Boston and its vicinity." There he ran upon his old master, Dr. F. Patten, at that time a surgeon in the United States Navy. Patten invited him to visit him in Chelsea, which he did "the same afternoon, and was kindly treated."[238] He raised about fifty dollars in New Bedford and nearly one hundred dollars in Providence, plus a promise that caused the clouds of sorrow to part for the sorely pressed father. We read of this good luck in Providence:

> I had been from home several months, and had collected in all about
> seven hundred dollars, but still lacked about four hundred to accom-
> plish my object. I was receiving letters every week from my Church
> and family, saying that my presence at home was greatly needed;
> but the idea of going home without accomplishing my great object,
> filled me with distress. While speaking to the meetings, and telling
> how God had delivered me from time to time out of trials, I felt
> such a sense of my condition, that for the moment I could not
> retrain my feelings—my heart became so full, that I stopped all utter-
> ance. At the close of the meeting, the people showed their sympathy

for me by giving me a collection of sixty-one dollars.—One dear
brother, (May the Lord bless him!) came forward, and presenting
me with a ten-dollar bill, said, "Brother Davis, give yourself no more
trouble about that daughter.—You say you have to stop in New
York. Let me say, that when you get home, whatever you lack of the
four hundred dollars, write to me, and I will send you a check for
the balance." This was spoken in the presence of the whole meeting.
I felt completely at a loss for words of gratitude and thanksgiving;
and merely said, the day is broke, and the Lord has appeared for me
indeed![239]

He "used every effort" in his power to prevent having to call upon this
generous friend in Providence, but in order to make up the amount still
needed in order to pay the purchase price of eleven hundred dollars, he found
it necessary to write and ask him for the sum of one hundred and forty-two
dollars, "which he immediately and generously supplied, by remitting me a
check for the full amount." On December 1, 1858, Davis went for his daughter, releasing her within one year from the time she was sold.

At the time he had negotiated for the purchase of his daughter, the young
man who had bought his two sons at the same sale had promised him that, if
he succeeded in paying for his daughter during that year, the master would
set a price on the two boys, that he might buy them. What plan to undertake
for this last project to purchase his own flesh and blood from slavery was now
the question. His church needed his presence sorely, so further touring was not
possible—besides, he felt he had asked as much as one person could expect
to obtain from all the churches he could find to visit. Helped by prayer and
meditation, the thought of writing the story of his life occurred to him. His
brave little book ends with the mention of the dawning of this new hope:

Could I not, by *making a book*, do something to relieve myself and
my children, and ultimately, by the same means, help my church,
under its heavy debt, and also relieve the Missionary Board from
helping me. This idea struck me with so much force, that I have
yielded to it—that is, to write a short Narrative of my own life,
setting forth the trials and difficulties the Lord has brought me
through to this day, and offer it for sale to my friends generally, as
well as to the public at large; and I hope it may not only aid me,
but may serve to encourage others, who meet with similar difficulties, to put their trust in God.[240]

A matter of interest that has not come definitely before the attention of
the reader, though mention has been made of it now and then, is the relation
of the free Negro father to his slave family. An unusually enlightening description of the psychology attending one such relationship is given in the naive,

truly homespun *Narrative of the Life and Labors of the Reverend G. W. Offley, A Colored Man, and Local Preacher*, which was published by himself in Hartford, Connecticut, in 1860. A man of fifty-two years at the time of the writing of this narrative, Offley was able to help many fugitive slaves on their way up through Connecticut and included narrative sketches of some of these courageous individuals within the covers of the interesting little fifteen-cent book. It is in the beginning of the narrative that we find ourselves particularly concerned, for the reasons given:

> My mother was born a slave in the State of Virginia, and sold in the State of Maryland, and there remained until married, and became the mother of three children. She was willed free at the death of her master; her three children were also willed free at the age of twenty-five. But my youngest brother was put on a second will, which was destroyed by the widow and the children, and he was subjected to bondage for life. My father was a free man, and therefore at the age of twenty years. He also bought my sister for a term of years, say until she was twenty-five years old. He gave her her freedom at the age of sixteen years. He bought my grandmother, who was too old to set free, that she might be exempted from servitude in her old age.[241]

The reader of Offley's account of how unfairly his free Negro master-father treated him receives a definite shock, as the record is without a parallel. Like Lunceford Lane, Offley had to work nights in order to earn money to buy whatever he needed, as his father allowed him nothing. He tells us:

> During my boyhood father hired me to a slaveholder for a term of four years to pay his house rent. . . . When I was ten years old I sat down and taking an old basket to pieces, learned myself to make baskets. After that I learned to make foot-mats and horse collars, not of leather but of corn husks; also two kinds of brooms. These articles I used to make nights and sell to get money for myself. When I was sixteen years old I commenced taking contracts of wood-chopping at fifty cents per cord, and hired slaves to chop for me nights, when the moon shone bright. In the fall and winter we would make our fire and chop until eleven or twelve at night. We used to catch oysters and fish nights, and hire other slaves to peddle them out on Sunday mornings. By this way I have helped some get their freedom.[242]

Through his mother's intervention, Offley's father finally decided to give his son his freedom when the latter was twenty-one. Offley reports that in appreciation he gave his father "one year's work to buy him a horse!"

Offley's first acquaintance with the world of letters came one day when he was going to work. He discovered "a piece of a chapter of an old Bible, *Genesis* XXV, concerning Isaac, Jacob, and Esau." An old black man who was working for his father read the section to him and then undertook to teach Offley his letters, giving him lessons at night and on Sunday morning. After the old man left, Offley made arrangements with the son of a poor slave-holder to teach him "the art of wrestling' boxing and fighting" in return for reading lessons. Later, when he went to work in a hotel at St. George, Delaware, he was able to continue his learning under the tutelage of a gambler's son, exchanging baskets of food for lessons in reading and writing.[243] It is obvious from the state of the composition that Offley's instruction was very far from complete, but none the less it furnished him with an equipment sufficient to allow him to record in writing a type of slave experience that probably had counterparts but that has not otherwise been registered.

The long-promised story of the escape from slavery in Georgia in 1848 of William and Ellen Craft was published in London in 1860, under the title *Running a Thousand Miles for Freedom; or, The Escape of William and Ellen Craft.*[244] The romantic nature of the reception of the young couple by abolitionists everywhere in Pennsylvania, New York, and New England, and in the British Isles is recounted elsewhere in this study.[245] The manner of their escape was one of the excitements of the age. It may have been the emphasis placed by the public upon the way in which they brought themselves up out of slavery that suggested to William Craft the outline plan for the narrative he undertook to write a dozen years later.

Declaring in his preface that his book was "not intended as a full history of the life of my wife, nor of myself; but merely as an account of our escape; together with other matter which I hope may be the means of creating in some minds a deeper abhorrence of the sinful and abominable practice of enslaving and brutifying our fellow-creatures," William Craft sets forth on his recital. The decision to flee from slavery had come about as the result of their inner conviction that no one had the right to hold them as "chattels," both by reason of God's having made of one blood all nations of men, and of the truths said to be "self-evident" by the American Declaration of Independence. Therefore, he says, "we felt perfectly justified in undertaking the dangerous and exciting task of running a thousand miles, in order to obtain those rights which are so vividly set forth in the Declaration." The plan was conceived early in the month of December, 1848, and put into execution eight days after they had thought of it.

Ellen Craft's first master was her father. His wife was so frequently and excessively annoyed by the fact that Ellen was mistaken for a child of the family that she gave the child to one of her daughters as a wedding present when Ellen was eleven years old. This change separated Ellen from her mother and other dear ones, but she was so glad to be away from the incessant cruelty of her old mistress that she did not grumble much at the transfer. But, now that she and her husband had set their hearts upon escape from the system of slavery, the white skin and straight hair and Anglo-Saxon features that had been the cause of so much of her special ill-treatment in her early years became the central prop in their plan.

The entire preparation for their disguise and escape was made the night they left, as they feared the secret might in some way leak out if any earlier steps were taken to transform Ellen into the figure of an invalided Southern gentleman traveling north to a hospital in Philadelphia under the care of her faithful slave. A poultice was put up in a kerchief for her to wear around her face—under the chin and up the cheeks—to hide her beardlessness and the feminine expression of her face. Green spectacles had been procured to shield her eyes from detection, as she would be thrown a great deal in the company of gentlemen in the hotels where they planned to stop on their way to Philadelphia. In the dead of that critical night, William Craft cut off his wife's fair hair, "square at the back of the head, and got her to dress in the disguise and stand out on the floor." Decided that she "made a most respectable-looking gentleman," they felt that the hour for flight had come. We attend them as they depart:

> When the time had arrived for us to start, we blew out the lights, knelt down, and prayed to our Heavenly Father mercifully to assist us, as he did his people of old, to escape from cruel bondage; and we shall ever feel that God heard and answered our prayer. . . .
>
> After this we rose and stood for a few moments in breathless silence,—we were afraid that some one might have been about the cottage listening and watching our movements. So I took my wife by the hand, stepped softly to the door, raised the latch, drew it open, and peeped out. Though there were trees all around the house, yet the foliage scarcely moved; in fact, everything appeared to be as still as death. I then whispered to my wife, "Come, my dear, let us make a desperate leap for liberty!" But, poor thing, she shrank back, in a state of trepidation. I turned and asked what was the matter; she made no reply, but burst into violent sobs, and threw her head upon my breast. . . . We both saw the many mountainous difficulties that rose one after the other before our view, and knew far too well what our sad fate would have been, were we caught and forced back into our slavish den. . . .
>
> However, the sobbing was soon over, and after a few moments of silent prayer she recovered her self-possession, and said, "Come, William, it is getting late, so now let us venture upon our perilous journey."
>
> We then opened the door, and stepped as softly out as "moonlight upon the water." I locked the door with my own key, which I

now have before me, and tiptoed across the yard into the street. I say tiptoed, because we were like persons near a tottering avalanche, afraid to move, or even breathe freely, for fear the sleeping tyrants should be aroused, and come down upon us with double vengeance, for daring to escape in the manner which we contemplated.

We shook hands, said farewell, and started in different directions for the railway station. I took the nearest possible way to the station, for fear I should be recognized by someone and got into the Negro car in which I knew I should have to ride; but my *master* (as I will now call my wife) took a longer way round.[246]

The young couple anticipated the problems that would befall them. They tied up the "master's" right arm in a sling so that "he" would not be expected to sign his name at the hotel registry desk or elsewhere. They pleaded extreme fatigue in order to get him to his room with his slave as soon as they arrived at the hotels and urged as swift means of transportation as possible in order that "Massa" get to the specialist in Philadelphia before it was too late. The excitement of their adventure is before us on the page, as vividly as words can convey the tension and bated breath and frantic prayers of that hazardous trip.

Artistically, the Crafts' narrative is weakened by frequent digressions, bolstered by means of excerpts from such antislavery favorites as Bourne's *Pictures of Slavery*. The exciting story was clogged by vindictive passages on the Dred Scott decision. The Crafts realized the appropriate appeal of such criticisms. It was not possible to accept the opinion of the highest tribunal of the Republic, that no black person could ever become a citizen of the United States, or have any rights which white men were bound to respect. Their anger was manifested in perhaps fifty of the one hundred and eleven pages of the narrative. Whether one wished to "read around" the digressions or straight through the narrative, *Running a Thousand Miles for Freedom, etc.* is an unforgettable contribution to the slave narrative.

The narratives by the slave women that appeared at the rate of one or two during each decade of the nineteenth century have not been considered before this point in our survey for the reason that it was deemed better to equip the reader with the grotesque essentials of the slave experience by way of the male slave before presenting him with the bizarre addenda that could be expected as part of the slave woman's plight. To the reader already conditioned by abolitionist campaigning against the sin of slavery, the helplessness of the slave woman depicted in the slave narrative might serve as a galvanizing agent, spurring lukewarm sympathies into active antislavery ferment. Without an adequate background of appreciation of the nature of the slave experience as a whole, however, it is difficult, if not impossible, to enter sympathetically into the narratives by the slave women. One must understand the violent invasion of the slaves' privacy and decency by the masters' unbridled lust, which became obvious as the complexion of the next generation of slaves changed in color. Having met a number of the slave women already as mothers and wives and sisters and daughters, we may by now expect that they can be rightly understood as authors.

Six narratives by slave women achieved popularity during the period of the flowering of woman authors generally, from the 1830s to the frankly feminine '50s: *The Narrative of Chloe Spear;*[247] *The Memoirs of Elleanor Eldridge;*[248] *The Narrative of Sojourner Truth; a Northern Slave, Emancipated from Bodily Servitude by the State of New York in 1828;*[249] *Janie Parker, the Fugitive;*[250] *Aunt Sally; or, The Cross the Way to Freedom;*[251] and, *Linda: Incidents in the Life of a Slave Girl, Written by Herself.*[252] The first in point of time, *The Narrative of Chloe Spear,* was written about 1815, shortly before the death of the dignified, godly slave, by a "Lady of Boston." It was revised for publication as one of the first ventures of the Boston branch of the American Anti-Slavery Society in 1832.

The Memoirs of Elleanor Eldridge was published in Providence, Rhode Island, in 1843 by friends of the then-sheltered and ladylike personal maid whose recollections of her early years added to the excitement of the anti-slavery lectures that became so popular all over New England in the 1840s. Sojourner Truth had already come into prominence as a woman suffragist with spectacular powers as a public speaker when an admirer, Olive Gilbert, took down the story of her life as a slave. Gilbert published the dictated account, together with excerpts from Sojourner Truth's stock of homely proverbs, in 1850. The book was reedited in 1855 with an introduction by Harriet Beecher Stowe.[253] Although an aura of mystic power hovered over the name and personality of Sojourner Truth because of her eccentric dress and her ability to capture and hold the attention of her audience by her gaunt majesty and sonorous address, the ever-widening circle of readers of her narrative of the degradations of slavery that she had experienced from birth to womanhood was brought to the realization that it was the slave experience—not mysticism, as many contemporaries insisted—that had opened Sojourner Truth's eyes so widely.

The popular, fictionalized style in which Emily Pierson dressed the fugitive Janie Parker's story of her life in 1851 probably doubled the market for the book but reduces its value as a slave record through the sentimentalization of scenes that needed no touching up. The two slave narratives enjoying the greatest vogue in this group by woman writers, seem to have been the last two on the list, the stories of "Aunt Sally" and of "Linda Brent."

Aunt Sally; or, The Cross the Way to Freedom is a full-sized narrative of the long and harrowing experience of the mother of one of the fugitive slaves who escaped to freedom and became a successful minister of the gospel in Detroit, Michigan, one Reverend Isaac Williams. We regret the modesty of the editor of this apparently painstakingly recorded story, for we have been given no inkling as to his identity beyond the intimation that he was a minister in Brooklyn, New York, in whose house "Aunt Sally" stayed for a short time on her way up from slavery in Alabama after her son had succeeded in tracing her and had sent the money for her purchase. The purpose of the book, we are told in the unsigned preface, is to enlighten the young people in the Sabbath Schools of the North as to the actual conditions of slavery, "so that the young may grow up imbued with the spirit of liberty, and rejoicing to labor for that oppressed and unhappy race which 'Aunt Sally' represents, so, at length, this unfortunate people shall be slaves no longer, but shall find that, to them all, the Cross has been the Way of Freedom." Born about 1796 as a slave on an estate near Fayetteville, North Carolina, "Aunt Sally" was a doughty little woman of more than sixty years at the time of her narration of the details of a life that had experienced every hardship and physical and spiritual torment known to the average female slave. Uncowed by her sufferings, she was still alertly responsive to what life was now offering her, eager to leave Brooklyn for Detroit to see the only grandchildren whom she would not lose to the auction block sooner or later.

The early years of "Aunt Sally" in North Carolina were saddened by the steady sale South of those nearest and dearest to her. Her girlhood was blackened by experiences common to slave girls, but it was not until she had to become accustomed to the sorrow of grieving over her children's sufferings that life became too distressing to bear. We read her ironic description of the fancy wedding her owners "got up" for her slave daughter and wince with her at the thought that a mere whim of the master of either slave might bring about immediate dissolution of the marriage her daughter and new son were entering into so happily. We watch her card yarn and spin cloth throughout the night hours so sorely needed for sleep in order to make clothes to cover her naked children or a little money to buy something to add to their boiled rice. Her husband was sold, suddenly, as punishment for gambling, and she never saw him again. Her sons and then her mother were sold, one by one.

Determined not to lose another dear one to the dread auction sale, "Aunt Sally" married a free man and helped him set up a business that became the envy of the whites. Her owner resented the "insolent" independence of the free black man. Encouraged by his friends, who hated seeing a free Negro succeed at anything, he pounced upon the adorable little three-year-old Lewis, "Aunt Sally's" son by the free husband, and sold him away in the South. The husband, frantic with grief, was torn still further by the decision of "Aunt Sally's" master to sell her in Alabama. We watch him, maddened by despair, beside the slave pen where she is confined while the "herd" is being assembled for the dreadful journey by foot to unknown trials in Alabama. They never saw each other again. "Aunt Sally" learned later, by way of the slaves' "grapevine," that her husband had taken to drink after seeing her disappear over the ridge of the hill in the snake-like winding of the slave coffle and had died soon after.

Life in Alabama was even worse than her worst fears. She was sent to the field by sunup, lashed constantly to encourage speed in the broiling sun, constantly troubled by the gnawing pangs of hunger, sickened by the witnessing of cruelties to others. Yet there were moments of deep beauty: the camp meeting in August, with the glowing vision of her coming home in Heaven, that made her life on earth seem but a temporary condition; the love of the little slave children, mothered by the oldest little girl of eight when their mother was sold away from them, whose troubles "Aunt Sally" was eager to help relieve; the deep interest and incredible sacrifices for each other among the slaves. Her mistress was a villainness of the deepest dye. One of the striking passages in the narrative is the account of leaving this cruel, evil-hearted old tyrant, who begged "Aunt Sally" to pray with her before she left![254] There is the story of the roundabout route in the depths of slavedom taken by a message from her son Isaac before it reached the mother who had last seen him as she wept beside the slave pen twenty years before when he had been sold South. It is a touching illustration of the cooperation of the slaves and their determination to preserve their identity, if by no other means than a scrap of cloth, or a verse from the Bible, chosen in the last frantic moment of separation through sale as the password by which they might know each other again. The message finally reached her through a cousin: she was to be released from slavery upon her son's sending down four hundred dollars in payment for her. The woman who had come through all the trials a slave could suffer stepped briskly forth from the train at Detroit to meet the son who had been more than lost to her for twenty years and a daughter-in-law and grandchildren whom she had never seen.

In contrast to the complete ignorance of the reader as to the identity of the "ghost writer" for "Aunt Sally's" narrative, the fact that Lydia Maria Child was the editor of *Linda: Incidents in the Life of a Slave Girl, Written by Herself* was widely proclaimed in the antislavery papers and in the introduction and appendix of the narrative. "Linda Brent" was the pseudonym adopted by the slave author, the fugitive Harriet Jacobs, to shield her from discovery, as the facts concerning her life that she disclosed in the narrative were of such a nature as to cause embarrassment to her among her friends if it were known that she was the author. In her introduction, Mrs. Child vouches for the authenticity of Harriet Jacobs' book, disclaiming any activity in connection with it that could be considered exceptional for an editor to perform. As it happened, Mrs. Jacobs' sensibilities were very similar to Mrs. Child's, so the tendency of critics has been to assign a greater part of the work of composition to Mrs. Child than she admits. Careful study of Mrs. Jacobs's text will show, however, remarkable consistency in the style of the whole book and an integral relationship between that style and the contents. The details of the narrative can be found paralleled in the mass records of the slave narratives obtained in the 1930s, but some of them have not been *preserved* in publications of earlier date. For this reason, it seems likely that what Mrs. Child has stated in the "Editor's Introduction" to this narrative is the truth. She writes:

> The author of the following autobiography is personally known to me, and her conversation and manners inspire me with confidence. During the last seventeen years, she has lived the greater part of the time with a distinguished family in New York, and has so deported herself as to be highly esteemed by them. This fact is sufficient, without further credentials of her character. I believe those who know her will not be disposed to doubt her veracity, though some incidents in her story are more romantic than fiction.
>
> At her request, I have revised her manuscript; but such changes as I have made have been mainly for purposes of condensation and orderly arrangement. I have not added any thing to the incidents, or changed the import of her very pertinent remarks. With trifling exceptions, both the ideas and the language are her own. I pruned excrescences a little, but otherwise I had no reason for changing her lively and dramatic way of telling her own story. The names of both persons and places are known to me; but for good reasons I suppress them.
>
> It will naturally excite surprise that a woman reared in Slavery should be able to write so well. But circumstances will explain this. In the first place, nature endowed her with quick perceptions. Secondly, the mistress, with whom she lived till she was twelve years old, was a kind, considerate friend, who taught her to read and spell. Thirdly, she was placed in favorable circumstances after she came to the North; having frequent intercourse with intelligent persons, who felt a friendly interest in her welfare, and were disposed to give her opportunities for self-improvement.
>
> I am well aware that many will accuse me of indecorum for presenting these pages to the public; for the experiences of this intelligent and much-injured woman belong to a class which some call delicate subjects, and others indelicate. This peculiar phase of slavery has generally been kept veiled; but the public ought to be made acquainted with its monstrous features, and I willingly take the responsibility of presenting them with the veil withdrawn. I do this for the sake of my sisters in bondage, who are suffering wrongs so foul, that our ears are too delicate to listen to them. I do it with the hope of arousing conscientious and reflecting women at the North to a sense of their duty in the exertion of moral influence on the ques-

tion of Slavery, on all possible occasions. I do it with the hope that every man who reads this narrative will solemnly swear before God that, so far as he had power to prevent it, no fugitive from Slavery shall ever be sent back to suffer in that loathsome den of corruption and cruelty.[255]

In the author's preface to *Linda: Incidents in the Life of a Slave Girl, etc.*, Mrs. Jacobs assures the reader that "this narrative is no fiction," incredible though some of the adventures may seem. The writing of the book was undertaken at irregular intervals, whenever she could "snatch an hour from household duties," on the advice of Bishop Paine of the African Methodist Episcopal Church and others. She describes her purpose in preparing the painful story of her life:

> When I first arrived in Philadelphia, Bishop Paine advised me to publish a sketch of my life, but I told him I was altogether incompetent to such an undertaking. Though I have improved my mind somewhat since that time, I still remain of the same opinion; but I trust my motives will excuse what might otherwise seem presumptuous. I have not written my experiences in order to attract attention to myself; on the contrary, it would have been more pleasant to me to have been silent about my own history. Neither do I care to excite sympathy for my own sufferings. But I do earnestly desire to arouse the women of the North to a realizing sense of the condition of two millions of women at the South, still in bondage, suffering what I suffered, and most of them far worse. I want to add my testimony to that of abler pens to convince the people of the Free States what Slavery really is. Only by experiences can any one realize how deep, and dark, and foul is that pit of abominations.[256]

The first twelve years of the life of Linda (the name that we, too, will adopt in designating the author for purposes of easy reference) were spent happily on a Virginia plantation somewhat resembling the plantation of which Noah Davis tells. Her father was a carpenter who put by some savings in the hope of being allowed to purchase himself and his family. But the opportunity was denied him. Linda's mother died when she was six years old, and Linda turned to her grandmother as her mother from that time. That remarkable woman was the mainstay of her children and grandchildren for many incredibly trying years. When Linda was twelve, her mistress died, and it was hoped by all in her family that she had been given her freedom by the terms of her mistress's will. Instead, the girl had been willed to the five-year-old daughter of her mistress's sister. All five of her grandmother's children were sold at the block.

Linda's new life as the slave of a child less than half her age was in the hands of the child's parents, a Dr. and Mrs. Flint, who were wonderfully cruel individuals in different ways. Linda soon found life a very different affair from what she had known. Concerning the provisions given her, she says:

> Little attention was paid to the slaves' meals in Dr. Flint's house. If they could catch a bit of food while it was going, well and good. I gave myself no trouble on that score, for on my various errands I passed my grandmother's house, where there was always something to spare for me. I was frequently threatened with punishment if I stopped there; and my grandmother, to avoid detaining me, often stood at the gate with something for my breakfast or dinner. I was indebted to *her* for all my comforts, spiritual or temporal. It was *her* labor that supplied my scanty wardrobe. I have a vivid recollection of the linsey-woolsey dress given me every winter by Mrs. Flint. How I hated it! It was one of the badges of slavery.[257]

Before long, she was initiated into the sights and sounds that few slaves were able to live twelve years without witnessing. She tells of the horrible punishments:

> When I had been in the family a few weeks, one of the plantation slaves was brought to town, by order of his master. It was near night when he arrived, and Dr. Flint ordered him to be taken to the work house, and tied up to the joist, so that his feet would just escape the ground. In that situation he was to wait till the doctor had taken his tea. I shall never forget that night. Never before, in my life, had I heard hundreds of blows fall, in succession, on a human being. His piteous groans, and his "O, pray don't, massa," rang in my ear for months afterwards. There were many conjectures as to the cause of this terrible punishment. Some said master accused him of stealing corn; others said the slave had quarrelled with his wife, in presence of the overseer, and had accused his master of being the father of her child. They were both black, and the child was very fair.
>
> I went into the work house next morning, and saw the cowhide still wet with blood, and the boards all covered with gore. The poor man lived, and continued to quarrel with his wife. A few months afterwards Dr. Flint handed them both over to a slave-trader. The guilty man put their value into his pocket, and had the satisfaction of knowing that they were out of sight and hearing. When the mother was delivered into the trader's hands, she said, "You *promised* to treat me well." To which he replied, "You have let your tongue run too far, damn you!" She had forgotten that it was a crime for a slave to tell who was the father of her child.[258]

As Dr. Flint came to figure very prominently in connection with Linda's sufferings, we stop for a bit of characterization that will help the reader understand that hateful individual:

> Dr. Flint was an epicure. The cook never sent a dinner to his table
> without fear and trembling; for if there happened to be a dish not
> to his liking, he would either order her to be whipped, or compel her
> to eat every mouthful of it in his presence. The poor, hungry crea-
> ture might not have objected to eating it; but she did object to
> having her master cram it down her throat till she choked.[259]

Lincoln's Emancipation Proclamation became effective on New Year's Day, and the significance of this fact to the slave cannot be fully understood unless one had learned what New Year's Day regularly signified on plantations throughout the South. Linda's account is typical of the slave narratives:

> Hiring-day at the south takes place on the 1st of January. On the 2d,
> the slaves are expected to go to their new masters. On a farm, they
> work until the corn and cotton are laid. They then have two holi-
> days. Some masters given them a good dinner under the trees. This
> over, they work until Christmas eve. If no heavy charges are mean-
> time brought against them, they are given four or five holidays. . . .
> Then comes New Year's eve; and they gather together their little
> alls, or more properly speaking, their little nothings, and wait
> anxiously for the dawning of day. At the appointed hour the
> grounds are thronged with men, women, and children, waiting, like
> criminals, to hear their doom pronounced. The slave is sure to know
> who is the most humane, or cruel master, within forty miles of him.
>   It is easy to find out, on that day, who clothes and feeds his
> slaves well; for he is surrounded by a crowd, begging, "Please,
> massa, hire me this year. I will work *very* hard, massa."
>   If a slave is unwilling to go with his new master, he is whipped,
> or locked up in jail, until he consents to go, and promises not to
> run away during the year. . . .
>   To the slave mother, New Year's day comes laden with peculiar
> sorrows. She sits on her cold cabin floor, watching the children who
> may all be torn from her the next morning; and often does she
> wish that she and they might die before the day dawns. She may be
> an ignorant creature, degraded by the system that has brutalized her
> from childhood; but she has a mother's instincts, and is capable of
> feeling a mother's agonies.[260]

Between her twelfth and her fifteenth year, nothing of especial importance happened to Linda herself, but she became permanently saddened by the terrible things that were happening to those less fortunate than she. Also, during that period, her beloved brother Willie had been dreadfully punished and imprisoned for trying to run away. He finally did make his escape to the North. When she was fifteen, however, her life began to be troubled by the chief plague in the slave girl's history. We read her account of a trial we have heard brothers tell of in connection with their sisters:

> I now entered on my fifteenth year—a sad epoch in my life of a slave girl. My master began to whisper foul words in my ear. Young as I was, I could not remain ignorant of their import. I tried to treat them with indifference or contempt. The master's age, my extreme youth, and the fear that his conduct would be reported to my grandmother, made him bear this treatment for many months. . . . I turned from him with disgust and hatred. But he was my master. . . . He told me I was his property; that I must subject to his will in all things. My soul revolted against the mean tyranny. But where could I turn for protection? No matter whether the slave girl be as black as ebony or as fair as her mistress. In either case, there is no shadow of law to protect her from insult, from violence, or even from death; all these are inflicted by fiends who bear the shape of men. . . . I know that some are too much brutalized by slavery to feel the humiliation shrink from the memory of it.[261]

Linda's mistress, instead of protecting the frightened young girl from Dr. Flint's advances, became jealous of her attraction and vented her anger on Linda in numberless vengeful ways. Deadly quarrels set in between the Flints as the master's obsession mounted, inflamed by Linda's refusal to bow to his wishes, even after promises had been made of a house of her own and luxuries of many kinds.

Meanwhile, Linda had fallen in love with a free Negro whom she had met at her grandmother's. One evening she was cruelly struck by her master for daring to see him, and the young man was forced to leave town and go North because of threats from Dr. Flint. How Linda, apparently on the rebound, submitted to the suit of a white man named Mr. Sands, a gentleman and friend of Dr. Flint, is a curious thing. Just at the point where Dr. Flint was certain that he had her as he wanted, she maddened him with the news that she was to become the mother of a child by one of his white friends. The child was a boy, born in her grandmother's house just before the Nat Turner insurrection. A second child was born to the same man, this time a girl. Linda's grandmother walked with her proud head bowed, wondering what could have come over Linda, and Linda wondered about herself. She could only explain that Mr. Sands had been kind, whereas Dr. Flint had been hateful. Mr. Sands wanted to buy the freedom of Linda and her children, but Dr. Flint took keen delight in refusing to sell them to him. Linda was put in charge of the new house for Dr. Flint's bride, a young woman he married shortly after the old mistress died of heartbreak. Things went fairly smoothly until Linda learned that her children were to be brought by her master from her grandmother's, to be "broken in" on the plantation. She decided to take flight, knowing that Dr. Flint would not bother to take the youngsters at such a troublesome age except to torment her. Before night of the day following her escape, she found the following notice posted "at every corner, and in every public place for miles around":

> $300 REWARD! Ran away from the subscriber, an intelligent, bright, mulatto girl, named Linda, 21 years of age. Five feet four inches high. Dark eyes, and black hair inclined to curl; but it can be made straight. Has a decayed spot on a front tooth. She can read and write, and in all probability will try to get to the Free States. All persons are forbidden, under penalty of the law, to harbor or employ said slave. $150 will be given to whoever takes her in the state, and $300 if taken out of the state and delivered to me, or lodged in jail.
>
> Dr. Flint[262]

Unfortunately, Linda was bitten in the leg by a poisonous snake while fleeing through the woods and had to jeopardize her own safety and the safety of a friend who harbored her and obtained information from an old woman as to how to make a dressing by steeping "a dozen coppers in vinegar over night." It was necessary for her to appeal to her grandmother, though the poor woman was so sorely laden with grief. Besides, her house was continually searched. Help in their crisis came from an unexpected source, as we learn:

> Among the ladies who were acquainted with my grandmother, was one who had known her from childhood, and always been very friendly to her. . . . At this crisis of affairs, she called to see my grandmother, as she not unfrequently did. She observed the sad and troubled expression of her face, and asked if she knew where Linda was. . . . My grandmother shook her head, without answering. "Come, Aunt Martha," said the kind lady, "tell me all about it. Perhaps I can do something to help you." The husband of this lady held many slaves, and bought and sold slaves. She also held a number in her own name; but she treated them kindly, and would never allow any of them to be sold. She was unlike the majority of slave-holders' wives. Something in the expression of her face said "Trust me!"[263]

The grandmother related the whole story of Linda's life since she was fifteen and her place of hiding at the moment. The woman promised to take Linda into her own home, concealing her in a small room above her own sleeping compartment with no one but herself and her cook, a jolly good woman named Betty, in on the secret. Linda stayed in that house, concealed by day from the rest of the household beneath a plank in the kitchen, until the suspicion of one of the house girls made it impossible for her to stay there any longer, since the mistress would have been severely punished, even though she was a slaveholder herself, if it had been known that Linda was being harbored under her roof.

The only place she knew to turn to was her grandmother's. For the next seven years, without benefit of a space even long enough for her to turn her body, Linda lay in a little shed attached to the roof of her grandmother's house. She tells the story of that living death: how she was worried by wind and rain, tormented "by hundreds of little red insects, fine as a needle's point, that pierced through my skin and produced an intolerable burning" until her grandmother found herbs that got rid of them, cramped almost to hysteria, and able to hear the voices of slavehunters passing in the street below, day in and day out. Once in a while she even heard her name mentioned with the wish to find her and collect the reward. A tiny hole in the floor of the shed allowed her glimpses of her two children playing below and also kept her mind tortured as she learned of various threats from Dr. Flint to sell them at auction, though he still refused to sell them to Mr. Sands for any sum. At the end of the seven years, by the combined efforts of her grandmother, an uncle, and a friend of the uncle, Linda was whisked away from her hiding place and put safely onto a boat for Philadelphia, in which city she arrived ten days later. This was in 1848. Haunted by fears of recapture and anxious to find some way to help get her children in addition to making a living for herself, she sought advice of the bishop of the black church mentioned earlier. Work was obtained, and in a statement printed in the appendix to her narrative we learn of the sympathy she inspired in the family for which she worked during the whole year of 1849, until forced to flee when her pursuers learned of her whereabouts. The statement, from one Amy Post, a Quaker, says:

[When I urged Linda to publish her narrative] she said, "You know a woman can whisper her cruel wrongs in the ear of a dear friend much easier than she can record them for the world to read." Even in talking with me, she wept so much, and seemed to suffer such mental agony, that I felt her story was too sacred to be drawn from her by inquisitive questions, and I left her free to tell as much, or as little, as she chose. Still, I urged upon her the duty of publishing her experiences, for the sake of the good it might do; and, at last, she undertook the task. Having been a slave so large a portion of her life, she is unlearned; she is obliged to earn her living by her own labor, and she has worked untiringly to procure education for her

children; several times she has been obliged to leave her employ-
ments, in order to fly from the man-hunters and woman-hunters of
our land; but she pressed through all these obstacles and overcame
them. After the labors of the day were over, she traced secretly and
wearily, by the midnight lamp, a truthful record of her eventful
life.[264]

It has not been possible, in the course of this chapter, to touch upon all
of the slave narratives of the period between 1836 and the Act of Emancipation.[265] Nor has it been possible to do justice to the individual narratives that
have been discussed. Excerpts are but a clumsy substitute for the experience
of reading the whole story. However, enough of an introduction has been
presented to produce a new image of the American Negro slave. Narration
of his story has continued from the time that his bonds were loosed, formally
at least, up to the 1940s. Signal honors have come to ex-slave narrators:
one has been elected to a position in the Hall of Fame;[266] one has had his
imagined birthday, January 5, set aside for national annual observance.[267]
Copies of the narratives published before 1863, in their day as plentiful in
publishing centers of the United States and England as today's comic book,
are now so rare that when scholars poking about in uncatalogued deposits of
public and private libraries and in second-hand book stalls turn them up,
they are ceremoniously put under lock and key as rare Americana. It is
time, therefore, that they be reedited as source material that must not be
overlooked in the current crusade for a reinterpretation of the "American
dilemma."

Chapter 4

The Trustworthiness
of the Slave Narrative

Doubt as to the trustworthiness of the slave narrative may be expected for three reasons: it was used as abolitionist propaganda in the only period during which it possessed literary importance; it depicts a social institution completely foreign to the modern mind; and it involves the element of unreliability natural to the autobiographic form, particularly when the autobiographer is in need of editorial assistance.

It is noteworthy that the *Narrative* of Moses Roper, the first to appear in the 1830–1860 period with definitely established authorship, was published under the auspices of English abolitionists in London in 1837. A half century earlier, English abolitionists had sponsored the publication of the narratives of the ex-slave Equiano and Gronniosaw, the great popularity of which has been observed in an earlier chapter. Isaac Knapp, Boston book publisher and printer of Garrison's *Liberator*, brought out in 1838 an edition of Equiano's two-volume autobiography that included a reprinting of a number of letters by English abolitionists that had been appended to earlier editions of the book, along with a copy of the special dedication written by Equiano for the occasion of the presentation of his narrative to Parliament in 1790. Knapp's advertisement of this edition emphasized the same features that had been advertised by London and Dublin and Rotterdam presses in the 1790s: the variety of romantic adventures in the experience of this "noble savage" who had "passed through a great variety of wonderful scenes, which give his narrative an interest scarcely surpassed by Robinson Crusoe."[1]

The forty copies of *The Liberator* that Garrison began sending to England regularly each week by the end of the paper's second year greatly impressed the English abolitionists, whose own crusade to blot out slavery in the British Empire was to culminate soon with victory in 1834. Therefore, by the time the slaves' exodus from the South began to reach the proportions of a concerted movement, there was a revival of the enthusiasm for helping the oppressed slave from the United States that had waxed so strong in English abolitionist circles fifty years before. Although circulation figures for the slave narratives are far from complete, the figures we do have lead to the conclusion that there were as many purchasers of the popular book-length slave narratives of the 1830s to 1860s on one side of the Atlantic as on the other, and as many publishers. One can appreciate the acute embarrassment to the South of this new liaison of abolitionists, especially in view of the fact that the South looked to England as her chief market for the slavery-produced cotton. Then, too, when the English abolitionists had sympathized with slaves from America at the end of the preceding century, it had been a matter pertaining to the whole United States, as the institution of slavery was not "peculiar" to the South at that time. Ex-slaves, not fugitive slaves, had either purchased their freedom or been manumitted by their owners and became special objects of interest in England and Holland in the 1790s. There was plainly not much that the Southerners could say about the slave narratives as they came hot from the presses except to dismiss them as gross fabrications "spun by abolitionist busybodies" in New England and old England. Since every slave narrator after 1840 was also an antislavery lecturer and in every case had told his story over and over again to many audiences before it reached the printed page, the readers of the harrowing stories of the slaves had supplementary means by which to determine the extent to which abolitionist scribes had exercised editor's license. According to reports that we have found, the chief difference between the slave lecture and the slave narrative was thought to lie in the superiority of the former in the creation of hair-raising and blood-curdling effects. Thus, the discrediting of the narratives by the Southerners was largely ignored until after the Emancipation Act. Since that time, however, the tendency to overlook the testimony of the slave narratives has been justified by the dubious worth of the literature of propaganda.

From the literary viewpoint, the abolitionists were the most important publishers the slave narrator ever had, but they were not the only publishers. About one-half of the more than six thousand narratives were published or kept in a state of preservation by five other sources of publication: the court record, the sensational journal, the church record, the independent printer, and the Federal Writers' Projects Administration during the 1930s. It is therefore possible to compare the data given in the slave narratives published under abolitionist auspices with the data given in the slave narratives unconnected with such auspices.

The publication of records connected with the due process of law in some phase or other has provided a rich and unwitting source of slave narratives, from the story of John Saffin's Adam in 1703 to the story of the fugitive slave John Anderson in 1863. The "editor" of fifty-six life histories discovered in this way was the court stenographer, whom it would be reasonable to credit with no interest in the words he was trying to take down from the lips of the slave in the dock beyond being paid for his work. Three of the slave narrators with full court histories also had abolitionist publishers for narratives they themselves wrote after their trials: Peter Randolph, Anthony

Burns, and John Anderson.[2] Without the evidence of external marks of identification, it is to be doubted whether the general reader would be able to
decide which of the versions was from the court record and which from the
abolitionist press in each of the three cases. Also, the combined testimony
in the fifty-six court records—both the minutiae and the general nature of
the slave experience—produces a variety of evidence that comes in very
handy as corroboration of one or another apparently flagrant exaggeration
of fact in statements from narratives published by the abolitionists.

The narrative of the slave Arthur, discussed elsewhere at length, belongs
to a curious series of slave narratives published from the 1760s to the 1790s
in the form of broadsides. They were the sensational "confessions" of slaves
about to be executed for some crime, made on the eve of their execution.[3]
These broadsides enjoyed great popularity due to an interest in the "rake's
progress" which Hogarth had made such an entertaining project at the beginning of the eighteenth century. Printers vied with each other in the obtaining and publishing of similar accounts. The search for likely copy finally
extended even to the cell of the condemned slave. Of the four slave narratives of this group, the *Life and Dying Speech of Arthur* seems to have been
the most popular, probably because of the almost irresistible waggishness
of that young rascal. We do not know who took down these narratives, but
it appears that the scribes were enterprising young apprentices to printers
in Worcester and Boston and Philadelphia who had noses for "good copy"
for a reading public that might have gone mad with delight over an issue
of the present-day tabloid newspaper. Certainly we can sense the effect on
the condemned slave of the vicarious enjoyment of his wild adventures by his
recorder: his memory simply raced along his past, pulling up short before the
details that would be sure to please his excited guest, then took off again for
more and more of the kind. It is doubtful that the reporter found it necessary to add to the slave's confession. From the looks of the incredibly packed
page of the broadside, which averaged fifty-seven by forty-eight centimeters,
or approximately twenty-three by nineteen inches, with the printing done on
type of the very tiniest size, the reporter's chief job was to get it all onto the
sheet, as fast as he could, so that the broadside might be peddled down Milk
Street or Broad Street the following morning as news of the latest dye.

Contemporary with the earliest of the "confession" narratives and resembling that group in that it abounds with the exciting experiences "off duty"
of a pleasure-seeking slave, the narrative of Briton Hammon, published in
Boston in 1760 under the title, *The Narrative of the Uncommon Sufferings
and Surprizing Deliverance of Briton Hammon, a Negro Man, Servant to
General Winslow of Marshfield, New-England, Who Returned to Boston after
Having Been Absent Almost Thirteen Years, etc.*, may have engaged the attention of its publisher, the Boston firm of Green and Russell, with its similarity
to other stories of surprising adventures then in vogue. In the general course

of tracking down the slave narratives, two contemporary narratives resembling Briton Hammon's have been discovered. They are listed in three great libraries as books on the Negro but prove upon close examination to be the narratives of an Englishman and of a Scotsman, kidnapped from their homes and sold into slavery in America.[4] The "uncommon sufferings" of Briton Hammon—none of which came from experiences at the hands of his owner but rather during the thirteen years of absence which he had taken without leave—probably attracted the same group of readers that had made successful the publication of the anonymous *Memoirs of an Unfortunate Young Nobleman, Return'd from a Thirteen Years Slavery in America Where He Had Been Sent by the Wicked Contrivances of His Cruel Uncle* when it was presented to the public in London in 1743. Just before the appearance of Hammon's narrative, the first of sixteen known editions of the popular narrative of Peter Williamson was published in York in 1758 (a second edition being the earliest copy located). *French and Indian Cruelty Exemplified in the Life and Various Vicissitudes of Fortune of Peter Williamson*, appeared steadily from that year until 1813 in London, Edinburgh, Liverpool, and Aberdeen, and in Albany and Hartford in the United States.[5] After the fifth edition, published in Edinburgh in 1762, the title under which the book was usually issued was *The Life and Curious Adventures of Peter Williamson, Who Was Carried Off from Aberdeen and Sold for a Slave in America, Written by Himself*. An unnamed printer in Aberdeen brought out an edition in 1841, entitled *Authentic Narrative of the Life and Surprizing Adventures of Peter Williamson, Who Was Kidnapped and Sold for a Slave in America, Written by Himself*. The book thus joined the ranks of abolitionist publications with the curious distinction of being a slave narrative by a Scotch ex-slave which was used in the crusade to arouse human sympathies to the point of abolishing slavery for the American Negro. Since Briton Hammon's narrative contained no internal evidence of his racial identity, the three narratives of adventure were closely enough linked by reason of their exciting stories of kidnappings, enforced slavery in foreign parts, and lucky escapes to account for their being popular together in the eighteenth century.

Church records have provided a third source of slave narratives, particularly the annals of the Quaker sect. Thirty-three short slave narratives and the long narrative of William Boen have been found among the Quaker records.[6] Six narratives of fair length have been located among Catholic records and six of similar length among the records of the African Methodist Episcopal Church, which also reprinted the slave narrative of its founder, originally published by an independent printer.[7] On the whole, the narratives of outstandingly religious slaves reveal individuals less troubled by the gruelling details of the earthly institution to which they were shackled than with the problem of their immortal souls. Therefore, the nature of their struggle with destiny emphasizes a defiance of mortal laws as against divine laws rather than a struggle of an enslaved individual against mortal slavery. William Boen refused to obey his master's command to cut down all the trees, because he was convinced that God had told him not to.[8] A number of slaves risked beating and even sale South because they felt called by God to attend forbidden prayer meetings.[9] One slave suffered his master to whip him until he died to prove his love for Christ.[10] But it is not only within the pages of church records that we find such testimonials of the power of faith in God to lift the slave above his heartache and despair. Slave narratives published by abolitionists are full of such evidence, and some reveal fuller details of the situation from which the slave prayed to be delivered. The reader may recall the cases of Gronniosaw, Equiano, Solomon Bayley, Lunceford Lane, Josiah Henson, John Thompson—in fact, *most* of the slave narrators, in some portion of their narrative, have attested to the strong dependence of the slave upon prayer for spiritual release from the degradation of the slave experience.

The publishing of slave narratives by their authors dates back as far as the first printing of Jupiter Hammon's story in 1787. There were many such ventures during the heyday of the 1840s to 1860s, and they were quickly absorbed into the general stream of antislavery publications. It was in this way that the popular narratives of Henry Watson, Henry Bibb, Peter Randolph, and Noah Davis, among others, reached the public market. After 1863, as the years brought a desire to record the story of their experiences to aging slaves in fairly comfortable circumstances, there were many who brought out the narratives of their lives as private projects.[11] Sometimes the cost of publication was met by local church groups, lodges, or similar organizations. The format for these publications ranged from inexpensive paper covers to very handsomely bound editions, resplendent with gold trimming and glossy pages.[12] Designed often as gift-books for their many friends in the church or lodge, these books today bespeak a racial pride that the social historian would do well to look into before coming to conclusions concerning attitudes of the American Negro with respect to himself.

The fifth nonabolitionist source of records of the slave is to be found in the labors of workers under the Federal Writers' Projects Administration in the field of the slave narratives. A total of twenty-three hundred slave testimonials has been collected as the result of the interviewing, between 1934 and 1938, of ex-slaves living in seventeen different states, who were at that time between the ages of seventy-two and one hundred and twelve years of age. They were slaves at ages ranging from eight to forty-eight in 1860. Much use has been made of these narratives. As will be seen further on in this chapter, these narratives have provided source material for corroboration of the data in the slave narratives published as abolitionist propaganda. Also, the director of the project during the years 1836 to 1938 has recently published an edited anthology of these records as a "folk history of slavery."[13]

Had the American Negro slave been the insensate creature that Dew and Calhoun and others fancied, there of course could not have been any slave narratives, as the autobiographic intention is found only in sensitive individuals in the first place.[14] It is interesting to note the fact that the autobiography as a literary form did not assume an important place in English and American literature until the latter part of the eighteenth century, when there was greater emphasis upon the worth of the individual.[15] The very word "autobiography" is apparently an invention of the early nineteenth century. The first use of the term recorded in the *Oxford New English Dictionary* appears in an article by Robert Southey in 1809. The title of Franklin's *Autobiography* was not given to his work until publication of the first American edition in 1818, though the work itself was begun in 1771 and completed in 1781. Thus the literature of autobiography came into prominence with the Romantic Movement. The form served particularly well as a vehicle of expression for the man with a grievance, for the individual whose faith in the existing order has been crushed by injustice in the life about him, but who has become inspirited suddenly by a new current of thought. Hence, for the slave.

Doubt concerning the reliability of the slave narratives as records spread as the result of a series of mix-ups following the publication in January, 1836, of *Slavery in the United States: A Narrative of the Life and Adventures of Charles Ball, a Black Man* in Lewiston, Pennsylvania, by the publisher J. W. Shugert. A prospectus for the book had been published in antislavery newspapers the preceding August, announcing that the narrative would be published by subscription at one dollar per copy, and recommending it to every citizen in the United States as an expose of "the actual condition of the slaves, moral as well as physical, mental as well as corporeal, with greater certainty, and with more accuracy of detail than could be obtained by many years of travel."[16] A special inducement was offered to "those who take delight in lonely and desperate undertakings, pursued with patient and unflinching courage," in the pages describing Charles Ball's "flight and journey from Georgia to Maryland, which exhibits the curious spectacle of a man wandering six months in the United States without speaking to a human creature."[17] A "Mr. Fisher" appeared in the preface as having prepared Ball's narrative from dictation, and the book had a fine reception and sale. A reviewer in the *Journal of Public Morals* declared it to be effective as:

A history of the exertions of a slave to obtain his freedom . . . a very impressive exhibition of the influence of slavery on the moral character both of the slave and his master. It is written in a charming style, and is calculated deeply to interest all classes. It resembles the story of Robinson Crusoe . . . and would seem utterly incredible to anyone who was not able to conceive the strength of the love of liberty as it burns in the heart of man. . . . It is natural to suppose that Charles, in relating his adventures, would give them in glowing style, and it is evident that while the Editor declares, that in all the statements relative to the Slave himself, he faithfully adheres to the facts as stated by him, he has, nevertheless, exerted a very high degree of skill, in the introduction of such illustrations as the varied scenery of the Southern and Middle States would be likely to furnish.[18]

Although there was plenty of protest from the South to the effect that *Slavery in the United States* was fictitious, the 1836 edition had sold out before the end of the year and a second edition was scheduled for 1837. Toward the end of 1836, however, there appeared in Boston the anonymous *The Slave; or, Memoirs of Archy Moore*, without even the name of a publisher on its title page or anywhere else. The book purported to be the autobiography of a Virginia slave, the son of his owner. It began at once to rival Charles Ball's narrative in the eyes of the public. Both books were sold out and ready for second editions in 1837. The *Memoirs of Archy Moore* was republished that year both in Boston and in London, where it received an elaborate review in the *Spectator* as well as in other literary periodicals.[19] While abolitionists were lauding the "slave Archy Moore" for the "broad blaze of light" which his narrative "throws down into every corner of the horrid caverns of slavery," it suddenly became known that the author of the book was the abolitionist Richard Hildreth, whom Schlesinger has spoken of as "one of the more enigmatic figures in American intellectual history," and whose history of banking was published at the same time as the second edition of *The Slave; or, Memoirs of Archy Moore*.[20] Immediately, both Hildreth's book and Ball's autobiography were widely reported as works of fiction by Southern sympathizers. The historian Hildreth admitted his authorship in the course of publishing his pamphlet, "Brief Remarks on Miss Catharine E. Beecher's Essay on Slavery and Abolitionism," in 1837, in refutation of Miss Beecher's charges that abolitionists had no right to act as "reprovers" of society. Neither the "Mr. Fisher" of *Slavery in the United States* nor Charles Ball ever appeared.

It soon was learned that Hildreth had left his home in Deerfield, Massachusetts, on the advice of his doctor, to spend a year and a half on a plantation in Georgia because of ill health. His passionate hatred of the workings of slavery, to which he could not give utterance for reasons of tact, Hildreth had poured out in the two-volume novel which anticipated the antislavery novel of more than a dozen years hence. This was in 1834-35. No publisher in New York or Boston would undertake to print the book at first, and a year later, the "brave" printer who decided he would risk publishing it would not risk placing his name in the book. But the book boomed. Though

it is still to be found listed in bibliographies and special studies as autobiography,[21] *The Liberator* recognized the *Memoirs of Archy Moore* as
fiction as early as January 14, 1837.[22] Two months later, however, such a
widely read antislavery paper as the *Herald of Freedom* was giving the opposition press copy for ridicule by insisting anew, after the book had been avowed
to be fiction:

> It purports to have been written by a Slave, and it is no more diffi-
> cult to imagine this to be the case, than to imagine who could write
> it, if a slave did not. Who but the spirit that had experienced it could
> draw this terrible portraiture of Slavery? . . . No sojourner amid
> the hospitalities of the Plantations could have achieved the book. No
> slaveholder born and bred to all the mysteries of this unearthly
> institution could have written it. A slave cannot be supposed to have
> done it. 'Stat nominis umbra.'[23]

To cap this to-do over whether the slave was or was not writing the slave
narrative came the *Narrative of James Williams, an American Slave, Who Was
for Several Years a Driver on a Cotton Plantation in Alabama*, published by
the American Anti-Slavery Society of Boston in May of 1838, as "Written
by John Greenleaf Whittier from the Verbal Narrative of James Williams."
According to the 5th Annual Report of the Executive Committee of that
society:

> No pains were spared to apply to the veracity of the narrator every
> test that the circumstances of the case admitted, and a large number
> of gentlemen were well satisfied that there could be no imposition
> in the story without attributing to its author such powers of mind
> as few men, either white or black, could justly lay claim to. It was
> published in connection with abundant facts, showing its statements
> to be at least within the bounds of probability. So far as any contra-
> diction has yet been made at the South, it is of a nature to confirm
> rather than shake belief.[24]

But soon the *Alabama Beacon* published allegations against the credibility
of the narrative, which were reprinted by the *Emancipator* in New York,
August 30, 1838. The *Emancipator* sent letters of inquiry, "without disclosing the antislavery background of the inquiry," to between forty and fifty
persons residing in Virginia, Alabama, and elsewhere in the South. Other
letters were sent to Southerners who were informed of the intent to determine the credibility of James Williams' *Narrative*. Williams had left the
country, presumably for England, before the investigation started. The
Emancipator published a full report of the evidence it received denying the
truth of seven "factual" assertions by Williams, to wit: that no Larrimores
owned the estate called Mount Pleasant, which actually existed in Powhatan

County, Virginia, but was of little value; that no one by the name of Larrimore had resided anywhere near Powhatan County or Richmond; that there had been no intermarriage between Larrimores and Roanes, Brockenbroughs, or Scotts "for the last fifty years, if ever;" that the late Mr. Brockenbrough of Charlotteville had never held a slave who was a brother to James Williams; that there was no record that any John Smoot, John Green, Benjamin Temple, or John Gatewood had ever resided in that county or elsewhere; that no Stephen Ransdell had been known to reside in Caroline County; that no John Scott had ever resided in Richmond.[25]

The Liberator, in an editorial for September 28, 1838, considered the type of evidence too "loose to condemn the narrative as false," adding:

> The portrait in the book is a very correct and striking likeness of
> the man who told the story, and can undoubtedly be identified by
> many in Virginia. . . . A young colored apprentice was bought free
> in Jamaica, by Joseph Sturge, and his narrative, which was published
> in England, was denied as positively by the slaveholders as our book
> has been; but the British government sent out orders to have the
> matter examined by commissioners on the spot, who reported that
> it was a great deal worse than James had related.[26]

The Executive Committee of the New York branch of the American Anti-Slavery Society, with James G. Birney and Lewis Tappan as co-chairmen, was initially disposed to credit the narrative but came forth with a signed retraction of the Williams narrative in an authorized statement printed in the *Liberator* for November 2, 1838, and in other antislavery papers. The statement directed the publisher to discontinue the sale of the book, declaring, in part:

> The committee called on, in the discharge of their duty . . . have
> scrupulously guarded themselves against the influence of the pre-
> vailing prejudice, which would lead them to decide of course, or
> hastily, against a black, where his testimony was contradicted by a
> white. Thus prepared, as they feel themselves to be, for impartially
> weighing all the circumstances of the case, they have been drawn
> fully to the conclusion, that the statements of the Narrative, so far
> as they are cited above, and contradicted by the writers of the
> letters, are wholly false, and therefore they cannot with propriety
> ask for the confidence of the community in any of the statements
> contained in the Narrative.[27]

The abolitionists, led by the former Alabaman and slaveholder James Birney, acted sensibly in discrediting the *Narrative of James Williams*. To be sure, the replies to the letters sent to more than three-score Southerners had not attacked the *substance* of the narrative to any considerable extent, but rather the *names* Williams had given his characters. Therefore, the most pain-staking investigation that it was possible to undertake, including both "blind" and informed Southern participants, did not shake the verity of the general picture Williams had dictated. Birney himself had declared Williams's account of slave life in Alabama to be a true relation of slave conditions as he had known them.[28] Many residents of Alabama and Virginia or Northerners who had previously lived in those states likewise testified to the general truth of the narrative. But the fact that Williams had (probably without thinking) selected the name of a real county in Virginia for some other county of his experience precipitated some real trouble. All that the residents of Powhatan County, Virginia, had to do to clinch their argument against the slave narra-tive was to prove the nonexistence in that county of the persons Williams had placed there. It is unfortunate that Williams was not sufficiently circum-spect to avoid naming the county, as in his treatment of Alabamans. The names of Charles Ball's narrative had been fictitious, too—as fictitious as those in "Archy Moore's." Williams's names should have been protected by a disclaimer to the effect that "any resemblance of the names in this story to persons living or dead is purely accidental and unintentional." But since no such precaution was taken, since a Powhatan County did exist in Virginia and a dumpy little estate in that county happened to have the very possible name of "Mount Pleasant" besides, the case was wholly ruined for the *Narra-tive of James Williams*. As Whittier wrote in the *Pennsylvania Freeman* while the abolitionists were waiting "with some anxiety" during September and October for full returns from the South in reply to the letters that had been sent down:

> Our cause needs no support of a doubtful character; and if the
> narrative in any essential particular is untrue, the slaveholders of
> Virginia and Alabama could confer a favor upon us by immediately
> producing testimony to that effect.[29]

This James Williams narrative thus left the publishing world. James Williams appears as the author of two other slave narratives. The *Life and Adventures of James Williams, a Fugitive Slave* was published in San Francisco in 1874 and again in Philadelphia in 1893. The *Life of James Williams, Better Known as Professor Jim, for Half a Century Janitor of Trinity College* was published in Hartford in 1873. A fourth James Williams wrote a *Narrative of the Cruel Treatment of a Negro Apprentice in Jamaica, from the First of August, 1834 Till the Purchase of His freedom in 1837*, published in Glasgow and in London in 1837. But this was a British slave who was never in the United States. The narrative of the only James Williams the abolitionists were con-cerned with was withdrawn from sale, because the accidental identification rendered certain other names "false." It was a wise move on the part of the abolitionists to peserve the effectualness of the slave narrative as propaganda.

Thereafter, slave narrators used actual names of persons and places and either skipped the country with a batch from the first issue of their narratives under their arms or got together enough money to buy their freedom, to be on the safe side.

Hildreth's novel appeared in the guise of fiction but had the same features of interest to those who wanted to know about slavery in its worse phases in the South. It went into its seventh edition by 1848, and the publishers offered an eager public its choice of copies ranging from $1.25 to 38 cents in price, according to the binding. It was rejacketed as *Archy Moore, the White Slave; or, Memoirs of a Fugitive* by Tappan and Whittemore in Boston during the tidal wave of interest in slave literature that washed the North in 1852. It was published the same year by Ingram and Cook in London as *The White Slave; or, Memoirs of a Fugitive. A Story of Slave Life in Virginia and Other Slave States of America*. It reached a sale of fifteen thousand before the end of the second month and was reissued by that firm as a companion volume to the fifth edition of *Uncle Tom's Cabin* that Ingram and Cook issued after three months. Ingram and Cook's edition gives no author, stating on the title page that the book was "edited by R. Hildreth, Esq., Author of *A History of the United States*." Thus, to an uninformed reading public in England, *The White Slave* was an actual autobiography, by one "Archy Moore."

An edition in 1853 followed Mrs. Stowe's 1853 example by providing a "key" to the sources for the book in the form of a lengthy section of "Notes to *The White Slave*" appended to the novel. The very first note suggests that the real key to Hildreth's sources is a book he had written near Savannah, Georgia, during the years 1834-1835. The book refers to the daring means of escape of the fugitive slaves William and Ellen Craft from a plantation near Macon, Georgia, to Philadelphia, *in December, 1848*, which suggested to Archy Moore a means whereby he and Cassy could escape![30] *The Liberator* reprinted from *Commonwealth* a report of a curious distinction that was accorded the book, saying that the novel,

> which has had a great run in Europe, having appeared at London in
> five or six different forms, and in French, German, and Italian
> translations at Paris, Berlin, and Rome, has just had the crowning
> honor of being prohibited by the Pope. It must be the general spirit
> of liberty which the book breathes, the same cause which has led
> to its prohibition generally, south of the Potomac.[31]

The book proved to be the most influential by far of all of Hildreth's writings, all of which showed, Schlesinger asserted, the abolitionist's "sturdy hostility to slavery which continued through his life." He cites Hildreth's contemporary, Charles Congdon, for crediting Hildreth with giving the *New York Tribune* its antislavery tone and concludes that "perhaps at that time he was in advance of its editor."[32] A belief in democracy that could not brook despotism based on slavery runs through Hildreth's works, which include, in addition to the *Memoirs of Archy Moore* and the histories of banking and of the United States already mentioned: *Despotism in America: An Inquiry into the Nature, Results, and Legal Basis of the Slaveholding System in the United States. By the Author of Archy Moore* (Boston, 1840 and 1854); and *Japan As It Was and As It Is* (Boston, c. 1855). Hildreth's bitter seriousness sets him apart from all the other white authors of antislavery novels, including Mrs. Stowe. It seems to be for this reason that his puzzling pseudo-slave narrative both helped to increase the popularity of the real slave narrative and to cast doubt upon the veracity of its contents.

Business-minded publishers realized that the sudden discovery in 1837 of the fictional character of the *Memoirs of Archy Moore* did not disprove the authenticity of the fugitive slave Charles Ball's narrative. They therefore brought out several later editions of *Slavery in the United States*—one in London in 1846, with a Mrs. Barnard as editor; an edition from the publishing house of J. T. Shryock of Pittsburg, in 1853; and the gala hoax on the part of the New York publishers H. Dayton and Asher, who in 1858 brought forth the narrative under the guise of a brand new arrival among slave narratives. Herbert Nelson has described the ruse well:

> Twenty-two years after it first appeared, the excellent narrative of
> Charles Ball was seized upon, condensed slightly, bound in a fiery
> red cover, with great wavering gilt letters staring out at the reader,
> and handed out to an eager public under the astonishing title, *Fifty
> Years in Chains*. The public was told, moreover, that the slave thus
> held for fifty years was still alive, and that revealing his name would
> make him liable to capture—this although his name had been
> blazoned abroad on title-pages for two decades—and whereas the
> brief preface intimated quite clearly that this was the first printing
> of the story, it had gone through at least two editions before.[33]

The venture of Dayton and Asher proved very successful. A new edition was issued in 1859, and more copies are to be found of this particular edition than are to be found of any other edition of this slave narrative, or any other slave narrative, in the libraries throughout this country. But the "discredited" *Narrative of James Williams* was never again to be touched by the abolitionists, even though it was as appealing as the other two books figuring in this controversy over the authenticity of the slave narrative, used exactly the same technique to hide the author's identity as the Ball narrative, and was taken down by the hand of honest John Greenleaf Whittier.

Garrison, characteristically enough, resented the common-sense decision of the Birney-led committee that framed the policy of the abolitionists in respect to Williams's narrative, since nothing had been disproved but a set of names. He found an opportunity to point up his opposition nearly a year later in an editorial in which he reviewed Theodore Weld's *Slavery As It Is*, that "handbook of the anti-slavery movement for ten years," which Simms declares "carried the assault upon slavery to vituperative heights not reached by any publication, except, perhaps, the *Liberator*."[34] The "facts" of this book, notwithstanding the reactions of Southerners, were actually culled from one thousand different items concerning slaves that appeared in leading Southern newspapers during the 1830s and are verifiable through the newspaper files. In his most typical manner, Garrison exclaimed:

> Abolitionists exaggerate the horrors of slavery? Impossible! They
> have never conceived half its horrors! . . . What a clamor was raised
> about the narrative of James Williams! 'Oh! how the dear good
> Christian slaveholders were slandered! What an incredible fiction!'
> Yes, truly. Let the narrative of James Williams go for a fiction! We
> are now inclined to think it must have been. The picture was not
> dark enough. It melts away before the *now authenticated* 'horrors'
> of the prison house.[35]

This turn of affairs in connection with the slave narrative forced court-record accuracy upon the choice of names for persons and places in the slave narrative, even at the price of exile or great personal danger to the slave narrator. Clearly, the connection between the abolitionist editor and the creative composition of the slave narrative he used for propaganda purposes had been very loose. A study of the question-and-answer method that regularly followed the lecture of the slave narrators further illustrates that connection.

The Northerners and Britishers who packed churches and lyceum halls to get a good look at fugitive slaves and hear them tell of slavery seem to have been restless listeners. Newspaper reporters frequently inserted phrases describing their reactions, and the period of questioning that followed the slave lecture was evidently a lively affair, especially when proslavery sympathizers were present at the antislavery meetings. What the slave had to tell was so incredible to persons who had never witnessed slavery in operation or had only seen a dress-parade version of it at places like Saratoga Springs and other resorts frequented by Southerners that they seemed eager to question the fugitive on every phase of his narrative and lecture. The fugitive slave Lewis Clarke built up an interesting appendix for the second edition of his *Narrative*, first published in Boston in 1845. The second edition came out in 1846 and included thirty-six of the questions most often asked after his lectures, along with his answers. The questions were:

> How many holidays in a year do slaves have?
> How do slaves spend the Sabbath?
> What if strangers come along and see you at work?

Why did you not learn to read?

What proportion of slaves attend church on the Sabbath?

How many slaves have you ever known that could read?

What do slaves know about the Bible?

Are families often separated?

How are the slave cabins usually built?

What amount of food do slaves have?

What is the clothing of a slave for a year?

Have you ever known a slave mother to kill her own children?

How is it that masters kill their slaves when they are worth so much money?

What do they do with old slaves who are past labor?

What makes them wash slaves in salt and water after they whip them?

Do not slaves often say that they love their masters very much?

Who are the patrols?

How do slaves get information of what is going on in the free states?

Don't slaves that run away return sometimes?

If the slaves were set free, would they cut the throats of their masters?

Did the slaves hear of the emancipation in the West Indies?

What do slaves think of the piety of their masters?

Do slaves have conscientious scruples about taking things from their masters?

Do you think it was right for you to run away and not pay anything for yourself?

Soon after you came into Ohio, did you let yourself to work?

Why do slaves dread so bad to go to the South, to Mississippi or Louisiana?

What is the highest price you ever knew a slave to sell for?

Why is a black slave-driver worse than a white one?

Are the masters afraid of insurrection?

What is the worst thing you ever saw in Kentucky?

Which is the worst, a master or a mistress?

How soon do the children begin to exercise their authority?

Do you suffer from cold in Kentucky?

What do they raise in Kentucky?

Do the masters drink a great deal?

Are you afraid they will try to catch you, and what will you do if they do?[36]

These questions and the answers to them that Clarke gives are typical of the questions and answers reported in stenographic accounts in abolitionist newspapers of lectures by both Lewis and Milton Clarke, Lunsford Lane, Douglass, William Wells Brown, Henry Bibb, Pennington, Moses Grandy, William and Ellen Craft, Austin Steward, Henry Watson, Henry Box Brown, and many other popular slave lecturers.

As only a few hundred of some fifty thousand fugitive slaves achieved popular acclaim, it is interesting to follow the fortunes of William and Ellen Craft from the time of their arrival in the free state of Pennsylvania, where they at once caught the attention of a fellow fugitive slave, William Wells Brown, in December, 1848. Brown ranked second only to Douglass in popularity as an abolitionist speaker, and, in some quarters, stood first since Douglass had "stooped" to ransom. His interest in the couple from Georgia immediately ushered them into the inner clique of slave lecturers. The romantic story of their escape struck their audience as without parallel in all history, but the slave narratives reveal use of the motif before as well as after the Crafts ran their thousand thrilling miles:[37] the white-looking woman slave, dressed in male attire and passing as a Southern slaveholder, goes from city to city on her way North and stops in the best hotels with the very dark slave husband passing as her servant. Since neither of them could read or write, they tied Ellen's right hand up as though it was injured so that she would not be called upon to write her name at the hotel registry desk. Everywhere they stopped, William begged that his "master" not be detained, as it was necessary that he get to Philadelphia at once for vital medical attention.

Brown arranged for a lecture tour for them throughout New England and the British Isles, and the three fugitive slaves had an almost royal journey of it. Typical of newspaper accounts of their many lectures is the following account of the reaction of a New Bedford audience in February of 1849:

> An expression of astonishment arose from the audience, as Ellen and her husband stood before them. Could it be possible that she was held as a slave? There she was, in the language of the slaveholder's advertisement, 'with regular features, straight hair, and so light as not to be distinguished from a white woman.'
>
> A lady in the audience wanted to know if they called her a 'nigger' at the South. 'Oh, yes,' said she, 'they didn't call me anything else; they said it would make me proud.'
>
> Surely, many of the mothers, wives, and sisters in that audience, must have felt the question of slavery brought close home to their hearts as they looked upon her. Slavery knows no color, but only condition: tens of thousands of mothers, wives and daughters, are held in the same condition by this nation.
>
> William, the husband, is a noble specimen of a man; he is said to resemble Cinques, the Amistad hero; he certainly does in his love of liberty; you may see it in his eye. . . .

William was asked what he expected to do, if an attempt was made to take him. Said he, with deep energy, 'I knew the consequences; I had made up my mind to kill or be killed, before I would be taken.'[38]

A gentleman in the audience, who had been a resident in Macon, Georgia, put a series of questions to the Crafts in regard to the topography of Macon, its leading inhabitants, etc., all of which were answered completely and satisfactorily until the questioner—who waxed testy as the audience tried to cut off his questions—asked the Crafts to name the last six governors of Georgia. This they could not do, and the interrogator showed a feeling of having triumphed over the fugitives at last. But when someone in the audience asked the former Georgian to name them himself, he could not.[39]

Four days later, Brown and his proteges—whom one reporter referred to as "three specimens of the peculiar property of the South"—had another exciting triumph at Northboro, concerning which Lyman Allen wrote to Garrison:

> Then came the separation; and what a rush, not to the door, but to take the hand that was so lately in chains! . . . I wish in my soul that Calhoun and Company could have seen it. This growing sympathy for the slave is more to be dreaded by the South than bullets and guns combined.[40]

One Sunday evening in April, the Crafts were given a public welcome at Boston's famed Tremont Temple, which was packed beyond capacity in spite of the admission fee charged. They were introduced first by Garrison and then by Brown. William Craft then told the story of their escape, the effect of which, according to one reporter, was as follows:

> [Mr. Craft's] manly dignity and evident sincerity at once secured the respect and confidence of the audience, and he was listened to with corresponding attention. His narrative showed that the ingenuity of the fugitives in laying their plans for escape, and their steadiness of nerve in their execution, would enable them amply to 'take care of themselves' under any circumstances. After Mr. Craft had closed, Wendell Phillips addressed the audience in his usually eloquent strain.[41]

The danger of recapture for the three fugitives so worried their powerless wellwishers in New England that William Wells Brown and the Crafts set sail for even greater triumphs in England, arriving in Liverpool in January, 1851, two years after the Crafts' flight from Georgia. *The Liberator* reprints an article from the *Leeds Mercury* in its issue for May 23, 1841, stating that the Crafts had been listed by one Mr. William Armistead of Leeds on the census report of March 30, as "fugitives from slavery in America, the land of their nativity." The article commented further that Ellen Craft was as "fair as British girls, and as intelligent," while William Craft was "very dark but of a reflective, intelligent countenance, and of manly and dignified deportment."[42]

From March to September, 1851, the Crafts accompanied Brown on a lecture tour of England and Scotland, but in September they had the good fortune to interest friends in their cherished dream of getting an education. The following account is from an article that appeared in the *London Morning Advertiser*, as reprinted in *The Liberator* for September 26, 1851:

> It is now their good fortune, with the assistance of friends, to be received as pupils in the Ockham Schools, near Ripley, Surrey. These schools, which are partly industrial, were established by Lady Byron for giving useful education to children residing in the rural districts.
>
> All the advantages the schools possess are afforded to the Crafts, in a mode which is in every respect considerate of their feelings. In addition to other branches of knowledge, Mr. Craft is cultivating his taste for drawing under an able master; he renders himself useful by giving the boys instruction in carpentering and cabinet-making, while Mrs. Craft exerts herself in communicating some of her varied manual acquirements to the girls. The children are greatly attached to her, and both she and her husband are happy, industrious, and making progress in their pursuits.[43]

William Craft's progress in the art of writing can be watched in the letters he wrote to Garrison on the average of one a year. His plan to write a slave narrative is mentioned in November of 1852,[44] an interesting fact with respect to the authenticity of the slave narrative, as the narrative itself did not appear until 1860. There were certainly scribes enough in the neighborhood in which the Crafts now resided to take down his words for him, just as they had taken down Moses Roper's, Moses Grandy's, Lewis and Milton Clarke's, and others. According to the evidence of his letters, each year brought improvement in William Craft's grammar, his ability to paragraph his material, and his style. There is no reason for questioning his ability to produce *Running a Thousand Miles for Freedom; or, the Escape of William and Ellen Craft from Slavery*, which was published in London by Tweedie in 1860, a dozen years after that escape. The Crafts lectured continually and kept in touch with the progress of the abolitionists' crusade in America through the *Liberator*, copies of which Garrison had sent them ever since they had left New England. One of the most interesting of William Craft's letters, written to Garrison in February, 1855, conveys his thanks for Garrison's kindness in sending him the paper and adds that he now wishes to *pay* for the paper, having arranged with Brown (who had returned to America) to settle with Garrison for a twelve-month subscription. The same letter reports the safe arrival of a child.[45]

The Crafts never returned to America. They were always very bitter over the injustice of the slave system, and their remarks, printed in the newspaper accounts of their many lectures, show that the asperity of their autobiography belonged to them, not to any editor. On one occasion in London, for example, they were asked, "Do you really think that the slaves are intelligent enough to take care of themselves?" Ellen Craft was reported in the *London Daily News* as replying: "At present, they take care of themselves and their masters too; if they were free, I think they would be able to take care of themselves."[46] It amused them that the publicity given their method of escape had redounded to the suspicion and discomfort of actual young Southern masters traveling north with a single slave attendant. The last episode we have found concerning them owes its existence to the romantic curiosity of Major General James H. Wilson, who took time enough off from his duties as Union commander in Macon to follow up Garrison's request that he try to find Maria Smith, the mother of Ellen Craft. The general wrote to Garrison:

> Having discovered her residence, I sent for her yesterday, and read your letter to her. She was delighted to hear from her daughter and son-in-law, and requests me to say that she wishes to join them just as soon as they can send the money necessary to pay her traveling expenses. She is in good health, very hale, and young looking for a woman of her age.[47]

The experiences of many fugitives similarly favored by abolitionist publicity rivaled the good fortunes of the Crafts. Josiah Henson shuttled back and forth between Dawn, Canada West, and Boston in the 1840s. In Boston he was frequently a guest of Congressman Samuel A. Eliot, to whom Henson dictated his *Life of Josiah Henson, Formerly a Slave, Now an Inhabitant of Canada, as Narrated by Himself*. Published in Boston in 1849, this slave narrative inspired the Reverend Ephraim Peabody to write what is probably the best essay that has been written on the "Narratives of Fugitive Slaves," a thirty-one page article that appeared in the *Christian Examiner* in July, 1849. Mrs. Stowe's guardian angel should have looked to the destruction of all copies of this issue upon the death of that gifted lady, for it is quite evident from her perfect silence concerning Peabody in her elaborate and "complete" *Key to Uncle Tom's Cabin* that she intended to keep the secret of the influence of that article upon her. Full discussion of that unsuspected secret will be given in a later chapter. At this point it is sufficient merely to correct a statement by a noted historian of the Negro to the effect that Josiah Henson's experiences in slavery were so strange and peculiarly romantic that on hearing his story Mrs. Harriet Beecher Stowe reconstructed and embellished it so as to produce the famous narrative known as *Uncle Tom's Cabin*."[48] Mrs. Stowe did not meet Henson until after her great book had carried her on tour to England in the wake of her novel's phenomenal reception. Henson was in England on business for the Canadian settlement, according to the papers he carried with him. The six-thousandth copy of his narrative had already been issued, as his London publisher, T. Binney, announced in the reprint edition of 1852. Only two scant pages were devoted to discussion of his narrative in the *Key to Uncle Tom's Cabin* that Mrs. Stowe had written in order to indicate the sources from which she drew the material inspiration for her book. It was not until 1858 that the idea seems to have occurred to Mrs. Stowe to assign more importance to Josiah Henson's narrative than she expresses in the casual passage beginning: "A last instance parallel with that of Uncle Tom is to be found in the published memoirs of the venerable Josiah Henson, now, as we have said, a clergyman in Canada."[49]

Perhaps because she felt that it was no longer likely that readers of the *Christian Examiner* would remember an article written nine years previously, Mrs. Stowe suddenly identified Henson as the "original Uncle Tom" in the preface to a revised edition of his narrative, which came out in Boston and in Cleveland in 1858 wih the new title: *Truth Stranger than Fiction: Father Henson's Story of His Own Life*. Perhaps she liked a quality she may have discovered in Henson upon making his acquaintance—a touch of the charlatan, which the Reverend Mr. Peabody never suspected, but which she herself could be expected to recognize as one of the special characteristics of the Beecher clan. However it happened, her decision changed Henson's life, from that year until his death, 1881, into a series of successes exactly to his liking. It was very fortunate for him that this happened. For it is a fact that Josiah Henson had got himself into the uncomfortable position of being exposed as an imposter by the residents of Dawn and the sheriff of Chatham, Canada, in February of 1851.

The publicity given the too-good-to-be-true credentials that Henson had provided for himself and was carrying around England led the fugitive slaves in the all-Negro settlement at Dawn to disclaim the papers, which purported to authorize Henson to receive donations for that settlement. In its issue for January 24, 1851, *The Liberator* carried an editorial describing these credentials as follows:

> As an introduction to those to whom he intended to appeal in Great Britain, the old man carried with him testimonials from the highest officers of the Canadian Government; and among them one, which, in its statement of a single, simple fact in the history of this good man's life, passed a higher eulogium upon his moral worth, and his character as a man and Christian, than was ever before paid in the loftiest strains of eloquence, or by the most gifted bard, to any

human being. It was the certificate of the Sheriff of the County in
Canada, where Father Henson resides, who testifies that during
fifteen years and with a black population of from three to four
thousand, not a single Negro has come under legal custody or animadversion for any crime or misdemeanor whatever, etc.

The slaves sent word to the abolition world through the *American Baptist* for
March, 1851, however, to refute this testimony, declaring that Henson

has never colonized or settled a community of Fugitive Slaves in this
country, and . . . is not the agent of any public society in Canada,
and has no rightful authority to collect funds in the name of the
colored people of this Province. . . . We consider it a duty of necessity to inform the benevolent of England, Ireland, and Scotland, that
Josiah Henson is a totally unworthy medium through which to transmit their donations for the poor fugitive slaves arriving in Canada,
as he has proved false; and we warn all concerned, that his statements are gratuitous and utterly without truth; that he has no
credentials worthy of credit, as will be seen by the subjoined certificate from the worthy Sheriff of Kent.[51]

The certificate, signed by a Sheriff J. Waddell of the County of Kent, Canada,
asserted that the sheriff had given Henson no such paper as the latter had
with him. The *Christian Register* carried the same refutation, reprinted from
the *American Baptist* in April, 1851. This was copied by the *Voice of the
Fugitive*, the fugitive slaves' own paper. Fortunately for Henson, there was
so much going on in abolitionist circles in 1851 that no further notice was
taken of the expose. His talent for convincing others of his martyr-like
service in the cause of religion and the uplift of his fellow fugitives kept
him in comfortable circumstances until the windfall of Mrs. Stowe's decision
to play him up as her own dramatic discovery set him squarely within the
heaven of publicity for which his type is made. Advance orders before publication for the "Stowe edition" of his narrative, at 75 cents a copy, totaled
1000 copies on May 14 and 5000 copies on May 28, 1858.[52] Presentation
to Queen Victoria was part of his reward for being the splendid self-propa-
gandizing agent that he was, and he was busy keeping his history up to date
until his death, at ninety years of age.

Of lesser calibre than Henson, but enjoying as much publicity at first,
because of the spectacular means by which he escaped from slavery, was
Henry Box Brown, whose *Narrative of Henry Box Brown, Who Escaped from
Slavery Enclosed in a Box Three Feet Long, Two and a Half Feet High* was
published in Boston in 1849 and in Manchester in 1851. New Engalnd audiences were satisfied with hearing Henry Box Brown describe over and over
again the agony of his twenty-six-hour ordeal in the box—including the period

of nearly two hours when the box had been turned so that he was standing on his head—on the journey in the baggage train from Richmond to Philadelphia. They had the corroboration of the testimony of Samuel J. May for Brown's story, as May had been present in the home of the Philadelphia abolitionist when the box was delivered. On May 31, 1849 he gave a huge audience at Faneuil Hall, a graphic description of the way Brown looked when he was taken out of the box. The English, however, seemed in need of proof that what Brown had done could be done. A box was made at Bradford to the specifications given in Brown's narrative, Brown was nailed inside it exactly as he had been in Richmond, and he was carried from Bradford to Leeds, a trip of two and three-quarters hours, preceded by a band of music and banners![53] To such lengths they went for verification of their priceless abolitionist propaganda!

Accounts of the public lives of dozens more popular slave narrators could be given in illustration of the point that the "facts" of the slave narratives came from the slaves and not from their abolitionist editors, who could no more have created the substance of the slave narratives than Americans today seem able to conceive of the state of society that engendered the atrocities of the slave camps in Europe and in the Far East in the 1930s and 1940s.

Judged beside the data in the slave narratives written either before or after the 1830–1860 period, the descriptions generally given of the machinery of slavery in operation during that period in the abolitionist-published narratives present as the norm experiences which in the other narratives appear only as exceptional instances. Various factors account for this difference: the actual degeneration of the slavery system in the newly developed "Cotton Kingdom" in the Black Belt—that region stretching across the deep South for more than a thousand miles, from South Carolina to San Antonio, Texas, the region which the slave dreaded worse than death; the fact that ninety percent of the book-length slave narratives of this period were by fugitive slaves, the majority of whom endured exceptional mistreatment in comparison with the treatment of the other slaves on their plantation for one reason or another— very often because they were mulattoes and therefore hated by the mistress or others; and the fact that his ability to sense the situation in which he now found himself, as favored specimen and lecturer and author and guest of romantically passionate haters of "those ogres, the slaveholders," led the slave narrator to follow the "director's" lead, in this drama that was scheduled to end with his own emancipation.

This adjustment of his material to the emotional bias of his abolitionist hosts, a characteristic of the slave already noted as stage presence, is natural for witnesses, according to an authority on judicial proof who says:

> Witnesses usually feel more or less complimented by the confidence
> that is placed in them by the party calling them to prove worthy of

this confidence. This feeling is unconscious on the part of the witness, and is usually not a strong enough motive to lead to actual perjury in its full extent; but it serves as a sufficient reason why the witness will almost unconsciously dilute or color the evidence to suit a particular purpose, and perhaps add only a bit here, or suppress one there, but this bit will make all the differences in the meaning.[54]

Thus it was to be expected that the slave narrator of the abolitionist period would draw a portrait of the slaveholder that resembled the abolitionist's preconception of a monster somewhat more closely than do the portraits of slaveholders in the slave narratives produced before or after that period. Also, the Southerners knew better than any other people could that the slave had a good right to judge him harshly. For, as a contemporary critic expressed it:

The best qualities of the master are likely to appear anywhere rather than in his connection with the slave. And except it be an easy kindness, the slave is in no position to estimate aright the virtues of one who, towards himself, appears simply as a power whom he cannot resist. They stand in such utterly false relations to each other, that their whole intercourse must necessarily be vitiated, and the worst qualities of each, and these almost exclusively, must be perpetually forced on the attention of the other.[55]

The critic hastens to leave room for admission of this chief weakness of the slave narrative of the 1830s to 1860s, however, by adding: "But human nature could not long exist were the great body of slaveholders like those whom these narratives describe." He was speaking of the five narratives upon which *Uncle Tom's Cabin* was based, the narratives of Douglass, the Clarkes, William Wells Brown, Pennington, and Henson. The testimony is pretty bad for the majority of the slaveholders in the other slave narratives of the period, too.

According to Wigmore, the "usual character of human testimony" can be described as "substantial truth under circumstantial variety."[56] It is therefore very interesting to note how closely the descriptions of the slave experience found in the slave narratives taken down from the lips of more than twenty-six hundred ex-slaves during the years 1934 to 1938 resemble the descriptions in the narratives published during the 1830 to 1860 period. All of the questions on how the slaves lived and felt that Lewis Clarke listed in the appendix to the second edition of his narrative, as discussed earlier in this chapter, have counterparts in the questions asked the aged ex-slaves by the interviewers in the Federal Writers' Project who collected slave narratives.[57]

Details concerning the selling apart of families of slaves, the plight of the slave girl, the housing conditions, methods of punishment, and other phases of the slave experience have the same general characteristics in the later narratives as in the group dependent upon abolitionist sponsors for publication, a resemblance that certainly suggests "substantial truth under circumstantial variety." For various reasons, however, the temptation to consider the genuineness of the slave narratives because of this resemblance of substance must be held in check.

Current attention to the first publication of narratives from the lips of ex-slaves shows clearly a rather general curiosity as to how the slave looked at slavery.[58] Wigmore's assertion that "we possess only the general understanding that, for perception the senses become less keen, and that for recollection, the recollection of earlier events becomes more active and that of recent events less active,"[59] may explain why some scholars today are disposed to give at least a measure of credence to the aged slaves' stories.[60] The net effect of the more than ten thousand pages of narratives by the ex-slaves is persuasive.

It must be remembered, none the less, that without doubt many of the answers of the ex-slaves to many of the questions were conventional, particularly in replies to the less skillful interviewers. The "proper way to answer white folks" that had been imprinted indelibly in the minds of some ex-slaves from their earliest years was obviously the motivation behind some of the answers. Also, as many of the persons interviewed were on federal relief and seemed to fear a direct connection between what they might say to employees on a federal project and their future on the relief board, it is probable that their frequently wary attempts to sound out their interviewers before making definite statements in answer to certain questions stemmed from a desire to please the representative from the "goose" allowing them the nearest thing to gold that they knew. If stories of superstitious beliefs among the slaves were what the interviewer wanted to hear, therefore, the ex-slave seemed to rack his memory to bring some forth. Similarly, the ex-slaves provided accounts of brutal treatments, poor food, and unfit housing conditions or, on the contrary, of kind treatment, good food, and pleasant housing conditions. It is interesting to observe, in this connection, how readers with different ideational perspectives react to this first published volume of selections from the narratives of the ex-slaves. One reader, a professional reviewer, is troubled by the impression that "through the scores of testimonies there runs, like a scarlet thread, the awful memory of the lash."[61] Another, one of the most eminent authorities on Negro history, complains that Botkin "doubtless included a disproportionate number of narratives of Negroes who were satisfied with slavery and unwillingly accepted freedom when it finally came. Other collections of slave narratives do not give such a bright picture as we find in this narrative."[62]

We must recognize the elements of untrustworthiness inherent in human testimony. Belief is a so purely mental product and memory often takes poetic license. We feel, however, that the slave narrative records from 1703 to 1865 have been enhanced by the Writers' Project interviews. In the absence of the objective standards of the scientist, any inferences that we may draw as to resemblances between the testimonies of slaves in the different periods are recognizedly tentative and imperfect. Perhaps subsequent developments in the study of American literary history will render more usable the narratives of illiterate groups.

"Why did you not learn to read?" was a natural question for members of the antislavery audience to ask of Lewis Clarke, in view of Clarke's general alertness. His answer, and the answer in hundreds of the ex-slave narratives, as well as in many of the narratives of Clarke's fellow fugitives, was that the slave might be killed if he did. This particular restraint upon the slave, which we have noticed especially in the narratives of John Thompson and Tom Jones, belongs more peculiarly to the 1830–60 period than even the selling apart of slave families. The reasons that some slaveholders gave for the denial of learning to the slave become clearer from the testimonies of the ex-slaves than from the earlier group alone, for the ex-slaves reveal also what often happened on a plantation when slaves like Thompson and Jones succeeded in learning to read and write. A "reading" slave could transmit news that the master wanted to keep secret, such as slave uprisings or the like. "Writing" slaves often forged "passes" and "free papers" for fugitive slaves. Sometimes the ability to write would lead to the playing of pranks upon the master, such as forging the master's name to a long list of eatables from the county grocer and "throwing a party" for the field hands. Sometimes grave disturbance to the smooth working of the system of slavery would result from the slave's knowledge of the "three R's." The punishments devised on some plantations for the offense of learning how to read and write thus served to protect the system.

We are told in many of the ex-slave narratives that knowledge of the punishments meted out to slaves who had been "caught" reading or writing kept many slaves from even glancing in the direction of a book. Others, however, persisted in spite of the danger. One ex-slave in the *Reddick Narratives*, Patsy Alexander, tells of an old man who taught himself to read:

> I used to see him peep around the corner and peep in his book.
> When somebody would be coming he would stuff it in his pocket
> and start singing like nothing was the matter.

The ex-slave Jeff Cox, in the same collection of narratives, tells of one "Steve," taught to read by white children, "who slipped around and done it; but later become a preacher and was run off." Lizzie Craig was taught to read by her master's children after she had cut out twenty-two blocks of wood, on which the children painted the letters with polk berries. Henrietta Davis tells of a slave who learned to read in a way similar to the way that Douglass learned:

> There was a slave that drove a team all the time. He didn't get home only once a week. He would go to the river to get things. He would watch the shipping clerk check things. He got so he could read things. Finally he got so he could read good and he would read the paper before he got home. He would tell us when there was going to be a sale. His name was Simon Morrow.

Cora Epps and many other ex-slave narrators tell of having watched the masters' children do their lessons, after which the slaves would slip off and try to write what the children had written. William Hendricks tells of how he practiced writing by cutting the bark from a tree and writing on the under side with his knife while the bark was still wet. He learned well. Mary Jones Parker tells of "an awful whipping" given both to her and to the master's child who was teaching her to read, adding: "They taught you not to look in the Bible, not even to look at pictures in a book." Candace Richardson observes, "If they had a good master and was ambition enough to steal books and such, that might help them to learn." Elizabeth Taylor tells of little white children who would teach the slaves to read, "but they would not teach them to write." Squire Lilly Wakefield says, "God taught me. Sometimes the white children would try to learn you the ABCs. Some got a touch of it that way." Bright Whitefield also tells of slaves learning by "being pets, or nurses close to children," who taught them secretly. The recipe for learning given by William Wells is simply: "Go off on Sundays and get down in the hollow where we could be hid, and there read and write." The smartest slave Gusta Winchester ever knew, he says, was a "dark-skinned butler who had learned to read the Bible by looking at the words when the master read aloud." The most unusual report among those of the forty-two slaves who told of masters who did not hinder and sometimes even helped slaves learn to read and write comes from ex-slave Pinkie Reese:

> If a slave got up the nerve to ask his master to teach him, the master would sometimes agree. But it would make it hard for him, because it would add extra whippings to his credit if he didn't learn fast.

One of the pleasant chapters that might be written on the subject of the relationship between the slave and the "Big House" is a history of the way hundreds of children in plantations all over the South would slip away from the mansion house at night to teach slave children in the field or barn or slave cabin.They usually had to carry out their plans with utter secrecy; to be discovered might mean a severe whipping to themselves and even death to the slave they were teaching, as in the case of the brother of the ex-slave

Julia Watts. Some mistresses also helped teach the slaves against the master's express orders. Thus the words "slip and learn," which appear again and again in the slave testimonials, may be applied to the entire process connected with the slave's fight to learn, despite the law.

However well the "slip and learn" course of study might turn out, there was still plenty for the abolitionist editor to do, we can be sure, before the slave narrative would be ready for the press. In the narrative of Zamba[63] we are given a literal copy of one of the first letters he wrote to his overseer, who taught him to read and write out of gratitude for Zamba's having saved him from drowning. The letter is prefaced with the remark that, while doubtless the spelling and diction would amuse the reader, the penmanship would seem even more humorous. Zamba writes:

Verry Gud Sar,

I am moch indett to yu for kindnes to poor Africann.—I'm stonish yu pay tension to grat to blak Slavv—if Scotsman al lik yu den Scotlan must shude bee vine cuntrey—yu teech me reed—reed Bibell.—Bibell telly me all bout God and Hevven an grat most eksselentest Saveeour Jesus who die for all men ever live and bleeve on Him.—Bibell telly me allsoe bout Hell, dat is de place vere al bad man goe—al Tyrands an Moorderurs an Teeves—dey will floggee Cow-skinn one anoder dere for punishe for sins dune in dis worlld— 'Low me tank yu Massa Tomson fur al yur tension an no morr till nicks time yu heere from mee Yur moss bedeent Sarvan

Zamba.[64]

An interesting study of two entirely different types of editing of narrative material from the same fugitive slave, neither of which seem to disturb the essential quality of the original versions, is to be found in the following testimony from the "lips" of Harriet Tubman. The first is by Benjamin Drew and appeared in 1856 in his *A North-Side View of Slavery. The Refugee: or, the Narratives of Fugitive Slaves in Canada*; the other is Lydia Francis Child, to be found among her *Letters*:

[Harriet Tubman] I grew up like a neglected weed,—ignorant of liberty, having no experience of it. Then I was not happy or contented: every time I saw a white man I was afraid of being carried away. I had two sisters carried away in a chain gang,—one of them left two children. We were always uneasy. Now I've been free, I know what a dreadful condition slavery is. I have seen hundreds of escaped slaves, but I never saw one who was willing to go back and be a slave. I have no opportunity to see my friends in my native land. We would rather stay in our native land, if we could be as free there as we are here. I think slavery is the next thing to hell. If a person would send another into bondage, he would, it appears to me, be bad enough to send him to hell if he could.[65]

[Mrs. Child wrote: "You have doubtless heard of Harriet Tubman . . . she said the other day . . ."] Dey may send de flower ob dair young men down South, to die ob de fever in de summer, and de agoo in de winter. Fur 'tis cold down dar, dough 'tis down South. Day may send dem one year, two year, three year, till day tired ob sendin', or till dey use up all de young men. All no use! God's ahead ob Massa Linkum. God won't let Massa Linkum beat de South till he do de right ting. Massa Linkum beat de South till he do de right ting. Massa Linkum he great man, and I'se poor nigger; but dis nigger can tell Massa Linkum how to save de money and de young men. He do it by setting de niggers free. S'pose dar was awfu' big snake down dar, on de floor. He bit you. Folks all skeered, 'cause you die. You send for doctor to cut de bite; but snake he rolled up dar, and while doctor dwine it, he bite you agin. De doctor cut out dat bite; but while he dwine it, de snake he spring up and bite you agin, and so he keep dwin, till you kill him. Dat's what Massa Linkum orter know.[66]

Which of these jobs of editorship is closer to Harriet Tubman's original utterance is a moot question. Both seem to have caught the same spirit and, in the absence of any words from her own hand, must be accepted with thanks. It is probable that there would be equal differences in styles of recording the narratives of Moses Roper, Lewis and Milton Clarke, Moses Grandy, Josiah Henson, Henry Box Brown, and others if we had more than one scribe for their dictation. But it does not seem likely that the substance or essential spirit of the slave narrators would be harmed.

"Written by Himself" can be accepted literally as the label for the slave narratives by Lunceford Lane, Frederick Douglass, William Wells Brown, Henry Bibb, Henry Watson, James W. C. Pennington, Solomon Northup, Thomas H. Jones, John Thompson, Peter Randolph, Samuel Ringgold Ward, Austin Steward, Noah Davis, G. W. Offley, William Craft, and Harriet Jacobs, from among the hundred book-length slave narratives published between 1836 and the Act of Emancipation. With the exception of Ward, who stands aside as an exception anyway because of his nominal connection with slavery, all of these narrators have had a story to tell of serious struggle to acquire their equipment for authorship. It is an achievement of which the American Negro can be proud, the first fruits of these slave authors. Of their other achievements, a contemporary has glowingly announced:

There are no incidents in history, or romance, more thrilling than the sufferings, perils, and hair-breadth escapes of American slaves. No Puritan pilgrim, or hero of '76 has manifested more courage and perseverance in the cause of freedom, than has been evinced, in thousands of instances, by this persecuted race. In future ages, popular ballads will be sung to commemorate their heroic achievements, and children more enlightened than ours will marvel at the tyranny of their white ancestors.[67]

Their autobiographies, though imperfect as literary monuments, offer much to the student of the American scene.

Chapter 5

The Most Important
Slave Narrative

Popular acquaintance with the work of Frederick Douglass does not extend
to his *Narrative of the Life of Frederick Douglass, an American Slave, Written
by Himself*, the publication of which in Boston in the month of May, 1845,
was a milestone in the history of the literary crusade to end slavery.

The first of four published versions of his life story is today rarely to be
found, outside of rare books divisions in main library collections of the
country. The second version of Douglass's autobiography is also hard to
find, his *My Bondage and My Freedom*, which appeared in 1855. The third
version, the *Life and Times of Frederick Douglass*, published in 1881, is the
version to be found in most library collections, although a reprinted edition
of the revised 1892 version of the *Life and Times of Frederick Douglass* in
1941 has recently been added to library files in connection with the centen-
nial commemoration of the first public appearance of Douglass in the role
of a fugitive slave.

The history of the reception of Douglass's slave narrative has been outlined earlier in this study. The "grandest slave of them all" had captured
the imagination of the abolitionist public from the time that he had emerged
from obscurity in 1841 as a fugitive slave in New Bedford, struggling hard
but happily to earn a living in a new land of "stolen" freedom. That he
rose quickly into favor we learn from a letter he sent Garrison on November
8, 1842, his first formal effort at writing as we learn in the apology contained
in the conclusion to that lengthy epistle.[1] The occasion for the letter was
Douglass's chagrin over being prevented by a bad cold from being able to
continue "speaking almost day and night, in public and in private" on behalf
of the fugitive slave George Latimer, who had been recaptured by slave
hunters and lodged in a Boston jail, pending extradition. Together with
Charles Remond, a free Negro who was the first member of his race to be
enlisted as an abolitionist speaker, Douglass had been making a tour of
Massachusetts with exhilarating success. He mentions the eagerness of the
inhabitants in one town to arrive in good time for an afternoon meeting
scheduled to follow a few hours after a morning meeting at which he had
"occupied about an hour, on the question as to whether a man is better

than a sheep." Douglass observes that "long before the drawling, lazy church bells commenced sounding their deathly notes, mighty crowds were making their way to the town hall. . . . As I gazed upon them, my soul leaped for joy; and, but for the thought that the time might be better employed. I could have shouted aloud."

A report of one of his early speeches, given at Concord, New Hampshire, in February of 1844, provides us with the first of a long line of reporters' analyses of Douglass's ability to demonstrate the right of the slave to be called a man. In view of its importance as one of the few records we have of Douglass before publication of his narrative made him a celebrity, we quote from the article at length:

> In the evening, Douglass made a masterly and most impressive
> speech. The house was crowded, and with the best of our people—no
> clergy—and but a few of the bigots who are past hearing. He began
> by a calm, deliberate, and very simple narrative of his life. After
> narrating his early life and briefly—his schooling, the beginning of
> the wife of his master's relative to teach him letters, and the stern
> forbidding of it, by her husband, which Frederick overheard—how
> he caught a little teaching here and there from the children in the
> streets (a fact, he said, which accounted to him for his extraordinary
> attachment to children)—after getting through this, in a somewhat
> suppressed and hesitant way—interesting all the while for its facts
> but dullish in manner—and giving, I suspect, no token to the
> audience of what was coming through, though I discerned, at times,
> symptoms of a brewing storm—he closed his slave narrative, and
> gradually let out the outraged humanity that was laboring in him, in
> indignant and terrible speech. It was not what you could describe
> as oratory or eloquence. It was sterner, darker, deeper than these. It
> was the volcanic outbreak of human nature, long pent up in slavery
> and at last bursting its imprisonment. It was the storm of insurrec-
> tion; and I could not but think, as he stalked to and fro on the plat-
> form, roused up like the Numidian lion, how that terrible voice of
> his would ring through the pine glades of the South, in the day of
> her visitation, calling the insurgents to battle, and striking terror to
> the hearts of the dismayed and despairing mastery. He reminded me
> of Toussaint among the plantations of Haiti. There was a great
> oratory in his speech, but more of dignity and earnestness than what
> we call eloquence. He was not up as a speaker, performing. He was
> an insurgent slave, taking hold on the right of speech, and charging
> on his tyrants the bondage of his race. One of our editors ventured
> to cross his path by a rash remark. He better have run upon a lion.
> It was a fearful, but magnificent, to see how magnanimously and

lion-like the royal fellow tore him to pieces, and left his untouched
fragments scattered around him.

There is a prospect of having Douglass here again, and in other
parts of New Hampshire. He is a surprizing lecturer. I would not
praise him, or describe him; but he is a colored man, a slave, of the
race who can't take care of themselves—our inferiors, and therefore to be kept in slavery—an abolitionist, and therefore to be
despised. . . . He is one of the most impressive and majestic speakers
I have ever heard. The close of his address Sunday was unrivalled.
. . . I have never seen a man leave the platform, or close a speech,
with more real dignity, and eloquent majesty.[4]

The antislavery journals during the last week in May and the entire month
of June, 1845, were uniform in agreement that Douglass's narrative was the
chief literary news of the day. Called by one enthusiast, his *"multum in
parvo,"* the book had the tremendous effect of putting into print Douglass's
powerful appeal to their sympathetic understanding. As one woman reader
wrote Garrison in a letter in which she enclosed five dollars to be spent with
"judgment and care" (in the promise of the Editor's note) on copies of the
narrative "for the extension of its publicity":

I have many times heard the author vividly portray the evils of
slavery. I have often heard him recount with deep feeling the endless
wrongs they are made to endure—but, oh! never before have I been
brought so completely in sympathy with the slave—never before have
I so fully realized the doctrine of our blessed Savior, 'Whatsoever ye
do unto the least one of these, ye do it unto me.' . . . May his narrative incite us to renewed diligence in our labors for the slave! May
the author become a mighty instrument to the pulling down of the
strongholds of iniquity, and to the establishing of righteousness in
our land![5]

Garrison's fatherly pride in Douglass's book showed itself in the many
reprintings that appear in the pages of *The Liberator* during the season of
the debut of the *Narrative of the Life of Frederick Douglass, an American
Slave. Written by Himself.* One of the reviews, reprinted from the *Lynn
Pioneer*, packed into fairly short space the dominant sentiments of the
readers of the book, as follows:

My readers will be delighted to learn that Frederick Douglass—the
fugitive slave—has at last concluded his narrative. All who know the
wonderful gifts of friend Douglass know that his narrative must, in
the nature of things, be written with great power. It is so indeed. It

is the most thrilling work which the American press ever issued—and the most important. If it does not open the eyes of this people, they must be petrified into eternal sleep.

The picture it presents of slavery is too horrible to look upon, and yet it is but a faint *picture* of what to millions is a vivid life. It is evidently drawn with a nice eye. . . . There are passages in it which would brighten the reputation of any living author,—while the book, as a whole, judged as a mere work of art, would widen the fame of Bunyan and DeFoe. A spirit of the loftiest integrity, and a vein of the purest religious sentiment, runs through its pages, and it must leave on every mind a deep conviction of the sale of at least twenty thousand in this country, and equally great in Europe. It will leave a mark upon this age which the busy finger of time will deepen at every touch. It will generate a public sentiment in this nation, in the presence of which our antislavery laws and constitutions shall be like chaff in the presence of fire. . . . Great efforts will be made in the name of the Constitution and the Bible, of James Polk and the Apostle Paul, to suppress it: but it will run through this nation from house to house and from heart to heart.[6]

Meanwhile, Douglass had fled the country, taking passage aboard the steamship *Cambria*, on the Cunard line. Of this voyage he wrote Garrison in a letter sent from Dublin, September 1, 1845: "There were slaveholders from Cuba and slaveholders from Georgia—we had anti-slavery singing and pro-slavery grumbling; and at the same time that Governor Hammond's letters were being read, my Narrative was being circulated."[7]

Proof of the authenticity of Douglass's narrative came by way of the Southern press. The editor of the *Raleigh Register*, after commenting upon publicity given Douglass in a Buffalo paper, proceeded to identify Douglass as a slave he himself had known. We read:

We speak from our own knowledge of facts, when we say that never was a slave treated with greater kindness and indulgence than this same boy. He was Governor Dudley's body-servant, was entrusted by him with money in considerable sums, and the most implicit confidence was reposed in him. In fact, he was regarded by the whole family, more as a friend than a slave. How little he deserved it all, is shown by his present conduct. But black as has been *his* ingratitude, he is a respectable man compared with his Northern aiders and abettors, who knowing him to be a Runaway (for so they advertise him), thus sustain and encourage him, to accomplish their own fiendish purposes.[8]

Douglass's excoriation of the slaveholder, which in this first of his four versions of his autobiography flayed the creature at times in true Garrisonian fashion, was naturally the chief reason why Southerners undertook to defend themselves by trying to invalidate his testimony. Douglass at length decided to prepare a public answer to an article attacking his narrative that had appeared in the autumn of 1845 in the *Delaware* (Wilmington) *Republican*, written by Mr. A. C. C. Thompson. Writing from Perth, Scotland, in January of 1846, after reading Thompson's article as reprinted in the *Liberator* for December 12 of the year just ended, Douglass began his long letter by observing the indiscretion of proslavery men in breaking silence as regarded the facts of slavery. Then he expressed his thanks to Mr. Thompson for his confirmation of the truth of his narrative in the very process of refuting it. It is an interesting expression of gratitude:

> I beg Mr. Thompson to accept my thanks for his full, free and unsolicited testimony, in regard to my identity. There now need be no doubt on that point, however much there might have been before. ... But for you, sir, the pro-slavery people in the North might have persisted, with some show of reason, in representing me as an imposter—a free Negro who had never been south of Mason and Dixon's line—one whom the abolitionists, acting on the jesuitical principle, that the end justifies the means, had educated and sent forth to attract attention to their faltering cause. I am greatly indebted to you, sir, for silencing those truly prejudicial insinuations. ... You have completely tripped up the heels of your pro-slavery friends, and laid them flat by the feet. You have done a piece of anti-slavery work which no anti-slavery man could do. Our cautious and truth-loving people in New England would never have believed this testimony, in proof of my identity, had it been borne by an abolitionist. ... Not that they really think an abolitionist capable of bearing false witness intentionally; but such persons are thought fanatical, and to look at everything through a distorted medium. They will believe you—they will believe a slaveholder. ... Your testimony ... will serve to give effect to my exposures of slavery, both at home and abroad. I hope I shall not administer to your vanity, when I tell you that you seem to have been raised up for this purpose! I came to this land (Scotland) with the highest testimonials from some of the most intelligent and distinguished abolitionists in the United States; yet some here have entertained and expressed doubt as to whether I have ever been a slave. You may easily imagine the perplexing and embarrassing nature of my situation, and how anxious I must have been to be relieved of it. You, sir,

have relieved me. I now stand before both the American and British public, endorsed by you as being just what I have ever represented myself to be—to wit, an *American slave.*[9]

The facts in Douglass's narrative that Mr. Thompson had been instrumental in verifying concerned the most important persons and events in the little one-hundred-twenty-five-page book. Mr. Thompson had said that he "knew this recreant slave by the name of Frederick Bailey," instead of Douglass, which testimony Douglass evaluated as "direct and perfect—just what I have long wanted." He said that he knew Douglass when the latter lived with Mr. Covey (Douglass's worst master), and that he was "intimately acquainted" with "most of the persons mentioned" in the narrative. He proceeded to describe those individuals: Colonel Lloyd, the wealthy planter; Mr. Gore (the basest character described in the narrative), formerly Colonel Lloyd's overseer but now a resident and church member at St. Michael's; Thomas Auld, Douglass's owner; and others. In recognition of the value of Mr. Thompson's "service" to him, Douglass made him a promise in his best sarcastic vein:

> Do allow me, once more, to thank you for this triumphant vindication of the truth of my statements; and to show you how highly I value your testimony, I will inform you that I am now publishing a second edition of my narrative in this country, having already disposed of the first. I will insert your article with my reply as an appendix to the edition now in progress. If you find any fault with my frequent thanks, you may find some excuse for me in the fact, that I have serious fears that you will be but poorly thanked by those whose characters you have felt it your duty to defend. I am almost certain they will regard you as running before you were sent, and as having spoken when you should have been silent. Under these trying circumstances, it is evidently the duty of those interested in your welfare to extend to you such words of consolation as may ease, if not remove, the pain of your sad disappointment![10]

As far as we have been able to discover, Douglass's promise to provide Mr. Thompson's article with longevity in back pages of his second edition did not materialize. No such edition has yet been located. (Douglass *may* have presented the current publisher with the article and letter in reply, and the publisher may have simply put them quietly aside, thinking them too lengthy for the appendix of a smallish book.) Douglass continues discussion of Mr. Thompson's article, point by point, including Thompson's denial of the cruelties to the slaves in Maryland that Douglass described, his defense of the slaveholders' "Christianity," and his doubt that Douglass wrote his narrative himself because at the time that Mr. Thompson knew him he seemed "an unlearned and rather an ordinary Negro." Concerning this last point, Douglass admits:

> Well, I have to admit I was rather an ordinary Negro when you knew me, and I do not claim to be a very extraordinary one now. But you knew me under very unfavorable circumstances. It was when I lived with Mr. Covey, the Negro-breaker, and member of the Methodist Church. I had just been living with my master Thomas Auld, where I had been reduced by hunger. Master Thomas did not allow me enough to eat. Well, when I lived with Mr. Covey, I was driven so hard, and whipt so often, that my soul was crushed and my spirits broken. I was a mere wreck. The degradation to which I was then subjected, as I now look back to it, seems more like a dream than a horrible reality. I can scarcely realize how I ever passed through it, without quite losing all my moral and intellectual energies. I can easily understand that you sincerely doubt if I wrote the narrative; for if any one had told me, seven years ago, I should ever be able to write such an one, I should have doubted as strongly as you do now.[11]

The effect of the exposure to the world of the details of his private affairs upon Douglass's owner, Thomas Auld (whom Douglass, in classifying slaveholders, placed in the third class, comprised of slaveholders-by-marriage), was to transfer ownership of Douglass to his brother, Hugh Auld. The latter was a mean man, whereas Thomas Auld was merely stingy. The cruelties to his slaves came from masters to whom Auld had hired them out rather than from Auld himself. Hugh Auld straightway set about making plans for the capture of Douglass. In a note to Garrison, one J. B. Sanderson of Lynn, Massachusetts, conveyed the report, by hearsay on a train from New York to Boston, of the following supposed plan:

> A gentleman . . . overheard several persons in the car, conversing about Douglass. One of them said a combination had been entered by a number of slaveholders, the object of which was to watch vessels leaving great Britain, to note where Douglass left; and if he arrived into any other American port except Boston, to be prepared and seize him immediately upon his landing.[12]

A Southerner, who was personally acquainted with the Lloyds, had read Douglass's narrative, and was inclined to accept it at face value, had also heard of some such purpose of Hugh Auld's, as we learn from an article that appeared in the *Western Citizen* in May of 1846. The author of the article stated that he had been informed of the determination of Douglass's owner to take him back again into slavery, "as sure as his feet shall touch American soil," and he did not doubt that the intention would be carried out if

Douglass should attempt to return. The "Southerner's" reaction to Douglass's book has value as revealing a person not to be identified ideationally with the mythical "solid South":

> It is only recently that I have had an opportunity of reading the life of this extraordinary man, and from my knowledge of slavery as it really exists . . . I am fully prepared to bear a decided testimony to the truth of all its assertions, with regard to the discipline upon the plantations of Maryland, as well as his descriptions of cruelty and murder. Of Colonel Lloyd, or his family, I have personally little knowledge, although during the years of my childhood and youth, I have occasionally met them in Annapolis, where they frequently visited. . . . Aristocratic in the extreme, they moved and lived in the style of the nobility of foreign lands, and however amiable the Colonel or his family might appear, I'll venture to say he was willing to wink at, and permit any cruelty or oppression which an un-principled overseer might say was necessary. . . . I have heard masters and mistresses too, say to their overseers, 'Knock them down or shoot them, or anything else sooner than not enforce and secure implicit obedience.'[13]

What most impressed Douglass about the whole matter was the fact that his master had broken his silence, finally, after nearly twelve months of publicity, to deny certain of Douglass's charges and deprive the public of the right to refer to him as the owner of Douglass by "giving" him to his brother. As Douglass wrote to Garrison from Glasgow, April 16, 1846:

> I doubt not that my old master is in a state of mind quite favorable to an attempt at re-capture. Not that he wishes to make money by selling me, or by holding me himself, but to feed his revenge. I know he feels keenly my exposures, and nothing would afford him more pleasure than to have me in his power. He has suffered goadings, or he would not have broken the silence of seven years to exculpate himself from the charges I have brought against him, by telling a positive lie. He says he can put his hand upon the Bible, and, with a clear conscience, swear he never struck me, or told anyone else to do so! . . . This positive denial, on his part, rather staggered me at first. I had no idea the gentleman would tell a downright untruth. He had certainly forgotten when a lamp was lost from the carriage, without my knowledge, that he came to the stable with the cart-whip, and with its heavy lash beat me over the head and shoulders, to make me tell how it was lost, until his brother Edward, who was at St. Michael's on a visit at the time, came forward, and besought him to desist; and that he beat me until he wearied himself. My

memory, in such matters, is better than his. . . . He finds fault with me for not mentioning his promise to set me free at twenty-five. I did not tell many things which I might have told. Had I told of that promise, I should have also told that he had never set one of his slaves free; and I had no reason to believe he would treat me with any more justice and humanity, than any other one of his slaves. But enough of this . . .[14]

The story of how the tempest created by the candor of Douglass's narrative was quieted at the end of two years by the payment of seven hundred and fifty dollars "cash money" as the price of Douglass's freedom, only to be raised again at once in the opposite camp, as abolitionists received with consternation the news of that transaction, has been told in an earlier chapter. We turn now to a consideration of the actual slave narrative, the little book that provoked all this excitement.

The eleven-page introduction to the *Narrative of the Life of Frederick Douglass, an American Slave, Written by Himself* was written by Garrison, who was the sponsor for the book and to a certain extent Douglass's mentor during this first period of his life as a freeman, but whose influence upon the actual subject matter of the narrative was less formative than has been supposed. Garrison's emphasis upon the evil natures to be found among slaveholders and the mockery made by such persons of religion is thoroughly characteristic, alternating in style between extravagant praise of Douglass as a man among men, and violent denunciation of his masters. The front matter of the little volume also includes a letter by Wendell Phillips, who lauds Douglass's powers as a thinker and a writer but fears that his risk of personal safety for the sake of revealing the whole truth may cut short his opportunities for further service in the important field of lecturing upon slavery.

The facts of Douglass's life as a slave, as presented in this first version of his autobiography, bear about the same relationship to the facts presented in each of his subsequent versions, as a series of pictures taken by a snapshot camera will bear to a series taken by time exposures of varying lengths. It is possible that Douglass's selection of details was consciously determined along Garrisonian lines of emphasis. But, as he says in later versions, abolitionist audiences preferred facts to reflections about the slave experience. As the mass records of the slave narratives prove, the facts of slavery were as sharp and unshaded by nature as a page full of Garrison's sentences on the subject. Besides, as a young man probably under thirty years of age, shudderingly close to the miserably sharp facts themselves and not beyond the fear of return to the dread state, it was but natural that his focal attention differed from the emphasis, later, of the man of forty, then of sixty-five, and lastly of seventy-five.

Douglass was born in Maryland, on a plantation in Tuckahoe, in Talbot County. The opening emphasis in the narrative is upon the fact that neither he nor any other slave that he had ever met could tell of his birthday, though the "white children could tell their ages." He believed that he must have been born about the year 1818, because he had heard his master say, sometime during 1835, that he was about seventeen years old.

We learn that his mother was a woman of very dark complexion, named Harriet Bailey. She was separated from him while he was yet an infant, and, Douglass says, he never saw her, "to know her as such, more than four or five times in my life; and each of these times was very short in duration, and at night." One of the favorite passages in the narrative describes her journey on foot, at night, from the plantation about twelve miles away where she was obliged to be on the field at sunrise or get a whipping, in order to see her little boy. He tells of her brief role in his experiences:

> I do not recollect of ever seeing my mother by the light of day. She
> was with me in the night. She would lie down with me, and get me
> to sleep, but long before I waked she was gone. Very little communi-
> cation ever took place between us. Death soon ended what little we
> could have while she lived, and with it her hardships and suffering.
> She died when I was about seven years old, on one of master's farms,
> near Lee's Mill. I was not allowed to be present during her illness, at
> her death, or burial. She was gone long before I knew anything
> about it. Never having enjoyed, to any considerable extent, her
> soothing presence, her tender and watchful care, I received the
> tidings of her death with much the same emotions I should probably
> felt at the death of a stranger.[15]

Douglass was left "without the slightest intimation of" who his father was, he says on the third page of his narrative, adding that the whisper he heard that his master was his father "may or may not be true." On the preceding page, however, he asserts flatly: "My father was a white man. He was admitted to be such by all I ever heard speak of my parentage." It is interest-ing to keep these items in mind, with the exact wording, for purposes of comparison with parallel passages in the later autobiographies. Douglass follows his passage on his parentage with a discussion of the plight of mulatto slaves, of whom he says that "it is worthy of remark that such slaves invari-ably suffer greater hardships, and have more to contend with than others." The special hatred of the mistress and frequent sale of such slaves South were the usual outcomes. Douglass's conclusion concerning that phase of slavery is certainly un-Garrisonian in manner, though it gives emphasis to the subject as Garrison emphasized it:

Every year brings with it multitudes of this class of slaves. It was doubtless in consequence of a knowledge of this fact, that one great statesman of the South predicted the downfall of slavery by the inevitable laws of population. Whether this prophecy is ever fulfilled or not, it is nevertheless plain that a very different-looking class of people are springing up at the South, and are now held in slavery, from those originally brought to this country from Africa; and if their increase will do no other good, it will do away the force of the argument, that God cursed Ham, and therefore American slavery is right. If the lineal descendants of Ham are alone to be scripturally enslaved, it is certain that slavery at the South must soon become unscriptural; for thousands are ushered into the world, annually, who, like myself, owe their existence to white fathers, and those fathers most frequently their own masters.[16]

Douglass's initiation into one of the slave's hardest roles, that of forced spectator at the beatings of the slaves by the master or overseer, took place shortly after his arrival at the master's house from his grandmother's house on the outskirts of the plantation where he spent his babyhood. The master, whose name was Captain Anthony, had been infuriated by a young woman Douglass calls "Aunt Hester" because she had been found in the company of a slave named Ned when the master had ordered her never to let him catch her in company with a young man. The fright of the little boy heightens the dreadful scene:

Before he commenced whipping Aunt Hester, he took her into the kitchen, and stripped her from neck to waist, leaving her neck, shoulders, and back, entirely naked. He then told her to cross her hands, calling her at the same time a d——b b——h. After crossing her hands, he tied them with a strong rope, and led her to a stool under a large hook in the joist, put in for the purpose. He made her get upon the stool, and tied her hands to the hook. She now stood fair for his infernal purpose. Her arms were stretched up their full length, so that she stood upon the ends of her toes. He then said to her, "Now, you d——d b——h, I'll learn you how to disobey my orders." and after rolling up his sleeves, he commenced to lay on the heavy cowskin, and soon the warm, red blood (amid heart-rending shrieks from her, and horrid oaths from him) came dripping to the floor. I was so terrified and horror-stricken at the sight, that I hid myself in a closet, and dared not venture out till long after the bloody transaction was over. I expected it would be my turn next.[17]

Captain Anthony did not belong to the first, or aristocratic, rank among slaveholders but "was what might be called the overseer of the overseers," as Douglass expressed it. He was the clerk and superintendent for one Colonel Lloyd, whose feudal estate of from three to four hundred slaves is described with increasing fullness of detail in the later autobiographies. The organization of the slaveholding community was strictly hierarchical—the overseer of the plantation "belonged" to the slaveholder of first rank (Colonel Lloyd in Douglass's situation). The slaveholder of second rank (Captain Anthony) often had an overseer who married his daughter, thereby becoming a slave-holder-by-marriage, or third rank (Thomas Auld, for example, although he was not an overseer at any time before becoming a slaveholder). Captain Anthony's overseers during Douglass's time included two brutal men, appropriately named Mr. Severe and Mr. Gore, and one "good overseer" who, though he whipped, "seemed to take no pleasure in it," and who, because of his decent inclinations, soon lost his job. Douglass's portrait of Mr. Austin Gore took its place in the 1840's beside Moses Roper's Mr. Gooch as one of the most memorable portraits in the slaveholders' gallery. We meet Mr. Gore:

> Mr. Hopkins was succeeded by Mr. Austin Gore, a man possessing, in an eminent degree, all those traits of character indispensable to what is called a first-rate overseer. Mr. Gore had served Colonel Lloyd in that capacity of overseer, upon one of the outfarms, and had shown himself worthy of the high station of overseer upon the home or Great House Farm.
>
> Mr. Gore was proud, ambitious, and persevering. He was artful, cruel, and obdurate. He was just the man for the place, and it was just the place for such a man. . . . He was one of those who could torture the slightest look, word, or gesture, on the part of the slave, into impudence, and would treat it accordingly. There must be no answering back to him; no explanation was allowed a slave, showing himself to have been wrongfully accused. Mr. Gore acted fully up to the maxim laid down by the slaveholders,—"It is better that a dozen slaves should suffer under the lash, than that the overseer should be convicted, in the presence of the slaves, of having been at fault." No matter how innocent a slave might be—it availed him nothing, when accused by Mr. Gore of any misdeameanor. To be accused was to be convicted and to be convicted was to be punished, the one always following the other with immutable certainty. To escape punishment was to escape accusation; and few slaves had the fortune to do either, under the overseership of Mr. Gore. He was just proud enough to demand the most debasing homage of the slave, and quite servile enough to crouch, himself, at the feet of the master. . . . He was, of all the overseers, the most dreaded by the

slaves. His presence was painful; his eye flashed confusion; and seldom was his sharp, shrill voice heard, without producing horror and trembling in their ranks. . . . Though a young man, he indulged in no jokes, said no funny words, seldom smiled. . . . He spoke but to command, and . . . dealt sparingly with his words, and bountifully with his whip, never using the former where the latter would answer as well. When he whipped, he seemed to do so from a sense of duty, and feared no consequences.[18]

The most barbarous of the many acts of savage character that were committed by this individual, who would have fit neatly into a Dickens novel if he had been two or three dozen shades less mean, was his murder of the slave Demby, who had bounded away from Mr. Gore while the latter was in the process of whipping him, and plunged into a creek to the depth of his shoulders, refusing to come out. Mr. Gore, with his usual "stone-like coolness," told Demby what he would do if Demby did not come out of the water at the third call, and he did, as we find out:

Mr. Gore told him that he would give him three calls, and that, if he did not come out at the third call, he would shoot him. The first was given. Demby made no response, but stood his ground. The second and third calls were given with the same result. Mr. Gore then, without consultation or deliberation with any one, not even giving Demby an additional call, raised his musket to his face, taking deadly aim at his standing victim, and in an instant poor Demby was no more. His mangled body sank out of sight, and blood and brains marked the water where he had stood.

A thrill of horror flashed through every soul upon the plantation, excepting Mr. Gore. . . . He was asked by Colonel Lloyd and my old master, why he resorted to this extraordinary expedient. His reply was, (as well as I can remember), that Demby had become unmanageable. . . . Mr. Gore's defence was satisfactory.[19]

These sights were the child slave's prelude to his own slave experience. They were the inevitable background of his earliest conscious memories, often coming more dreadfully close to his consciousness than was the case with Douglass because they involved a father, as with Josiah Henson, or a mother, as with James Curry, or other kin. Douglass's description of the treatment of the slave children on Colonel Lloyd's plantation gives a typical picture:

My own treatment . . . was very similar to that of the other slave children. I was not old enough to work in the field, and there being little else than field work to do, I had a great deal of leisure time. The most I had to do was to drive up the cows at evening, keep the fowls out of the garden, keep the front yard clean, and run on errands for my master's daughter, Mrs. Lucretia Auld. The most of my leisure time I spent in helping Master Daniel Lloyd in finding his birds, after he had shot them. My connection with Master Daniel was of some advantage to me. He became quite attached to me, and was a sort of protector of me. He would not allow the older boys to impose upon me, and would divide his cakes with me.

I was seldom whipped by my old master, and suffered little from anything else than hunger and cold. I suffered much from hunger, but much more from cold. In the hottest summer and coldest winter, I was kept almost naked—no shoes, no stockings, no jacket, no trousers, nothing on but a coarse tow linen shirt, reaching only to my knees. I must have perished with cold, but that, the coldest nights, I used to steal a bag which was used for carrying corn to the mill. I would crawl into this bag, and there sleep on the cold, damp, clay floor, with my head in and feet out. My feet have been so cracked with the frost, that the pen with which I am writing might be laid in the gashes.

We were not regularly allowanced. Our food was coarse corn meal boiled. . . . It was put into a large wooden tray or trough, and set down upon the ground. The children were then called, like so many pigs, and like so many pigs they would come and devour the mush; some with oyster-shells, others with pieces of shingle, some with naked hands, and none with spoons. He that ate fastest got most; and few left the trough satisfied.[20]

Douglass's discussion of the significance of the slaves' singing was widely commented upon in the contemporary reviews of his narrative, and he himself quoted the passage at length in his later autobiographies. It is one of the important testimonies concerning the origin of the slave songs:

The slaves selected to go to the Great House Farm, for the monthly allowance for themselves and their fellow-slaves, were peculiarly enthusiastic. While on their way, they would make the dense old woods, for miles around, reverberate with their wild songs, revealing at once the highest joy and the deepest sadness. They would compose and sing as they went along, consulting neither time nor tune. The thought that came up, came out—if not in the word, in the sound;—and as frequently in the one as in the other. They would sometimes sing the most pathetic sentiment in the most rapturous tone, and the most rapturous sentiment in the most pathetic tone. Into all of their songs they would manage to weave something of the Great House Farm. Especially would they do this, when leaving home. They would then sing most exultingly the following words:

> "I am going away to the Great House Farm!
> O, yea! O, yea! O!"

This they would sing, as a chorus, to words which to many would seem unmeaning jargon, but which, nevertheless, were full of meaning to themselves. I have sometimes thought that the mere hearing of these songs would do more to impress some minds with the horrible character of slavery, than the reading of whole volumes of philosophy on the subject could do.

I did not, when a slave, understand the deep meaning of those rude and apparently incoherent songs. I was myself within the circle; so that I neither saw nor heard as those without might see and hear. They told a tale of woe which was then altogether beyond my feeble comprehension; they were tones loud, long, and deep; they breathed the prayer and complaint of souls boiling over with the bitterest anguish. Every tone was a testimony against slavery, and a prayer to God for deliverance from chains. The hearing of those wild notes always depressed my spirit, and filled me with ineffable sadness. . . . To those songs I trace my first glimmering conception of the dehumanizing character of slavery. I can never get rid of that conception. Those songs still follow me, to deepen my hatred of slavery, and quicken my sympathies for my brethren in bonds. If anyone wishes to be impressed with the soul-killing effects of slavery, let him go to Colonel Lloyd's plantation, and, on allowance day, place himself in the deep pine woods, and there let him, in silence, analyze the sounds that shall pass through the chambers of his soul. . . .

I have often been utterly astonished, since I came to the North, to find persons who could speak of the singing, among slaves, as evidence of their contentment and happiness. It is impossible to conceive of a greater mistake. Slaves sing most when they are most unhappy. The songs of the slave represent sorrows of his heart; and he is relieved by them, only as an aching heart is relieved by its tears. . . . Crying for joy, and singing for joy, were alike uncommon to me while in the jaws of slavery. The singing of a man cast away upon a desolate island might be as appropriately considered as evidence of contentment and happiness, as the singing of a slave; the songs of one and of the other are prompted by the same emotion.

The first period of Douglass's life as a slave, this prelude to the experience of being an actual slave laborer, ended in his eighth year. At that time, Captain Anthony, his owner, decided to send him to Baltimore as the houseboy of his son-in-law's brother, Mr. Hugh Auld.

Douglass described the news that he was to be sent to Baltimore, which he received three days before the actual departure, as probably the happiest intelligence of his entire life as a slave. He had already been inspired with a strong desire to see Baltimore by descriptions of the city by his cousin Tom, an older slave little given to fluency of speech except in this one connection. Douglass tells of the impression upon him of the older boy's praise of the place, declaring: "I could never point out any thing at the Great House, no matter how beautiful or powerful, but that he had seen something at Baltimore far exceeding, both in beauty and strength, the object which I pointed out to him."

There were no ties binding Douglass to the Lloyd plantation. His mother was dead. His grandmother lived so far off that he seldom saw her; and, though he had two sisters and a brother living in the same house with him, their early separation had, as he says, "well nigh blotted the fact of our relationship from our memories." He was confident that the new home could not promise less than his old home had given him—hardship, hunger, whipping, nakedness, and sadness of spirit—and he felt hopeful that it would mean something better. Preparation for the departure consisted mainly of three days of scrubbing in the creek, "washing off the plantation scurf," crowned by his first reward, a first pair of trousers, which Mrs. Lucretia promised him if he scrubbed off all of the dirt. The trip was taken by boat on a beautiful Saturday morning, up the Miles River and into the bay. The little boy gave to the Lloyd plantation what he hoped "would be the last look," as the boat set sail. He then placed himself in the bows of the sloop, becoming interested in watching "what was in the distance rather than in things near by or behind."

He was a slave for seven years in the house of Mr. Hugh and Mrs. Sophia Auld and their little son Thomas. As slave situations went it was a most fortunate situation for a slave boy during those formative years. His new mistress was a source of great rapture to him, at first, and Douglass's description of their meeting captures that joy:

> Here I saw what I had never seen before; it was a white face beaming with the most kindly emotions; it was the face of my new mistress, Sophia Auld. I wish I could describe the rapture that flashed through my soul as I beheld it. It was a new and strange sight to me, brightening up my pathway with the light of happiness. Little Thomas was told, there was his Freddy,—and I was told to take care of little Thomas; and thus I entered upon the duties of my new home with the most cheering prospect ahead.[21]

Douglass was the first slave Mrs. Auld had ever had under her control. Before her marriage she had earned her living as a weaver, and thus, as

Douglass explains it, "by constant application to her business, she had been in a good degree preserved from the blighting and dehumanizing effects of slavery." He found it difficult to know how to act before her, as "the crouching servility, usually so acceptable a quality in a slave, did not answer when manifested toward her." She was very pleasant of disposition and had "a face made of heavenly smiles" and a "voice of tranquil music." As one of her first actions, she began to teach the eager little boy who had come to live with them how to read.

It was her husband's anger at Mrs. Auld's instruction of Douglass that opened the lad's eyes to a reason for a mystery that had been puzzling him sadly. Mr. Auld forbade her to instruct Douglass any further, telling her that it was against the law to teach a slave to read and unwisely explaining why this was so in the presence of their little slave. What his words meant to Douglass, we learn:

> To use his own words, . . . he said, "If you give a nigger an inch, he
> will take an ell. A nigger should know nothing but to obey his
> master—to do as he is told to do. Learning would *spoil* the best
> nigger in the world." Now, said he, "if you teach that nigger (speak-
> ing of myself) how to read, there would be no keeping him. It would
> forever unfit him to be a slave. He would at once become unmanage-
> able, and of no value to his master. As to himself, it could do him no
> good, but a great deal of harm. It would make him discontented and
> unhappy." These words sank deep into my heart, and called into
> existence an entirely new train of thought. It was a new and special
> revelation, explaining dark and mysterious things, with which my
> youthful understanding had struggled, but struggled in vain. I now
> understood what had been to me a most perplexing difficulty—to
> wit, the white man's power to enslave the black man. It was a grand
> achievement, and I prized it highly. From that moment, I under-
> stood the pathway from slavery to freedom. It was just what I
> wanted, and I got it at a time when I least expected it. Whilst I was
> saddened by the thought of losing the aid of my kind mistress, I was
> gladdened by the invaluable instruction which, by the merest acci-
> dent, I had gained from my master. Though conscious of the diffi-
> culty of learning without a teacher, I set out with high hope, and a
> fixed purpose, at whatever cost of trouble, to learn how to read. The
> very decided manner with which he spoke, and strove to impress his
> wife with the evil consequences of giving me instruction, served to
> convince me that he was deeply sensible of the truths he was utter-
> ing. It gave me the best assurance that I might rely with the utmost
> confidence on the results which, he said, would flow from teaching
> me to read.[22]

Mrs. Auld was equally transformed by her husband's words, but in her case they imbued her with the necessity for developing a technique befitting a slaveholder's wife. In his own mind, Douglass's road ahead was clear. Young as he was, he realized that by keeping his high resolve hidden from everyone around him and yet snatching every conceivable chance to learn to read, there was a vague chance that something better might come to him than what the grown slaves he had known were experiencing. The Aulds fed him well and kept him neatly clothed. He was rarely punished. This manner of treating the slaves in Baltimore contrasted sharply with treatment on the plantations, he observed, as the slaveholder in the city was curbed by nonslaveholding neighbors from indulging in "those outbreaks of atrocious cruelty so commonly enacted upon the plantation." As he says:

> He is a desperate slaveholder, who will shock the humanity of his
> non-slaveholding neighbors with the cries of his lacerated slave. Few
> are willing to incur the odium attaching to the reputation of being a
> cruel master; and above all things, they would not be known as not
> giving a slave enough to eat. Every city slaveholder is anxious to have
> it known of him, that he feeds his slaves well; and it is due to them
> to say, that most of them do give their slaves enough to eat.[23]

The only real hardship he experienced during the seven years that he lived with the Aulds, was the difficulty connected with his determination to learn to read and write.

A tiger-like fierceness soon took the place of the "lamblike disposition" that Douglass had first known in Mrs. Auld. She resolved that she would see to it that "Freddy" got no more education. She became even more violent in her opposition than her husband himself. Douglass says of her:

> She was not satisfied with simply doing as well as he had com-
> manded; she seemed anxious to do better. Nothing seemed to make
> her more angry than to see me with a newspaper. She seemed to
> think that here lay the danger. I have had her rush at me with a
> face made all up of fury, and snatch from me a newspaper, in a
> manner that fully revealed her apprehension. . . . From this time I
> was most narrowly watched. If I was in a separate room any con-
> sierable length of time, I was sure to be suspected of having a book,
> and was at once called to give an account of myself. All this, how-
> ever, was too late. The first step had been taken. Mistress, in teach-
> ing me the alphabet, had given me the *inch*, and no precaution could
> prevent me from taking the *ell.*[24]

Douglass adopted a strategy, however, that furthered his progress in the realm of learning with the aid of some poor little white children who lived on

Philpot Street, near a shipyard. The little children were always half-starved, so Douglass used to carry bread and his book in his pockets when sent on errands. He accomplished his errand in double-quick time and obtained a lesson from the poor children in exchange for the bread before returning to the house. When he was about twelve years old, he came into the possession of a little book that had a prodigious effect upon him. We read of this awakening, through literature:

> I was now about twelve years old, and the thought of being *a slave for life* began to bear heavily upon my heart. Just about this time, I got hold of a book entitled "The Columbian Orator." Every opportunity I got, I used to read this book. Among much of other interesting matter, I found in it a dialogue between a master and his slave. The slave was represented as having run away from his master three times. The dialogue represented the conversation which took place between them, when the slave was retaken the third time. In this dialogue, the whole argument in behalf of slavery was brought forward by the master, all of which was disposed of by the slave. The slave was made to say some very smart as well as impressive things in his reply to his master—things which had the desired though unexpected effect; for the conversation resulted in the voluntary emancipation of the slave on the part of the master.
>
> In the same book, I met with one of Sheridan's mighty speeches on and in behalf of Catholic emancipation. These were choice documents to me. I read them over and over again with unabated interest. They gave tongue to interesting thoughts of my own soul, which had frequently flashed through my mind, and died away for want of utterance. The moral which I gained from the dialogue was the power of truth over the conscience of even a slaveholder. What I got from Sheridan was a bold denunciation of slavery, and a powerful vindication of human rights. The reading of these documents enabled me to utter my thoughts, and to meet the arguments brought forth to sustain slavery; but while they relieved me of one difficulty, they brought on another even more painful than the one of which I was relieved. The more I read, the more I was led to abhor and detest my enslavers. I could regard them in no other light than a band of successful robbers, who had left their homes, and gone to Africa, and stolen us from our homes, and in a strange land reduced us to slavery. I loathed them as being the meanest as well as the most wicked of men. As I read and contemplated the subject, behold! that very discontentment which Master Hugh had predicted would follow my learning to read had already come, to torment and sting my soul to unutterable anguish.[25]

The hand of fate, which was to deflect the course of Douglass's life from the position on the brink of civilization which he enjoyed while living with the Aulds to the very depths of degradation in the "very jaws of slavery," was mercifully held off for another two years, until Douglass could acquire the art of writing. This he learned by way of his duties in the shipyard with which his master was connected. Watching the shipmen mark timbers with letters to designate the part of the ship for which they were intended, he secretly spent his time copying the letters while they were away at lunch until he had learned to write them with ease. When there were no new labels to learn, he began to "swap" his ability to write letters with chalk on pavements and fences, urging on the little boys he saw to "beat that if they could." In this way he finally acquired a rudimentary knowledge of writing. But he kept on practicing, copying all of the words in italic print in Webster's speller and filling in the blank lines in young Master Thomas's highly prized copy books (which would have brought him into inconceivably serious trouble, had he been caught not only learning to write but, in addition, marring the care-fully laid away copy books of the son of the house). Like Thomas Jones, he also secreted a flour barrel in his room to serve as a desk and copied passages from the Bible or from the Methodist hymn book by the light of a candle while the family was asleep.

Just as he was becoming somewhat pleased with his proficiency in both reading and writing, however, fate struck him his worst blow: he was ordered sent back to the plantation, now the property of Mr. Thomas Auld since the death of the latter's father-in-law, Douglass's former master, Captain Anthony. The reason for the change had to do with a private feud that had developed between the brothers Thomas and Hugh Auld over an imbecile slave girl named Henny, whom nobody wanted. The details of the story are complex, and concerned Douglass only in the outcome, his return to "real" slavery, for the first time as an actual laborer on a slave gang. Master Thomas immediately hired him out on the first day of January, 1834. His purpose in regard to Douglass, a well-formed and strapping boy of about fifteen or sixteen years, was to make money from the sale of his labor for the rest of his natural life, although he did tell Douglass at one time, according to an admission in one of Douglass's letters already quoted, that he would set him free at the age of twenty-five. (Douglass mentions this promise in his later versions, also.) The man to whom Douglass was hired out was a Mr. Edward Covey, notorious far and wide for his "fierce and savage disposition." Douglass's only "consolation in going to live with him," he says dryly, "was the certainty of finding him precisely as represented by common fame."

Mr. Covey's formula for success as a slaveholder was the lash, which Douglass received at least once a week during the first six months of the year he remained with him. "Aching bones and a sore back" were his constant companions, he writes of his harrowing routine:

Frequent as the lash was used, Mr. Covey thought less of it, as a means of breaking down my spirit, than that of hard and long continued labor. He worked me steadily, up to the point of my powers of endurance. From the dawn of day in the morning, till the darkness was complete in the evening, I was kept at hard work, in the field or in the woods. At certain seasons of the year, we were all kept in the field till eleven and twelve o'clock at night. At these times, Covey would attend us in the field, and urge us on with words or blows, as it seemed best to him. He had, in his life, been an overseer, and he well understood the business of slave driving. There was no deceiving him. He knew just what a man or boy could do, and he held both to strict account. When he pleased, he would work himself, like a very Turk, making everything fly before him. It was, however, scarcely necessary for Mr. Covey to be really present in the field, to have his work go on industriously. He had the faculty of making us feel that he was always present. By a series of adroitly managed surprises, which he practiced, I was prepared to expect him at any moment. His plan was, never to approach the spot where his hands were at work, in an open, manly and direct manner. . . . He would creep and crawl, in ditches and gullies; hide behind stumps and bushes, and practice so much of the cunning of the serpent, that Bill Smith and I—between ourselves—never called him by any other name than "*the snake*." . . . One half of his proficiency in the art of Negro breaking consisted, I should think, in this species of cunning. We were never secure. . . . He was, to me, behind every stump, tree, bush and fence on the plantation. He carried this kind of trickery so far, that he would sometimes mount his horse, and make believe he was going to St. Michael's; and, in thirty minutes afterward, you might find his horse tied in the woods, and the snake-like Covey lying flat in the ditch, with his head lifted above its edge, or in a fence corner, watching every movement of the slaves![26]

The description of Mr. Covey matches the man to his practices:

He was a man to whom a slave seldom felt any disposition to speak. Cold, distant, morose, with a face wearing all the marks of captious pride and malicious sternness, he repelled all advances. . . . He was only about five feet ten inches in height, I should think; short-necked, round shoulders; of quick and wiry motion, of thin and wolfish visage; with a pair of small, greenish-gray eyes, set well back under a forehead without dignity, and constantly in motion, and floating his passion, rather than his thoughts, in sight. . . . When he spoke, it was from the corner of his mouth, and in a sort of light growl, like a dog, when an attempt is made to take a bone from him.[27]

Six months of such treatment, at such hands, brought Douglass to the "bitterest dregs of slavery." Mr. Covey succeeded in breaking him. He says of this period, "My natural elasticity was crushed; my intellect languished; the disposition to read departed; the cheerful spark that lingered about my eye died; the dark night of slavery closed in upon me; and behold a man transformed into a brute!" Sunday was his only leisure time, and he spent it "in a sort of beast-like stupor, between sleep and wake, under some large tree." At times he thought of taking his life, after taking Mr. Covey's, "but was prevented by a combination of hope and fear." Recalling his sufferings during that half year, they seemed from a distance more like a nightmare than an actuality. Their plantation bordered upon Chesapeake Bay, and sometimes as he lay under a tree on Sunday, he would look out upon the "sails from every quarter of the habitable globe" that covered the bosom of the bay. His reaction to that normally uplifting sight was a true index to his condition:

> Those beautiful vessels, robed in purest white, so delightful to the
> eye of freemen, were to me so many shrouded ghosts, to terrify
> and torment me with thoughts of my wretched condition . . . and
> there, with no audience but the Almighty, I would pour out my soul's
> complaint in my rude way, with an apostrophe to the moving
> multitude of ships:
> 'You are loosed from your moorings, and free; I am fast in my
> chains, and am a slave! You move merrily before the gentle gale,
> and I sadly before the bloody whip! You are freedom's swift winged
> angels, that fly around the world; I am confined in bonds of iron!
> O, that I were free! O, that I were on one of your gallant decks, and
> under your protecting wing! Alas! betwixt me and you the turbid
> waters roll. Go on, go on. O that I could also go! CouldI but swim!
> If I could fly! O, why was I born a man, of whom to make a brute!
> The glad ship is gone; she hides in the dim distance. I am left in the
> hottest hell of unending slavery. O God, save me! God, deliver me!
> Let me be free! Is there any God? Why am I a slave? I will run
> away. I will not stand it. Get caught, or get clear, I'll try it. . . . I
> had as well be killed running as die standing. Only think of it; one
> hundred miles straight north, and I am free! Try it? Yes! God help-
> ing me, I will. . . . Let but the first opportunity offer, and, come
> what will, I am off. Meanwhile, I will try to bear up under the yoke.
> I am not the only slave in the world. Why should I fret? I can bear as
> much as any of them. Besides, I am but a boy, and all boys are
> bound to some one. It may be that my misery in slavery will only
> increase my happiness when I get free. There is a better day
> coming.[28]

Goaded finally to the point where physical sickness caught up with mental sickness, Douglass fled to Master Thomas Auld, begging him to find him another master. Auld merely gave him a huge dose of epsom salts (which, Douglass asserted, was about the only medicine given to slaves) and sent him back to Covey, explaining that his contract with Covey was for the entire year, only half of which was up. Douglass hid in the woods near Covey's plantation, too sick to face "the snake's chastisement," and during the Sunday lull—when he was sure Covey was at church, all smiles, for he was a faithful church attendant—Douglass went to see a friendly colored man in the neighborhood, "a genuine African" called Sandy, for advice as to what to do. Sandy gave him a "magic" root to try to keep Covey from beating him, since his "book learning had not kept Covey off." Douglass took it to please him, because "Sandy was so earnest, and so confident of the good qualities of this weed." The rest of Sandy's advice included going bravely back to Covey's with all speed as though nothing had happened. Covey greeted him with his "Sabbath smile" just as he came into the yard, which happened to be at the very moment that the Coveys were returning from the services.

The next morning, however, as Douglass was obeying his order to feed the horses, "Covey sneaked into the stable, in his peculiar snake-like way" and seized Douglass suddenly by the leg, throwing his "newly mended body" to the stable floor as he skillfully endeavored to "get a slip-knot" on his legs before he could draw up his feet. And that was the last beating Covey ever gave Douglass. From somewhere had come "the fighting madness" upon Douglass's spirit, and he found his strong fingers firmly attached to his tormentor's throat, so that Covey's blood "followed [his] nails." Feeling daring and as supple as a cat, he parried Covey's every blow, and flung him on the ground several times when Covey had tried to hurl him there. Soon Covey "cried out lustily for help" and was answered in the person of his cousin Hughes, to whom Douglass dealt a painful kick, sending him staggering away in agony, in preference to having Hughes tie up his right hand. Frightened by that time lest he be worsted by his infuriated slave, Covey took the fight out into the cow yard, with Douglass meeting every blow with a better one. He called for help from his hired man and from a strong slave woman named Caroline, but neither would touch Douglass. After about two hours, Covey "gave up the contest," and he never whipped Douglass again during the six months that remained of the contract. By law, a slave resisting his master was to be hanged. Pressed for an explanation of the fact that Covey did not take him before the Maryland authorities, Douglass decided that Covey kept silent about the whole episode because he would otherwise have lost his "very valuable reputation, of being a first rate overseer and Negro breaker" through the humiliating experience of defeat at the hands of a sixteen-year-old boy. It is in the effect upon Douglass himself of this critical skirmish that we take most interest:

Well, my dear reader, this battle with Mr. Covey,—undignified as it was, and as I fear my narration of it is—was the turning point in my *life as a slave*. It rekindled in my breast the smouldering embers of liberty; it brought up my Baltimore dreams, and revived a sense of my own manhood. I was a changed being after that fight. I was *nothing* before; I WAS A MAN NOW. . . . After resisting Covey, I felt as I had never felt before. . . . I was no longer a servile coward, trembling under the frown of a brother worm of the dust, but, my long-cowed spirit was roused to the point, at which I was *not afraid to die*. This spirit made me a freeman in *fact*, while I remained a slave in *form*. When a slave cannot be flogged he is more than half free. . . . From this time, until that of my escape from slavery, I was never fairly whipped. Several attempts were made to whip me, but they were always unsuccessful. Bruises I did get, as I shall hereafter inform the reader; but the case I have been describing, was the end of the brutification to which slavery had subjected me.[29]

Four years were to pass, however, before Douglass was actually to escape from slavery. He worked out the remaining six months of his contract with Mr. Covey without anything eventful happening. On January 1 of the next year, 1836, he was hired out to a Mr. William Freeland, a pleasant slave-holder, as slaveholders went. He fed his slaves well, seldom worked them longer than from sun-up to sun-down, and was disposed toward fair-minded-ness. In addition to the physical improvement in his position, Douglass found four congenial companions among Mr. Freeland's slaves: Henry Harris, John Harris, Handy Caldwell, and Sandy Jenkins, the man who had given him the "magic" root to prevent his being harmed by Mr. Covey and who duly claimed credit for the outcome of that struggle. Full of his new, spiritual freedom, Douglass soon began to proselytize these slave friends, using his *Columbian Orator* material as a starting point. Before long he had formed a "Sabbath School" of between twenty and thirty young men, all slaves, meet-ing Sundays under the trees with spelling books which had been cast off by their young masters or mistresses. Although their masters would not have minded their forming an association "to drink whiskey, to wrestle, fight, and to do other unseemly things," they all knew that it would go very hard with them if they were discovered meeting "for the purpose of improving the mind and heart," by learning to read the sacred scriptures; therefore "all were impressed with keeping the matter as private as possible." The school *was* broken up, before long, by three church leaders who rushed in "fero-ciously. . . armed with mob-like missiles, and forbade our meeting again, on pain of having our backs made bloody by the lash," as Douglass reported. One of the men who broke up their school, Garrison West, had been Douglass's "class leader" before that event. "He led me no more after that," is Douglass's comment. This was not the actual end of their school, we learn:

> After getting the school into operation, the second time—holding it in the woods, behind the barn, and in the shade of trees—I succeeded in inducing a free colored man, who lived several miles from our house, to permit me to hold my school in a room at his house. He, very kindly, gave me this liberty; but he incurred much peril in doing so, for the assemblage was an unlawful one. . . . I had, at one time, more than forty scholars, all of the right sort; and many of them succeeded in learning to read. I have met several slaves from Maryland, who were once my scholars; and who obtained their freedom. I doubt not, partly in consequence of the ideas imparted to them in that school. I have had various employments during my short life; but I look back to *none* with more satisfaction, than to that afforded by my Sunday school. An attachment, deep and lasting, sprung up between me and my persecuted pupils, which made my parting from them intensely grievous; and, when I think that most of these dear souls are yet shut up in this abject thralldom, I am overwhelmed with grief.[30]

In addition to the school that met each Sunday, Douglass spent three evenings a week during the winter teaching the slaves to read, hiding with them in barns and woods and fields, in grave danger if any of them should be discovered. Mr. Freeland was a good master; in fact, Douglass went so far as to say of him: "To the credit of Mr. Freeland,—irreligious though he was—it must be stated, that he was the best master I ever had, until I became my own mster, and assumed for myself, as I had a right to do, the responsibility of my own existence and the exercise of my own powers."[31] Probably in consequence of their having a good master, the slaves of his plantation were very genial and friendly. In their actions they were "generally a unit, and moved together." Mr. Freeland renewed the contract for Douglass's time for the year 1837, but Douglass was already in the midst of plans to make his escape from slavery, so that it did not mean to him, as otherwise it might have, that he was assured of a "nice place" for the coming twelve months.

There were five young men besides Douglass among the conspirators striking out for their freedom. "The very flower of the neighborhood," each of them was worth "one thousand dollars in the home market" and "fifteen hundred dollars, a piece, and perhaps more" at New Orleans. They were Henry and John Harris, Sandy Jenkins, Charles Roberts, and Henry Baily. Douglass was almost the youngest member of the group but had "the advantage of them all, in experience, and in a knowledge of letters." He was the leading force and admitted entire responsibility for putting it into their heads to run away. The plans were discovered, somehow, and the five were led most ignominiously to the jail at Easton. As Douglass describes the scene:

> Could the kind reader have been quietly riding along the main road to or from Easton, that morning, his eye would have met a painful sight. He would have seen five young men, guilty of no crime, save that of preferring *liberty* to a life of *bondage*, drawn along the public highway—firmly bound together tramping through dust and heat, bare-footed and bare-headed—fastened to three strong horses, whose riders were armed to the teeth, with pistols and daggers—on their way to prison, like felons, and suffering every possible insult from the crowds of idle, vulgar people, who clustered around, and heartlessly made their failure the occasion for all manner of ribaldry and sport. . . . It seemed to me . . . that everybody we met knew the cause of our arrest, and were out, awaiting our passing by, to feast their vindictive eyes on our misery and to gloat over our ruin. Some said, *I ought to be hanged*, and others, *I ought to be burnt*; other, I ought to have the *"hide"* taken from my back; while no one gave us a kind word or sympathizing look, except the poor slaves, who were lifting their heavy hoes, and who cautiously glanced at us through the post-and-rail fences, behind which they were at work.[32]

The young fellows had every reason for fearing the worst—sale to the Georgia traders, at the very least. But what actually happened to them seemed almost a miracle. First, after a fairly short period, the two slaveholders who owned the other five men in the conspiracy appeared at the jail to take them back home. Douglass was left in prison for being the instigator, without whose "evil whispers" the other slaves would never have "thought of running off." Douglass was reduced to the depths of misery, left alone without the others and with thoughts of lifelong slavery in Georgia or Louisiana or Alabama. By the end of a month of loneliness and uncertainty, Douglass found himself actually glad to see his master, Thomas Auld, even though it was with the promise that he would be sent to Alabama "with a cousin" in a few days. No "cousin" came, however, and so before long Douglass had the unexpected good luck to be sent to Baltimore to be the slave of his owner's brother Hugh again. The brothers were now "at peace" with each other, and Thomas Auld apparently had found no buyer for such an "insurgent" slave.

This was in the spring of 1837. For the next eight months, Douglass was hired out by Hugh Auld to a Mr. Gardiner to learn the caulking trade. It did not happen to be a very good time to be taught that trade, however, as Mr. Gardiner was at that time "engaged in building two large man-of-war vessels, professedly for the Mexican government," which were to be launched in July of that year. As failure to meet the contract would result in the forfeiture of a very considerable sum of money, Mr. Gardiner had all hands working to the limit. Douglass tells of his role in this new environment:

> There was no time to learn anything. Every man had to do that which he knew how to do. In entering the shipyard, my orders from Mr. Gardiner were, to do whatever the carpenters commanded me to do. This was placing me at the beck and call of about seventy-five men. I was to regard all these as masters. Their word was to be my law. My situation was a most trying one. At times I needed a dozen pair of hands. I was called a dozen ways in the space of a single minute. Three or four voices would strike my ear at the same moment. It was −'Fred., come help me to cant this timber here.'− 'Fred., come carry this timber yonder.'−'Fred., bring that roller here.'−'Fred., go get a fresh can of water.'−'Fred., come help saw off the end of this timber.'−'Fred., go quick and get the crowbar.'− 'Fred., hold on the end of this fall.'−'Fred., go to the blacksmith's shop, and get a new punch.'−'Hurra, Fred.! run and bring me a cold chisel.'−'I say, Fred., bear a hand, and get up a fire as quick as lightning under that steam-box.'−'Halloo, nigger! come, turn this grindstone.'−'Come, come! move, move! and *bowse* this timber forward.'−'I say, darkey, blast your eyes, why don't you heat up some pitch?'−'Halloo! halloo! halloo!' (Three voices at the same time.) 'Come here!−Go there!−Hold on where you are! D——n you, if you move, I'll knock your brains out!'[33]

Release from this "training school" in the caulker's trade came about as the result of a race riot in the shipyard among the laborers. The white mechanics periodically showed their resentment against unfair competition with slave laborers. They were not so open in their methods as to refuse to work "by the side of slaves;" instead, they chose cowardly attacks on the free black mechanics in the shipyard. Douglass's discussion of the beginning of this type of trouble in Baltimore is of particular interest:

> Until a very little while before I went there, white and black ship carpenters worked side by side, in the shipyards of Mr. Gardiner, Mr. Duncan, Mr. Walter Price and Mr. Robb. Nobody seemed to see any impropriety in it. To outward seeming, all hands were well satisfied. Some of the blacks were first-rate workmen, and were given jobs requiring the highest skill. All at once, however, the white carpenters knocked off, and swore that they would no longer work on the same stage with free Negroes. Taking advantage of the heavy contract resting upon Mr. Gardiner, to have the war vessels for Mexico ready to launch in July, and of the difficulty of getting other

hands at that season of the year, they swore they would not strike
another blow for him, unless he would discharge his free colored
workmen.[34]

In the melee that followed, Douglass was seriously beaten up by four ship
hands. Mr. Auld was very angry about the damage done to his "property"
and tried to obtain redress. Douglass was dryly amused to watch Auld's
mounting exasperation over the law that was this time hurting the slaveholder, in its refusal to accept the testimony of a slave against white assail-
ants. Douglass was unable to work until his wounds had healed, after which
interim Mr. Auld hired him out for a year in Mr. Price's shipyard, where
Douglass learned the caulker's trade and "in the course of a single year . . .
was able to command the highest wages paid to journeymen caulkers in
Baltimore."

By May, 1838, therefore, Douglass had become "of some pecuniary
value" to his master, earning from six to nine dollars a week. He made his
own contacts and contracts for work at the rate of a dollar and a half a day
and handed over his earnings to "Master Hugh" every Saturday night—
except one. The Saturday that he missed, preferring to be late with his
master's money than to be late to camp meeting, occurred early in August.
His master was so angered that he withdrew from Douglass the privilege of
hiring out his own time and commanded him to bring his tools and other
belongings and "come home" to master. Douglass did so and sat down for
an entire week, "awaiting orders." His master glowered and said nothing
until Saturday night arrived. Douglass had no money, he said, because he
had been given no work. Mr. Auld changed that: he found him work early
Monday morning, and Douglass very promptly brought him nine dollars for
three Saturday nights. Then on Monday morning, September 3, 1838,
Douglass made his escape from his master and slavery and Baltimore and the
South. He did not choose to reveal the manner of his escape until he wrote
the third version of his autobiography.

His immediate destination was New York, where, after wandering about
fearful of pursuers and troubled by lack of funds, he was befriended by a
sailor whose face he thought "trustworthy." He took Douglass to his home
and put him in touch with the abolitionist David Ruggles. Ruggles advised
him to go to New Bedford, a good place for the kind of work he could do.
First, however, Douglass was married to Anna, the free colored woman to
whom he sent word to meet him, by the Rev. J. W. C. Pennington (whom no
one at that time knew to be a fugitive slave himself, as he did not make that
surprising announcement for another eleven years). He then set off for New
Bedford. There, the young fugitive and his bride found a home with a kindly
colored man, a Mr. Nathan Johnson, who had just been reading the *Lady of
the Lake* when the newcomers were introduced and induced his guest to

change his name from "Frederick Bailey" to "Frederick Douglass" as one of his first deeds.

As David Ruggles had said, there was much work at New Bedford for caulkers to do, but there was no work for a Negro caulker, as Douglass soon found out. We read of a situation reminding us of his experience at Gardiner's in Baltimore:

> It so happened that Mr. Rodney French, late mayor of the city of New Bedford, had a ship fitting out for sea, and to which there was a large job of caulking and coppering to be done. I applied to that noble-hearted man for employment, and he promptly told me to go to work; but going on the float-stage for the purpose, I was informed that every white man would leave the ship if I struck a blow upon her. "Well, well," thought I, "this is a hardship, but yet not a very serious one for me." The difference between the wages of a caulker and that of a common day laborer, was an hunder per cent, in favor of the former; but then I was free, and free to work, though not at my trade. I now prepared myself to do anything which came to hand in the way of turning an honest penny.[35]

During those first three years, he sawed wood, dug cellars, shoveled coal, swept chimneys, rolled oil casks on the wharves, helped load and unload vessels, and worked in a candle factory and in a brass foundry. Food prices were high, and they were "closely pinched" to make ends meet. There was another little mouth to feed by the end of the first year, but the little family managed happily. Douglass joined the Methodist church and became a member of its organizations for the spiritual advancement of young men. He found in *The Liberator* what he had been looking for: the crusade to which he wished wholeheartedly to attach himself, the cause of the slave still in bondage.

The details of Douglass's life from the time that he became affliated with the antislavery movement need not be rehearsed here, though the actual facts of his life as a freeman are so intermingled with mythical matter as to tempt one to turn aside from the business of *the slave* and lay them out straight. The Douglass of the later days is the same person we have watched grow up—sensitive, imaginative, deeply concerned with the "under dog," magnetic, honest. The misconceptions that attended some of his public moves stemmed from the hysteria attending the stupendous purpose of the abolitionist forces. Naturally, Douglass could not clear the picture that had been built up in some quarters as to his presumed chauvinism, no matter how many versions of his autobiography he prepared. The job awaits doing and should be done.

Considering Douglass's autobiography from the literary historian's viewpoint, we have unhesitatingly assigned to it the position of top-ranking slave narrative. The fact that Douglass was himself the most important American Negro slave is in no wise responsible for this decision in regard to his autobiographical achievement, for the latter holds its ground on the basis of its own merits. Even when read without benefit of adequate understanding of the general nature of the slave experience, the *Narrative of Frederick Douglass, an American Slave, Written by Himself* is an arresting book. When read after one has acquired that understanding through the knowledge of "the inmost thoughts" of thousands of slave narrators, Douglass's narrative commands unstinted praise. It is the veritable ambassador before the world of the soul of the American Negro imprisoned as a slave. In the words of a contemporary reviewer writing for the *New York Tribune* in June, 1845:

> Considered merely as a narrative, we have never read one more
> simple, true, coherent, and warm with genuine feeling. It is an excel-
> lent piece of writing, and on that score to be prized as a specimen of
> the powers of the black race, which prejudice persists in disputing.
> We prize highly all evidence of this kind, and it is becoming more
> abundant. The Cross of the Legion of Honor has just been conferred
> in France on Dumas and Soulie.[36]

The second version of Douglass's *Narrative* appeared under the title *My Bondage and My Freedom* in 1855. The initial sale of five thousand copies in two days gives one an insight into its welcome by the public,[37] which continued to buy the book eagerly throughout the 1850s. The one hundred twenty pages of the first version were expanded into three hundred thirty pages for "Part I—Life as a Slave" and an additional one hundred and thirty-four for "Part II—Life as a Freeman." More important than the swelling of the pages was the change in sponsor and publisher for this second auto-biography. The book was dedicated, in an impressive display of font on the page following the title page, to Gerrit Smith, "as a slight token of esteem for his character, admiration for his genius and benevolence, affection for his person, and gratitude for his friendship, etc." It was published by the firm of Miller, Orton, and Mulligan, of Auburn, New York. The unsigned "Editor's Preface" includes a letter from Douglass in reply to a request for an up-to-date history of his life. Expressing his "somewhat positive repugnance" to writing or speaking of matters that would lead others to impute his motive to publicity-seeking, he says:

> I have . . . felt that it was best for those having histories worth the
> writing—or supposed to be so—to commit such work to hands other
> than their own. To write of oneself, in such a manner as not to incur
> the imputation of weakness, vanity, and egotism, is a work within
> the ability of but few; and I have little reason to believe that I
> belong to that fortunate few.

These considerations caused me to hesitate, when first you kindly urged me to prepare for publication a full account of my life as a slave, and my life as a freeman.

Nevertheless, I see with you, many reasons for regarding my auto-biography as exceptional in its character, and as being, in some sense, naturally beyond the reach of those reproaches which honorable and sensitive minds dislike to incur. It is not to illustrate any heroic achievements of a man, but to vindicate a just and beneficent princi-ple, in its application to the whole human family, by letting in the light of truth upon a system. . . . I agree with you, that this system is now at the bar of public opinion—not only of this country, but of the whole civilized world—for judgment. . . . Any facts, either from slaves, slaveholders, or by-standers, calculated to enlighten the public mind, by revealing the true character, nature, and tendency of the slave system, are in order, and can scarcely be innocently withheld.

I see, too, that there are special reasons why I should write my own biography, in preference to employing another to do it. Not only is slavery on trial, but unfortunately, the enslaved people are also on trial. It is alleged, that they are, naturally, inferior; that they are *so low* in the scale of humanity, and so utterly stupid, that they are unconscious of their wrongs, and do not apprehend their rights. Looking, then, at your request, from this standpoint, and wishing everything of which you think me capable to go to the benefit of my afflicted people, I part with my doubts and hesitation, and proceed to furnish you the desired manuscript; hoping that you may be able to make such arrangements for its publication as shall be best adapted to accomplish that good which you so enthusiastically anticipate.[38]

The chief difference between the first and second autobiographies is to be found in the amplification, in the second, of all expository passages in the first, where Douglass seemed to feel that the reader's understanding of the basic machinery of the institution of slavery might be in need of help. The emphasis in the introduction to the book, written by James M'Cune Smith, reveals the wide interest—we might even say worldwide interest—at that time in the question of Douglass's paternity. Douglass's new version recognizes that curiosity in his expansion of the brief passage in his first book into a ten-page chapter entitled "The Author's Parentage." A lengthy table of contents, with subdivisions that serve as a subject index, further equips the book with aids to the understanding. There are also steelpoint engravings of representa-tive scenes in a slave's life. The passages in the 1845 version which are impor-tant for their beauty of expression or power are to be found, literally unchanged for the most part, in the 1855 version. It is also significant that, though Douglass's hero is now the more tolerant Gerrit Smith and not Garrison, there is no change in his handling of the slaveholders, with the exception of the slight "softening" of his portrait of Mr. Thomas Auld, obtained by inclusion of that master's verbal promise to set Douglas free at the age of twenty-five. Douglass announced publicly in 1847 that he had neglected to mention that promise earlier because he did not believe that Mr. Auld meant what he was saying.[39] It can therefore be safely assumed that the influence upon Douglass of Garrison's views in regard to the slaveholder was more superficial than actual.

Conscious of the weighty discussions during the 1840s and 1850s as to whether *any* of his powers could be attributed to any heritage but his "white father," Douglass does a good job of complicating the puzzle in the third chapter of the 1855 version. It is his mother's chapter. Of his father, Douglass says, this time:

> I say nothing of *father*, for he is shrouded in a mystery I have never been able to penetrate. Slavery does away with fathers, as it does away with families. . . . The name of the child is not expected to be that of its father, and his condition does not necessarily affect that of the child. He may be the slave of Mr. Filgman; and his child, when born, may be the slave of Mr. Gross. He may be a *freeman*; and yet his child may be a *chattel*. He may be white, glorying in the purity of his Anglo-Saxon blood; and his child may be ranked with the blackest slaves. Indeed, he *may* be, and often *is*, master and father to the same child . . . and may sell his child without incurring reproach. . . . My father was a white man, or nearly white. It was sometimes whispered that my master was my father.[40]

It may as well be mentioned at this point that in the 1881 version of his autobiography Douglass says briefly, in this connection, "Of my father I know nothing."[41] In the 1892 version he says the same thing,[42] adding later, in commenting upon the hearsay that his mother was the only slave around Tuckahoe who could read, "In view of this fact, I am happy to attribute any love of letters I may have, not to my presumed Anglo-Saxon paternity, but to the native genius of my sable, unprotected and uncultivated mother—a woman who belonged to a race whose mental endowments are still disparaged and despised."[43] From the 1855 version on, Douglass adds to his original description of his mother as a tall, dark, well-formed woman, "remarkable sedateness" in her manner, "a deep black glossy complexion," and regular features of which he says he was always reminded by the picture on page 157 of *Prichard's Natural History of Man*. The outline story of his mother's visits to him by night at the risk of her life for going off the plantation without permission, to say nothing of the twenty-four miles round trip on foot between the weariness of one day's work and the coming arduousness of the next is spun out longer and longer from 1855 to 1892. A horrid cook named Aunt Katy is brought in "fresh," as a foil character to his loving mother. Still claiming not to be deeply attached to his mother—as he says, "certainly not so deeply as I should have been had our relations in childhood been different"[44]—Douglass yet succeeds in drawing a beautiful picture of the love of a slave mother for her child.

One of the passages added to the second version shows Douglass's deep interest in the situation of the slaves still in the South and his care lest he write anything that might reduce their chances for escape. The passage explains his refusal to relate to the public the manner of his escape from slavery. He writes:

> The practice of publishing every new invention by which a slave is known to have escaped from slavery, has neither wisdom nor necessity to sustain it. Had not Henry Box Brown and his friends attracted slaveholding attention to the manner of his escape, we might have had a thousand *Box Browns* per annum. The singularly original plan adopted by William and Ellen Crafts, perished with the first using, because every slaveholder in the land was apprised of it. The *salt water slave* who hung in the guards of a steamer, being washed three days and three nights—like another Jonah—by the waves of the sea, has, by the publicity given to the circumstances, set a spy on the guards of every steamer departing from southern ports. . . . Nothing is more evident, than that such disclosures are a positive evil to the slaves remaining, and seeking to escape. In publishing such accounts, the anti-slavery man addresses the slaveholder, *not the slave*; this stimulates the former to greater watchfulness, and adds to his facilities for capturing the slave. We owe something to the slaves south of Mason and Dixon's line, as well as to those north of it; and, in discharging the duty of aiding the latter, on their way to freedom, we should be careful to do nothing which would be likely to hinder the former, in making their escape from slavery.[45]

Therefore we wait until we come to the third version of Douglass's autobiography, the *Life and Times of Frederick Douglass, Written by Himself*, published in Hartford, Connecticut, in 1881, for the story of the particular means by which Douglass got away from the slaveholder.

Although the slave in Baltimore was never far removed from facilities for escape in the form of the train or boats, the necessity of showing "free papers" whenever asked for them rendered the chance to escape by one of these means more difficult than might be assumed. The ways by which slaves managed to forge free papers were incredibly ingenious in some cases and very risky in others. In the 1881 narration we learn of the risks Douglass took:

I had one friend—a sailor—who owned a sailor's protection, which answered somewhat the purpose of free papers—describing his person, and certifying to the fact that he was a free American sailor. The instrument had at its head the American eagle, which gave it the appearance at once of an authorized document. This protection did not, when in my hands, describe its bearer very accurately. Indeed, it called for a man much darker than myself, and close examination of it would have caused my arrest at the start. In order to avoid this fatal scrutiny on the part of the railroad official, I had arranged with Isaac Rolls, a hackman, to bring my baggage to the train just on the moment of its starting, and jumped upon the car myself when the train was already in motion. Had I gone into the station and offered to purchase a ticket, I should have been instantly and carefully examined, and undoubtedly arrested. In choosing this plan upon which to act, I considered the jostle of the train, and the natural haste of the conductor, in a train crowded with passengers, and relied upon my skill and address in playing the sailor as described in my protection, to do the rest. One element in my favor was the kind feeling which prevailed in Baltimore and other seaports at that time, towards "those who go down to the sea in ships." "Free trade and sailors' rights expressed the sentiment of the country just then. In my clothing I was rigged out in sailor style. I had on a red shirt and a tarpaulin hat and black cravat, tied in sailor fashion, carelessly and loosely about my neck. My knowledge of ships and sailor's talk came much to my assistance, for I knew a ship from stem to stern, and from keelson to crosstrees, and could talk sailor like an "old salt." On sped the train, and I was well on the way to Havre de Grace before the conductor came into the Negro car to collect tickets and examine the papers of his black passengers. This was a critical moment in the drama. My whole future depended upon the decision of this conductor. Agitated I was while this ceremony was proceeding, but still externally, at least, I was apparently calm and self-possessed. He went on with his duty—examining several colored passengers before reaching me. He was somewhat harsh in tone, and peremptory in manner until he reached me, when, strangely enough, and to my surprise and relief, his whole manner changed. Seeing that I did not readily produce my free papers, as the other colored persons in the car had done, he said to me in a friendly contrast with that observed towards the others: "I suppose you have your free papers?" To which I answered: "No, sir; I never carry my free papers to sea with me." "But you have something to show that you are a free man, have you not?" "Yes, sir," I answered; "I have a paper with the American eagle on it, and that will carry me round the world." With this I drew from my deep sailor's pocket my sea-man's protection, as before described. The merest glace at the paper satisfied him, and he took my fare and went about his business.[46]

The crisis thus passed, Douglass could begin to breathe again, though not yet easily, as he was "still in Maryland, and subject to arrest at any moment." Especially on the passage by ferry over the Susquehanna River, he was worried by the attentions of a person who insisted upon knowing him. There was also a German blacksmith on the train with him who really recognized Douglass, the latter believed, "but had no heart to betray" him and "held his peace." There was danger during the change from train to steamboat at Wilmington, but no one disturbed him there. Soon he was in Philadelphia and then in New York. The whole journey took less than twenty-four hours.

The account of his method of escape from slavery is one of the most important of the contributions of the 1881 autobiography to the story of Douglass as a slave. Only two hundred of the five hundred and sixteen pages of the *Life and Times of Frederick Douglass* are devoted to that period of his life, more than a hundred fewer than in the 1855 version. The other three hundred pages describe the times—one hundred conventions he took part in, his impressions abroad, John Brown, Mrs. Stowe, Abraham Lincoln, the Proclamation of 1863, and various phases of the turmoil during Reconstruction. Douglass feels more sentimental about his visit, "forty years after," to see his old master, Thomas Auld, at the old plantation at St. Michael's. Stricken with palsy, the bedridden old man had sent for Douglass when he learned that his former slave was in the neighborhood. The chief point of interest in their reunion would seem to be Mr. Auld's reply to Douglass's frank question as to what Mr. Auld had thought of his conduct in running away and going north. In the words of Douglass's report: "He hesitated a moment as if to properly formulate his reply, and said: 'Frederick, I always knew you were too smart to be a slave, and had I been in your place I should have done as you did.'" The account continues:

> I said, "Captain Auld, I am glad to hear you say this, I did not run away from you, but from *slavery*; it was not that I loved Caesar less, but Rome more." I told him that I had made a mistake in my narrative, a copy of which I had sent him, in attributing to him ungrateful and cruel treatment of my grandmother; that I had done so on the supposition that in the division of the property of my old master, Mr. Aaron Anthony, my grandmother had fallen to him, and that he had left her in her old age, when she could be no longer of service to him, to pick up her living in solitude with none to help her, or in other words had been turned out to die like an old horse. "Ah!" he said, "that was a mistake, I never owned your grandmother; she in the division of the slaves was awarded to my brother-in-law, Andrew

Anthony; but," he added quickly, "I brought her down here and took care of her as long as she lived." The fact is, that after writing my narrative describing the condition of my grandmother, Captain Auld's attention being thus called to it, he rescued her from her destitution. I told him that this mistake of mine was corrected as soon as I discovered it, and that I had at no time any wish to do him injustice; that I regarded both of us as victims of a system. "Oh, I never liked slavery," he said, "and I meant to emancipate all of my slaves when they reached the age of twenty-five years." I told him I had always been curious to know how old I was, that it had been a serious trouble to me, not to know when my birthday was. He said he could not tell me, but he thought I was born in February, 1818. . . . The whole interview did not last more than twenty minutes, and we parted to meet no more. His death was soon after announced in the papers, and the fact that he had once owned me as a slave was cited as rendering that event noteworthy.[47]

In the revised version of *The Life and Times of Frederick Douglass, Written by Himself*, which was published in Boston in 1892, the narrative first told in 1845 comes into full bloom. Except for excision of polemical additions to the 1855 version no longer needed, everything reappears that was in the three preceding volumes, viewed now from the vantage point of three score years and fourteen. Details unconsciously absorbed by the sensitive child that the man nearing thirty was too distracted to recall show forth surprisingly clearly and naturally on the retina of old age. Though monsters still, even Mr. Gore and Mr. Covey do not jump from the page in 1892. Douglass's story of his life has become a saga, the saga of the slave.

Colonel Lloyd's plantation on the Wye River in Talbot County, Maryland, becomes the classic slave plantation. Far away from "the great thoroughfares of travel and commerce, and proximate to no town or village," there was neither schoolhouse nor townhouse in its neighborhood. The master's children and grandchildren were taught by a private tutor from Massachusetts "who did not speak a dozen words to a slave in a whole year, and the overseer's children were sent "off somewhere in the State to school" so that they could not bring any "foreign or dangerous influence from abroad to embarrass the natural operation of the slave system of the place." The community was made up of three classes: slaveholders, overseers, and slaves. Its blacksmiths, wheelwrights, shoemakers, weavers, and "coopers" were all slaves. Every "leaf and grain of the products of this plantation and those of the neighboring farms belonging to Colonel Lloyd" were carried to Baltimore in Colonel Lloyd's own vessels, manned by his own slaves, the captain alone being excepted. Everything entering the plantation from outside came in through the same channel.

The plantation was "a most strikingly interesting place, full of life, activity, and spirit." There was a large windmill with wide-sweeping "white wings," a river called the "Swash," with a large sloop, the "Sally Lloyd," named in honor of the Colonel's favorite daughter, lying quietly at anchor, ready to take the master's family in to Baltimore. A little red house up the road was occupied by the overseer, the first of "a great many houses, human habitations full of the mysteries of life at every stage of it." Between the overseer's house and the "Big House" was the "long quarter," a long, low building "literally alive with slaves of all ages, sexes, conditions, sizes, and colors." A tall, dilapidated old brick building, originally designed for some other purpose, had also been turned into slave quarters. Besides these two buildings there were "numerous other slave houses and huts scattered around in the neighborhood, every nook and corner of which were completely occupied." Douglass's master's house, as the house of the chief overseer, was a long brick building, independent of the rule of the plantation. In addition to these houses, there were "barns, stables, store-houses, tobacco-houses, blacksmith shops, wheelwright shops, cooper shops; but above all there stood the grandest building my young eyes had ever beheld, called by every one on the plantation the *great* house." Kitchens, washhouses, dairies, summer houses, greenhouses, henhouses, turkey houses, pigeon houses, and arbors of many types, "all neatly painted or whitewashed, interspersed with grand old trees, ornamental and primitive," framed the *great* house from the rear.

The carriage entrace to the Colonel's mansion was through a large gate a quarter of a mile distant. The intermediate space between the gate and the large white wooden building with wings on three sides and a broad, columned portico extending the entire length of the building was a beautiful lawn, dotted thickly over with trees and flowers. The road from the gate, richly paved with white pebbles from the beach, formed a complete circle around the lawn. Rabbits, deer, and other wild game sported in the parks outside the estate. There was the family cemetery, with its "vast tombs, embowered beneath the weeping willow and the fir tree." Colonel Lloyd was the owner and head of the entire establishment, which numbered not less than a thousand slaves at any time, for, "though scarcely a month passed without the sale to the Georgia traders, of one or more lost, there was no apparent diminution in the number of his human stock."

There was always much bustle and noise on the plantation on the two days at the end of each month when the slaves belonging to the thirty different branch farms "assembled here by their representatives, to obtain their monthly allowances of corn-meal and pork": one bushel of the meal, "unbolted, of which quite fifteen per cent was more fit for pigs than for men" and eight pounds of pickled pork (often tainted) or its equivalent in fish. One pint of salt added to this, constituted "the entire monthly allowance of a full-grown slave, working constantly in the open field from morning till night every day in the month except Sunday."

The yearly allowance of clothing was not more generous than the food supply: two linen shirts, so coarse that the skin was constantly itching from the tow threads; one pair of trousers of the same material for summer and a woolen jacket and a pair of woolen trousers for winter; and one pair of shoes of the "coarsest description" and a pair of yarn stockings. Children under ten had "neither shoes, stockings, jackets, nor trousers," and when their two tow linen shirts per year wore out, "they went naked until the next allowance day." There were no beds for the slaves. Only the men and the women were given bedding, in the form of one coarse blanket. But less concern was felt by the slaves for the privation of bedding than for the lack of time to take care of their personal needs and still get their much-needed sleep. We read:

> Time to sleep was of far greater importance. For when the day's work was done most of these had their washing, mending, and cooking to do, and having few or no facilities for doing such things, very many of their needed sleeping hours were consumed in necessary preparations for the labors of the coming day. The sleeping compartments, if they could have been properly called such, had little regard to comfort or decency. Old and young, male and female, married and single, dropped down upon the common clay floor, each covering up with his or her blanket, their only protection from cold or exposure. The night, however, was shortened at both ends. The slaves worked as long as they could see, and were late in cooking and mending for the coming day, and at the first streak of the morning they were summoned to the field by the overseer's horn. They were whipped for over-sleeping more than for any other fault. Neither age nor sex found any favor. The overseer stood at the quarter door, armed with stick and whip, ready to deal heavy blows upon any who might be a little behind time. When the horn was blown there was a rush for the door, for the hindermost one was sure to get a blow from the overseer. Young mothers who worked in the field were allowed an hour about ten o'clock in the morning to go home to nurse their children. This was when they were not required to take them to the field with them, and leave them upon "turning row," or in the corner of the fences."[48]

The slaves were "expected to sing as well as to work." A silent slave was not liked by either the master or the overseer. They were constantly being told, when silent, to "Make a noise there! Make a noise there!"—a means of telling the overseer "where they were and what they were about." As a rule, they did not go to their quarters for their meals at the Lloyd plantation but took their ash-cake and piece of pork or salt herring with them when they went out onto the field at dawn. As for the inmates of the mansion, we learn:

> The close-fisted stinginess that fed the poor slave on coarse corn-meal and tainted meat, that clothed him in crashy tow-linen and hurried him on to toil through the field in all weather, with wind and rain beating through his tattered garments, and that scarcely gave even the young slave-mother time to nurse her infant in the fence-corner, wholly vanished on approaching the sacred precincts of the "Great House" itself. There the scriptural phrase descriptive of the wealthy found exact illustration. The highly favored inmates of this mansion were literally arrayed in "purple and fine linen, and fared sumptuously every day." The table of this house groaned under the blood-bought luxuries gathered with pains-taking care at home and abroad. Fields, forests, rivers, and seas were made tributary. Immense wealth and its lavish expenditures filled the Great House with all that could please the eye or tempt the taste. Fish, flesh, and fowl were here in profusion. Chickens of all breeds; ducks of all kinds, wild and tame, the common and the huge Muscovite; Guinea fowls, turkeys, geese, and pea-fowls; all were fat and fattening for the destined vortex. Here the graceful swan, the mongrel, the black-necked wild goose, partridges, quails, pheasants, pigeons and choice water-fowl, with all their strange varieties, were caught in this huge net. Beef, veal, mutton, and venison, of the most select kinds and quality, rolled in bounteous profusion to this grand consumer. The teeming riches of the Chesapeake Bay, its rock perch, drums, crocus, trout, oysters, crabs, and terrapin were drawn hither to adorn the glittering table. The dairy, too, the finest then on the eastern shore of Maryland, supplied by cattle of the best English stock, imported for the express purpose, poured its rich donations of fragrant cheese, golden butter, and delicious cream to heighten the attractions of the gorgeous, unending round of feastings. Nor were the fruits of the earth overlooked. The fertile garden, many acres in size, constituting a separate establishment distinct from the common farm, with its scientific gardener direct from Scotland, a Mr. McDermott, and four men under his direction, was not behind, either in the abundance or in the delicacy of its contributions. The tender asparagus, the crispy celery, and the delicate cauliflower, egg plants, beets, lettuce, parsnips, peas, and French beans, early and late; radishes, cantelopes, melons of all kinds; and fruits of all climes and of every description, from the hardy apples of the north to the lemon and orange of the south, culminated at this point. Here were

gathered figs, raisins, almonds, and grapes from Spain, wines and brandies from France, teas of various flavor from China, and rich, aromatic coffee from Java, all conspiring to swell the tide of high life, where pride and indolence lounged in magnificence and satiety.[49]

The fifteen slaves selected to wait upon the master's family formed "a sort of black aristocracy," resembling the field hands "in nothing except their color, and in this they held the advantage of a velvetlike glossiness, rich and beautiful." They were selected with a view not only to their "capacity and adeptness, but with special regard to their personal appearance, their graceful agility, and pleasing address." The girls and women were dressed in the "scarcely-worn silk" of the mistress and her daughters, "while the serving men were equally well attired from the overflowing wardrobe of their young masters, so that in dress, as well as in form and feature, in manner and speech, in tastes and habits, the distance between these favored few and the sorrow and hunger-smitten multitudes of the quarter and the field was immense."

In the stables were thirty-five horses "of the best approved blood, both for speed and beauty," and a house built specially for dogs contained "a pack of twenty-five or thirty, the fare for which would have made glad the hearts of a dozen slaves." Two slaves, "Old Barney" and his son, were in charge of these animals, and were whipped almost to the point of death, more than once, when the master or his sons took objection to the looks of a horse's mane or a dog's ear. In the carriage houses were "gigs, phaetons, barouches, sulkeys, and sleighs," and the saddles and harnesses were "beautifully wrought and richly mounted." Hospitality was the order of the day, with many a health-seeking "divine or merchant from the north" being astonished and charmed by the Lloyds' grandeur. Indeed, Douglass concludes, "viewed from his table, and *not* from the field, Colonel Lloyd was a model of generous hospitality."

The little slave boy Frederick, as he grew older and "more thoughtful," became more and more conscious of the contrast between the wretchedness of the slave and the pageant-like splendor of the master's family. Douglass writes:

> The unkindness of Aunt Katy [the cook], the hunger and cold I
> suffered, and the terrible reports of wrongs and outrages which came
> to my ear, together with what I almost daily witnessed, led me to
> wish I had never been born. I used to contrast my condition with
> that of the blackbirds, in whose wild and sweet songs I fancied
> them so happy. Their apparent joy only deepened the shades of my
> sorrow. There are thoughtful days in the lives of children—at least
> there were in mine—when they grapple with the great primary sub-
> ject of knowledge, and reach in a moment conclusions which no

subsequent experience can shake. I was just as well aware of the unjust, unnatural and murderous character of slavery, when nine years old, as I am now. Without any appeals to books, to laws, or to authorities of any kind, to regard God as "Our Father," condemned slavery as a crime.[50]

This discontent, natural to the thousands of slaves of reflective disposition, was augmented within a few years as the result of Douglass's initiation into the world of books. His *Columbian Orator*, we learn here, cost fifty cents. Douglass's purchase of the book was inspired "by hearing some little boys say that they were going to learn some pieces out of it for the exhibition." Douglass dwells further upon the extent to which his discontent was increased by book learning, as Mr. Hugh Auld had predicted to his wife:

Light had penetrated the moral dungeon where I had lain, and I saw the bloody whip for my back and the iron chain for my feet, and my *good, kind* master was the author of my situation, and made me gloomy and miserable. As I writhed under the sting and torment of this knowledge I almost envied my fellow slaves their stupid indifference. It opened my eyes to the horrible pit, and revealed the teeth of the frightful dragon that was ready to pounce upon me; but alas, it opened no way for my escape. I wished myself a beast, a bird, anything rather than a slave. I was wretched and gloomy beyond my ability to describe. This everlasting thinking distressed and tormented me; and yet there was no getting rid of this subject of my thoughts. Liberty, as the inestimable birthright of every man, converted every object into an asserter of this right. I heard it in every sound, and saw it in every object. It was ever present to torment me with a sense of my wretchedness. The more beautiful and charming were the smiles of nature, the more horrible and desolate was my condition. I saw nothing without seeing it, and I heard nothing without hearing it. I do not exaggerate when I say that it looked at me in every star, smiled in every calm, breathed in every wind, and moved in every storm.[51]

Religion came to the rescue of the despairing thirteen-year-old lad as it had for thousands and thousands of other despairing slaves. The preaching of a white Methodist minister "named Hanson" was the means of bringing him to feel that in God he had a "father and protector" to whom he could go in his "loneliness and destitution." Although the boy did not understand what the minister meant by his preaching about the sins of "all men, great and small, bond and free" in the sight of God, which must be repented of before the soul could be reconciled to God through Christ, he did understand one part of the good minister's sermon—that God had promised to give rest to all who were wretched if they would come to him. We read:

> I consulted a good colored man named Charles Lawson, and in tones
> of holy affection he told me to pray, and to "cast all my care upon
> God." This I sought to do; and though for weeks I was a poor,
> broken-hearted mourner, traveling through doubts and fears, I
> finally found my burden lightened, and my heart relieved. I loved all
> mankind, slaveholders not excepted, though I abhorred slavery
> more than ever. I saw the world in a new light, and my great con-
> cern was to have eveybody converted. My desire to learn increased,
> and especially did I want a thorough acquaintance withe the con-
> tents of the Bible. I have gathered scattered pages of the Bible from
> the filthy street-gutters, and washed and dried them, that in
> moments of leisure I might get a word or two of wisdom from them.
> While thus religiously seeking knowledge, I became acquainted
> with . . . Lawson. This man not only prayed three times a day, but
> he prayed as he walked through the streets, at his work, on his
> dray—everywhere. His life was a life of prayer, and his words when
> he spoke to any one, were about a better world. Uncle Lawson lived
> near Master Hugh's house, and becoming deeply attached to him, I
> went often with him to prayer-meeting and spent much of my
> leisure time on Sunday with him. The old man could read a little,
> and I was a great help to him in making out the hard words, for I
> was a better reader than he. I could teach him "the letter," but he
> could teach me "the spirit," and refreshing times we had together,
> in singing and praying. These meetings went on for a long time
> without the knowledge either of Master Hugh or my mistress. Both
> knew, however, that I had become religious, and seemed to respect
> my conscientious piety.[52]

After a time, however, his master began to suspect that the influence of "Uncle Lawson" might not be good for Douglass, and he forbade Douglass to see him again in pain of a whipping. But it was too late: Lawson had already told Douglas that the "Lord had a great work" for him to do. Though Douglass did not see how that could really be accomplished, he was inspired by the suggestion and decided to go to see the old man, as usual, despite Mr. Auld's "persecution." In connection with this situation Douglass writes:

> He fanned my already intense love of knowledge into a flame by
> assuring me that I was to be a useful man in the world. When I
> would say to him, "How can these things be?" he simply replied,
> *"Trust in the Lord."* When I would tell him, "I am a slave, and a
> slave for life, how can I do anything?" he would quietly answer,

"The *Lord* can make you free, my dear; all things are possible with Him; only have *faith* in God. 'Ask, and it shall be given you.' If you want liberty, ask the Lord for it *in* FAITH, *and He will give it to you.*"[53]

During this same period, the thought of obtaining his freedom by the process of running away was suggested to him by two Irishmen whom Douglass helped, unasked, with their task of unloading a scow. They seemed deeply affected when Douglas answered one of their questions by saying that he was "a slave for life." They told him that he ought to run away to the north, where he would find friends and "then he as free as anybody." Douglass had heard of slaves being decoyed by white men who pretended to be helping them escape from slavery, only to "kidnap" them and return them to their masters after a reward had been posted for their capture, so he did not show any outward interest in what they were saying. Inwardly, however, his thoughts were quite active, as we learn:

> I . . . remembered their words and their advice, and looked forward to an escape to the north as a possible means of gaining the liberty for which my heart panted. It was not my enslavement at the then present time which most affected me; the being a slave *for life* was the saddest thought. I was too young to think of running away immediately; besides, I wished to learn to write before going, as I might have occasion to write my own pass. I now not only had the hope of freedom, but a foreshadowing of the means by which I might some day gain that inestimable boon.[54]

Austin Steward's reception of the phenomenon of the sun's eclipse comes to mind as we read Douglass's account of another natural phenomenon that took place the year that his hopes seemed permanently blasted by his return to plantation slavery at St. Michaels in March 1838. Douglass writes:

> I know the year, because it was the one succeeding the first cholera in Baltimore, and was also the year of that strange phenomenon when the heavens seemed about to part with their starry train. I witnessed this gorgeous spectacle, and was awestruck. The air seemed filled with bright descending messengers from the sky. It was about daybreak when I saw this sublime scene. I was not without the suggestion, at the moment, that it might be the harbinger of the coming of the Son of Man; and in my then state of mind I was prepared to hail Him as my friend and deliverer. I had read that the "stars shall fall from heaven," and they were now falling. I was suffering very much in my mind. It did seem that every time the young tendrils of my affection became attached they were rudely

broken by some unnatural outside power; and I was looking away
to heaven for the rest denied me on earth.[55]

Feeling himself "the sport of a power" which made no account of his
welfare or of his happiness, Douglass took his way to Mr. Covey's on the first
of January, 1834, "its chilling wind and pinching frost quite in harmony with
the winter in [his] own mind," to begin the four degrading years that we
have already described. Douglass reveals very clearly the state of mind which
led to his plan for escape from Mr. Freeland's plantation, at the very time
his lot as a slave was pleasantest:

> Notwithstanding all the improvements in my relations, notwith-
> standing the many advantages I had gained by my new home and my
> new master, I was still restless and discontented. I was about as *diffi-
> cult* to be pleased by a master as a master is by a slave. The freedom
> from bodily torture and unceasing labor had given my mind an
> increased sensibility and imparted to it greater activity. I was not yet
> in exactly right relations.... When entombed at Covey's and
> shrouded in darkness and physical wretchedness, temporal well-being
> was the grand desideratum; but, temporal wants supplied, the spiri-
> tual put in its claims. Beat and cuff the slave, keep him hungry and
> spiritless, and he will follow the chain of his master like a dog; but
> feed and clothe him well, work him moderately and surround him
> with physical comfort, and dreams of freedom will intrude. Give
> him a *bad* master and he aspires to a good master; give him a good
> master, and he wishes to become his own master. Such is human
> nature.... Thus elevated a little at Freeland's, the dreams called
> into being by that good man, Father Lawson, when in Baltimore,
> began to visit me again. Shoots from the tree of liberty began to
> put forth buds, and dim hopes of the future began to dawn.[56]

From this time until he finally walked out upon the streets of New York
City, "the thought of being only a creature of the *present* and the *past*"
troubled Douglass, and he "longed to have a *future*—a future with hope in
it." All was not to prove rosy during the first years after his escape from
slavery into the new life which he entered "in the full gush of unsuspecting
enthusiasm." But the young Douglass had been tempered in the world's
hardest school, so with the spring of supple steel he bounded up from re-
buffs—which seemed mild in comparison with the sufferings he had known—
to become famous throughout the Western world before seven years had
passed after his escape.

In 1941, in celebration of the one-hundredth anniversary of Douglass's
emergence into the "world of men" through his "discovery" by the Garri-

sonians, a handsome reprint edition of the 1892 version of Douglass's autobiography was published.[57] Introduced by the social historian Alain Locke,
this edition brings into the present scene the slave narrative that startled a
considerable portion of the English-speaking world into active and anti-
slavery consciousness in the middle 1840s.

Chapter 6

The Literary Significance
of the Slave Narratives

The slave narratives, on the whole, are admittedly low in artistic value. Their primary significance, their picture of the institution of slavery as seen through the eyes of the bondsman himself, concerns the social historian. Some of the narratives achieve a degree of literary distinction in some passages, and the narratives of Equiano and Douglass are readily acceptable as literary achievements. But the untutored condition of the slave authors and the rush market for their stories as abolitionist propaganda militated against the development of literary excellence in the slave narratives. Social history apart, therefore, the significance of the narratives rests largely upon their germinating influence on American letters in the 1850s and 1860s and upon their revelation of the mind of the American Negro author as a slave.

Popular interest in the life of the Negro slave extends further back than the history of the narrative by a slave or an ex-slave. It seems to have begun in the latter part of the seventeenth century with the publication in 1688 of Mrs. Behn's *Oroonoko*, the story of an idealized African slave martyr, recently described as notable "for its early statement of a theme that was to become the darling of the revolutionary novelists during the romantic movement—the theme of the noble savage and of the tyranny that afflicted him."[1] The interest waned during the first half of the eighteenth century, when urbanization became a chief concern, but it waxed strong again in England toward the end of the century. The slave poetry of Cowper and Blake and the narratives of Gronniosaw and Equiano brought the slave into the picture of the common man then occupying the central position. With the rise of periodical literature in America as well as in England during the first quarter of the nineteenth century, the slave's story reached the journals.

Two types of slave narrative appeared side by side in the periodicals until 1852. The formula that Mrs. Behn had launched nearly a century and a half before was the basis for an idealized portrait of a cultured and sensitive slave bearing wrongs from his oppressor with remarkably Anglo-Saxon philosophizing. At the same time, there appeared the realistic portrait of the ambitious but frustrated slave finding his way out of slavery into freedom. Fusion of the two types appeared but rarely before the 1850s. The idealized narrative generally went its highly polished way with much style and little substance, and the "natural" narrative blundered along with inept expressions.

Idealized slave narrative sketches formed an important part of the contents of the antislavery periodicals, from the opening pages of Elihu Embree's *The Emancipator* in April of 1820 to the closing pages of Garrison's *The Liberator* in December of 1865. Often highly sentimental in tone, the sketches were written by leading abolitionist writers of the day: Mrs. Child, Edmund Quincy, Harriet Martineau, Maria Weston Chapman, Isaac Hopper, Julia Griffiths, William Adam, and others. Even more highly sentimentalized poems in the style of Cowper appeared beside the narratives, contributed to the periodicals by William Cullen Bryant, Whittier, Elizabeth Barrett Browning, Longfellow, and numerous poetasters. Created by authors almost totally ignorant of the actual slave scene, these slave narrative sketches and poems lacked life, though as literary exercises they were sometimes admirable.

Collection of these "parlor" pieces on the life of the slave were reprinted in permanent book form as early as 1826, when Abigail Field Mott published the first of five series of *Biographical Sketches and Interesting Anecdotes of Persons of Color.*[2] This was followed by Harriet Martineau's sketches of slaves of Columbia, South Carolina, reprinted in her two-volume account of *Society in America*, published in London in 1932. Adopting the format of the elegant "gift books" in vogue in the 1830s, Mrs. Child brought together a group of the sketches and poems, published as *The Oasis*, in 1834. Her lead was followed by Mrs. Chapman, who, with the aid of a talented editorial board united under the name "Friends of Freedom," prepared handsome volumes of the antislavery "gift book" annual, *The Liberty Bell*, for sale in connection with the annual Massachusetts Anti-Slavery Fair. *The Liberty Bell* appeared annually from 1839 to 1858, except for the years 1840, 1850, 1854, 1855, and 1857. Other antislavery "gift books" made sporadic appearances, including the volumes entitled *Freedom's Gift* (1840), *North Star* (1840), *Star of Emancipation* (1841), *Liberty Chimes* (1845), and *Autographs for Freedom* (1853 and 1854). A collection of slave narrative sketches designed for children was gathered from the pages of *The Slave's Friend* and other periodicals and printed as *The Anti-Slavery Alphabet* for sale at the antislavery fair at Philadelphia in 1847. From first to last, these treatments of the noble savage theme attest to the efforts of authors of the day to interpret the plight of the slave in the only way they could, by imaginatively identifying themselves with persons they had never really known and the like of whose besetting problems they had never even seen. What these authors lacked in verity they endeavored to make up for with fine writing. The paper upon which their pieces were printed was also very fine, and the bindings and other subsidiary attractions were generally elegant.

Contrasting sharply with these pieces were the undressed narratives of the slave by the slave, after the school of Arthur and Venture Smith, William

Grimes, and Richard Allen. Nearly three hundred slave stories of this type
appear in the pages of *The Liberator*. Other antislavery periodicals contain an
additional hundred. Theodore Weld gathered approximately a hundred more
to include among his "thousand witnesses" of *Slavery as It Is*. This accounts
in large measure for the amazing popularity of that "anti-slavery handbook"
from the time of its publication in 1839. The printer J. W. Barber contributed
thirty-six real-life sketches of slaves direct from Africa to the growing store
of slave testimonials in his publication of the result of his personal interviews (with the aid of an African who understood a number of native dialects
and spoke English) with the insurgents on the *Amistad* slave ship. These
appeared together with phrenological studies of the captives in New Haven
in 1840, under the title, *The History of the Amistad Captives*. By the 1840s,
therefore, readers of the various antislavery publications were being copiously
supplied with the raw materials of the slave's story, direct from his lips to
the reporter's page.

The authors of the idealized slave sketches were the quickest of all the
friends of the fugitives to appreciate the superior strength of the real slave
story in comparison with the imagined one. Some of them at once became
scribes and editors for the slaves' narrations. Whittier recorded the ill-starred
story of James Williams. Joseph Lovejoy acted as scribe for the Clarke
brothers. Wendell Phillips consulted with Douglass over his manuscript.
Edmund Quincy helped William Wells Brown with his. The obviously tam-
pered state of Zamba's narrative is the work of its many different editors,
whose liberties with Zamba's text were taken as an excuse by the last editor,
Peter Neilson, for additional changes of his own. Samuel Eliot prepared
Josiah Henson's story; Olive Gilbert wrote Sojourner Truth's; Chamerovzow
wrote John Brown's. Mrs. Child edited Harriet Jacobs's. Although it is plain
that the hand of the scribe was sometimes taking down dictation from his
own brain, especially in introductory and transitional passages, even cursory
comparison of the content material of the abolitionist author's signed slave
story with the slave story he edited will discourage belief that he was the
creator of the latter. A recent student of the slave narratives, who is by no
means inclined towards allowing the slave author undue credit, presents his
decision as to the genesis of those writings:

> Curiously enough, of the many slave autobiographies, or biog-
> raphies—for they were often "edited" by friends of the slave—all but
> three or four seem to be forgotten. For this neglect students of
> literature are easily excusable, because the narratives are seldom
> works of art; not so the historians, however, whose need is always
> for just such illuminating documents. Although filled with the most
> vociferous propaganda, in parts embittered and untrue, even the
> worst of them record as nothing else does the workaday life of the

ante-bellum South. A reader soon learns to distinguish, in the large, the true portions from the falsified, and having done so, he finds himself confronted with pictures of slavery as it was; he discovers how both slaves and masters of the old South actually talked, dressed, carried on their occupations, amused themselves—in short, what their social background was, the world in which they moved.[3]

Dearth of attention to the slave narratives as literature was not a characteristic of contemporary chronicles, however.[4] The tenor of the frequent reviews and criticisms in current periodicals of all types ranged from highest praise to dire disgust. One of the most sustained of the contemporary studies was an article by a Reverend Ephraim Peabody, entitled "Narratives of Fugitive Slaves," which appeared in the *Christian Examiner* in July, 1849. The article was published shortly after publication of the narrative of Josiah Henson, which had produced a profound effect upon the writer because it had seemed to him to contain all of the points of strength of the slave narratives previously published but was free from their chief defect, a one-sided picture of the slaveholder.

Describing the recent vogue of narratives by slaves, Peabody placed their volumes "without hesitation among the most remarkable productions of the age—remarkable as being pictures of slavery by the slave, remarkable as disclosing under a new light the mixed elements of American civilization, and not less remarkable as a vivid exhibition of the force and working of the native love of freedom in the individual mind."[5] Ordinary romances were tame, he thought, by the side of the incredible adventures of the fugitive slaves. Dwelling further upon the nature of the slave experience, Peabody writes:

> [The fugitive slaves] encounter a whole Iliad of woes, not in plundering and enslaving others, but in recovering for themselves those rights of which they have been deprived from birth. Or if the Iliad should be thought not to present a parallel case, we know not where one who wished to write a modern Odyssey could find a better subject than in the adventures of a fugitive slave. What a combination of qualities and deeds and sufferings most fitted to attract human sympathy in each particular case![6]

Five slave narratives are included in Peabody's specific discussion of the "very wide influence on public opinion" exerted by the slave narratives "scattered over the whole of the North," compared with which, he believed, "all theoretical arguments for or against slavery" were "feeble." The narratives were the autobiographies of Douglass (1845 version), Lewis and Milton Clarke (1846), William Wells Brown (1847), James W. C. Pennington (1849), and Josiah Henson (1849). Concerning Douglass and Henson, both of whom he declared he had known personally. Peabody says, "Apart from the internal evidence of truth which their stories afford, we have every reason to put confidence in them as men of veracity." Most of the thirty-pages of this article are devoted to analysis of their books.

Douglass's narrative was somewhat of a disappointment to Peabody, who was sorry to find in the "life of a superior man" like Douglass a "severity of judgment and a one-sidedness of view." Peabody believed that a person with Douglass's ability to "make all he says effective, through candor and a just appreciation of the difficulties that beset the subject of emancipation" should be careful not to diminish his power as an advocate of the antislavery cause by alienating antislavery sympathizers in the South. He inserted a personal message to Douglass in his article, directing his attention to the discussion that followed of the two kinds of slaveholders. Without minimizing the perpetual danger to the slave inherent in the system under which he existed, even under the best of slave environments, Peabody pleaded earnestly for a more understanding attitude toward the Southerners who recognized slavery as "a pernicious institution, injurious to the higher interests of all who are affected by it." Though fewer in number than those who cared only for "the advantages which they imagine may accrue to themselves personally from the present state of things," such slaveholders did exist, he pointed out, and it was vitally important to early solution of the problem of emancipation that pivotal figures like Douglass learn to regard "the friends of freedom at the South with the profoundest interest and sympathy." In fact, Peabody concluded in this connection that such Southerners composed "the only class of antislavery men whose existence is absolutely vital and essential to freedom—freedom can dispense with the efforts of others, but not with theirs."[7]

Peabody objected to the narratives of the Clarkes, Brown, Pennington, and Douglass because of the impression they give that "the Slave States constitute one vast prison-house, of which all the whites without exceptions are the mere keepers, with no interest in the slaves further than they can be made subservient to the pleasure or profit of their owners."[8] But the objection did not extend to the narrative of Josiah Henson. Declaring that he considered that narrative "to be the best picture of the evils incident to slave life on the plantations which can be found," Peabody devoted the entire second half of his essay to analysis of that individual, for whom he recommended the title of "Moses of the regenerated Africans in Canada." It might be interesting to the reader to compare Peabody's conception of Henson with the reader's own impressions from the narrative. To be sure, Peabody had the added advantage of personal acquaintance with the man, which we may keep in mind as we read his summary of Henson's treatment of slavery as a system:

> Those who know Henson will not doubt his statement of facts; and
> there is a freedom of [sic] exaggeration, a tolerance of judgment,

and an absence of personal bitterness which give additional weight to
his testimony. He does not represent all the whites in the Slave
States as demons; but they appear in his narrative such as they are
in reality,—human beings with the average virtues and vices of mankind, but their characters modified by the institutions under which
they live. Among the whites he had kind friends—he knew those who
were opposed to slavery; even those among his several masters who,
in particular cases, treated him the worst, he looks upon with kindness. He sees that the masters, in their worst vices, are hardly less the
victims of this disastrous institution than are the slaves in their
degradation. There is no disposition to nurse his indignation against
the wrongs he has received, or to bring them forward as a complete
picture of slavery.[9]

The "peculiar air of trustworthiness to what he says" had the effect of
making more emphatic the evils inherent in the slave system, particularly
that chief fear of the slave even on happy plantations—the fear of being sold
away from his loved ones. Concerning this evil, so clearly depicted in Henson's story, Peabody writes:

If we leave out of view the physical horrors of the Middle Passage,
we believe that this internal slave trade is a system more accursed,
more deserving of execration, the cause of more suffering, than the
direct trade from Africa. It is a horrible phantom, making miserable
the whole slave population of the South. They who are never made
the victims of this traffic, who live and die on the same plantation,
know that, at any moment,—sometimes from the selfishness of
avaricious masters, sometimes from the misfortunes or death of the
kind-hearted,—they are liable to be sold to the slave-dealer who will
bid highest, and sent to some other region. . . . When added to all
other deprivations and sufferings, this horrible fear, weighing inces-
santly on the thoughts of millions of men and women, is in itself an
evil of terrible magnitude.[10]

Considered as an ideational unit, Peabody's analysis of the narratives of
fugitive slaves pulses with suggestions for a subject-hunting fiction writer in
that crucially important year of the slavery question, 1849 to 1850. Therefore, since Mrs. Harriet Beecher Stowe did come forth before the public
in 1857 with the dramatic declaration that Josiah Henson was the prototype
for her immortal Uncle Tom, and since for various reasons it is inconceivable
that her interpretation of that character would have accidentally conformed
to the fifteen-page interpretation of the Reverend Mr. Peabody rather than to
a somewhat less myopic view of the contents of Henson's narrative, we

believe that Mrs. Stowe found the ideational groundwork for her masterpiece in Peabody's study.

Mrs. Stowe's career as a fiction writer had been launched in the middle 1840s in the pages of *Godey's Lady's Book*. The editor of that "monthly annual" was the enterprising Mrs. Sarah Josepha Hale, author of the first slave novel written in America, *Northwood; or, Life North and South* (1827), the success of which had brought prominence to the little woman who was also owner and editor of the first "female" monthly magazine in the country, published in Boston. Louis Godey had bought out her magazine and transported Mrs. Hale to Philadelphia to become the editor of his new magazine for the rapidly expanding public of women readers. By 1850, Mrs. Hale had built up the subscription list to the fashionable *Godey's Lady's Book* to a monthly circulation of 150,000 copies and had presented to the public, through its pages, such outstanding literary "finds" as the Carey sisters, the Warner sisters, and Margaret Fuller. It is to be imagined that Mrs. Stowe, with her inherited "Beecher" ambition and eye for opportunities, was on the lookout for the formula underlying the sensational successes of some of her associates on Mrs. Hale's staff. Nor would it take long to ascertain the ingredients of the Susan Warner success motif: the domestic scene, sentiment "Dickenized into sentimentality," predominating femininity, and "always the humanitarian motif," as one critic has analyzed the best-seller of the day.[11]

For the indispensable humanitarian theme, nothing could have suggested itself to a subject-hunting novelist as more likely to attract the masses than the slave story, given the inflamed state of popular opinion in the North in the days surrounding the passage of the drastic Fugitive Slave Law of 1850. As to precedents in use of the theme in fiction, there was Mrs. Hale's own first novel, which had gone through four editions in a few years, and there was Richard Hildreth's slave novel, *Memoirs of Archy Moore*, which had enjoyed even wider success. The autobiographies of popular fugitive slave lecturers had been occupying the limelight in the 1840s, but their public was largely limited to the antislavery world. Borrowing their materials, rich in the ingredients of "sentiment-jerkers," as Peabody had so clearly pointed out, it would be possible to graft the slave's theme upon the *Wide, Wide World* formula and, instead of thousands of readers, capture tens of thousands! Thus do we imagine the course of Mrs. Stowe's musing in her quest for a theme rivaling that of her coworkers in appeal. At about that time she must surely have come upon Peabody's article in a magazine that few people besides preachers like her husband read.

This is not the place to trace exhaustively the apparently seminal relationship between Peabody's "Narratives of Fugitive Slaves" and *Uncle Tom's Cabin*. In the *Key to Uncle Tom's Cabin* which Mrs. Stowe prepared for the publishers directly after the appearance of her novel in order to satisfy the avalanche of requests from the reading world that she present the "original facts and documents upon which the story is founded, together with corroborative statements verifying the truth of the work,"[12] there is no mention of the Reverend Ephraim Peabody. On the other hand, the narrative of Josiah Henson, which in 1857 she cited as the chief original source for her book in her glowing introduction to the special "Harriet Beecher Stowe Edition" dedicated to her and republished in that year,[13] receives less space in the *Key, etc.*, than do any of the other four slave narratives which Mrs. Stowe acknowledged as the source of her main materials. These same five narratives were the ones that Peabody had presented from among a number of popular narratives by fugitives. A conjecture as to Mrs. Stowe's reason for ever deciding to claim Henson as the prototype for Uncle Tom has been given elsewhere in this study.[14] In so hectic a period as the 1850s, when escaping slaves were shooting up one street and slave hunters down another, when the emissaries of the law were ordered to be extra vigilant lest any but the latter be served, a matter like the genesis of Mrs. Stowe's great idea seemed trifling. Nearly a hundred years later, however, in the course of tracing ideational growth from 1830 to the 1860's, it becomes important to examine the notion that Mrs. Stowe simply "thought up" her novel, after the day's dishes were done and the children tucked safely in bed, that she drew it from the depths of her great compassion for the slaves she often saw and helped on their hurried passage northward through Cincinnati.

First described by Mrs. Stowe as "simply a *tale*, a story, the scenes of which lie among a race hitherto ignored by the associations of polite and refined society,"[15] *Uncle Tom's Cabin* brought about a fusion of the two types of slave story: the raw material of the slave's account and the sentimental material of the imagined account. As Peabody had observed, the lives of the struggling slaves made the ordinary characters of romance seem dull and tame. He did not know "where one who wished to write a modern Odyssey could find a better . . . combination of qualities and deeds and sufferings . . . fitted to attract human sympathy."[16] We have been on the Shelby plantation before—at the Lloyd plantation in Douglass's narrative, at the Campbell plantation in the Clarke brothers' story, and at the Tilghman plantation in Pennington's narrative. George Harris is a composite picture of Douglass and William Wells Brown; Legree combines Messrs. Gore and Covey; Mr. St. Clair looks like Mr. Freeland; and we met Haley and Marks and Tom Loker when we went down to New Orleans with Henson. Clarke's sister Delia looks out from Cassy's eyes; Eliza is Henson's Charlotte; Little Evas run through dozens of slave testimonials telling of the loyalty and affection of the children of the Big House, who would openly defy the scorn of older members of their family to go dress the wounds of a favorite slave beaten dreadfully for some trifle or other and run the risk of punishment themselves for slipping off to teach slave children the rudiments of learning denied them. Mrs. Stowe's New England need not be looked to as the only possible source for Ophelia and St. Clair's Yankee brother; New Englanders appear on a number of the plantations, in the narratives of the slaves. The scenes on the cotton field, in front of the cabins, on the auction block, and beside the whipping post are made up of authentic details repeatedly corroborated in the mass slave records. The distress of the separated members of the loving slave family, the outrageous nature of punishments administered because of the slave's refusal to bend as low as the master's command, the hairbreadth escapes and breathtaking adventures of the spirited young slave, the transcendent power of religious faith over the degradation of the slave experience—from a mass of real happenings teeming with sensation the inspired author created unity by means of the idealized figure of Uncle Tom.

Uncle Tom was Peabody's conception of Josiah Henson, not Henson's. Mrs. Stowe must have realized this after she met the interesting "ambassador for the fugitives" in England in the course of her triumphal tour. Wishing to find a slave sufficiently philosophical in his thinking to look at the slave scene steadily and see it in terms of a whole, Peabody found passages enough in Henson's narrative to satisfy him. He completely missed this man's irony, it would seem, as well as the picture of a slaveholder given by Douglass in Mr. Freeland, which is superior to Henson's Master Amos or any of the others. Henson's remarkable description of his conversion deeply affected Peabody and inspired a moving interpretation of the very able and by no means self-effacing plantation overseer.

The idealized Henson becomes Mrs. Stowe's Uncle Tom. His ending cannot be the same. George Harris escapes to a colony in Liberia (in deference, perhaps, to the cherished antislavery plan of Mr. Birney, who was the first buyer of Mrs. Stowe's story), but Uncle Tom must die a victim of the system that he understood too profoundly to pack his children in a duffel bag and flee to the north, like the real Josiah Henson! In his concern that the slave narrative serve the antislavery cause effectively, stirring all hearts by the compelling power of true revelations of evils but at the same time avoiding "censorious, loose, and violent treatment" of the slaveholders as a class, the Reverend Mr. Peabody unwittingly joined hands with those who wrote of the "noble savage" with more style than substance. The one step remaining to be taken to weld fact and fancy into the novel of novels is the step taken by Mrs. Stowe.

Thus, to the student of the slave narrative, the novel that, according to Lincoln, started the Civil War is an intriguing composite of two literary streams: the sentimentally imagined slave story and the real slave autobiography. None of the events in the whole eventful story is without its parallel in the slave records. But whereas the slave author, in the full flush of his release from the dreadful reality of slavery, felt its wrongs too deeply for tears, the sentimental writer required equal portions of fact and tears to fulfill the stock formula. How well Mrs. Stowe succeeded in meeting the requirements we can deduce from the chiding of her master in the field of the sentimental novel, Charles Dickens. Asked by Mrs. Stowe for an opinion of *Uncle Tom's Cabin*, he is said to have written:

> You go too far and seek to prove too much. The wrongs and atrocities of slavery are, God knows! case enough. I doubt if there be any warrant for making out the African race to be a great race, or for supposing the future destinies of the world to lie in that direction.[17]

It was to an antislavery paper, we will do well to remember, not to *Godey's Lady's Book*, that Mrs. Stowe sold the serial rights to her slave novel. The conservative abolitionists, Mr. and Mrs. James G. Birney, bought her story for the journal they had founded in 1846, *The National Era*, a paper forever to be distinguished among antislavery publications as the medium through which the reading world first obtained Whittier's *Leaves from Margaret Smith's Journal in the Province of Massachusetts Bay, 1678-1679* (1849) and Hawthorne's *The Scarlet Letter* (1850), as well as *Uncle Tom's Cabin*, which was the serial feature from June 5, 1851, until April 1, 1852.[18] Just before the appearance of the last installment as a serial, on March 12, 1852, the novel was published reluctantly in book form by the firm of John P. Jewett and Company of Boston.

The history of the popular reception of this book almost exceeds belief. Early newspaper reports credited its "immense circulation" to the "extraordinary exertion of the abolitionists" who, according to one paper, were everywhere "exulting in the sale of this pernicious work," and, according to another, were rejoicing over the cause "this admirable work" was serving—the downfall of slavery. By the first of May, the publishers canceled all other printing orders, busying themselves for the next eleven months with turning out nothing but copies of the novel they were loathe to publish in the first place for fear that they would lose money on the venture. Ten thousand copies per week were printed, fifty thousand having already been sold by the first of May.[19] Extant copies of issues from the John P. Jewett press with the 1852 imprint give the information "10th thousand," "30th thousand," "40th thousand," "70th thousand," "85th thousand," "100th thousand," "120th thousand," "183rd thousand," and "285th thousand"![20] Reporting the sale of the novel in England, an authority states that between April and December, 1852, eighteen different publishing houses had reprinted and sold one-and-a-half million copies of *Uncle Tom's Cabin*. One publisher sending out to his agents as many as 10,000 copies per day. In conclusion, the writer says:

> Of all the American works reprinted in Great Britain during the century, by all odds *Uncle Tom's Cabin* had the largest immediate

or relatively immediate sale. Indeed, this work supplied the English booktrade with its first example of "best sellerism" in the modern sense, far surpassing anything by Scott or Dickens in its initial success.[21]

In 1853, the book was being issued in translations to German, French, Flemish, Dutch, Italian, Spanish, Portuguese, Greek, and Celtic, in editions ranging in price from thirty-seven-and-a-half cents to five dollars. A letter sent to Garrison from Constantinople, in midsummer of 1853, reported that *Uncle Tom's Cabin*, which was being published in that city by a Greek newspaper as a weekly serial, was "taking the literary world by storm" and that "Shelby, St. Clair, 'Uncle Tom.' Casey, and Legree [had become] household words."[22] In May of 1853, Mrs. Stowe's *Key to Uncle Tom's Cabin* was ready for distribution. Jewett and Company announced that 59,300 copies of the initial edition of 80,000 copies had been ordered in advance of publication.[23] The book was soon issued in bindings conforming to the various bindings for the novel as a companion-piece, in editions ranging from the twenty-five cent copy "for the million," to the five-dollar, turkey-red octavo for the luxury-minded. Translations of the *Key, etc.* were published in German, French, and Celtic.

Miniature "Uncle Tom flags" were being circulated as choice souvenirs at church fairs,[24] and the praises of "the story of the age" were being sung either *ex tempore* or in the words of Whittier's poem "Little Eva, Uncle Tom's Guardian," as set to music by Manuel Emilio in July of 1852. Meanwhile, a grumbling undercurrent in opposition to the novel was striving to make itself felt. One newspaper correspondent denounced the book as a "mischievous, dangerous work, got up on purpose for evil," and considered Eve's sinful sharing of the apple the only adequate parallel to the harm done.[25] The students of the University of Virginia, learning that Mrs. Stowe was visiting in the neighborhood, got up a great mock serenade and burnt her in effigy.[26] A black man in Dorchester County, Maryland, received a sentence of ten years in the State Penitentiary for having "incendiary publications"—that is, a copy of *Uncle Tom's Cabin*—in his house, though it was not proved that he had read it to any other black people in the neighborhood or even that he knew how to read it himself.[27] A curious group of opposers to the novel consisted of radical abolitionists of the type that had fought Douglass's ransoming of himself. They were greatly disturbed by Mrs. Stowe's "gentle" handling of the slaveholder. One irate correspondent, after having declared himself "an abolitionist heart and soul," wound up a heated letter with the following splutter:

> I fear the book will raise jeers and jests. . . . If this book be really a faithful record of what slavery is in America, and of what slaves are, let slavery remain and work out its own cure. No missionaries will

ever make the converts which the "niggers" will of their masters, if
they are like Uncle Tom, and no laborers in our European countries
lead half such happy lives as the majority of "niggers" do in the slave
States, according to this novel.[28]

The reaction of readers in New Orleans, as avowed in a letter from a resident of that city to the editor of the *New York Independent*, shows a viewpoint among Southerners that Peabody had discussed. Writing from New
Orleans, August 18, 1852, the resident says:

> When *Uncle Tom's Cabin* was first issued, it was predicted in your
> paper that it would be read in New Orleans; and it has indeed found
> its way here, and numbers of our citizens have, as with avidity they
> persued its deeply interesting narratives, been alternately moved to
> tears, or convulsed with laughter. I sent to New York for the book,
> and when I carried it home and laid it upon the table, it was taken
> up and read by a young Southern friend then present, who has traf-
> ficked in slaves; and he soon remarked, 'This description is true to
> the life; the writer must have had some personal experience of
> slavery!' He asked and obtained the first loan of the book. Since
> then, it has been going the rounds, and before one is through, it is
> engaged by another.
>   Our papers occasionally copy notices of the work, such as the
> extent of the sales, the profits of the author, etc.,—but I have seen
> only one notice upon the merits of the book, and that was in the
> *Bulletin*, whose editor pronounced it "a pack of lies." But I will
> venture the assertion, that he never read the book, and probably
> never saw it. My own view is, that Mrs. Stowe has presented the
> institution of slavery in too favorable a light. As to the truthfulness
> of the barbarities she describes, abundant confirmation may be had
> by any one who will take the trouble to collect the facts. This very
> day, a Southern lady, a slaveholder, detailed to me scenes of cruelty
> she had witnessed, equaling in atrocity the worst representation in
> *Uncle Tom's Cabin*.[29]

The whole front page of *The Liberator* for the issue of March 4, 1853, was
devoted to reprintings of reviews of *Uncle Tom's Cabin* from newspapers
throughout the world in honor of the phenomenal first-year record of that
best-selling novel. At the same time that Garrison was glorying in the book's
power, George R. Graham, owner, publisher and editor of *Graham's Magazine*, was sending slips to the nineteen hundred editors with whom he
exchanged," in order to "make clear the principles" of his periodical in
connection with the current "incursion of the blacks" into the pressroom.
Among other things, Graham tells the editors:

> Mrs. Stowe's *Uncle Tom's Cabin* is a *bad book*. It is badly con-
> structed, badly timed, and made up for a bad purpose. The work has
> been successful pecuniarily—but there is such a thing as blood
> money, speedily gained by nefarious doings. . . . Uncle Tom has
> served its purpose—it has made excitement and money—but we must
> be excused from falling down and worshipping so false and mean a
> thing. . . . Our female agitators have abandoned Bloomers in despair,
> and are just now bestride a new hobby—an intense love of black
> folks, in fashionable novels. A plague of all black faces![30]

Two months earlier, after a long stampede on *Uncle Tom's Cabin* in particular and the interest of the public in "black letters" in general, including
interest in the "literary nigritudes" and "tadpoles of the press" in the form
of the slave autobiographies, the sad-hearted author posed a worried query in
an unsigned article appearing in *Graham's Magazine* for January of 1853,
entitled "Black Letters; or, Uncle Tom-foolery in Literature":

> The population of reader has gone a wool-gathering. . . . Seriously
> speaking—our writers who would take the public ear, would turn to
> someting worthier than these Negro subjects. Where is the great need
> of going to the black section of the population in quest of themes,
> while the broader and richer domains of the better races lie before
> them?[31]

Despite such pleas to the writers of the day, however, the "great need" of
taking advantage of Mrs. Stowe's popular invention of the stickily sentimental novel based on the actual and grotesque facts of the slave system
struck antislavery agitators, proslavery agitators, and writers in search of good
potboilers. Because it was a formula that almost any writer of the day might
imitate to some sort of advantage, a flurry of imitations of *Uncle Tom's
Cabin* rose like dust particles, many of them settling again almost as quickly.
In superficial design, these "poor relations of Uncle Tom," as one recent
critic has named the slave novels deluging the market in the 1850s,[32] resembled each other. The front matter of the volumes usually announced the
author's purpose of portraying "slavery in the cabins and the mansions of
the South as it really is" or something very similar. And in their final effect,
probably, the import of the novels by antislavery or proslavery thinkers was
probably very similar: the focusing of the world's attention on the lives of
four million human beings who, whether oppressed by direst sufferings or
pampered with luxury, were one and all denied the freedom of movement of
other human beings. In their advertised purpose, however, the basic unity of
the slave story was divided into two treatments: books denying or books
affirming cruelty to the slave by the slave system.

Literary and social historians of the 1850s have adopted the rather obvious statement that "at least fourteen proslavery novels" followed close upon publication of *Uncle Tom's Cabin*.[33] At least fourteen have *survived*. Judging from contemporary notices, the actual number that appeared must have been wearying.[34] The best, like Mrs. Eastman's *Aunt Phillis' Cabin* (1852), J. Thornton Randolph's *The Cabin and the Parlor* (1852), Mrs. Emily Pearson's *Cousin Frank's Household* (1852), J. P. Kennedy's 1852 revision of *Swallow Barn* (originally published in 1832), and J. H. Ingraham's *The Sunny South* (1860), received wide recognition for their "corrections" of Mrs. Stowe's pictures of the South's "patriarchal institution." The worst, like W.L.G. Smith's *Uncle Tom's Cabin as It Is* (1852) and Wilson's *Our Nig* (1853), provoked the ridicule of the press for conspicuous wasting of fine paper and good ink in printing them. On the whole, however, the many "answers to *Uncle Tom's Cabin*" that appeared, particularly in 1852 and from 1859 to 1860, in the wake of the John Brown tragedy, were of run-of-the-mill quality, no better and no worse than the second- and third-rate fiction of any literary period. As social documents revealing the mental atmosphere of the decade, they are of value today, for they show the unthinking sentimentality with which millions of Americans glossed over the evils of slavery rather than be faced with the troublesome task of changing the status quo. From a historical point of view, one of the most enlightening of the proslavery publications was the republishing in 1857 of *Northwood; or, Life North and South*, which had appeared in 1827 as the first slave novel. Originally written in the hope of improving the understanding of the difference between social conditions north and south of the Mason-Dixon line, Mrs. Hale's novel was antislavery in tone but stressed preservation of the Union through appreciation of sectional problems. In 1857, in her introduction to the revised edition, which enjoyed great financial success because of the important position of its author and the nature of its publication history, Mrs. Hale expressed regret that the humanitarian question at the basis of the vogue for novels on slavery was being confused with political issues.[35] Forced to take a stand, therefore, either for or against "the South," she was now launching her previously antislavery book on the side of the proslavery sympathizers.

Meanwhile, the abolitionists were also "answering" *Uncle Tom's Cabin* with fewer volumes, distinctly belligerent in tone. Mrs. Stowe's treatment of certain aspects of slavery had troubled many in the antislavery ranks, and there was sharp purpose behind the didactic "fiction" that resulted. Richard Hildreth's *Memoirs of Archy Moore*, which had never really left the book stands from the time of its appearance in 1836, came forth in 1852 in a new version, buttressed with a "key" to its sources in the newly added appendix and variously titled *The White Slave: or, Memoirs of a Fugitive; The Slave: or, Memoirs of Archy Moore;* and, *The White Slave: or, Negro Life in the Slave States of America*.[36] William Wells Brown, from his exiled position in

England as a fugitive from slavery, adopted the slave novel form for his own picture of the life of the mulatto slave in *Clotel: or, The President's Daughter*, a very popular addition to antislavery publications in England in 1853.[37] Mrs. Stowe's *Dred*, which appeared in 1856 and sold 165,000 copies within the course of three months, no longer "straddled the fence" after the manner of Peabody's wishes (and with the certain result of catapulting her master-piece into fame and fortune). Based on the *Confessions of Nat Turner* and attentive to the complaints of abolitionists concerning the "milk of human kindness" that they felt unnecessary and even harmful to antislavery litera-ture, *Dred* was a much stronger novel than *Uncle Tom's Cabin* and makes for better reading today. But the change in the formula from her initial combi-nation of ingredients left only the facts and kept *Dred* from becoming popu-lar outside of abolitionist groups, except on the basis of "another novel by the author of *Uncle Tom's Cabin*."

The slave narratives were closely imitated by the abolitionist authors of slave novels after 1852, and it was frequently impossible to tell one from the other when the author was not publicly known. The anonymous *Auto-biography of a Female Slave* (1856) was probably the most successfully disguised of the slave novels. Its author, Mattie Griffiths Browne, was a young white woman, a former slaveholder in Kentucky, who had enlisted whole-heartedly in the abolitionist cause and had emancipated all of her slaves, even though she was thus confronted with the prospect of poverty and the derision of the only society she had ever known. Befriended in Boston by Mrs. Child, the young woman wrote short sketches and antislavery poems for the journal Mrs. Child was editing, *The National Anti-Slavery Standard*, before preparing one of the most powerfully authentic of the slave novels. Sentiment-ridden and intolerant of slavery, the book still possesses strength as a work of fiction, and its details, which Mrs. Browne declared were true in every respect, are authenticated in the mass testimony of the slave records. It was long believed to be an actual autobiography. During the late 1850s and early 1860s, few readers stopped to investigate or to care. The annals of the lowly slave were eagerly sought and were so strange even in mild histories that whether a work was factual or fictional or a combination ceased to concern the popular mind. In an atmosphere saturated with slave stories, fact and fancy came together to form one thing: books on slavery.

Commingling of the materials continued throughout the nineteenth cen-tury in post-Civil War stories of the slave. With the disappearance from sight and memory of the harassed, hunted fugitive, popular conception in the North of the Negro as a "brother but in chains" faded, and a stereotyping along the line of the "Topsy" motif began to take place. In the South, the wreck of the entire social fabric and the poverty everywhere precluded interest in the ubiquitous black man as a man. Social research in the present day, however, is leading to analyses that separate fact and fancy in the social history of the slave. In the field of his literary history, equal advances can be made.

This pioneer study of the slave narratives must be considered as merely "getting our guns into position" for projecting the mind of the slave into the records of American literary history. The narratives before 1836 and after 1865 reveal the same person that we find in the autobiographies winnowed from the stacks of slave literature of the 1830s to the 1860s: the American Negro, without benefit of society.

He is a very thoughtful individual, this American Negro slave. Saffin's Adam, Gronniosaw, Equiano, Venture Smith, Robert Voorhis, Solomon Bayley, Richard Allen, William Grimes, Lunceford Lane, Henry Bibbs, Austin Steward, John Thompson—the mere names call forth their sensitive reflections on the nature of the environment in which fate had placed them, on plans for effecting an improvement in their lot, on analysis of their fellow man. The absence of humor in their narratives does not mean an absolute absence of that essential quality in their lives. In the process of focusing their attention upon the underlying pattern of their experiences as slaves, in meeting the demands of the autobiography as a literary form, humor would assume a very negative position. Unconsciously, however, the slave narrator sometimes reveals the very soul of humor, even in the midst of harrowing experiences: Solomon Bayley's overhearing of the slavehunters coming back from their search for him, or the little dog that worried Pennington as he lay afraid even to tremble on the bed of cornshucks that crackled like pistols when he but breathed, or Lunceford Lane's indecision in choosing to work all night to earn money to buy himself or to sleep all night so that he would not get beaten for not working fast enough during the day.

The ambition of the slave of the narratives and his struggle against dreadful odds to achieve learning, decent standards of living, security, and freedom make the slave narratives an impressive record of human behavior. Undoubtedly, the record concerns superior slaves in the main, especially in the book-length narratives. It is probable that only superior slaves were able to inspire enough interest in themselves to bring the story of their lives to permanent records. None the less, the narrators Venture Smith and Tom Jones, James Curry and Moses Grandy, Henry Watson and Henry Box Brown were not telling of themselves alone. With very few exceptions, the narratives tell of the ambitions of other slaves on the plantation, of cooperation between slaves within a plantation and between plantations. The mysterious "grapevine" that carried slave messages so bafflingly in all parts of the slave area was a monument to the slaves' interest and desire to help others acquire the opportunity to escape from slavery if humanly possible. There are numerous accounts of the ways in which house slaves steered the projects of escaping slaves, welcoming their opportunity to keep informed at the Big House of happenings of importance to the slaves in general. They ran the risk of being whipped to death for learning to read, in order that they might convey to the other slaves information from the newspapers and other printed matter. Thousands of slaves who attempted flight were caught, beaten, "demoted" to harder work, sold to the deep South. Only a relative few, an estimated sixty thousand, managed to reach free soil.

The slave authors were a select group of that number of successful fugitives. It is possible that they were not fewer proportionally, however, than the percentile relationship between authors and readers in the free world of their time. Ideationally, the slave narrator and the slave seem to be one.

Present-day reviewers are complaining, with increasing frequency, of the "bitterness" and "emotion" expressed in the writings of Richard Wright, Chester Himes, W. E. B. DuBois, Langston Hughes, J. Saunders Redding, and most of the rest of the growing circle of popular Negro authors. Their market, today, reminds us of the market of the fugitive slave one hundred years ago. A crusade is again in process, this time for the purpose of emancipating humankind from the neurosis of racial prejudice. A Mrs. Stowe is again needed to fuse the Negro's story and the imaginings of wishful thinkers.

Summary

The slave narratives comprise a group of autobiographical or semiautobiographical records of American Negro slaves, separately published in book form, preserved in records of the court and church, discovered in the files of periodical publications, or massed together in unpublished collections. In all about six thousand records have been found, one half of the number belonging to the period when the slave was still a slave, the other half the result of recent attempts to capture the story from the now aged survivors of slavery.

Adventure is the dominant characteristic of the slave narratives. The narratives before 1836 present individual slaves concerned with individual escape from bondage. After 1836, however, the attitude of the slave narrator is imbued with a class consciousness. Race and slave status are grouped together in the narratives of this period ending with the Civil War. No use of the post-Civil War narratives has been made in this introductory study except for purposes of comparison with the material in the narratives of the most disputed and most significant period of 1830 to 1860.

The trustworthiness of the substance of the slave narratives can not be satisfactorily established. It seems reasonable to conclude that the chief contributions of abolitionist editors were in the form of outline plans and the mechanics of composition. Several obviously unaided narratives provide illustrations of the kind of narratives that would have been put upon the market generally had slave narrators been given no more aid than was given Noah Davis, Henry Watson, and G. W. Offley. But no means for discovering a line of division between "substantial truth" and fancy has been found.

While the majority of the slave narratives are below standard as literary expressions, passages of literary merit are to be found in many of the narratives, and a number of them possess considerable literary worth. The four versions of the autobiography of Frederick Douglass comprise the most important example of the narratives.

The important influence of the slave narratives upon the slave novels of the 1850s is clear. The publication of *Uncle Tom's Cabin* is the literary high point in their history. That phenomenally successful novel not only stemmed from five slave narratives published in the 1840s, but also precipitated the break between the proslavery and the antislavery novelists. For both groups, the slave narratives furnished the substance, and by the middle 1850s the narrative itself was becoming patently fictionalized. The history of the influence of these narratives upon Mrs. Stowe's masterpiece and its successors needs to be written.

Future studies of the slave narratives may direct their attention to the rich gallery of self-portraits of the American Negro as a slave provided by the narratives. In the long view, this approach may show the chief contribution of the narratives to the universal brotherhood of man. They represent the most illuminating phase, without doubt, in the long and fascinating autobiographical record of a race under the yoke of a grotesque institution.

Notes

In the years since 1946, parts of the original dissertation have been lost. A few of the notes that follow are therefore incomplete or missing. Much of the source material was fragile and inaccessible even in 1946, and it has not been possible to reconstruct all of the data. Such cases are designated by a bracketed note indicating the reference is no longer available.

Foreword

1. Writings that have been carefully consulted include, among others, U. B. Phillips, *American Negro Slavery* (1918, 1936), *Life and Labor in the Old South* (1929), *The Course of the South to Secession* (1939), and the papers in the Ulrich B. Phillips Collection, Yale University; Frederic Bancroft, *Slave Trading in the Old South* (1931); Lorenzo Greene, *The Negro in Colonial New England* (1942); and studies in slavery in North Carolina (R. H. Taylor), Virginia (J. C. Ballagh), Maryland (J. P. Brackett), Georgia (R. Brett Flanders), Mississippi (C. S. Sydnor), and Kentucky (J. W. Coleman).
2. In W. E. B. DuBois and Guy B. Johnson, ed., *The Negro Encyclopedia* (1945).
3. A quotation, not documented, from Richard Allen, following details drawn from Allen's narrative: "I soon saw a large field open in seeking and instructing my African Brethren who had been a long-forgotten people, and few of them attended public worship." The sentence can be found in Richard Allen, *Life, Experiences, and Gospel Labors of the Right Reverend Richard Allen* (c. 1887 edition, in the Schomburg Collection), p. 13. Quoted, without reference to source, in Woodson, *The Negro in Our History* (1941), p. 147.
4. Lorenzo Dow Turner, *Anti-Slavery Sentiment Prior to 1865*, (Ph.D. diss., University of Chicago, 1925), published in Washington, 1929.
5. See pages 337–338.
6. See *Journal of Negro History*, vols. 1, 4, 11, 15, 16, 20.
7. See *American Literature* 17, no. 4:380; *Book Week*, 9 December 1945, p. 3; *Saturday Review of Literature*, 15 December 1945, p. 22;

Weekly Book Review (Herald Tribune), 15 December 1945; New York *Times Book Review*, 6 January 1946, p. 4; and *Phylon*, January 1946, pp. 96–97. Also, *Journal of Negro History*, January 1946, pp. 119–121.

8. John Herbert Nelson, *The Negro in American Fiction* (1926), p. 61.
9. See page 337 and following.
10. See pages 339–350.
11. John Henry Wigmore, *The Principles of Judicial Proof; or, The Process of Proof as Given by Logic, Psychology, and General Experience and Illustrated in Judicial Trials*, 2d ed., rev., 1931.
12. See page 337.
13. See pages 339–350.
14. Carter Woodson, *Education of the Negro Prior to 1861* (1915), p. 207. Some of the sources that Dr. Woodson gives are Mott (*Biographical Sketches*), Redpath (*Roving Editor*), Drew (*Refugee*), Francis Kemble (*Journal*), and Catherine Birney (*Grimke Sisters*)—for which see Bibliography, below.
15. Woodson, *Education of the Negro Prior to 1861* (1915), p. 230. He also lists, as sources, Siebert's *Underground Railroad* and J. D. Long's *Pictures of Slavery*, both of which have been used in collecting narratives for this study.
16. Woodson, *The Mind of the Negro as Reflected in Letters Written during the Crisis 1800-1860* (1926), p. i.
17. See bibliography of separately published narratives.
18. Woodson, *The Mind of the Negro*, p. v.
19. E. Franklin Frazier, *The Negro Family in the United States* (1929), Chapters I and II.
20. Check index, under "Frazier," in Melville Herskovits, *Myth of the Negro Past* (1942). The only direct reference to a slave narrative is the reference to Douglass, *My Bondage and My Freedom*.
21. U. B. Phillips, *The Course of the South to Secession: An Interpretation*, ed. E. Merton Coulter (1939), p. 101.
22. Merle Curti, *Growth of American Thought* (1943), p. 309ff.
23. Cf. *American Literature* 17:380 and *Phylon* 7:96–97.
24. Benjamin Botkin, *Lay My Burden Down* (1945), p. 1.
25. Coleman Rosenberger, in the *Weekly Book Review*, 23 December 1945, p. 5.
26. Lloyd Lewis, in the *New York Times Book Review*, p. 4.
27. See page 243.
28. Carter G. Woodson, in the *Journal of Negro History* 31, no. 1:119–120.

Chapter One: Background

1. Jesse Macy, *The Anti-Slavery Crusade: A Chronicle of the Gathering Storm*, p. 2.
2. Lorenzo Dow Turner, *Anti-Slavery Sentiment in American Literature Prior to 1865*, pp. 1–3.

3. Paul Kaufman, "The Romantic Movement," in Norman Foerster, *The Re-Interpretation of American Literature*, p. 134.

4. Ephraim Peabody, "Narratives of Fugitive Slaves," *Christian Examiner*, July 1894, p. 61.

5. "Black Letters," *Graham's Magazine* 42 (January 1853):215.

6. Turner, *Anti-Slavery Sentiment*, p. 1.

7. James Madison, *The Papers of James Madison*, 1:24.

8. John Woolman, *Some Considerations on the Keeping of Negroes Recommended to the Professors of Christianity of Every Denomination*, Part II, p. 209.

9. Benjamin Franklin, *Observations concerning the Increase of Mankind and the Peopling of Countries*, p. 10.

10. Peter Bestes et al., *Petition of Slaves to the Massachusetts Legislature, 1773*.

11. Herbert Aptheker, *Essays in the History of the American Negro*, p. 77.

12. Ibid.

13. Ibid.

14. Phillis Wheatley, *Poems on Various Subjects, Religious and Moral*, p. 18.

15. Trumbull, John, *New Haven Correspondent* 8 (6 July 1770); see also Turner, *Anti-Slavery Sentiment*, Appendix.

16. Jupiter Hammon, *An Address to the Negroes in the State of New York*.

17. Dorothy Porter, "Early American Negro Writings," in *The Papers of the Bibliographical Society of America* 39 (1945):236.

18. See Aptheker, *American Negro Slave Revolts*; also, Harvey Wish, "American Slave Insurrections before 1861," *Journal of Negro History* 29, no. 193:299–320.

19. Aptheker, *Essays in the History of the American Negro*, pp. 209–210.

20. Ibid., p. 23.

21. Ibid., pp. 23–24.

22. Ibid., p. 4.

23. Ibid.

24. Ibid., pp. 209–210.

25. Ibid., p. 30 and pp. 27–28.

26. Philip A. Shelley, "Crevecoeur's Contribution to Herder's Neger-Idyllen," *Journal of English and Germanic Philology* 38, no. 1 (1938):48–64.

27. Edward D. Seeber, *Anti-Slavery Opinion in France during the Second Half of the Eighteenth Century*, pp. 118–119.

28. Turner, *Anti-Slavery Sentiment*, p. 2.

29. Nelson F. Adkins, Graduate Lecture, New York University, 27 April 1945.

30. Timothy Dwight, *Greenfield Hill: A Poem in Seven Parts*, Part II, 11. 221–234, 238–248, 253–260, 265–266, 271–278, 295–312.

31. Aptheker, *Essays*, p. 25.

32. Anti-Slavery Pamphlets, George Washington Collection, at the Boston Athenaeum, Boston, Massachuestts.

33. Virginius Dabney, *Liberalism in the South*, p. 64.
34. Merle Curti, *Growth of American Thought*, p. 198.
35. Aptheker, *Essays*, p. 62.
36. Ibid., p. 29.
37. Thomas Wentworth Higginson, *Travellers and Outlaws*, p. 204.
38. Ibid., pp. 196–204.
39. *Atlantic Monthly* 7 (June 1861):744.
40. Higginson, *Travellers*, pp. 259–261.
41. Lionel H. Kennedy and Thomas Parger, *An Official Report of the Trials of Sundry Negroes, Charged with an Attempt to Raise an Insurrection in the State of South Carolina, Prepared and Published at the Request of the Court. Charleston, 1822*, p. 26.
42. Ibid., pp. 26–27.
43. Ibid., pp. 180–181.
44. Ibid., p. 21.
45. Ibid., p. 179.
46. Macy, *The Anti-Slavery Crusade*, p. 12.
47. Elihu Embree, *The Emancipator*, Jonesborough, Tennessee, 1820.
48. Macy, *The Anti-Slavery Crusade*, p. 31; also Stephen B. Weeks, "Anti-Slavery Sentiment in the South," *Southern Historical Association Publications* 2 (1898):88–89.
49. *The Genius of Universal Emancipation* moved to Philadelphia in 1833, where it appeared at intervals until 1837, when it moved to Illinois until Lundy's death in 1839. Sporadic revivals appeared under other editors in the 1840s. A nearly complete file is to be found at the Johns Hopkins University, Baltimore.
50. Samuel Miller, *A Sermon, Preached at New-Ark, October 22, 1823, before the Synod of New Jersey, in behalf of the African School.*
51. Schlesinger, Arthur, in Foerster, *Re-Interpretation*, p. 173.
52. Ibid., p. 174.
53. See *The Liberator* 35:206ff.
54. W. P. Garrison and F. J. Garrison, *William Lloyd Garrison*, vol. 2, pp. 430–432.
55. Oswald G. Villard, *Some Newspapers and Newspaper Men*, p. 312.
56. *The Liberator* 4 (30 August 1834):139.
57. Ibid., 5 (21 February 1835):27.
58. Frederick Douglass, *My Bondage and My Freedom*, p. 361.
59. *The Liberator*, [balance of reference no longer available].
60. Ibid., 2 (11 August 1832):127.
61. Villard, *Some Newspapers*, p. 304.
62. Curti, *American Thought*, p. 447.
63. Alice Adams, *The Neglected Period of Anti-Slavery in America, 1808–1831*, pp. 116–118.
64. Henry Simms, "A Critical Analysis of Abolition Literature, 1830–1840," *Journal of Southern History* 6 (1940):381.
65. George Rockwood, "George Barrell Cheever, Protagonist of Abolition," in *Proceedings of the American Antiquarian Society* 45 (1936):86.

66. Ibid., p. 88.
67. E. Douglass Branch, *The Sentimental Years, 1836–1860*, p. 402.
68. Lydia Maria Francis Child, *An Appeal in Behalf of That Class of Americans Called Africans*, preface.
69. Child, *Letters*, pp. 258–259.
70. Christopher Hollis, *The American Heresey*, pp. 107–108.
71. See files of the *Richmond Enquirer, New Orleans Picayune*, and *Richmond Whig*.
72. Vernon Parrington, *The Romantic Revolution*, p. 70.
73. Simms, *Abolition Literature*, p. 382.
74. Macy, *The Anti-Slavery Crusade*, p. 62.
75. Ibid., pp. 63–64.
76. Thomas Roderick Dew, *Review of the Debate in the Virginia Legislature of 1831 and 1832*, p. 7.
77. Ibid., p. 8.
78. Ibid., p. 48.
79. B. D. R. Midgette, "Thomas R. Dew," in *The John P. Branch Historical Papers of Randolph-Macon College, 1909*, p. 11.
80. Dew, *Review*, pp. 7–8.
81. William E. Dodd, *The Cotton Kingdom: A Chronicle of the Old South*, pp. 49–50.
82. Dew, *Review*, pp. 47–48.
83. *The Liberator* 9 (8 November 1839):179.
84. Ibid., 9:104, reprinted from the *Emancipator*.
85. Leo Tolstoi, first sentence in *Anna Karenina*.
86–87. [References no longer available.]
88. *The Liberator* 5 (4 April 1835):53.
89. Ibid., 7 (6 October 1837):164, reprinted from the *Rutherford Gazette*.
90. Ibid., 11 (8 October 1841):161.
91. Ibid., 7 (8 October 1837):192.
92. See Simms, *Abolition Literature*, pp. 373–374; also Gilbert Barnes, *The Anti-Slavery Impulse*, p. 231.
93. Douglass, *My Bondage*, pp. 360–361.
94. *The Liberator* 23 (18 March 1853):4.
95. See Henrietta Henkle, *Let My People Go*, the bibliography.
96. *The Liberator* (12 October 1838):164.
97. John Brown, *Slave Life in Georgia*, pp. 159–166.
98. T. Watson Smith, *The Slave in Canada*, p. 134.
99. Ibid., p. 135.
100. Wilbur H. Siebert, "A Quaker Section of the Underground Railroad in Northern Ohio," *Ohio Archaeological and Historical Publications* 39 (1930):502.
101. Ibid., pp. 494–495.
102. Ibid., p. 490.
103. *The Liberator* 17 (30 July 1847):122.
104. Ibid., 18 (25 February 1848):31.
105. Sampson Low, *British Catalog of Books, 1837–1852*.

106. Low, *British Catalog of Books, 1835–1863*.
107. Clarence Gohdes, *American Literature in Nineteenth Century England*, p. 19.
108. Peabody, "Narratives," p. 62.
109. Ibid., p. 64.
110. "Black Letters," pp. 214–215.
111. *The Liberator* 20 (24 May 1850):83.
112. Noah Davis, *Narrative*, p. 2.
113. L. D. Reddick, in introduction to Kate Pickard, *The Kidnapped and the Ransomed* (reprint edition, 1941), p. 12.
114. James Freeman Clarke, *Anti-Slavery Days*, p. 101.
115. *The Liberator* 20 (27 September 1850):156.
116. Ibid., 21 (25 July 1851): 118.
117. Ibid., 39:155.
118. Ibid., 15:190.
119. Ibid., 16:21.
120. Ibid., p. 25.
121. Ibid., p. 34.
122. Ibid., p. 59.
123. Ibid., pp. 85–86.
124. Ibid., p. 139.
125. Ibid., p. 139.
126. Ibid., 17 (15 January 1847):6.
127. Ibid., p. 10.
128. Ibid., p. 11.
129. Ibid., 17 (29 January 1847):10.
130. Ibid., p. 18.
131. Ibid.
132. Ibid.
133. Ibid., 18 (4 February 1848):19.
134. Ibid., 19 (2 November 1849):173.
135. Ibid., 24 (26 May 1854):82.
136. Ibid., 21 (20 June 1851):82.
137. William Wells Brown, *The Rising Son; or, The Antecedents and Advancement of the Colored Race*, pp. 393–412.
138. Branch, *The Sentimental Years*, p. 403.
139. Ibid., pp. 403–404.
140. Wright, Louis B., "Myth-Makers and the South's Dilemma," *Sewanee Review* 53 (1945):557.

Chapter Two: The Slave Narrative Before 1836

1. In *A Narrative of the Uncommon Sufferings and Surprising Deliverance of Briton Hammon, a Negro Man, etc.*
2. See Thomas Cooper, *Narrative of the Life of Thomas Cooper*; and William Boen, *Anecdotes and Memoirs of William Boen*; among others.

3. "Adam Negro's Tryall," in *Publications of the Colonial Society of Massachusetts Transactions, 1892–1894*, pp. 103–112.

4. John Saffin, *A Brief and Candid Answer to a Late Printed Sheet, entitled, The Selling of Joseph, etc.*

5. "Adam Negro's Tryall," p. 105.

6. Ibid., p. 114.

7. Briton Hammon, *A Narrative of the Uncommon Sufferings and Surprising Deliverance of Briton Hammon, A Negro Man, etc.* (Boston: Green and Russell, 1760).

8. See Oscar Wegelin, *Jupiter Hammon*.

9. Jupiter Hammon, *An Address to the Negroes in the State of New York* (New York: Carroll and Patterson).

10. Jupiter Hammon, *An Address*, p. 2.

11. Ibid., p. 11.

12. Ibid., p. 47.

13. Ibid., p. 11.

14. Ibid., p. 3.

15. Ibid., pp. 6–7.

16. Ibid., p. 14.

17. Margaretta Odell, *Phillis Wheatley: A Memoir*.

18. See number 6, above.

19. Phillis Wheatley, *Letters of Phillis Wheatley, the Negro-Slave Poet of Boston* (Boston: John Wilson and Son, 1864). See also *The Proceedings of the Massachusetts Historical Society for 1864*.

20. Wheatley, *Letters*, p. 12.

21. Ibid., pp. 13–14.

22. Ibid., pp. 14–15.

23. Ibid., pp. 16–17.

24. Dorothy Porter, "Early American Negro Writings," *Papers of the Bibliographical Society of America* 39 (1945):233–234.

25. See bibliography of separately published slave narratives for those by Gronniosaw, Equiano, Venture Smith, and Zamba.

26. James Albert Ukawsaw Gronniosaw, *A Narrative of the Most Remarkable Particulars in the Life of James Albert Ukawsaw Gronniosaw, An African Prince, as Related by Himself* (Leeds: Davies and Booth, 1814).

27. Ibid., p. 7.

28. Ibid., p. 8.

29. Ibid., pp. 9–10.

30. Ibid., p. 10.

31. Ibid., p. 11.

32. Ibid., p. 12.

33. Ibid., p. 13.

34. Ibid., p. 15.

35. Ibid., p. 25.

36. Ibid., p. 26.

37. Ibid., p. 32.

38. See bibliography of separately published slave narratives.

39. See bibliography of separately published slave narratives.
40. See Benjamin Brawley, *Early Negro American Writers*; Carter Woodson, *The Negro in Our History*; and Vernon Loggins, *The Negro Author*.
41. Olaudah Equinao, *The Interesting Narrative of the Life of Olaudah Equiano, or Gustavus Vassa, The African, Written by Himself*, vol. I (New York: W. Duell, 1791).
42. Ibid., pp. 42–43.
43. Ibid., pp. 50–51.
44. Ibid., p. 53.
45. Ibid., p. 66.
46. Ibid., p. 68.
47. Ibid., p. 75.
48. Ibid., p. 77.
49. Ibid., p. 108.
50. Ibid., p. 123.
51. Ibid., pp. 125–126.
52. Ibid., p. 129.
53. Ibid., p. 181.
54. Ibid., p. 192.
55. Ibid., pp. 193–194.
56. Ibid., vol. 2, pp. 2–3.
57. Ibid., p. 4.
58. Ibid., pp. 9–10.
59. Ibid., p. 16.
60. Ibid., p. 62.
61. Venture Smith, *A Narrative of the Life and Adventures of Venture, A Native of Africa; But Resident above Sixty Years in the United States of America, Related by Himself* (New London: C. Holt, 1798).
62. Ibid., p. 9.
63. Ibid., p. 10.
64. Ibid., pp. 11–12.
65. Ibid., p. 14.
66. Ibid., p. 15.
67. Ibid., p. 13.
68. Ibid., p. 16.
69. Ibid., p. 18.
70. Ibid., pp. 18–19.
71. Ibid., p. 19.
72. Ibid., p. 21.
73. See Bibliography.
74. Richmond Legh, *The Negro Servant* (London: printed by J. Tilling for the Religious Tract Society, n.d.), p. 28. Also, Tract 119.
75. See Bibliography. William, *The Negro Servant*, under "Separately Published Slave Narratives."
76. Legh, *The Negro Servant*, p. 4.
77. Ibid., p. 7.

78. Ibid., p. 15.
79. George White, *A Brief Account of the Life, Experiences, Travels, and Gospel Labours of George White, An African; Written by Himself and Revised by a Friend* (New York: J. C. Tottle, 1810).
80. Ibid., p. 5.
81. Ibid., pp. 5-6.
82. Ibid., p. 7.
83. Ibid.
84. Abraham Johnstone, *The Address of Abraham Johnstone, a Black Man, Who Was Hanged at Woodbury in the County of Gloucester, and State of New Jersey, etc.* (Philadelphia: printed for the purchasers, 1797).
85. Ibid., p. 15.
86. William Henry Smith, "The First Fugitive Slave Case of Record in Ohio," *Annual Report, American Historical Society Association*, 1894, pp. 91-100.
87. Ibid., p. 100.
88. William Grimes, *Life of William Grimes, the Runaway Slave, Written by Himself* (New York, 1825).
89. Ibid., p. 26.
90. Ibid., p. 27.
91. Solomon Bayley, *Narrative of Some Remarkable Incidents in the Life of Solomon Bayley* (London, 1825).
92. Ibid., p. vii.
93. Ibid., p. ix.
94. Ibid., pp. 2-3.
95. Ibid., p. 10.
96. Ibid., p. 13.
97. Ibid., pp. 18-19.
98. Ibid., p. 47.
99. Robert Voorhis, *Life and Adventures of Robert Voorhis, the Hermit of Massachusetts, Who Has Lived for Fourteen Years in a Cave, Secluded from Human Society, etc.* (Providence, 1829).
100. Ibid., p. 26.
101. Thomas R. Gray, *The Confessions of Nat Turner, the Leader of the Late Insurrection in Southampton, Virginia, as Fully and Voluntarily Made to Thomas R. Gray, in the Prison Where He was Confined, etc.* (Baltimore, 1831). For a critical study of this work see Herbert Aptheker, *Nat Turner's Revolt*. (M.A. thesis, Columbia University, 1937).
102. *The Liberator* 1 (17 December 1831): 202-203.
103. Ibid., p. 202.
104. Whomas Wentworth Higginson, *Travellers and Outlaws*, p. 278.
105. Ibid., pp. 281-282.
106. For example, see narrative material on the slave Gabriel in the *Salem Gazette*, 7 October 1800, and Lionel Kennedy, and Thomas Parker, *An Official Report of the Trials of Sundry Negroes, Charged with an Attempt to Raise an Insurrection in the State of Carolina, etc.*, for the

accounts of Denmark Vesey's slave accomplices Peter Poyas, Gullah Jack, Rollo, and Ned.

107. Thomas Cooper, *Narrative of the Life of Thomas Cooper* (New York, 1832).
108. Ibid., p. 13.
109. Ibid., p. 27.
110. Thomas Cooper, *The African Pilgrim Hymns* (London: Bertrand, 1820).
111. Richard Allen, *The Life, Experience, and Gospel Labours of the Right Reverend Richard Allen. To Which Is Annexed the Rise and Progress of the African Methodist Episcopal Church in the United States of America, etc.* (Philadelphia, 1841). For a biographical study of Allen, see Charles Wesley, *Richard Allen, Apostle of Freedom*.
112. Allen, *Life, Experience, and Gospel*, pp. 5–7.
113. Ibid., p. 8.
114. Ibid., p. 8.
115. Ibid., pp. 13–14.
116. Ibid., pp. 19–24.

Chapter Three: The Slave Narrative After 1836

1. See pages 147–148.
2. *American Anti-Slavery Almanac*, published by the Boston Anti-Slavery Society from 1836 to 1840, then by the New York Anti-Slavery Society, until about 1847.
3. *The Chronotype*, published in Boston, c. 1836 to 1847?
4. *The Liberator*, edited by Garrison and published in Boston from 1831 to 1865.
5. *The American Anti-Slavery Record*, published by the New York Anti-Slavery Society from 1835 to 1839, began as the *Anti-Slavery Reporter* in 1833. The name was changed in 1834 to the *American Anti-Slavery Reporter* and changed again in 1835.
6. *Anti-Slavery Examiner*, published by the New York Anti-Slavery Society from 1836 to 1845.
7. *Anti-Slavery Record*, published by the New York Anti-Slavery Society from 1835 to 1839.
8. *The Emancipator*, published variously by New York and Boston from 1833 to 1850 by the American Anti-Slavery Society. The title changed to *The Republican* in the 1840s. Not to be confused with Elihu Embree's *The Emancipator*, published in 1820 in Jonesborough, Tennessee.
9. *Human Rights*, published by the New York Anti-Slavery Society, from 1835 to 1837.
10. *Quarterly Anti-Slavery Magazine*, published by the New York Anti-Slavery Society from 1835 to 1837.

11. *Slave's Friend*, a magazine for juveniles, published by the New York Anti-Slavery Society from 1836 to 1839.

12. *National Enquirer*, Benjamin Lundy's paper, with which he merged the *Genius of Universal Emancipation*, published in Philadelphia from 1836 to 1839.

13. *Observer*, edited by Elijah P. Lovejoy and published in St. Louis from 1833 to 1837 and in Alton, Illinois, in 1837.

14. For example, *The Liberator* published a review in four of its issues of Solomon Bayley's *Narrative*. The review appeared in a column entitled "Memorials of a Slave," in *The Liberator* 4:23, 22, 30, 41, 46.

15. Charles Ball, *Slavery in the United States: A Narrative of the Life and Adventures of Charles Ball, a Black Man.* (Lewistown, Pennsylvania, 1836).

16. *The Liberator* 5 (29 August 1835):140.

17. See Chapter 4.

18. *The Liberator* 8:51.

19. See bibliography of separately published slave narratives.

20. Moses Roper, *Narrative of the Adventures and Escape of Moses Roper from American Slavery* (London, 1837), p. 4.

21. Ibid., p. 1.

22. Compare the fate of Delia Clarke, in Lewis Clarke, *Narrative of the Life and Sufferings, etc.*, Appendix; and in Harriet Jacobs, *Incidents in the Life of a Slave Girl*.

23. Roper, *Narrative*, pp. 7–8.

24. Ibid., p. 11.

25. Ibid.

26. Ibid., pp. 19–20.

27. Ibid., p. 21.

28. Ibid., p. 26.

29. Ibid., p. 6.

30. *The Liberator* 8 (26 October 1838):170.

31. James Williams, *Narrative of James Williams, an American Slave*, ed. John Greenleaf Whittier (New York: Anti-Slavery Society, 1838).

32. See Chapter 4.

33. *Herald of Freedom*, published in Concord, Massachusetts, 1837 to 1840.

34. *The Liberator*, 8:150.

35. Reprinted in *The Liberator* 9 (3 May 1839):74.

36. Ibid.

37. Ibid.

38. *The Liberator* 10:7. All references to the Curry narrative are to be found on this one vast page.

39. It is noteworthy that answers can be found in Curry's narrative to pracically all of the questions on the Reddick Questionnaire, prepared in 1934 as a guide in interviewing ex-slaves. See Chapter 4.

40. Reprinted from the *St. Louis Gazette* in *The Liberator* 11 (30 July 1841):124.

41. Lunceford Lane, *Narrative of Lunceford Lane* (Boston: printed by Howes and Watson for the author, 1842).
42. Ibid., p. iii.
43. Ibid., p. 7.
44. Ibid., pp. 7–8.
45. Ibid., p. 9.
46. Ibid., pp. 10–11.
47. Ibid., p. 14.
48. Ibid., p. 15.
49. Ibid., p. 16.
50. Ibid., p. 17.
51. Moses Grandy, *Narrative of the Life of Moses Grandy, Late a Slave in the United States of America*, p. 2.
52. Ibid., p. 8.
53. Ibid., pp. 10–11.
54. See Chapter 5.
55. Lewis Clarke, *Narrative of the Sufferings of Lewis Clarke, during a Captivity of More than Twenty-Five Years among the Algerines of Kentucky* (Boston: D. H. Eli, 1845).
56. Ibid., p. 12.
57. Ibid., p. 17.
58. Ibid., p. 22.
59. Ibid., p. 25.
60. Harriet Beecher Stowe, *Key to Uncle Tom's Cabin*, pp. 13–14.
61. Leonard Black, *The Life and Sufferings of Leonard Black, a Fugitive from Slavery, Written by Himself* (New Bedford: Press of Benjamin Lindsay, 1847).
62. Contemporary slave narratives of similar type are: William Hayden, *Narrative of William Hayden, Containing a Faithful Account of His Travels for a Number of Years, Whilst a Slave in the South, Written by Himself* (Cincinnati: published for the author, 1846); and Andrew Jackson, *Narrative and Writings of Andrew Jackson; Containing an Account of His Birth and Twenty-Six Years of His Life While a Slave; His Escape; Five Years of Freedom, etc.* (Syracuse: *Daily and Weekly Star* office, 1847).
63. Zamba, *Life and Adventures of Zamba, an African Negro King, and His Experiences of Slavery in South Carolina, Written by Himself, Corrected and Arranged by Peter Neilson* (London: Smith, Elder and Company, 1847).
64. William Wells Brown, *Narrative of William Wells Brown, a Fugitive Slave, Written by Himself* (Boston: American Anti-Slavery Office, 1847).
65. See pages 32–33.
66. Zamba, *Life and Adventures*, p. x.
67. Ibid., p. xii.
68. Ibid., p. xiv.

69. Ibid., p. 90.
70. Ibid., pp. 161–162.
71. Ibid., p. 167.
72. Ibid., p. 187.
73. Zamba, *Der Negerkonig Zamba, Eine Sklavengeschichte Seitenstuck zu Onkel Tom's Hutte* (Stuttgart, 1853).
74. Zamba, *Life and Adventures, etc.*, pp. 249–250.
75. Zamba, *Der Negerkonig Zamba, u.s.w.*, p. 5.
76. Zamba, *Life and Adventures, etc.*, p. 252.
77. Ibid., p. 256.
78. William Wells Brown, *Narrative*.
79. *The Liberator* 19 (1 June 1849):87.
80. Brown, *Narrative*, pp. vi–vii.
81. Ibid., p. 2.
82. Josephine Brown, *Biography of an American Bondman, by His Daughter*, p. 1.
83. Brown, *Narrative*, p. 16.
84. Ibid., pp. 95–96.
85. Ibid., pp. 97–99.
86. Ibid., p. 104.
87. *The Liberator* 17 (30 July 1847):122.
88. Ibid., 24 (29 January 1854):9.
89. William Wells Brown, *Clotel; or, The President's Daughter* (London: Partridge and Oakey, 1853).
90. ____, *A Description of William Wells Brown's Original Panoramic Views of the Scenes in the Life of an American Slave, etc.* (London, 1849).
91. ____, *Illustrated Edition of Life and Escape of William Wells Brown* (London: C. Gilpin, 1851).
92. ____, *Three Years in Europe* (London, 1852). Enlarged as *The American Fugitive in Europe, Sketches of Places and People Abroad, with a Memoir by the Author* (Boston and New York, 1855).
93. *The Liberator* 24 (20 January 1854):9.
94. William Wells Brown, *Places and People Abroad, by William Wells Brown, a Fugitive Slave* (Boston: John P. Jewett, 1854).
95. ____, *The American Fugitive in Europe, etc.*
96. ____, *Three Years in Europe*, pp. 216–219.
97. *The Liberator* 25 (12 January 1855):5.
98. Compare the statement, "There is no work by an American Negro that does not have racial wretchedness for its theme," made by Vernon Loggins in *The Negro Author*, p. 34. Some exceptions do exist, however; e.g., Phillis Wheatley's poems.
99. *The Liberator* 25:5.
100. Josephine Brown, *Biography*.
101. Ibid., pp. 96–97.
102. *The Liberator* 26 (21 November 1857):186.

103. William Wells Brown, *Experience: or, How to Give a Northern Man a Backbone* (Boston: Anti-Slavery Society, 1858). See also *The Liberator* 26:186.

104. ____, *Escape; or, A Leap for Freedom* (Boston: Anti-Slavery Society, 1858). See also *The Liberator* 30:136. ____ *Jeremiah Adderson* (Worcester, 1856). See also *The Liberator* 26:124.

105. ____, *Black Man* (Boston, 1863). Published in June, 1863; second edition, enlarged, published in July, the first edition having already been exhausted.

106. ____, *My Southern Home* (Boston, 1872).

107. ____, *The Rising Son* (Boston, 1881).

108. *The Liberator* 18 (17 March 1848):143.

109. Henry Watson, *Narrative* (Boston: Bela Marsh, 1848).

110. Ibid., pp. 35–36.

111. Henry Bibb, *Narrative of the Life and Adventures of Henry Bibb, an American Slave, Written by Himself*, 3d. stereotyped edition (New York: published by the author, 1849).

112. *The Liberator* 17 (21 May 1847):80.

113. Ibid., 18 (18 February 1848):27.

114. Ibid., 17 (18 June 1847):97.

115. Bibb, *Narrative*, pp. ii–ix.

116. Ibid., pp. ii–ii.

117. Ibid., p. xii.

118. *The Voice of the Fugitive*, edited by Henry Bibb, published bi-monthly, 1851 to 1853, at Sandwich, Canada, as an organ through which the slaves could be heard.

119. Bibb, *Narrative* p. xii.

120. Ibid., pp. 78–79.

121. Ibid., p. 79.

122. Ibid., p. 88.

123. Ibid., p. 98.

124. Ibid., p. 100.

125. Ibid., p. 108.

126. Ibid., p. 110.

127. Ibid., pp. 124–128.

128. *The Liberator* 17 (15 Jan. 1847):12.

129. See page 36.

130. James W. C. Pennington, *The Fugitive Blacksmith, or, Events in the History of James W. C. Pennington, Pastor of a Presbyterian Church, New York, Formerly a Slave in the State of Maryland, United States*, 2d ed. (London: C. Gilpin, 1849).

131. Ibid., preface.

132. Ibid.

133. Ibid., pp. 5–6.

134. Ibid., p. 7.

135. Ibid., pp. 8–9.

136. Ibid., pp. 33–34.

137. Ibid., pp. 35-37.
138. See Chapter 4.
139. Josiah Henson, *Life of Josiah Henson, Formerly a Slave, Now an Inhabitant of Canada, as Related by Himself* (Boston: Arthur D. Phelps, 1849).
140. Ibid., pp. 7-8.
141. See Chapter 4.
142. Henson, *Life*, p. 9.
143. Ibid., p. 10.
144. Rev. Ephraim Peabody, "Narratives of Fugitive Slaves," *Christian Examiner*, July 1849, pp. 81-93.
145. Henson, *Life*, pp. 11-12.
146. Ibid., p. 13.
147. Ibid., pp. 34-35.
148. Ibid., p. 45.
149. Ibid., p. 47.
150. Ibid., pp. 48-49.
151. Ibid., p. 50.
152. Ibid., pp. 64-65.
153. Henry Box Brown, *Narrative of Henry Box Brown, Who Escaped from Slavery Enclosed in a Box Three Feet Long, Two Feet Wide, and Two and a Half Feet High, Written from a Statement of Facts Made by Himself* (Boston: Brown and Stearns, 1849).
154. See Chapter 4.
155. Henry Box Brown, *Narrative*, p. ii.
156. Ibid., p. 19.
157. Ibid., pp. 50-51.
158. Ibid., p. 53.
159. Ibid., pp. 55-56.
160. Ibid., pp. 53-55.
161. Ibid., p. 58.
162. *The Liberator* 15 (25 July 1845):120.
163. *Suppressed Book about Slavery* (New York: Carleton, 1864), pp. 282-283.
164. Lydia Maria Francis Child, *The Duty of Disobedience to the Fugitive Slave Act: An Appeal to the Legislators of Massachusetts*, pp. 15-16.
165. Solomon Northup, *Twelve Years a Slave* (Auburn, New York: Derby and Miller, 1853).
166. *Memoirs of an Unfortunate Young Nobleman, Returned from a Thirteen Years Slavery in America, Where He Had Been Sent by the Wicked Contrivances of His Cruel Uncle* (London: J. Freeman, 1743).
167. Peter Williamson, *The Life and Curious Adventures of Peter Williamson, Who Was Carried Off from Aberdeen and Sold as a Slave*, 2d ed. (London, 1759).
168. See Chapter 2.
169. *The Liberator* 1:127.
170. Ibid., 1 (27 August 1831):139.

171. Ibid., 2 (2 June 1832):87.
172. Ibid., 3 (18 May 1833):20.
173. Ibid., 4 (7 June 1834):90.
174. Ibid.
175. Olaudah Equiano, *Interesting Narrative of the Life of Olaudah Equiano, etc.,* vol. 2, pp. 51–52.
176. Northup, *Twelve Years,* p. 255.
177. *The Liberator* 25 (23 March 1855):57.
178. Kate E. R. Pickard, *The Kidnapped and the Ransomed, Being the Personal Recollections of Peter Still and His Wife "Vina," after Forty Years of Slavery,* 3d ed. (Syracuse: William T. Hamilton, 1856).
179. Ibid., p. xxii.
180. Kate Pickard, *The Kidnapped and the Ransomed.,* series 1, no. 1 (New York: Negro Publications Society of America, 1941).
181. Kate Pickard, *The Kidnapped and the Ransomed* (1856 ed.), p. i.
182. Ibid., p. xvii.
183. Thomas H. Jones, *The Experiences and Personal Narrative of Uncle Tom Jones, Who Was for Forty Years a Slave* (New York: G. C. Holbrook, 1854).
184. Ibid., p. 9.
185. Ibid., p. 6.
186. Ibid., p. 19.
187. Ibid., pp. 20–21.
188. Ibid., p. 32.
189. John Thompson, *The Life of John Thompson, a Fugitive, Containing His History of Twenty-Five Years in Bondage, and His Providential Escape, Written by Himself* (Worcester: published by John Thompson, 1856).
190. *The Liberator* 26 (22 August 1856):138.
191. Thompson, *The Life of John Thompson,* pp. 49–50.
192. Ibid., p. 33.
193. Ibid., p. 81.
194. Ibid., p. 110.
195. Ibid., p. 82.
196. John Brown, *Slave Life in Georgia: A Narrative of the Life, Sufferings, and Escape of John Brown, a Fugitive Slave, Now in England,* 2d ed. (London: W. M. Watts, 1855).
197. Ibid., p. 3.
198. Ibid., p. 202.
199. Ibid., p. 160.
200. Peter Randolph, *Sketches of Slave Life: or, Illustrations of the 'Peculiar Institution,' by Reverend Peter Randolph, an Emancipated Slave,* 2d ed. (Boston: published for the author, 1855).
201. Samuel Ringgold Ward, *Autobiography of a Fugitive Negro: His Anti-Slavery Labors in the United States, Canada, and England* (London: J. Snow, 1855).
202. Randolph, *Sketches,* p. 11.

...

203. Ibid., p. 12.
204. *The Liberator* 26 (15 February 1856):27.
205. J. H. Nelson, *The Negro Character in American Fiction*.
206. Ward, *Autobiography*, p. iii.
207. "A Slave's Story," *Putnam's Monthly* 9 (June 1856):614–620.
208. Ibid., p. 614.
209. *The Liberator*, 3 (13 April 1833):58.
210. Austin Steward, *Twenty-Two Years a Slave, and Forty Years a Freeman* (Rochester, New York: Allings and Cory, 1857).
211. Ibid., p. vi.
212. Ibid., p. xii.
213. Ibid., p. 83.
214. Ibid., p. 91.
215. Ibid., p. 96.
216. Ibid., pp. 101–102.
217. Ibid., p. 107.
218. Ibid., p. 111.
219. Jermain W. Loguen, *Reverend Jermain W. Loguen, as a Slave and as a Freeman* (Syracuse: Office of the *Daily Journal*, 1859).
220. Ibid., p. v.
221. See Franklin E. Frazier, *The Negro Family in the United States*, which cites Loguen frequently in Chapter 2, "Human All Too Human," and in Chapter 3, "Motherhood in Bondage." (This is considered the definitive study on the Negro family.) Other scholars who cite Loguen as an authentic primary reference include Aptheker in his *American Negro Slave Revolts*; Charles S. Johnson in his *Shadow of the Plantation*; and W. E. B. DuBois and Guy Johnson in *Negro Encyclopedia*.
222. Reprinted from the *Syracuse* (New York) *Standard* in *The Liberator* 30 (27 April 1860):64.
223. Ibid.
224. Loguen, *Reverend Jeremain W. Loguen*, p. viii.
225. Noah Davis, *A Narrative of the Life of Reverend Noah Davis, a Colored Man, Written by Himself, at the Age of Fifty-Four* (Baltimore: published by John F. Weishampl, Jr., 1859).
226. Ibid., p. 9.
227. Ibid., p. 13.
228. Ibid., pp. 14–15.
229. Ibid., p. 16.
230. Ibid., p. 17.
231. Ibid., pp. 19–24.
232. Ibid., pp. 26–27.
233. Ibid., p. 30.
234. Ibid., pp. 31–32.
235. Ibid., p. 36.
236. Ibid., pp. 41–42.
237. Ibid., pp. 55–56.
238. Ibid., pp. 57–59.

239. Ibid., pp. 66–67.
240. Ibid., pp. 71–72.
241. Reverend G. W. Offley, *A Narrative of the Life and Labors of the Reverend G. W. Offley, A Colored Man and Local Preacher, Written by Himself* (Hartford, 1860).
242. Ibid., pp. 3–8.
243. Ibid., pp. 11–12.
244. William Craft, *Running a Thousand Miles for Freedom; or, The Escape of William and Ellen Craft from Slavery* (London: William Tweedie, 1860).
245. See pages 235–238.
246. Craft, *Running a Thousand Miles*, pp. 41–42.
247. Chloe Spear, *Narrative of Chloe Spear. By a "Lady of Boston"* (Boston: American Anti-Slavery Society, 1832).
248. Elleanor Eldridge, *Memoirs of Elleanor Eldridge* (Providence, 1843).
249. Sojourner Truth, *Narrative of Sojourner Truth, a Northern Slave, Emancipated from Bodily Servitude by the State of New York in 1828* (Boston, 1850).
250. Janie Parker, *Janie Parker, the Fugitive* (Boston, 1851).
251. *Aunt Sally; or, The Cross the Way to Freedom* (Cincinnati: American Reform Tract and Book Society, 1858).
252. Harriet Jacobs, *Linda: Incidents in the Life of a Slave Girl, Written by Herself* (Boston, 1861).
253. Truth, *Narrative* . . . (Boston, 1855).
254. *Aunt Sally, etc.*, p. 190.
255. Jacobs, *Linda*, pp. 7–8.
256. Ibid., p. 6.
257. Ibid., pp. 19–20.
258. Ibid., pp. 23–24.
259. Ibid., p. 22.
260. Ibid., pp. 25–26.
261. Ibid., pp. 45–46.
262. Ibid., p. 149.
263. Ibid., pp. 151–152.
264. Ibid., p. 302.
265. See bibliography.
266. Booker T. Washington, in 1945. See his *Up from Slavery* (New York, 1900).
267. George Washington Carver, in 1946. See Rackham Holt, *George Washington Carver, an American Biography*; and Raleigh Merritt, *From Captivity to Fame*.

Chapter Four: Trustworthiness of the Narratives

1. *The Liberator* 7 (23 June 1837): 103.

2. Peter Randolph, *Sketches of Slave Life; or, Illustrations of the 'Peculiar Institution,' etc.*; Anthony Burns, *Narrative*; and John Anderson, *Story of John Anderson, Fugitive Slave.*

3 *The Life and Dying Speech of Arthur* (Worcester, 1868); Edmund Fortes, *The Last Words and Dying Speech of Edmund Fortes, A Negro Man* (Exeter, 1796); Abraham Johnstone, *The Address of Abraham Johnstone, A Black Man* (Philadelphia, 1797); and Joseph Mountain, *Sketches of the Life of Joseph Mountain* (New Haven, 1790).

4. See Chapter 2.

5. The known editions of the Peter Williamson narrative are all to be found in the New York Public Library, Rare Books Room.

6. William Boen, *Anecdotes and Memoirs of William Boen, a Colored Man Who Lived and Died near Mount Holly, New Jersey* (Philadelphia, 1934).

7. See bibliography.

8. Boen, *Anecdotes*, p. 5.

9. E.g., Solomon Northup, *Twelve Years a Slave* (Buffalo, 1853).

10. Catherine Birney, *Grimke Sisters; Sarah and Angeline Grimke.*

11. See bibligraphy of separately published slave narratives.

12. E.g., Isaac Mason, *Life of Isaac Mason, as a Slave* (Worcester, 1893).

13. Benjamin A. Botkin, *Lay My Burden Down* (Chicago, 1945).

14. A. R. Burr, *The Autobiography*, p. 44.

15. Waldo H. Dunn, *English Biography before 1700*, p. 130.

16. *The Liberator*, 5 (29 August 1835):140.

17. Ibid.

18. Cited in *The Liberator* 7 (28 April 1837):72.

19. E. A. Duyckinck, and G. L. Duyckinck, *Cyclopedia of American Literature*, p. 462.

20. Arthur M. Schlesinger, Jr., "Richard Hildreth," *New England Quarterly* 13:223.

21. E.g., M. G. McDougall, *Fugitive Slaves, 1619-1865*; and Monroe Work, *Bibliography of the Negro*.

22. *The Liberator* 7 (14 January 1837):9.

23. Ibid., 7 (31 March 1837):56.

24. Ibid., 8 (13 May 1838):78.

25. Ibid., 8 (2 November 1838):173.

26. Ibid., p. 153.

27. Ibid., p. 173.

28. Ibid., 8 (21 September 1838):150.

29. Ibid.

30. Richard Hildreth, *The White Slave; or, Negro Life in the Slave States of America* (London, n.d., c. 1852), p. 301.

31. *The Liberator* 23 (1 April 1853):51.

32. Schlesinger, "Richard Hildreth," p. 230.

33. John Herbert Nelson, *The Negro Character in American Literature*, p. 61.

34. Henry H. Simms, "A Critical Analysis of Abolition Literature, 1830-1840," *Journal of Southern History* 6 (1940):374.

35. *The Liberator* 9 (14 June 1839):96.
36. Lewis Clarke and Milton Clarke, *Narratives of the Sufferings of Lewis and Milton Clarke, Sons of a Soldier of the Revolution; during a Captivity of More than Twenty Years among the Slaveholders of Kentucky, One of the So-Called Christian States of North America*, pp. 108–123.
37. See Chapter 2.
38. *The Liberator* 19 (16 February 1849):27.
39. Ibid., pp. 27–28.
40. Ibid., (2 March 1849):35.
41. Ibid., 19 (6 April 1849):54.
42. Ibid., 21 (23 May 1851):82.
43. Ibid., 21 (26 September 1851):156.
44. Ibid., 22 (5 November 1852):179.
45. Ibid., 25 (23 February 1855):31.
46. Ibid., 23:45.
47. Ibid., 35:122.
48. Carter Woodson, *The Negro in Our History*, 6th ed., pp. 277–278.
49. Harriet B. Stowe, *A Key to Uncle Tom's Cabin, Presenting the Original Facts and Documents upon Which the Story Is Founded*, pp. 26–27.
50. *The Liberator*, 21:13–14.
51. Ibid., 21:60.
52. Ibid., 28 (28 May 1858).
53. Ibid., 21:110.
54. John Henry Wigmore, *The Principles of Judicial Proof; or, The Process of Proof as Given by Logic, Psychology, and General Experience and Illustrated in Judicial Trials*, p. 322.
55. Rev. Ephraim Peabody, "Narratives of Fugitive Slaves," *Christian Examiner* (July 1849), p. 69.
56. Wigmore, *The Principles*, p. 582.
57. The *Reddick Narratives* (260) of the Federal Writers' Project, deposited in typescript form in the Schomburg Collection, New York Public Library.
58. See Foreword, pp. xvii–xix.
59. Wigmore, *The Principles*.
60. Benjamin A. Botkin, *Lay My Burden Down*, p. 1.
61. Lloyd Lewis, in *New York Times Book Review*, 6 January 1946, p. 4.
62. Carter Woodson, in *Journal of Negro History* (January 1946), p. 120.
63. Zamba, *Life and Adventures of Zamba, an African Negro King and His Experiences of Slavery in South Carolina* (London, 1847).
64. Ibid., p. 171.
65. Benjamin Drew, *A Northside View of Slavery*, p. 30.
66. L. M. F. Child, *Letters*, p. 161.
67. _____, *The Duty of Disobedience to the Fugitive Slave, etc.*, p. 12.

Chapter Five: The Most Important Narrative

1. W. E. B. DuBois, "*A Look into the Past*," *Chicago Defender* (5 January 1946):11.
2. Ibid.
3. *Liberator* 11 (9 December 1842):182.
4. Ibid., 12:182.
5. Ibid., 14:29.
6. Ibid., 15:86.
7. Ibid., 15:155.
8. Ibid., 15:140.
9. Ibid., 16:35.
10. Ibid.
11. Ibid.
12. *The Liberator* 16:78.
13. Ibid.
14. Ibid.
15. Frederick Douglass, *Narrative of Frederick Douglass, an American Slave, Written by Himself* (Boston, 1845), p. 3.
16. Ibid., pp. 4–5.
17. Ibid., pp. 7–8.
18. Ibid., pp. 21–22.
19. Ibid., pp. 22–23.
20. Ibid., pp. 13–15.
21. Ibid., p. 30.
22. Ibid., pp. 31–32.
23. Ibid., p. 35.
24. Ibid., pp. 37–38.
25. Ibid., pp. 39–40.
26. Ibid., p. 40.
27. Ibid., pp. 60–61.
28. Ibid., pp. 64–65.
29. Ibid., p. 73.
30. Ibid., p. 80.
31. Ibid., p. 81.
32. Ibid., pp. 90–91.
33. Ibid., pp. 94–95.
34. Ibid., p. 97.
35. Ibid.
36. *The Liberator* 15 (20 June 1845):96. Reprinted from the *New York Tribune*.
37. Ibid., 25 (24 August 1855):135.
38. Frederick Douglass, *My Bondage and My Freedom* (New York, 1855), pp. vi–viii.
39. See Chapter 5.
40. Douglass, *My Bondage*, pp. 51–52.

41. Frederick Douglass, *Life and Times of Frederick Douglass, Written by Himself* (Hartford, 1881), p. 15.
42. ____, *Life and Times of Frederick Douglass, Written by Himself* (Boston, 1892), p. 27.
43. Ibid., p. 39.
44. Douglass, *My Bondage and My Freedom*, p. 52.
45. Ibid., pp. 324–325.
46. Douglass, *Life and Times, etc.* (Hartford, 1881), pp. 198–199.
47. Ibid., pp. 448–449.
48. Douglass, *Life and Times, etc.* (Boston, 1892), pp. 63–64.
49. Ibid., pp. 65–66.
50. Ibid., p. 86.
51. Ibid., pp. 105–106.
52. Ibid., p. 111.
53. Ibid., pp. 112–113.
54. Ibid., pp. 113–114.
55. Ibid., p. 127.
56. Ibid., pp. 185–186.
57. Frederick Douglass, *Life and Times of Frederick Douglass, Written by Himself* (New York: Pathway Press, c. 1941). Published for the Frederick Douglass Historical and Cultural League.

Chapter Six: The Literary Significance of the Slave Narratives

1. George B. Woods, Homer A. Watt, and George B. Anderson, *The Literature of England*, vol. 1, p. 717.
2. Abigail Field Mott, *Biographical Sketches and Interesting Anecdotes of Persons of Color*. Published first in 1826; then in 1828; enlarged with short narratives of escaped slaves in 1837 and 1838; reprinted in 1875 and 1882 as *Narratives of Coloured Americans*.
3. John Herbert Nelson, *The Negro in American Fiction*, p. 61.
4. For literary studies of the slave narrative, see: Vernon Loggins, *The Negro Author*; J. H. Nelson, *The Negro*; and Ephraim Peabody, "Narratives of Fugitive Slaves," *Christian Examiner*, July 1849. For references to slave narratives by social historians, see: Herbert Aptheker, *American Negro Slave Revolts*; E. Franklin Frazier, *The Negro Family in the United States*; and L. D. Reddick, introduction to Kate Pickard, *The Kidnapped and the Ransomed* (New York, 1941). Surprising absence of mention of the slave narratives is to be noted in the work of Carter Woodson in various phases of the history of slavery and in Lorenzo D. Turner's *Anti-Slavery Sentiment in American Literature Prior to 1865*. Very scant reference is made to the narratives in the work of Benjamin Brawley, only a few being mentioned in his *Early Negro American Writers*.
5. Reverend Ephraim Peabody, "Narratives of Fugitive Slaves," *Christian Examiner*, July 1849, pp. 61–62.

6. Ibid., p. 62.
7. Ibid., p. 67.
8. Ibid., p. 64.
9. Ibid., p. 80.
10. Ibid., p. 72.
11. Fred Pattee, *First Century of American Literature*, p. 570.
12. See title page of Mrs. Stowe's *Key to Uncle Tom's Cabin, etc.*
13. See bibliography for Josiah Henson, *Stranger than Fiction*.
14. See Chapter 4.
15. *The Liberator*, 22 (17 September 1852):152.
16. Peabody, "Narratives," p. 62.
17. Pattee, *First Century*, p. 572.
18. Whittier was an associate editor of the *National Era*, which was published in Philadelphia and in Washington between 1840 and 1860.
19. *The Liberator* (11 June 1852):93.
20. See Harvard College Library Union Catalog.
21. Clarence Gohdes, *American Literature in Nineteenth Century England*, p. 129. Also, see Herbert Brown, *The Sentimental Novel*; and the chapters on *Uncle Tom's Cabin* in Forrest Wilson, *Crusader in Crinoline*.
22. *The Liberator* 29 (11 March 1859):38.
23. Ibid., 23 (13 May 1853):75.
24. Ibid., 23 (11 March 1853):36.
25. Ibid., 22 (3 September 1852):141.
26. Ibid., 25 (1 June 1855):86, reprinted from *New York Tribune*.
27. Ibid., 27 (4 September 1857):143.
28. Ibid., 22 (22 October 1852):170, reprinted from the *London Times*.
29. See Chapter 4.
30. Cited in Pattee, *First Century*, p. 572.
31. *Graham's Magazine* 42 (January 1853):209.
32–37. [References no longer available.]

Introduction to Bibliographies

Rounding up the slave narratives for this study of the group as a literary genre has been an adventure. Two of the total of 6006 records are to be found in practically every public library: the autobiographies of Frederick Douglass and of Booker T. Washington. But this is the extent of the offerings of most libraries.

Bibliographic aids have been scant. The outstanding contribution in this field is Porter's "Early American Negro Writings: A Bibliographic Study," an admirable checklist of the published writings of American Negroes between 1760 and 1835, listing seventeen slave autobiographies. Augusta Johnson's special study of the editions of Equiano's narrative is the most thorough bibliography that we have. Work's *Bibliography of the Negro* is not reliable in its data on "Slave Narratives." Quinn's *Literary Crusade against Slavery* and Turner's *Anti-Slavery Sentiment in American Literature Prior to 1865* are surprising in that they do not refer to a single narrative. Nelson's *Negro Character in American Fiction* discusses twenty; Loggins's *Negro Author*, nine; and Brawley's *Early Negro American Writers*, three. References to slave narratives by social historians include citations from twenty in Frazier's *Negro Family in the United States*; Aptheker's *American Negro Slave Revolts* mentions seven; Reddick's introduction to the 1941 reprint edition of Pickard's *The Kidnapped and the Ransomed* mentions nine; and DuBois and Johnson's *Negro Encyclopedia*, seventeen. Biographical studies of slave narrators include biographies of Jupiter Hammon, Phillis Wheatley, Richard Allen, Nat Turner, William Wells Brown, Frederick Douglass, Harriet Tubman, Booker T. Washington, and George Washington Carver. Contemporary publishers' lists and the usual guides to periodical literature furnished additional help.

The literature of American slavery as a whole suggests the existence of much more material, however, than was discoverable by means of the aforementioned aids. Nelson, while speaking of just twenty slave narratives, admits that a conservative estimate would put the number of separately published narratives in existence in the 1830-60 period at "more than a hundred," not to mention "numerous briefer sketches which appeared in *The Liberator* and anti-slavery anthologies." Merle Curti speaks of the "hundred-odd auto-biographies written or directed after escape to the North," though he mentions only two. Thus it became necessary to go systematically through the card catalogs of the libraries designated as the most likely depositories of slave literature. Entries under the words "Narrative," "Negro," "Slave," "Slavery," "Autobiography," and "Biography" were checked, because special catalog entries labeled "Slave Narratives" proved to be deceptive. Examination of the actual books and card catalog data revealed numerous errors as well as some exciting discoveries. The files of antislavery newspapers and periodicals were similarly combed, page by page, for the narratives closely hidden within the many volumes. Unpublished manuscript collections were kindly placed at the writer's disposition in the final stage of this quest to bring together in one place the records of the mind and thought of the American Negro slave.

In listing the separately published slave narratives, the date and place of the first editions located have been given, along with subsequent editions that differed from earlier editions in some respect other than merely a later date. Therefore, no mention has been made of reissues of previous editions, as this would necessitate extending the bibliography unduly.

Most of the separately published slave narratives that have been located are deposited in special reference collections. The Schomburg Collection of Negro Literature of the New York Public Library contains the largest number of these narratives; therefore, in designating the place where individual editions are to be found, reference is made to the Schomburg Collection if the copy is there. If it is not in that collection, the place where it is located is given. Some of the narratives listed under "Schomburg" are also to be found elsewhere, but space limitations demand the single listing. Similarly, in some instances there are files or partial files of antislavery newspapers other than the particular collections listed. In each case, the file listed is, in the writer's opinion, the most complete or best-preserved and most convenient of the available sources.

Separately Published
Slave Narratives

Aaron. *Light of Truth and Slavery. Aaron's History in Virginia, New Jersey, and Rhode Island*. Worcester, Massachusetts, n.d. At Library of Congress.

"Adam Negro's Tryall." Edited by Abner C. Goodell. In *Publications of the Colonial Society of Massachusetts Transactions*, pp. 103–112.

Adams, John Quincy, *Narrative of the Life of John Quincy Adams, When in Slavery and Now as a Freeman*. Harrisburg, Pennsylvania, 1872. At the Schomburg.

Alexander, Archer. *The Story of Alexander Archer, from Slavery to Freedom, March 30, 1863*. As related to William Greenleaf Eliot. Boston: Cupples, Upham, and Company, 1855. At Massachusetts State Library.

Allen, Richard. *The Life, Experiences, and Gospel Labors of the Right Reverend Richard Allen*. Philadelphia: Martin and Boden, 1833. At the Schomburg.

Anderson, John. *Story of John Anderson, Fugitive Slave*. Edited by Harper Twelvetrees, Chairman, John Anderson Committee. London: W. Tweedie, 1863. At Schomburg.

Anderson, Robert. *From Slavery to Affluence, Memoirs of Robert Anderson, Ex-Slave*. Hemingsford, Nebraska, 1927. At New York Public Library.

Anderson, Thomas. *Interesting Account of Thomas Anderson, a Slave, "Taken from His Own Lips."* Dictated to J. P. Clark. n.p., 1854? At Oberlin.

Archer, Armstrong. *A Compendium of Slavery as It Exists in the Present Day*. London: J. Haddon, 1844. At Massachusetts State Library.

Arthur. *The Life and Dying Speech of Arthur*. A Broadside. Boston: printed and sold at Milk Street, 1768. New York Historical Society copy.

Aunt Sally; or, The Cross the Way to Freedom. Narrative of the Slave Life and Purchase of the Mother of Reverend Isaac Williams of Detroit, Michigan. Cincinnati: Western Tract and Book Society, 1858. At Schomburg.

_____. American Reform Tract and Book Society, 1862. At Schomburg.

Ball, Charles. *Slavery in the United States: a Narrative of the Life and Adventures of Charles Ball, a Black Man, Who Lived Forty Years in Maryland, South Carolina, and Georgia as a Slave*. Prepared by Fisher from the verbal narrative by Ball. Lewiston, Pennsylvania: J. W. Shugert, 1836. At Schomburg.

_____. _____. New York: J. S. Taylor, 1837. At Andover Seminary.

_____. _____. Edited by Mrs. Alfred Barnard. London, 1846. Harvard Library.

_____. _____. Pittsburgh: J. T. Shryock, 1853. At Library of Congress.

_____. *Fifty Years in Chains; or, The Life of an American Slave*. New York: Dayton and Asher, 1858. At Library of Congress.

_____. _____. New York and Indianapolis: Dayton and Asher, 1859. At Schomburg.

Bayley, Solomon. *Incidents in the Life of Solomon Bayley*. Philadelphia: Tract Association of Friends, No. 99, c. 1820. At Harvard.

_____. *Narrative of Some Remarkable Incidents in the Life of Solomon Bayley, Formerly a Slave in the State of Delaware, Written by Himself, Published for His Benefit by Richard Hunard*. London, 1825. At Schomburg.

Bibb, Henry. *Narrative of the Life and Adventures of Henry Bibb, an American Slave, Written by Himself*. Introduction by Lucius C. Matlack. New York: published for the author, 1849. At Schomburg.

_____. _____. New York, 1850. At Massachusetts State Library.

Black, Leonard. *Life and Sufferings of Leonard Black, a Fugitive from Slavery, Written by Himself*. New York: Press of Benjamin Lindsay, 1847. At Schomburg.

Blake, Jane. *Memoirs of Margaret Jane Blake*. Related to Sarah R. Levering, Baltimore, whose father had owned Jane Blake. Philadelphia: Innes and Son, 1897. At Library of Congress.

Boen, William. *Anecdotes and Memoir of William Boen, a Colored Man, Who Lived and Died near Mount Holly, New Jersey. To Which Is Added the Testimony of Friends of Mount Holly Monthly Meeting Concerning Him*. Philadelphia: Printed by John Richards, 1834. At New York Historical Society.

Brown, Henry Box. *Narrative of Henry Box Brown, Who Escaped from Slavery Enclosed in a Box Three Feet Long, Two Wide, and Two and a Half High. Written from a Statement of Facts Made by Himself*. With remarks upon the remedy for slavery by Charles Stearns. Boston: Brown and Stearns, 1849. At Schomburg.

_____. _____. Manchester, England, 1851. At Library of Congress.

Brown, Jane. *Narrative of the Life of Jane Brown and Her Two Children*. Related to the Reverend G. W. Offley. Hartford: Published for G. W. Offley, 1860. At Schomburg.

Brown, John. *Slave Life in Georgia: a Narrative of the Life, Sufferings, and Escape of John Brown, a Fugitive Slave, Now in England*. Edited by L. A. Chamerovzow. London: W. M. Watts, 1855. At Schomburg.

Brown, William Wells. *Narrative of William Wells Brown, a Fugitive Slave, Written by Himself*. Boston: The Anti-Slavery Office, 1847. At Schomburg.

_____. *Life of William Wells Brown*. Boston: Bela Marsh, 1848. At Boston Public Library.

_____. *Narrative of the Life of William Wells Brown*. Boston: Bela Marsh, 1849. At Harvard.

_____. *Illustrated Edition of the Life and Escape of William Wells Brown*. London: C. Gilpin, 1851. New York Public Library.

_____. *Three Years in Europe; or, Places I have Seen and People I Have Met*. With a memoir of the author, by William Farmer. London: C. Gilpin, 1852. At Boston Public Library.

_____. *Clotel; or, The President's Daughter: A Narrative of Slave Life in the United States, with a Sketch of the Author's Life*. London: Partridge and Oakey, 1853. At Boston Public Library.

_____. *Places and People Abroad, by William Wells Brown, a Fugitive Slave, with a Memoir of the Author*. Boston: John P. Jewett, 1854. At Schomburg.

_____. *The American Fugitive in Europe; Sketches of Places and People Abroad, with a Memoir of the Author*. Boston: Jewett and Company, 1855. At Schomburg.

Bruce, Henry Clay. *The New Man: Twenty-Nine Years a Slave, Twenty-Nine Years a Free Man*. Recollections of H. C. Bruce. York, Pennsylvania: P. Anstadt and Sons, 1895. At Schomburg.

Bruner, Peter. *A Slave's Advances toward Freedom, Not Fiction, but the True Story of a Struggle*. Oxford, Ohio, n.d. At Schomburg.

Burns, Anthony. *Narrative*. Boston, 1858. At Boston Public Library.

Burton, Annie L. *Memories of Childhood's Slavery Days*. Boston, 1919. At Schomburg.

Campbell, Israel. *Bond and Free; or, Yearnings for Freedom, from My Green Brier House; Being the Story of My Life in Bondage and My Life in Freedom*. Philadelphia, 1861. At Schomburg.

Carver, George Washington. *From Captivity to Fame*. Written by Raleigh H. Merritt. Boston: Meador Publishing Company, c. 1929.

Chandler, Charles. *The Story of a Slave*. n.p., 1894. At Schomburg.

Clarke, Lewis. *Narrative of the Sufferings of Lewis Clarke, during a Captivity of More than Twenty-Five Years among the Algerines of Kentucky*. Dictated by himself, written by Joseph C. Lovejoy. Boston: D. H. Eli, 1845. At Schomburg.

_____, Lewis Garrard, and Clarke, Milton. *Narratives of the Sufferings of Lewis and Milton Clarke, Sons of a Soldier of the Revolution; during a Captivity of More than Twenty Years among the Slaveholders of Kentucky, One of the So-Called Christian States of North America*. Boston: Bela Marsh, 1848. At Schomburg.

Cooper, Thomas. *Narrative of the Life of Thomas Cooper*. New York: Isaac T. Hopper, 1832. Moorland Foundation.

_____. _____. 4th ed. New York: Isaac T. Hopper, 1837. Arthur Spingarn Library, New York City.

Craft, William. *Running a Thousand Miles for Freedom; or, The Escape of William and Ellen Craft from Slavery*. London: W. Tweedie, 1860. At Schomburg.

Davis, Noah. *A Narrative of the Life of Reverend Noah Davis, a Colored Man, Written by Himself*. Baltimore: J. F. Weishampel, Jr., 1859. At Schomburg.

Dinah. *The Story of Dinah, as Related to John Hawkins Simpson, after Her Escape from the Horrors of the Virginia Slave Trade, to London.* London: A. W. Bennett, 1863. At Library of Congress.

Dormigold, Kate. *A Slave Girl's Story, The Autobiography of Kate Dorrigold.* Brooklyn, New York, 1898. At Library of Congress.

Douglass, Frederick. *Narrative of the Life of Frederick Douglass, an American Slave, Written by Himself.* Boston: Published at the Anti-Slavery Office, 1845. At the Schomburg.

_____. _____. Dublin: Webb and Chapman, 1845. At Schomburg.

_____. _____. 3d English ed. Wortley, near Leeds: Printed by J. Barker, 1846. Boston Public Library.

_____. _____. Boston: Bela Marsh, 1850. At Boston Public Library.

_____. *Vie de Frederic Douglass, esclave americain, ecrite par lui-meme.* Tr. de l'anglais par S. K. Parkes. Paris: Pagnerre, 1848. At Boston Public Library.

_____. *My Bondage and My Freedom.* Part I: "Life as a Slave," Part II: "Life as a Freeman." New York and Auburn: Miller, Orton, and Mulligan, 1855. At Schomburg.

_____. *Sclaverie und Freiheit Autobiographie.* Aus dem englischen ubertragen von Ottilie Assing. Hamburg: Hoffman und Campe, 1860. At Boston Public Library.

_____. *The Life and Times of Frederick Douglass.* Harford: Connecticut Park Publishing Company, 1881. At Schomburg.

_____. _____. new rev. ed. Boston: De Wolfe, Fiske, and Company, 1892. At Schomberg.

_____. _____. Published for the Frederick Douglass Historical and Cultural League, in preparation for the One Hundredth Anniversary of Douglass's First Public Appearance in the Cause of Emancipation. Substantially a reprint of the last revised and complete work. Introduction by Alaine Locke. New York: Pathway Press, 1941. Also, Centenary Memorial Subscribers' Edition. New York Public Library.

Eldridge, Elleanor. *Elleanor's Second Book.* Providence, 1839. At Library of Congress.

_____. *Memoirs of Elleanor Eldridge.* Providence, 1843. At Moorland Foundation.

_____. *Memoirs.* Providence, 1846. At Boston Public Library.

Equiano, Olaudah. *The Interesting Narrative of the Life of Olaudah Equiano, or Gustavus Vassa, the African, Written by Himself.* London: Entered at Stationers' Hall, 1789. At Schomburg.

_____. _____. 2d ed. London, 1789. At Library Company, Ridgeway Brothers, Philadelphia.

_____. _____. 3d ed., enlarged. London, 1790. At Schomburg.

_____. *Merkwaardige Lebensgevallen van Olaudah Equiano or Gustavus Vassa, den Afrikaan, eertyds een Negerslaaf.* Rotterdam, 1790. At Boston Public Library.

_____. *The Interesting Narrative of Olaudah Equiano, etc.* 1st American ed. New York: W. Durell, 1791. At Schomburg.

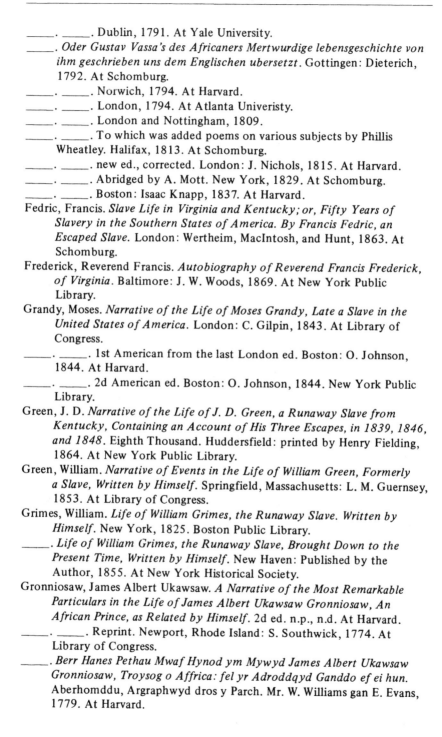

_____. _____. Dublin, 1791. At Yale University.

_____. *Oder Gustav Vassa's des Africaners Mertwurdige lebensgeschichte von ihm geschrieben uns dem Englischen ubersetzt*. Gottingen: Dieterich, 1792. At Schomburg.

_____. _____. Norwich, 1794. At Harvard.

_____. _____. London, 1794. At Atlanta Univeristy.

_____. _____. London and Nottingham, 1809.

_____. _____. To which was added poems on various subjects by Phillis Wheatley. Halifax, 1813. At Schomburg.

_____. _____. new ed., corrected. London: J. Nichols, 1815. At Harvard.

_____. _____. Abridged by A. Mott. New York, 1829. At Schomburg.

_____. _____. Boston: Isaac Knapp, 1837. At Harvard.

Fedric, Francis. *Slave Life in Virginia and Kentucky; or, Fifty Years of Slavery in the Southern States of America. By Francis Fedric, an Escaped Slave*. London: Wertheim, MacIntosh, and Hunt, 1863. At Schomburg.

Frederick, Reverend Francis. *Autobiography of Reverend Francis Frederick, of Virginia*. Baltimore: J. W. Woods, 1869. At New York Public Library.

Grandy, Moses. *Narrative of the Life of Moses Grandy, Late a Slave in the United States of America*. London: C. Gilpin, 1843. At Library of Congress.

_____. _____. 1st American from the last London ed. Boston: O. Johnson, 1844. At Harvard.

_____. _____. 2d American ed. Boston: O. Johnson, 1844. New York Public Library.

Green, J. D. *Narrative of the Life of J. D. Green, a Runaway Slave from Kentucky, Containing an Account of His Three Escapes, in 1839, 1846, and 1848*. Eighth Thousand. Huddersfield: printed by Henry Fielding, 1864. At New York Public Library.

Green, William. *Narrative of Events in the Life of William Green, Formerly a Slave, Written by Himself*. Springfield, Massachusetts: L. M. Guernsey, 1853. At Library of Congress.

Grimes, William. *Life of William Grimes, the Runaway Slave. Written by Himself*. New York, 1825. Boston Public Library.

_____. *Life of William Grimes, the Runaway Slave, Brought Down to the Present Time, Written by Himself*. New Haven: Published by the Author, 1855. At New York Historical Society.

Gronniosaw, James Albert Ukawsaw. *A Narrative of the Most Remarkable Particulars in the Life of James Albert Ukawsaw Gronniosaw, An African Prince, as Related by Himself*. 2d ed. n.p., n.d. At Harvard.

_____. _____. Reprint. Newport, Rhode Island: S. Southwick, 1774. At Library of Congress.

_____. *Berr Hanes Pethau Mwaf Hynod ym Mywyd James Albert Ukawsaw Gronniosaw, Troysog o Affrica: fel yr Adroddqyd Ganddo ef ei hun*. Aberhomddu, Argraphwyd dros y Parch. Mr. W. Williams gan E. Evans, 1779. At Harvard.

_____. *A Narrative of the Most Remakable Particulars in the Life of James Albert Ukawsaw Gronniosaw, an African Prince, etc.* Bath: W. Gye and T. Mills, 1780? At New York Public Library.

_____. *A Narrative of the Most Remarkable Particulars in the Life of James Albert Akawsaw [sic]; as Dictated by Himself.* 2d American ed. Catskill, New York: Printed at the Eagle Office, 1810. At the American Antiquarian Society.

_____. *A Narrative of the Most Remarkable Particulars in the Life of James Albert Ukawsaw Gronniosaw, an African Prince as Related by Himself.* Leeds: Printed by Davies and Booth, at the Stanhope Press, Vicar-Lane, 1814. At the New York Historical Society.

Hall, Elder Samuel. *Forty-Seven Years a Slave; a Brief Story of His Life as a Slave and After Freedom.* Washington, Georgia, 1912. At Atlanta University.

Hammon, Briton. *A Narrative of the Uncommon Sufferings, and Surprizing [sic] Deliverance of Briton Hammon, a Negro Man,—Servant to General Winslow, of Marshfield, in New-England; Who Returned to Boston, after having been absent almost Thirteen Years. Containing an Account of the many Hardships he underwent from the time he left his master's house, in the year 1747, to the Time of his Return to Boston.—How he was cast away in the Capes of Florida;—the horrid Cruelty and inhuman barbarity of the Indians in murdering the whole Ship's Crew;—the Manner of his being carry'd by them into captivity. Also, An Account of his being Confined Four Years and Seven Months in a close Dungeon.— and the remarkable Manner in which he met with his good old Master in London; who returned to New-England, a Passenger, in the same Ship.* Boston: Printed and sold by Green and Russell, in Queen-Street, 1760. At New York Historical Society.

Hammon, Jupiter. *An Address to the Negroes in the State of New York. By Jupiter Hammon, Servant of John Lloyd, jun. Esq. of the Manor of Queen's Village, Long Island.* New York: Printed by Carroll and Patterson, 1787. At New York Historical Society.

_____. _____. Philadelphia: reprinted by David Humphreys, in Spruce Street, 1787. New York Public Library.

_____. _____. New York: Samuel Wood, 1806. Arthur Spingarn Library.

Hayden, William. *Narrative of William Hayden, containing a Faithful Account of His Travels for a Number of Years, Whilst a Slave in the South, Written by Himself.* Cincinnati: Published for the Author, 1846. At Boston Public Library.

Henson, Josiah. *The Life of Josiah Henson, Formerly a Slave, Now an Inhabitant of Canada, as Narrated by Himself to Samuel Eliot.* Boston: A. D. Phelps, 1849. At Schomburg.

_____. _____. With preface by T. Binney. London, 1851. At Schomburg.

_____. _____. 6th Thousand. London, 1852. At Harvard.

_____. *Truth Stranger than Fiction. Father Henson's Story of His Own Life.* With an introduction by Harriet B. Stowe. Boston: J. P. Jewett and

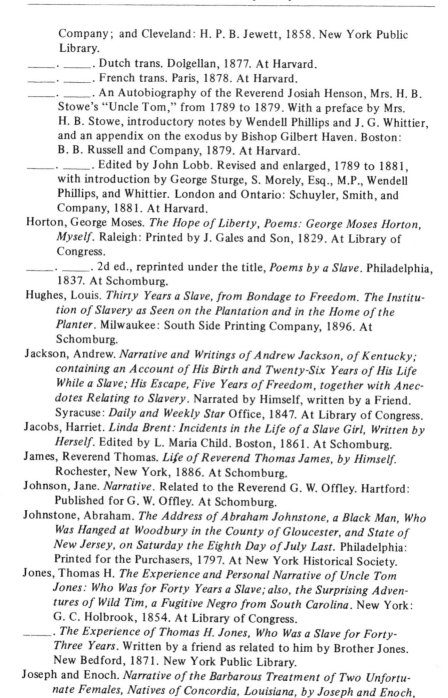

Company; and Cleveland: H. P. B. Jewett, 1858. New York Public Library.

_____. _____. Dutch trans. Dolgellan, 1877. At Harvard.

_____. _____. French trans. Paris, 1878. At Harvard.

_____. _____. An Autobiography of the Reverend Josiah Henson, Mrs. H. B. Stowe's "Uncle Tom," from 1789 to 1879. With a preface by Mrs. H. B. Stowe, introductory notes by Wendell Phillips and J. G. Whittier, and an appendix on the exodus by Bishop Gilbert Haven. Boston: B. B. Russell and Company, 1879. At Harvard.

_____. _____. Edited by John Lobb. Revised and enlarged, 1789 to 1881, with introduction by George Sturge, S. Morely, Esq., M.P., Wendell Phillips, and Whittier. London and Ontario: Schuyler, Smith, and Company, 1881. At Harvard.

Horton, George Moses. *The Hope of Liberty, Poems: George Moses Horton, Myself*. Raleigh: Printed by J. Gales and Son, 1829. At Library of Congress.

_____. _____. 2d ed., reprinted under the title, *Poems by a Slave*. Philadelphia, 1837. At Schomburg.

Hughes, Louis. *Thirty Years a Slave, from Bondage to Freedom. The Institution of Slavery as Seen on the Plantation and in the Home of the Planter*. Milwaukee: South Side Printing Company, 1896. At Schomburg.

Jackson, Andrew. *Narrative and Writings of Andrew Jackson, of Kentucky; containing an Account of His Birth and Twenty-Six Years of His Life While a Slave; His Escape, Five Years of Freedom, together with Anecdotes Relating to Slavery*. Narrated by Himself, written by a Friend. Syracuse: *Daily and Weekly Star* Office, 1847. At Library of Congress.

Jacobs, Harriet. *Linda Brent: Incidents in the Life of a Slave Girl, Written by Herself*. Edited by L. Maria Child. Boston, 1861. At Schomburg.

James, Reverend Thomas. *Life of Reverend Thomas James, by Himself*. Rochester, New York, 1886. At Schomburg.

Johnson, Jane. *Narrative*. Related to the Reverend G. W. Offley. Hartford: Published for G. W. Offley. At Schomburg.

Johnstone, Abraham. *The Address of Abraham Johnstone, a Black Man, Who Was Hanged at Woodbury in the County of Gloucester, and State of New Jersey, on Saturday the Eighth Day of July Last*. Philadelphia: Printed for the Purchasers, 1797. At New York Historical Society.

Jones, Thomas H. *The Experience and Personal Narrative of Uncle Tom Jones: Who Was for Forty Years a Slave; also, the Surprising Adventures of Wild Tim, a Fugitive Negro from South Carolina*. New York: G. C. Holbrook, 1854. At Library of Congress.

_____. *The Experience of Thomas H. Jones, Who Was a Slave for Forty-Three Years*. Written by a friend as related to him by Brother Jones. New Bedford, 1871. New York Public Library.

Joseph and Enoch. *Narrative of the Barbarous Treatment of Two Unfortunate Females, Natives of Concordia, Louisiana, by Joseph and Enoch,*

Runaway Slaves. As told by Mrs. Todd and Miss Harrington. New York: Printed for the Publishers, 1842. Massachusetts State Library.

Joyce, John. *Confession of John Joyce*. Related to Richard Allen. Philadelphia, 1818. Arthur Spingarn Library.

Keckley, Elizabeth. *Behind the Scenes; or, Thirty Years a Slave and Four Years in the White House, as Mrs. Lincoln's Maid*. New York: G. W. Carleton and Company, 1868. At Schomburg.

Lane, Lunceford. *Narrative of Lunceford Lane, Published by Himself*. Boston: Printed by Hewes and Watson for the Author, 1842. At Schomburg.

Langston, John Mercer. *From Plantation to Congress*. Hartford: American Publishing Company, 1894. At Library of Congress.

Lewis, Joseph Vance. *Out of the Ditch; A True Story of an Ex-Slave, by J. Vance Lewis*. Houston, Texas: Rein and Sons, 1910. At Schomburg.

Loguen, Jermain W. *The Reverend Jermain W. Loguen, as a Slave and as a Freeman. A Narrative of Real Life*. Syracuse: Office of the *Daily Journal*, 1859. New York Public Library.

Maddison, Reuben. *A True Story*. Birmingham, England, 1832. At Moorland Foundation.

Mallory, William. *Old Plantation Days*. 3d ed. Canada, 1901? In Daniel Murray Collection, Library of Congress.

Mars, James. *Life of James Mars, Written by Himself*. n.p., 1864. At Schomburg.

_____. *Life of James Mars, a Slave Born and Sold in Connecticut, Written Himself*. Hartford: Case, Lockwood and Company, 1865. At Schomburg.

_____. _____. 6th ed., enlarged. Hartford: Case, Lockwood and Company, 1865. At Boston Public Library.

Mason, Isaac. *Life of Isaac Mason, as a Slave*. Worcester, Massachusetts, 1893. At Schomburg.

Meachum, John B. *An Address to the Colored Citizens of the United States, Prefaced by a Narrative of the Author as a Slave in Virginia*. Philadelphia, 1846. At Library of Congress.

Mountain, Joseph. *Sketches of the Life of Joseph Mountain, a Negro, Who Was Executed at New-Haven, on the 20th Day of October, 1790, For a Rape, Committed on the 26th Day of May last*. New-Haven: Printed and Sold by T. and S. Green, 1790. At Yale University.

Northup, Solomon. *Twelve Years a Slave, Narrative of Solomon Northup, a Citizen of New York, Kidnapped in Washington City in 1841 and Rescued in January, 1853, from a Cotton Plantation near Red River, in Louisiana*. Dedicated to Mrs. Stowe. Auburn, Buffalo, and London: Derby and Miller, 1853. At Schomburg.

Offley, Reverend G. W. *Narrative of the Life and Labors of the Reverend G. W. Offley, a Colored Man and Local Preacher, Written by Himself*. Hartford: Published for the Author, 1860. At Schomburg.

O'Neal, William. *Life and History of William O'Neal; or, The Man Who Sold His Wife*. St. Louis: A. R. Fleming and Company, 1896. Arthur Spingarn Library.

Paige, C. F. *Twenty-Two Years of Freedom*. n.p., 1876? In Daniel Murray Collection, Library of Congress.

Parker, Janie. *Janie Parker, the Fugitive*. Related to Mrs. Emily Pierson. n.p., 1851. New York Public Library.

Pennington, James W. C. *The Fugitive Blacksmith; or, Events in the History of James W. C. Pennington, Pastor of a Presbyterian Church, New York, Formerly a Slave in the State of Maryland, United States*. 2d ed. London: C. Gilpin, 1849. At Schomburg.

_____. _____. 3d ed. London: C. Gilpin, 1850. At Harvard.

Peterson, D. H. *The Looking Glass: Being a True Narrative of the Life of the Reverend D. H. Peterson*. n.p., 1854. At Schomburg.

_____. _____. 2d ed., rev. and enlarged. Boston: Published for the Author, 1855. At Library of Congress.

_____. *From Slave Cabin to Pulpit; the Autobiography of Peter Randolph, the Southern Question Illustrated, Sketches of Slave Life*. Preface by Samuel May, Jr. Boston: Published for the Author, 1893. At Schomburg.

Roberts, Ralph. "A Slave's Story." Told by His Owner. *Putnam's Monthly* 9 (June 1857):614–620. At New York Public Library.

Roper, Moses. *A Narrative of Moses Roper's Adventures and Escape from American Slavery; with a Preface by Reverend T. Price*. London: Darton, Harvey, and Darton, 1837. At New York Historical Society.

_____. _____. 2d London ed. London: Harvey and Darton, 1838. At Harvard.

_____. _____. 1st American from the London ed. Philadelphia: Printed by Merrihew and Gunn, 1838. At Library of Congress.

_____. _____. 4th ed. London: Harvey and Darton, 1840. At Schomburg.

_____. _____. Celtic trans. Llanelli: Gan Rees a Thomas, 1841. At Harvard.

_____. _____. Berwick-upon Tweed: The Author, 1846. At Boston Public Library.

_____. _____. Berwick-upon-Tweed: The Author, 1848. At Boston Public Library.

Sambo. *Sambo: the Slave of Long Ago*. Related by Orrie M. MacDonnell, n.p., 1924. At New York Public Library.

Smith, Harry. *Fifty Years of Slavery in the United States of America*. Grand Rapids, Michigan: Western Michigan Printing Company, 1891. At Library of Congress.

Smith, James L. *Autobiography, including also Reminiscences of Slave Life*. Norwich, Connecticut: Bulletin Company, 1881. At Library of Congress.

Smith, Venture. *A Narrative of the Life and Adventures of Venture, a Native of Africa; but Resident about Sixty Years in the United States of America. Related by Himself*. New London: Printed by C. Holt, 1798. Arthur Spingarn Library.

_____. _____. New London: Reprinted and Published by a Descendant of Venture, 1835. At Schomburg.

_____. _____. rev. and republished, with traditions by H. M. Selden, of East Haddam. Haddam, Connecticut: 1896. At Library of Congress.

_____. _____. Middletown, Connecticut: J. S. Stewart, printer, 1897. At
  Library of Congress.
Spear, Chloe. *Narrative of Chloe Spear*. By a "Lady of Boston." Boston:
  American Anti-Slavery Society, 1832. At New York Historical Society.
Steward, Austin. *Twenty-Two Years a Slave and Fifty Years a Freeman*. New
  York: W. Alling, 1857. At Harvard.
_____. _____. 3d ed. Rochester: W. Alling, 1861. At Schomburg.
Still, James. *Early Recollections and Life of Dr. James Still*. Philadelphia:
  Printed for the Author by Lippincott, 1877. At Moorland Foundation.
Still, Peter. *The Kidnapped and the Ransomed: Narrative of Peter Still and
  His Wife "Vina."* Related to Mrs. Kate E. R. Pickard. Syracuse: W. T.
  Hamilton Press, 1856. At Schomburg.
Still, William *The Underground Railroad*. Preface to the revised edition.
  Philadelphia: Anti-Slavery Society, 1878. At Schomburg.
Stroyer, Jacob. *Sketches of My Life in the South*. Part I. Salem, 1879. At
  Schomburg.
_____. _____. New and enlarged ed. Salem: Salem Observer Book and Job
  Printing, 1885. At Harvard.
_____. _____. 3d ed. Salem: Salem Observer Book and Job Printing, 1890.
  At Harvard.
Thompson, John. *Life of John Thompson, a Fugitive Slave; containing His
  History of Twenty-Five Years in Bondage, and His Providential Escape:
  Written by Himself*. Worcester, 1856. At Schomburg.
Tilmon, Levin. *A Brief Miscellaneous Narrative of the More Early Part of the
  Life of Levin Tilmon, Pastor of a Colored Methodist Church, New
  York City*. Jersey City: W. and L. Pratt, 1853. At Library of Congress.
_____. _____. 2d ed., enlarged. Jersey City: W. and L. Pratt, 1853. At Harvard.
Tomlinson, Jane. "The First Fugitive Slave Case of Record in Ohio." *Annual
  Report*, American Historical Society Association, Washington, 1896,
  pp. 91–100. Massachusetts State Library.
Truth, Sojourner. *Narrative of Sojourner Truth, a Northern Slave, Emanci-
  pated from Bodily Servitude by the State of New York, in 1828*.
  Narrated to Olive Gilbert, including Sojourner Truth's *Book of Life*,
  and a dialogue. Boston, 1850. At Library of Congress.
_____. _____. Boston: Published for Sojourner Truth, 1853. At Schomburg.
_____. _____. With introduction by Harriet B. Stowe. Boston, 1855. At
  Library of Congress.
_____. *Narrative of Sojourner Truth, a Bondswoman of Olden Time, Emanci-
  pated by the New York Legislature in the Early Part of the Present
  Century*. Edited by Mrs. Francis W. Titus. Battle Creek: *Review and
  Herald* Office, 1884. At Massachusetts State Library.
Tubman, Harriet. *Scenes in the Life of Harriet Tubman*. As told by Sarah
  Bradford. New York and Auburn, 1869. At Schomburg.
Turner, Nat. *The Confessions of Nat Turner, the Leader of the Late Insurrec-
  tion in Southampton, Virginia*. As fully and voluntarily made to
  Thomas R. Gray, in the prison where he was confined, and acknowl-
  edged by him to be such when read before the court of Southampton,

with the certificate under the seal of the court convened at Jerusalem, November 5, 1831, for his trial. Baltimore: Thomas R. Gray, Lucas and Deaver, printers, 1831. At Schomburg.

Voorhis, Robert. *Life and Adventures of Robert Voorhis, the Hermit of Massachusetts, Who Has Lived Fourteen Years in a Cave, Secluded from Human Society. Comprising an account of his Birth, Parentage, Sufferings, and Providential Escape from Unjust and Cruel Bondage in Early Life–and His Reasons for Becoming a Recluse*. Taken from his own mouth by Henry Trumbull, and published for his benefit. Providence: Printed for Henry Trumbull, 1829. At Schomburg.

Ward, Samuel Ringgold. *Autobiography of a Fugitive Negro: His Anti-Slavery Labours in the United States, Canada, and England*. London: J. Snow, 1855. At Schomburg.

Washington, Booker Taliaferro. "Up from Slavery: an Autobiography." *Outlook*, November 3, 1900 to February 23, 1901.

_____. *Up from Slavery: an Autobiography*. New York: A. L. Burt Company, 1900. At New York Public Library.

_____. _____. New York: Doubleday Page and Company, 1901. At Boston Public Library.

_____. _____. London: T. Nelson, 1910. New York Public Library.

_____. _____. School ed. New York: Thompson, Brown and Company, 1915.

_____. _____. Johannes Knudsen's translation into Danish. Copenhagen: G. E. C. Gao, 1917. New York Public Library.

_____. _____. Garden City: Doubleday Doran, 1929.

Washington, Madison. *The Heroic Slave, A Thrilling Narrative of the Adventures of Madison Washington, in Pursuit of Liberty*. As told by Frederick Douglass. Boston: Jewett and Company, 1853. At Schomburg.

Watkins, James. *Narrative of the Life of James Watkins, Formerly a Chattel in Maryland, United States*. Bolton, Kenyon, and Abbott, printers, 1852. At Schomburg.

Watson, Henry. *Narrative of Henry Watson, a Fugitive Slave; Written by Himself*. Dedicated to Henry Holt. Boston: Henry Holt, 1848. At Schomburg.

Webb, William. *History of William Webb. Composed by Himself*. Detroit: e. Hoekstra, 1873. At Schomburg.

Wheatley, Phillis. *Letters of Phillis Wheatley, the Negro Slave Poet of Boston*. Boston: Printed by John Wilson and Son, 1864. At Schomburg. Also printed in the *Proceedings of the Colonial Society of Massachusetts* for 1864; and in Woodson, Carter, *Mind of the Negro Prior to 1860*, in the Introduction.

Wheeler, Peter. *Chains and Freedom; or, The Life and Adventures of Peter Wheeler, a Colored Man Yet Living*. Related to C. E. Lester. New York: E. S. Arnold and Company, 1839. At Oberlin.

White, George. *Account of Life, Experience, Travels, and Gospel Labours of an African. Written by Himself and Revised by a Friend*. New York: J. C. Tottle, 1810. Arthur Spingarn Library.

Wilkerson, James. *History of His Travels and Labors in the United States as a Missionary, since Purchase of His Liberty in New Orleans.* Columbus, Ohio, 1861. At Oberlin.

William. *The Negro Servant.* Related by Reverend Richmond Legh. London: Religious Tract Society, printed by J. Tilling, n.d. At Harvard.

_____. *The Negro Servant. An Authentic Narrative of a Young Negro, Showing How He Was Made a Slave in Africa; and Carried to Jamaica, Where He Was Sold to a Captain in His Majesty's Navy, and Taken to America, Where He Became a Christian; and Afterwards Brought to England, and Baptised.* Kilmarnock: H. Crawford, 1815. At Harvard.

_____. _____. Boston: New England Tract Society; Tract no. 53, 1816. At Harvard.

Williams, Isaac. *Sunshine and Shadow of Slave Life. Reminiscences Told to William Ferguson Goldie by Isaac Williams.* East Saginaw, Michigan: Evening News, 1885. At Library of Congress.

Williams, James. *Narrative of James Williams, An American Slave; Who Was for Several Years a Driver on a Cotton Plantation in Alabama.* As related to John Greenleaf Whittier. New York: n.d.

_____. *Narrative of James Williams, an American Slave.* Abolitionist's Library, No. 3. Boston: Massachusetts Anti-Slavery Society, 1838. Written by John Greenleaf Whittier from Verbal Narrative. In Library of Congress.

_____. *Narrative of James Williams, an American Slave; Who Was for Several Years a Driver on a Cotton Plantation in Alabama.* As related to J. G. Whittier. Second edition. Boston: J. F. Trow, printer, 1838. At Harvard.

Williams, James (not the same as above). *Life and Adventures of James Williams, a Fugitive Slave, with a Full Description of the Underground Railroad.* San Francisco: Woman's Union Print, 1873. At Schomburg.

_____. _____. Contains additional narrative sketches. Fourth edition. San Francisco: Women's Union Book and Job Printing Office, 1874. At Harvard.

_____. _____. 5th ed. Preface signed "John Thomas Evans, now James Williams." Philadelphia: A. H. Sickler and Company, 1893. At Harvard.

Zamba. *Life and Adventures of Zamba, an African Negro King, and His Experiences of Slavery in South Carolina, Written by Himself, Corrected and Arranged by Peter Neilson.* London: Smith, Elder, and Company, 1847. At Schomburg.

_____. *Der Negerkonig Zamba, Eine Sklavengeschichte Seitenstuck zu "Onkel Tom's Hutte."* Nach dem Englischen bearbeitet von Dr. Chr. G. Barth. Stuttgart, 1853. At Schomburg.

Primary Sources in Which
Slave Narrative Sketches Were Found

Unpublished Collections

The John B. Cade Manuscripts, at Southern University, Scotlandville,
Louisiana. A collection of eighty-two narratives of ex-slaves interviewed by thirty-six students under the direction of Mr. Cade in 1929
in the State of Louisiana. For Mr. Cade's statement concerning these
narratives see his article, "Out of the Mouths of Ex-Slaves." *Journal
of Negro History* 20 (1935):294–337.

The Library of Congress Collection of Slave Narratives, in the Rare Books
Division of the Library of Congress. A collection of more than two
thousand narratives of ex-slaves interviewed by workers on the Federal
Writers Project, 1936–1938, deposited in seventeen typescript volumes
corresponding to the seventeen states in which the ex-slaves were
found. A study of this manuscript collection as "a folk history of
slavery in the Unite States" has been published by the director of the
project, Dr. Benjamin A. Botkin, under the title *Lay My Burden Down*.
Chicago: University of Chicago Press, 1915.

The Library of Congress Collection of Slave Papers, in the Daniel Murray
Collection of Negro Materials. An Uncatalogued collection, containing
twenty-one slave narratives, not studied hitherto.

The Reddick Manuscripts, in the Schomburg Collection of the New York
Public Library. A collection of 260 narratives of ex-slaves interviewed
by twelve graduate students under the direction of Dr. L. D. Reddick
in 1934–1935 in the five states bordering the Ohio River. These manuscripts have not been studied hitherto.

The Wilbur H. Siebert Manuscript Collection. A mammoth collection of
source materials on the activities of the Quakers from the 1830s to the
1860s. In forty manuscript volumes in Dr. Siebert's possession at Ohio
State University, Columbus, Ohio. Contains nearly four hundred slave
narratives not hitherto found.

Contemporary Newspapers and Priodicals

Abolitionist: or, Record of the New England Anti-Slavery Society. Published
in Boston, 12 vols., beginning January, 1833. Files at Library of Con-

gress; the New York Public Library; the Boston Public Library; and the Cornell, Oberlin, and Harvard College libraries. Contains seventeen narrative sketches.

African Observer, The. Published monthly at Philadelphia, April 1827 to March 1828. Files at Oberlin College and Harvard College. Contains five narrative sketches.

American Anti-Slavery Almanac. Published in Boston and in New York, 1836 to c. 1847. No complete files exist, but volumes are to be found in the Daniel Murray Collection at the Library of Congress, at Cornell University, and at the Watkinson Library, Hartford. Twenty-eight narrative sketches were found.

American Anti-Slavery Reporter. Published by the American Anti-Slavery Society, New York, from January to August, 1834, superseding the *Anti-Slavery Reporter*. Files at Oberlin College, Cornell University, the Boston Public Library, and the Library of Congress. Contains ten narrative sketches.

American Convention for Promoting the Abolition of Slavery, and Improving the Condition of the African Race, Minutes of the Proceedings at Philadelphia, 1794–1827. File at the Library of Congress. Contains ten narrative sketches.

American and Foreign Anti-Slavery Society Annual Reports, 1840(?) to 1849(?). In the Daniel Murray Collection, Library of Congress. Contains thirty narrative sketches.

Anti-Slavery Advocate. Published in London, from October 1852 to May 1863. Files at Cornell University and the Boston Public Library. Contains twenty narrative sketches.

Anti-Slavery Bugle, The, edited at various places by Oliver Johnson and M. R. Robinson, 1850–1857 (12 volumes). File at the Library of Congress. Contains ten narrative sketches.

Anti-Slavery Examiner. Published by the American Anti-Slavery Society, New York, 1836–1845. Files at the Congregational Library in Boston, and at Cornell University. Contains twenty-five narrative sketches.

Anti-Slavery Record. Published in New York, 1835–1839. Files in the New York State Library and the Library of Congress. Contains ten narrative sketches.

Anti-Slavery Reporter. Published in New York from June to November, 1833, after which it was superseded by the *American Anti-Slavery Reporter*. Files at the Library of Congress, Oberlin College, Harvard College, and the Boston Public Library. Contains six narrative sketches.

Anti-Slavery Reporter and Aborigines' Friend. Published by the Anti-Slavery and Aborigines' Protection Society, 1840–1851. File in the Library of Congress. Contains twenty-eight narrative sketches.

Anti-Slavery Tracts. Published by the American Anti-Slavery Society, New York, 1855–1861. Files at Cornell University and the Historical Society of Pennsylvania, Philadelphia. Contains twenty narrative sketches.

Anti-Slavery Watchman, a Magazine of English and American Abolitionism. Published in London, 1853 to January 1854(?). Files at Cornell University. Contains forty-eight narrative sketches.

Christian Examiner, The. Contains fifteen narrative sketches in issues from the years 1824–1869.

Christian Recorder, The. Published by the African Methodist Episcopal Book Concern, Philadelphia, from 1852 to (?). Contains eighteen narrative sketches.

Emancipator, The. Published by Elihu Embree at Jonesborough, Tennessee, from April to October, 1820. (Re-printed by B. H. Murphy, Nashville, 1932.) Contains eight narrative sketches.

Emancipator and Republican. Published by the American Anti-Slavery Society in New York and Boston, 1833–1850 under various titles. The paper appeared also as the *Emancipator, Emancipator and Journal of Public Morals, Free American,* and *Weekly Chronicle*. No complete file extant, but copies are to be found at the Library of Congress, Cornell University, and the Boston Public Library. Contains ten narrative sketches.

Genius of Liberty. Published by the La Salle County Anti-Slavery Society, Lowell, Illinois, from December 1840 to April 1842. Only extant copy is of vol. I, no. 1, at the Library of Congress, which contains two narrative sketches.

Genius of Universal Emancipation. Founded in Mount Pleasant, Ohio, in 1821, by Benjamin Lundy; published variously in Jonesborough, Tennessee, Baltimore, Washington, and Philadelphia, with Lundy as editor, for nearly seventeen years. Nearly complete file at Johns Hopkins University. Contains fifty-three narrative sketches.

Herald of Freedom, The. Published by the New Hampshire Anti-Slavery Society, Concord, New Hampshire, March 7, 1835 to March 7, 1845. File in the Library of Congress. Contains more than three hundred narrative sketches.

Human Rights. Published by the American Anti-Slavery Society, New York, 1835–1839. No complete file exists, but partial files are to be found at the Library of Congress, the Boston Public Library, and Harvard College. Contains eighty-three narrative sketches.

Journal of Negro History. Published by the Association for the Study of Negro Life and History, Carter G. Woodson, editor, Washington, 1916–. Contains more than fifty narrative sketches.

Liberator, The. Published by Garrison at Boston, 1831–1865. Contains 207 narrative sketches.

Liberty Almanac. Published by the American and Foreign Anti-Slavery Society, 1844–1852. Complete file at Cornell University; incomplete files at Yale University, Harvard College, the Library of Congress, and the Boston Public Library. Contains one hundred narrative sketches.

Liberty Bell, The. Published by the "Friends of Freedom," in connection with the American Anti-Slavery Society Annual Fair at Boston, Mrs. Maria Chapman, editor, 1839–1859 (except that there were no volumes

prepared for the years 1840, 1850, 1854–55, and 1857). Complete files
at the Boston Athenaeum and the Brooklyn Public Library (Plaza).
Contains thirty narrative sketches.

National Standard, A Temperance and Literary Journal. Published by the
American Anti-Slavery Society at New York, 1840–1870, also under
the title *National Anti-Slavery Standard.* Contains ninety-two narrative sketches.

Putnam's Magazine. Contains six narratives and narrative sketches in issues
from the years 1852–1857.

Quarterly Anti-Slavery Magazine. Published by the American Anti-Slavery
Society, New York, 1835–1837. Files at Cornell Unversity, Oberlin,
Yale, and Library of Congress. Contains five narrative sketches.

Slave's Friend. Published by American Anti-Slavery Society, New York,
1836–1839. Complete files at the American Antiquarian Society and
the Library of Congress. Contains twenty-nine narrative sketches.

Voice of the Fugitive. Published in Sandwich, Canada, Henry Bibb, editor,
1851–1852. Files at Harvard College and the Library of Congress. Contains over thirty narrative sketches.

Books Containing Slave Narrative Sketches

Adams, H. G. *God's Image in Ebony: Being a Series of Biographical Sketches,
Facts, Anecdotes, Etc., Demonstrative of the Mental Powers and Intellectual Capacities of the Negro Race.* London, 1854. Contains twenty
narrative sketches.

Albert, Octavia V. R. *The House of Bondage; or, Charlotte Brooks and Other
Slaves.* New York, 1890. Contains nine narrative sketches.

Anti-Slavery Alphabet. Printed at Philadelphia for the annual antislavery
fair, 1847. (Oberlin Collection of Children's Anti-Slavery Literature.)
Contains fifteen narrative sketches.

Armistead, Wilson. *Five Hundred Thousand Strokes for Freedom.* London:
W. and F. Cash and William Tweedie, 1853. Contains ten narrative
sketches.

_____. *A Tribute for the Negro: Being a Vindication of the Moral, Intellec-
tual, and Religious Capabilities of the Colored Portion of Mankind;
with Particular Reference to the African Race.* London: Charles Gilpin,
1848. Contains thirty narrative sketches.

Armstrong, Orland Kay. *Old Massa's People: The Old Slaves Tell Their Story.*
Indianapolis: Bobbs-Merrill, 1931. Contains twenty narrative sketches.

Barber, J. Warner. *History of the Amistad Captives.* New Haven, 1840. Contains thirty-three narrative sketches.

Barker, Joseph, ed. *Interesting Memoirs and Documents Relating to American
Slavery.* London: Chapman Bros., 1846. Contains twelve narratives and
narrative sketches.

Brown, Hollie Q. *Homespun Heroines and Other Women of Distinction.*
1926. Contains narrative sketches of six slave women.

Catterall, Helen T., ed. *Judicial Cases concerning American Slavery and the Negro*. 5 vols. Washington: Carnegie Institute, 1926–1937. Contains more than a hundred narrative sketches.

Child, Lydia Maria Francis. *The Duty of Disobedience to the Fugitive Slave Act: An Appeal to the Legislators of Massachusetts*. Boston: Anti-Slavery Tracts, no. 9, new series, American Anti-Slavery Society, 1860. Contains five narrative sketches.

_____. *The Freedman's Book*. Boston: Ticknor and Fields, 1865. Contains nine narrative sketches.

_____. *The Patriarchal Institution, as Described by Members of Its Own Family*. Boston: American Anti-Slavery Society, 1860. Contains seven narrative sketches.

Child's Anti-Slavery Book. Edited by Julia Colman. New York: Carlton and Porter, 1859. At Oberlin and the Schomburg Collection, New York Public Library. Contains six narrative sketches.

Coffin, Levi. *Reminiscences of the Reputed President of the Underground Railroad*. Boston: American Anti-Slavery Society, 1876. Twenty narrative sketches.

Curtis, Anna L. *Stories of the Underground Railroad*. New York: Island Workshop Press Co-Operative, 1941. Contains twenty-two narrative sketches.

Drew, Benjamin. *The Northside View of Slavery, the Canadian Refugees' Own Narratives*. Boston: John P. Jewett, 1855. Contains 191 narrative sketches.

Emerson, William C. *Stories and Spirituals of the Negro Slave*. Boston: Badger and Company, c. 1930. Contains eleven narrative sketches.

Fairchild, James H. *Underground Railroad*. Cleveland: Western Reserve Historical Society, c. 1877. Contains thirty narrative sketches.

Griffiths, Julia. *Autographs for Freedom*. Rochester, 1853; 1854. Contains twenty narrative sketches.

Johnson, Homer Uri. *From Dixie to Canada. Romances and Realities of the Underground Railroad*. Buffalo: Chas. Wells Moulton, 1894. Contains nine narrative sketches.

Kemble, Frances Anne. *Journal of a Residence on a Georgia Planation in 1838–1839*. London: Longmans, 1863. Contains seven narrative sketches.

Kennedy, Lionel H. and Parker, Thomas. *An Official Report of the Trials of Sundry Negroes, Charged with an Attempt to Raise an Insurrection in the State of South Carolina*. Charleston: James R. Schenck, printer, 1822. Contains nine sketches of slaves.

Long, John Dixon. *Pictures of Slavery in Church and State, Biographical Sketches, Anecdotes, Etc*. Philadelphia, 1857. Fifteen narrative sketches included.

Martineau, Harriet. *Society in America*. 2 vols. London, 1832. Contains eleven narrative sketches.

May, Samuel. *The Fugitive Slave Law and Its Victims*. New York: American Anti-Slavery Society Tracts, no. 18, 1856. Contains twelve narrative sketches.

Mitchell, William M. *Underground Railroad from Slavery to Freedom*. 2d ed. London: W. Tweedie, 1860. Contains seventeen narrative sketches.

Moore, Frank. *The Rebellion Record. A Diary of American Events, with Documents, Narratives, Incidents, Etc.* New York: G. P. Putnam, 1861–1862. Contains ten slave narrative sketches.

Mott, Abigail Field. *Biographical Sketches and Interesting Anecdotes of Persons of Color*. New York: printed by M. Day, 1826; by W. Alexander, 1828; by Mahlon Day, 1837, 1838; and by order of the estate of Lindley Murray 1875, 1882. Contains forty narrative sketches.

Murray, M. "Stories of the Underground Railroad. *Canadian Methodist Magazine*, September, 1898. Contains ten slave narrative sketches.

Nordhoff, Charles. *The Freedmen of South Carolina*. New York: Charles T. Evans, 1863. Contains fourteen narrative sketches.

Parsons, C. G. *Inside View of Slavery; or, A Tour among the Planters*. Boston: John P. Jewett, 1855. Contains fourteen narrative sketches.

Redpath, James. *The Roving Reporter*. Boston: John P. Jewett, 1857. Contains thirty-nine narrative sketches.

Ross, Alexander. *Recollections and Experiences of an Abolitionist; from 1855 to 1865*. 2d ed. Toronto: Rowsell and Hutchinson, 1876. Contains twenty-one narrative sketches.

Smith, E. *Uncle Tom's Kindred: or, the Wrongs of the Lowly. Sketches and Narratives*. 10 vols. Mansfield, Ohio: Wesleyan Methodist Connection of America, 1853. At Oberlin. Contains sixty-two narrative sketches.

Smith, T. Watson. *The Slave in Canada*. Collections of the Nova Scotia Historical Society, 1896–98. vol. 10 (1899), pp. 1–161. Contains fifteen narrative sketches.

Still, James. *Early Recollections and Life of Dr. James Still*. New York: Lippincott, 1877. Contains six narrative sketches.

Stowe, Harriet B. *Key to Uncle Tom's Cabin, etc.* Boston: John P. Jewett, 1853. Contains twenty narrative sketches.

Suppressed Book about Slavery, The. New York: Carleton, 1864. Contains more than fifty narrative sketches.

Weld, Theodore, compiler. *American Slavery as It is: Testimony of a Thousand Witnesses*. New York: American Anti-Slavery Society, 1839. Contains more than a hundred slave narrative sketches.

Williams, James. *Life and Adventures of James Williams, etc.* San Francisco: Women's Union, 1873. Contains six narrative sketches.

General Bibliography

Adams, Alice Dana. *Neglected Period of Anti-Slavery in America, 1808-1831.* Radcliffe College Monograph, no. 14. Boston: Harvard University Press, 1908.

Aptheker, Herbert. *American Negro Slave Revolts.* New York: Columbia University Press, 1943.

_____. *Essays in the History of the American Negro.* New York: International Publishers, Inc., 1945.

Barnes, Gilbert H. *The Anti-Slavery Impulse, 1830-1844.* New York and London: D. Appleton-Century, 1933.

Bartlett, J. R. *The Literature of the Rebellion, with Works on American Slavery.* Boston: Draper, 1866.

Bassett, John S. *The Southern Plantation Overseer, as Revealed in the Letters of James Knox Polk.* Northampton: Smith College, 1925.

Baxter, Charles N. and Dearborn, James. *List of Books, Newspapers, Maps, Music, and Miscellaneous Matter Printed in the Confederacy.* Boston: Boston Athenaeum, 1917.

Bestes, Peter et al. *Petition of Slaves to the Massachusetts Legislature, April 20, 1773.* A Broadside. Boston, 1773. (Copy in the New York Historical Society.

Bingham, Caleb. *The Columbian Orator: Containing a Variety of Original and Selected Pieces together with Rules, Calculated to Improve Youth and Others in the Ornamental and Useful Art of Eloquence.* Troy: Parker and Bliss, 1928.

Birney, Catherine H. *Grimke Sisters, Sarah and Angelina Grimke: The First American Women Advocators of Abolition and Woman's Rights.* Boston: Lee, 1885.

Birney, William. "Bibliography of Anti-Slavery Works Published or Republished in the United States before 1831." Appendix A of *James G. Birney and His Times.* New York: Appleton, 1890.

"Black Letters." *Graham's Magazine* 42 (January 1853):209-215.

Botkin, Benjamin A. *Lay My Burden Down.* Chicago: University of Chicago Press, 1945.

_____. "The Slave His Own Interpreter." *Quarterly Journal of Current Acquisitions to the Library of Congress* 2, no. 1 (November 1944): 37-63.

...

358 The Slave Narrative

Branch, E. Douglass. *The Sentimental Years, 1836–1860*. New York: Appleton-Century Company, 1934.

Brawley, Benjamin. *Early Negro American Writers*. Chapel Hill: University of North Carolina Press, 1939.

Brown, Herbert Ross. *The Sentimental Novel in America, 1789–1860*. Durham: Duke University Press, 1940.

Burr, Anna Robeson. *The Autobiography: A Critical and Comparative Study*. Boston: Houghton Mifflin, 1909.

Carroll, Joseph C. *Slave Insurrections in the United States*. Boston: Chapman and Grimes, 1938.

Challen, Howard. *Publishers and Stationers Trade List Directory*. Philadelphia, 1867–1869.

Charvat, William. *Origins of American Critical Thought, 1810–1835*. Philadelphia: University of Pennsylvania Press, 1936.

Child, Lydia Maria Francis. *An Appeal in Favor of That Class of Americans Called Africans*. Boston: Allen and Ticknor, 1833.

_____. *The Duty of Disobedience to the Fugitive Slave Act: An Appeal to the Legislators of Massachusetts*. Anti-Slavery Tracts, new series, no. 9. Boston: Boston Anti-Slavery Society, 1860.

_____. *Letters of Lydia Maria Francis Child*. Boston: Houghton, Mifflin, 1883.

Clarke, James Freeman. *Anti-Slavery Days; a Sketch of the Struggle Which Ended in the Abolition of Slavery in the United States*. New York: Worthington, 1884.

Curti, Merle. *The Growth of American Thought*. New York: Harper, 1943.

Cushing, William. *Index to the North American Review, 1815–1877*. Cambridge, Massachusetts, 1878.

Dabney, Virginius. *Liberalism in the South*. Chapel Hill: University of North Carolina Press, 1932.

Dew, Thomas Roderick. *A Digest of Laws, Customs, Manners, and Institutions of the Ancient and Modern Nations*. New York: D. Appleton and Company, 1856.

_____. *Review of the Debate in the Virginia Legislature of 1831 and 1832*. Richmond, T. W. White, 1832.

Dodd, William E. *The Cotton Kingdom. A Chronicle of the Old South*. Chronicles of America Series, edited by Allen Johnson, vol. 27. New Haven: Yale University Press, 1919.

DuBois, W. E. Burghardt. "A Look into the Past." *Chicago Defender*, 5 January 1946, p. 11.

_____. *The Suppression of the African Slave Trade to the United States of America, 1638–1870*. Harvard Historical Studies, no. 1. New York, London, and Bombay, 1896.

_____, and Johnson, Guy B. eds. *Encyclopedia of the Negro*. New York: Phelps-Stokes, 1945.

Dunlap, William C. *Quaker Education in Baltimore and Virginia Yearly Meetings*. Philadelphia: University of Pennsylvania, 1936.

Dunn, Waldo. *English Biography*. London: J. M. Dent and Sons, 1913.

Duyckinck, Evert A. and George L. *Cyclopedia of American Literature*.
New York: Scribner's, 1855.

Dwight, Timothy. *Greenfield Hill: a Poem in Seven Parts*. New York:
Childs and Swaine, 1794.

Dykes, Eva Beatrice. *Negro in English Romantic Thought*. Washington:
Associated Publishers, 1941.

Earle, Thomas. *The Life, Travels, and Opinions of Benjamin Lundy, including His Journeys to Texas and Mexico*. Philadelphia, 1847.

Fairchild, Hoxie Neale. *The Noble Savage: A Study in Romantic Naturalism*.
New York: 1928.

Finley, Ruth E. *The Lady of Godey's Sarah Josepha Hale*. Philadelphia and
London: J. B. Lippincott, 1931.

Flanders, Ralph Betts. *Plantation Slavery in Georgia*. Chapel Hill: University
of North Carolina Press, 1933.

Foerster, Norman, ed. *Literary Scholarship, Its Aims and Methods*. Chapel
Hill: University of North Carolina Press, 1941.

_____, ed. *The Re-Interpretation of American Literature: Some Contributions
toward the Understanding of Its Historical Development*. New York:
Harcourt, Brace, 1928.

Ford, W. C. *Broadsides, Ballads, etc. Printed in Massachusetts, 1639-1800*.
Boston: Massachusetts Historical Society, 1922.

Fox, Early Lee. *The American Colonization Society, 1817-1840*. Baltimore:
Johns Hopkins University, 1919.

Franklin, Benjamin. *Observations Concerning the Increase of Mankind and
the Peopling of Countries*. Smythe Edition, vol. III. New York:
Macmillan, 1905.

Frazier, E. Franklin. *The Negro Family in the United States*. Chicago: The
University of Chicago Press, 1939.

Gaines, Francis Pendleton. *The Southern Plantation: A Study in the Development and Accuracy of a Tradition*. New York: Columbia University
Press, 1925.

Garrison, William Lloyd. *The Papers of William Lloyd Garrison*. (Boston
Public Library, Rare Books Room.)

Garrison, W. P. and F. J. *William Lloyd Garrison, 1805-1879. The Story
of His Life*. 4 vols. New York and Boston: Houghton Mifflin,
1885.

Godkin, Edwin L. *Life and Letters of Edwin Lawrence Godkin*. Edited by
Rollo Ogden. New York: Macmillan, 1907.

Gohdes, Clarence. *American Literature in Nineteenth Century England*
New York: Columbia University Press, 1944.

Gordon, Asa H. "The Struggle of the Slave for Freedom" *Journal of Negro
History* 13 (1926):22-36.

Govan, Thomas P. "Was Plantation Slavery Profitable?" *Journal of Southern
History* 8 (1942):513-535.

Greene, Lorenzo J. *The Negro in Colonial New England*. Columbia University
Studies in History, Economics, and Public Law, no. 494. New York:
Columbia University Press, 1942.

Greenlaw, Edwin. *The Province of Literary History*. Baltimore: Johns
    Hopkins University, 1931.
Gregoire, Abbe Henri, *An Enquiry concerning the Intelligence and Moral
    Faculties and Literature of the Negroe*. Paris, 1918.
Hall, Prince, *A Charge Delivered to the African Lodge, June 24, 1797, at
    Menotomy*. Boston: published at request of the lodge, 1797.
_____. *A Charge Delivered to the Brethren of the African Lodge, on the
    25th of June, 1792, at the Hall of Brother William Smith in Charleston,
    Massachusetts*. Boston: published at request of the lodge, 1792.
Harper's Encyclopedia of United States History. New York: Harper and
    Bros., 1905.
Henkle, Henrietta. *Let My People Go*. New York: Harper, 1941.
Higginson, Thomas W. "Denmark Vesey." *Atlantic Monthly* 7 (1861):
    728–744.
_____. "Gabriel's Plot." *Atlantic Monthly* 10 (1962):337–345.
_____. *Travellers and Outlaws: Episodes in American History*. Boston: Lee
    and Shepard, 1889.
Hill, James D. "Some Economic Aspects of Slavery, 1850–1860." *Southern
    Atlantic Quarterly* 26 (1927):161–177.
Hollis, Christopher. *The American Heresy*. New York: Minton, Balch and
    Company, 1930.
Jefferson, Thomas. *Notes on the State of Virginia*. 2d American ed. Phila-
    delphia, 1794.
Jenkins, W. S. *Pro-Slavery Thought in the Old South*. Chapel Hill: University
    of North Carolina Press, 1935.
Johnson, August. *The Autobiography of Gustavus Vassa*. M.A. thesis, Atlanta
    University, c. 1939.
Johnson, Charles S. *Shadow of the Plantation*. Chicago: University of Chicago
    Press, 1934.
Johnson, James Hugo. "A New Interpretation of the Domestic Slave
    System." *Journal of Negro History* 18 (1933):38–45.
Kain, Richard M. "The Problem of Civilization in English Abolition Litera-
    ture, 1772–1808." *Philological Quarterly* 15 (April 1936).
Locke, Mary Stoughton. *Anti-Slavery Movements in America from the Intro-
    duction of African Slaves to the Prohibition of the Slave Trade, 1619–
    1808*. Radcliffe College Monograph, no. 11. Cambridge, Mass.: Harvard
    University Press, 1901.
Loggins, Vernon. *The Negro Author*. New York: Columbia University Press,
    1931.
Low, Sampson. *British Catalog of Books, 1837–1852*. London, 1853.
_____. *British Catalog of Books, 1835–1863*. London, 1864.
McDougall, Marion Gleason. *Fugitive Slaves, 1619–1865*. Radcliffe College,
    Fay House Monographs, no. 3. Cambridge, Mass.: Harvard University
    Press, 1891.
Macy, Jesse. *The Anti-Slavery Crusade: A Chronicle of the Gathering Storm*.
    Chronicles of America Series, vol. 28, edited by Allen Johnson. New
    Haven: Yale University Press, 1921.

Madison, James. *The Writings of James Madison*. Edited by Gaillard Hunt. New York, 1900–1912.

Mather, Cotton. *The Negro Christianized. An Essay to Excite and Assist That Good Work, the Instruction of Negro Servants in Christianity*. Boston, 1706.

_____. *Rules for the Society of Negroes, 1693*. New York: Lenox Library; reprinted by George H. Moore, 1888.

May, S. J. "Catalog of Anti-Slavery Publications in America." *Proceedings of the American Anti-Slavery Society at Its Third Decade*. New York, 1864.

Memoirs of an Unfortunate Young Nobleman, Returned from a Thirteen Years Slavery in America, Where He Had Been Sent by the Wicked Contrivances of His Cruel Uncle. London: J. Freeman, 1743.

Midgette, B. D. Ralph, Jr. *Thomas Roderick Dew*. The John P. Branch Historical Papers of Randolph-Macon College, 3, 1909.

Miller, Samuel. *A Sermon, Preached at New-Ark, October 22d, 1823, before the Synod of New Jersey, for the Benefit of the African School, under the Care of the Synod*. Trenton: printed by George Sherman, 1823. Moorland Foundation. *A Catalog of Books in the Moorland Foundation of Howard University*. Howard University, c. 1937.

Nelson, John Herbert. *The Negro Character in American Literature*. University of Kansas Humanistic Studies, 4, no. 1, 1926.

Parrington, Vernon. *The Romantic Revolution*. New York: Harcourt Brace, 1927.

Pattee, Fred Lewis. *The First Century of American Literature, 1770–1870*. New York: Apple-Century, 1935.

Peabody, Ephraim. "Narratives of Fugitive Slaves." *Christian Examiner*, July, 1849, pp. 61–92.

Phillips, Ulrich. *Life and Labor in the Old South*. Boston: Little, Brown, 1929.

Porter, Dorothy. "Early American Negro Writings." *The Papers of the Bibliographical Society of America*, 39, 1945.

Quinn, Arthur H. *The Literary Crusade against Slavery, The* Philadelphia, c. 1929.

Reddick, Lawrence D. Introduction to *The Kidnapped and the Ransomed*, by Kate Pickard. Negro Publication Society of America, series 1, no. 1, 1941.

_____. *Negro in New Orleans Press*. Chicago: University of Chicago, 1939.

Rockwood, George L. "George Barrell Cheever, Protagonist of Abolition: Religious Emotionalism the Underlying Factor in the Causes of the Civil War." *Proceedings of the American Antiquarian Society* 46, part I, 1936, pp. 81–113.

Rouse, Michael. *Study of the Development of Negro Education under Catholic Auspices*. Baltimore: Johns Hopkins University, 1935.

Russell, Robert R. "The General Effects of Slavery upon Southern Economic Progress." *Journal of Southern History* 4 (1938):34–54.

Saffin, John. *A Brief and Candid Answer to a Late Printed Sheet, Entitled, The Selling of Joseph, Whereunto Is Annexed a True and Particular*

Narrative by Way of Vindication of the Author's Dealing with and Prosecution of His Negro Man Servant for His Vile and Exorbitant Behaviour towards His Master, and His Tenant, Thomas Shepard; Which Hath Been Wrongfully Represented to Their Pejudice [sic] and Defamation. Boston, 1701.

Savage, W. Sherman. *The Controversy over the Distribution of Abolition Literature, 1830–1860.* Washington: Associated Publishers, 1938.

Schlesinger, Arthur M., Jr. "The Problem of Richard Hildreth." *New England Quarterly*, June, 1940, pp. 223–245.

Seeber, Edward D. *Anti-Slavery Opinion in France during the Second Half of the Eighteenth Century.* Johns Hopkins Studies in Romance Literatures and Languages, extra vol. to. Baltimore: Johns Hopkins Press, 1937.

Sewall, Samuel. *The Selling of Joseph.* Boston, 1700. Reprinted in Massachusetts Historical Society Collections, 5th series, no. 6, pp. 16–20.

Shelley, Philip Alison. "Crevecoeur's Contribution to Herder's Neger-Idyllen." *Journal of English and Germanic Philology* 37, no. 1 (1938):48–64.

Siebert, Wilbur H. "A Quaker Section of the Underground Railroad in Northern Ohio." *Ohio Archaeological and Historical Publications* 39. Columbus, 1930.

Simms, Henry H. "A Critical Analysis of Abolition Literature, 1830–1840." *Journal of Southern History* 6 (1940):368–382.

Stowe, Harriet B. *A Key to Uncle Tom's Cabin, Presenting the Original Facts and Documents upon Which the Story Is Founded.* Boston: John P. Jewett and Company; Cleveland: Jewett, Proctor and Worthington; London: Low and Co., 1853.

Styron, Arthur. *The Cast-Iron Man. John C. Calhoun, and American Democracy.* New York and Toronto: Longmans Green and Company, 1935.

Sydnor, Charles S. *Slavery in Mississippi.* New York and London: D. Appleton-Century, 1933.

Tandy, Jeannette. "Pro-Slavery Propaganda in American Fiction in the Fifties." *South Atlantic Quarterly* 21 (January-March 1922):41–51; 170–178.

Thompson, Ralph. *American Literary Annuals and Gift Books. 1825–1865.* New York: The H. W. Wilson Company, 1936.

Trumbull, John. "The Correspondent." *Connecticut Journal and New Haven Post-Boy*, 8, July 6, 1770.

Turner, Lorenzo Dow. *Anti-Slavery Sentiment in American Literature prior to 1865.* Washington: Association for the Study of Negro Life and History, 1929.

Van Evrie, John H. *Negroes and Negro Slavery: The First, an Inferior Race— the Latter, Its Normal Condition.* Baltimore: J. D. Toy, 1853.

Villard, Oswald. *Some Newspapers and Newspapermen.* New York: Alfred A. Knopf, 1933.

Warner, Robert Austin. *New Haven Negroes: A Social Study.* New Haven: Yale University Press, 1940.

Wegelin, Oscar. *Jupiter Hammon, American Negro Poet*. New York: C. F.
    Heartman, 1915.
Weeks, Stephen B. *Southern Quakers and Slavery, A Study in Institutional
    History*. Johns Hopkins University Studies 15. Baltimore, 1896.
Wesley, Charles. *Richard Allen, Apostle of Freedom*. Washington: Associated
    Press, 1936.
Wigmore, John Henry. *The Principles of Judicial Proof; or, The Process of
    Proof as Given by Logic, Psychology, and General Experience and
    Illustrated in Judicial Trials*. 2d rev. ed. Boston: Little, Brown, 1931.
Williamson, Peter. *French and Indian Cruelty Exemplified in the Life and
    Various Vicissitudes of Fortune of Peter Williamson*. 2d ed. London,
    1759.
Wilson, Forrest. *Crusader in Crinoline*. New York, 1941.
Wish, Harvey. "American Slave Insurrections before 1861." *Journal of Negro
    History* 29 (1937):299–320.
Woods, George B.; Watt, Homer A.; and Anderson, George B. *The Literature
    of England*. vol. 1. New York, 1938.
Woodson, Carter G. *Education of the Negro prior to 1861*. New York:
    G.P. Putnam and Sons, 1915.
_____. *The Mind of the Negro as Reflected in Letters Written during the
    Crisis 1800–1860*. Washington: Associated Publishers, 1926.
_____. *The Negro in Our History*. 6th ed. Washington: Associated Publishers,
    1941.
Woolman, John. *Some Considerations on the Keeping of Negroes; Recom-
    mended to the Professors of Christianity of Every Denomination*.
    Philadelphia: Benjamin Franklin and David Hall, 1762.
Work, Monroe N. *Bibliography of the Negro*. New York: H. W. Wilson Com-
    pany, 1928.
Wright, L. H. *A Statistical Survey of American Fiction, 1774–1850*. San
    Marino, California, n.d.
Wright, Louis B. "Myth-Makers and the South's Dilemma." *Sewanee Review*
    53 (1945).

Index

Children
    antislavery material for—295
    orphan slaves—120-121
    teachers of slaves—69, 177, 244-246,
      266-267
Church, Charles—82
Churches. *See also* specific denominations.
    in antislavery movement—24, 211
    slave narratives in records of—224
Cinques—235
Clark—51
Clarke, Christiana—130
Clarke, Cyrus—130
Clarke, Delia—130, 301
Clarke, Dennis—130
Clarke, Lewis—129-132, 185, 233-235,
    237, 242, 244, 247, 296, 297, 298, 301
Clarke, Manda—130
Clarke, Milton—130, 132, 235, 237, 242,
    247, 296, 297, 298
Clay—122
Clotel (Brown)—144, 307-308
Coffin, Captain—53
Colonization—147-148, 157-158, 189
Columbia, S.C.—295
Columbian Orator—267, 272, 289
Congdon, Charles—231
Congo River—134-135
Congress
    slavery debates—7, 25
Connecticut
    slavery in—9-11, 53, 55
Cooper—110
Cooper, Thomas—9, 100-101
Cotton culture—12, 25, 241
Court records
    source of slave narratives—222
Couter, Jack—14
Covey, Edward—254, 255, 268-272, 284,
    292, 301
Cowper, William—294, 295
Cox, F. A.—108
Cox, Jeff—244
Craft, William and Ellen—36, 39, 207-
    209, 231, 235-238, 247, 281
Craig, Lizzie—244-245
Crevecoeur—8-9
Curry, James—117-121, 158, 172, 173,
    260, 309
Curti, Merle—xix
Curtis, Martha—125

Daniel—70
Davis, Henrietta—245
Davis, Noah—38, 196-205, 214, 225, 247,
    311

Declaration of Independence—2, 6, 207
Demby—261
Detroit Liberty Association—148
Devereaux, Thomas—125
Dew, Thomas Roderick—25, 26-29, 236
Dickens, Charles—145, 303
Doran, Captain—71-73
Douglass, Anna—276
Douglass, Frederick
    in antislavery movement—39-46, 143,
      147, 235, 249-250, 277
    autobiographies—xviii, 142, 247, 296
      changes in tone—129, 257, 279-
        280, 284
      content—249-293
      literary merit—251-252, 277-278,
        294, 311
      Peabody's analysis—297-298
      popularity—3, 37, 40, 249, 292-
        293
    escape from slavery—272-274, 277,
      281-283, 291-292
    and Garrison—20, 40, 44, 49, 251,
      253, 257
    in Great Britain—39-42, 147-148
    literacy—245, 249, 265-268, 272-273,
      289
    paternity—258-259, 279-280
    prototypes in *Uncle Tom's Cabin*—
      242, 301, 302
    public speaking style—40, 250-251
    purchased emancipation—40-46, 143,
      257
    on slave life—259-276, 279-281, 284-
      292
Drayton and Asher—232
Dred (Stowe)—308
Dred Scott decision—209
Dresser, Amos—21-22
Drew, Benjamin—246
DuBois, W. E. B.—xvii, 49, 310
Dudley—115
Dudley, Governor—252
[Dudley], Robert—115-117, 131
Duncan—275
Durham—110
Dwight, Timothy—9

Eastman, Mrs.—307
Eboue tribe—67
Economic affairs
    conditions of slave revolts—7
    sectional differences—25
Edloe—186